NORTHERN IRELAND
INTERNATIONAL FOOTBALL FACTS

DEAN HAYES

Appletree Press

First published in 2006 by
Appletree Press Ltd
The Old Potato Station
14 Howard Street South
Belfast BT7 1AP

Tel: +44 (028) 90 24 30 74
Fax: +44 (0) 28 90 24 67 56
Email: reception@appletree.ie
Web: www.appletree.ie

The publisher would like to acknowledge the kind assistance of Lee Purcell.

A catalogue record of this book is available from the British Library.

Northern Ireland – International Football Facts

ISBN-10: 0 86281 874 5
ISBN-13: 978 0 86281 874 6

Desk & Marketing Editor: Jean Brown
Copy-editor: Jim Black
Designer: Stuart Wilkinson
Production Manager: Paul McAvoy

9 8 7 6 5 4 3 2 1

AP3329

Author's Notes

All details are believed correct and whilst every effort has been made to ensure accuracy, information cannot be guaranteed. In the event of any error the publisher and author would welcome any further information and offer their sincere apologies.

CONTENTS

CHAPTER ONE
THE NORTHERN IRELAND STORY

The Irish FA was founded on 18 November 1880 at the Queen's Hotel, Belfast, becoming the fourth oldest governing body in the world, behind the three other home associations. This inaugural meeting was at the behest of the Cliftonville club – the oldest in Ireland – and clubs in Belfast and District created a unifying constitution and set of rules, adhering to those laid down by the Scottish FA some seven years earlier in 1873. The aims of this embryonic organisation were to promote, foster and develop the game of football throughout the whole of Ireland.

Football itself first came to Ireland a couple of years earlier when Scottish clubs Queen's Park and the Caledonians staged an exhibition match at the Ulster Cricket Ground, Ballynafeigh after John M McAlery, first secretary of the new association, had discovered the game whilst on honeymoon in Edinburgh. The Irish FA's first international match was against England at the Knock Ground, Bloomfield in East Belfast in 1882. Ireland lost 13-0 but the gate receipts amounted to £9 19s 7d. Captain of the Irish side that day was McAlery, who was distraught and sat in the dressing-room with tears running down his cheeks! A week later, and Ireland lost 7-1 to Wales at Wrexham with Distillery's Johnston netting his country's first goal in the international arena.

Qualification for internationals was not nearly so strict as it is today. If players were born in Ireland or had seven years residence, they could wear the St Patrick blue jersey – the nation's first colours. It changed to green against England on 17 October 1931 to avoid a clash with Scotland's dark blue. Professionalism became a debating point at the start of the 1885-86 season, with Scotland inviting the Irish FA delegation to a conference at Liverpool, but as England decided not to attend, there was no Irish representative there either. Though professionalism became legalised in England and Scotland that year, the Irish FA remained quite adamant that 'only amateurs should play in international matches'.

> DID YOU KNOW?
> The first brothers to score goals for Ireland were Joe Sherrard v Wales (12 March 1887) and Willie Sherrard v Wales (16 March 1895).

In March 1887, five years after their first-ever international match and some very heavy defeats, Ireland won their first-ever game when they beat Wales 4-1 at Oldpark Avenue in Belfast. In February 1899 Ireland again conceded 13 goals against England, this time at Sunderland's Roker Park. It was the first-ever international staged at that famous ground and on returning to Belfast, the Irish team found their bags had been chalk-marked with a huge '13' by disgruntled fans on the cross-channel ferry!

International football remained insular, played in the confines of the British Isles and, as a result, England, Scotland and Wales and of course Ireland had an inflated opinion of their skills compared with the European nations.

In February 1902 Ireland beat Wales 3-0 at Cardiff Arms Park with Andrew Gara of Preston North End netting all three goals. This was not the first international hat-trick scored by an Irishman – that honour went to Ollie Stansfield, who hit three in a 7-2 defeat of Wales in Belfast in 1891.

Ireland won two international in 1903 against Wales and Scotland but had to wait until February 1913 for their first success against England – a 2-1 win at Windsor Park with Billy Gillespie scoring both goals.

Ireland's playing fortunes had been mixed since those humiliating early defeats. There were the odd occasions when the side were victorious but in the main they were the underdogs. However, in 1913-14, Ireland won the Home International Championship outright, beating Wales 2-1 and England 3-0 but just missed out on the Triple Crown as a result of a 1-1 draw with Scotland. A blend had been found in the side and there were a number of experienced players now representing their country. Billy Gillespie scored in the wins over Wales and England, while Billy Lacey netted the other two goals in the defeat of England at Ayresome Park. In the game against Scotland, Fred McKee was injured just before half-time, forcing Billy Lacey to move into goal. The Irish did well to earn a point and thus win the Championship during a campaign in which each of the original teams chosen had been drastically altered by injuries and unavailability.

The final table read:

	P	W	D	L	F	A	Pts
Ireland	3	2	1	0	6	2	5
Scotland	3	1	2	0	2	4	4
England	3	1	0	2	3	6	2
Wales	2	0	1	2	1	4	1

Upon the partition of Ireland in 1921, the FAIFS (now the FAI) was set up to regulate the game in the Irish Free State (now the Republic of Ireland). Those behind the FAIFS believed that soccer should be regulated by a federation based in Ireland's capital, Dublin. The IFA's supporters argued that the federation should be based where the game was mainly played – Ulster and its principal city Belfast. Both federations claimed to represent the whole of the island, both competed as Ireland and both picked players from the two rival leagues – which also split at this time.

On 1 February 1930, Ireland recorded their biggest-ever win in international football when they defeated Wales 7-0 at Celtic Park. Joe Bambrick netted six of his side's goals – a record which not surprisingly still stands, while Andy McCluggage scored the other goal from a penalty. The following year, the national side changed their shirt colour from blue to green. The official reason at the time was that, due to Scotland's navy strip, they were forced to wear white shirts in games against them. Back then, it would have represented one-third of their games. Probably as influential – though never quoted as an official reason – was the off-the-field contest between the IFA and the Free State to be recognised as the 'true' national side of Ireland. Whereas the IFA blue shirt had an old-style Celtic cross badge with a harp in the middle, the Free State badge was of shamrocks. The IFA changed their badge to shamrocks in the mid 1930s.

When Ireland entertained Scotland at Windsor Park in October 1934, an overhead cable fault at Shaftesbury Square led to a break down in the tram service. This meant thousands of fans streamed in late into Windsor Park. Scotland led 1-0 at half-time but when the second-half started, Ireland resumed without goalkeeper Elisha Scott. McMillan went in goal and performed heroics as the 10-men team won 2-1 with two late goals from Martin and Coulter.

In 1948 the Irish FA joined FIFA in order to compete in the World Cup. Northern Ireland had the honour of hosting the first 'British' World Cup qualifier when Scotland visited Windsor Park in October 1949. The Scots raced into a three-goal half-time lead and though Sammy Smyth scored twice after the break, the visitors ran out comfortable winners 8-2. Ireland then played England at Maine Road but as in the Scotland game, it was over as a contest by half-time – England eventually

winning 9-2. The Irish secured their first World Cup point with a goalless draw against Wales at Wrexham's Racecourse Ground. This match was the last one that players born in the Republic of Ireland played for Ireland.

As with the 1950 qualifiers, FIFA elected to use the 1953-54 British Championships as qualification for the finals in Switzerland. Following defeats by Scotland and England, Ireland then recorded their first-ever World Cup qualifying when Peter McParland scored both his side's goals in a 2-1 defeat of Wales.

In the summer of 1954 FIFA ordered the Irish FA to name their international team Northern Ireland. FIFA also ordered the Football Association of Ireland to name their international team the Republic of Ireland.

When Northern Ireland were paired with Italy and Portugal in the qualifiers for the 1958 World Cup in Sweden, few fans held out much hope of this campaign being any different than the previous two. But of course, we now know that what followed was the zenith of Irish FA history. Northern Ireland began their World Cup campaign in January 1957 against Portugal in Lisbon, a match that kicked off at 10.30pm. It was a game that began one day and finished the next! In what was a physical encounter, a goal from Billy Bingham earned the Irish a point. Most fans thought it was a flash in the pan, few thinking it would lead to an era of glory. Those views were reinforced when over three months later, Italy beat Northern Ireland 1-0 and qualification seemed a long way off. However, eyebrows were raised just six days later when Northern Ireland defeated Portugal 3-0 with goals from Simpson, McIlroy and Casey. Later that month, the Portuguese beat the Italians by a similar margin. Italian qualification was now not a foregone conclusion, and it became even more worrying for them when Northern Ireland beat England 3-2 at Wembley.

This was a great boost to Northern Ireland's morale and so when they were due to meet Italy at Windsor Park on 4 December 1957, they needed a win, their opponents a draw. But what happened next has gone down in footballing folklore the world over. Hungarian referee Istvan Zolt, manager of the Budapest Opera House was appointed to officiate the game but he was fogbound at London Airport. However, Irish FA secretary Billy Drennan had Arthur Ellis, then rated the world's No.1 referee standing by to catch a train for Stranraer and the ferry to Larne.

No agreement could be reached, with the Italians insisting that the weather would improve sufficiently for Zolt to arrive the next day. But it didn't and by then it was too late for Ellis to make the journey across the Irish Sea. A local referee was also ruled out so it was decided to play the game as a friendly and arrange the World Cup tie for the following month. The friendly, in which tackles went in thick and fast, ended all-square at 2-2 but before the rematch, the Italians defeated Portugal to top the group. Northern Ireland's players knew nothing other than a win would suffice and thanks to goals from Jimmy McIroy and Wilbur Cush, a win by 2-1 is just what they got.

Now, for the first time in the history of the Irish FA, Northern Ireland had reached the World Cup Finals. This is how the group finished:

	P	W	D	L	F	A	Pts
NORTHERN IRELAND	4	2	1	1	6	3	5
Italy	4	2	0	2	5	5	4
Portugal	4	1	1	2	4	7	3

However, in the months after qualifying for the finals and the finals themselves, Northern Ireland only played one international match, that a draw with fellow qualifiers Wales.

When the draw was made for the 1958 Finals, Northern Ireland found themselves paired with reigning champions West Germany as the well as the much-fancied Czechoslovakia and Argentina. However, Northern Ireland's achievement in reaching the finals was tinged with controversy. Two of Ireland's matches in Sweden were arranged for Sundays and under the articles of the Irish FA, these were banned, thus casting doubt on the nation's participation in the tournament. A compromise was reached with the team permitted to play on the Sabbath and the rule remained unaltered: Sunday football was permitted outside Northern Ireland.

With Jackie Blanchflower still recovering from the Munich air disaster, it meant that Northern Ireland only took 17 players and this was reduced to 16 before a ball was kicked when Rangers' Billy Simpson was injured in the very first training session.

The opening match against Czechoslovakia was played at Halmstad – the first-ever occasion when an Irish FA XI had played on a Sunday. To the surprise of every one present, Northern Ireland triumphed 1-0 with Wilbur Cush getting the all-important goal. Northern Ireland's next opponents at the same venue three days later were Argentina, who were stunned just three minutes into the game when Peter McParland put the Irish ahead. However, the South American side hit back to win 3-1. Then it was on to Malmo for yet another Sunday match, this time against the current world champions West Germany. This match has gone down in both Irish and German sporting folklore, for with Harry Gregg in outstanding form and two goals from Peter McParland, Northern Ireland led 2-1 with just seven minutes to play. Just as the shock of the tournament was about to materialise, up popped a young Uwe Seeler to net the equaliser. With Czechoslovakia having surprisingly beaten Argentina 6-1, they finished equal on points with Northern Ireland, thus necessitating a play-off for a place in the quarter-finals.

The group table read:

	P	W	D	L	F	A	Pts
West Germany	3	1	2	0	7	4	4
Czechoslovakia	3	1	1	1	8	4	3
NORTHERN IRELAND	3	1	1	1	4	5	3
Argentina	3	1	0	2	5	10	2

Following their defeat of the Argentinians, Czechoslovakia were expected to exact their revenge on Northern Ireland for that opening defeat and progress to the quarter-finals where France lay in wait. There followed another victory for the Irish, albeit after extra-time with Peter McParland scoring twice in a 2-1 scoreline. Northern Ireland had reached the last eight of the World Cup but the preparation for the game against France – just two days after the play-off with Czechoslovakia – was not helped by an ever-growing injury list and the 10-hour journey across Sweden to Norrkoping. Unfortunately, the meeting with the French, who had players of the calibre of Raymond Kopa and Just Fontaine in their ranks, proved beyond Northern Ireland and they crashed out of the competition 4-0. It was a sad end to the fairytale story that had captured the imagination of the football world.

Within six months of the completion of the World Cup Finals, a future Northern Ireland international, Johnny Crossan, who was playing for Coleraine, was found guilty by the Irish League Management of being paid as an amateur and asking for more than the £750 permitted from a transfer fee – he was banned for life from British football! He had started out with Derry City where his ability on the ball attracted attention from a host of English clubs but after his relationship with Derry City deteriorated, in stepped Coleraine to sign him as an amateur. He later signed for Peter Doherty's Bristol City but the registration was not accepted by the Football League, thus

forcing the Irish authorities to act in the way they did. Appeals to the Irish FA were rejected and Crossan left to play his football on the continent, initially with Sparta Rotterdam. In November 1959, Crossan astonishingly found himself selected to play for Northern Ireland against England – a selection frowned upon by both the Football League and the Irish FA. Though he won 23 caps, he didn't appear again until 1962 but after a spell with Standard Liège, the ban was finally lifted and he went on to join Sunderland, whom he helped win promotion to the top flight.

The qualifiers for the 1962 World Cup Finals in Chile saw Northern Ireland placed in the same group as their old adversaries from the previous finals, West Germany, and Greece. The opening game saw Billy McAdams net a magnificent hat-trick for Ireland in front of a 40,000 strong Windsor Park crowd but the visiting Germans still triumphed 4-3. The Germans then virtually sealed qualification with a 3-0 win over Greece in Athens. Though the Irish were not mathematically eliminated, they did need to win themselves in Greece to stand any chance of qualification but they went down 2-1. A week later, a similar scoreline saw Northern Ireland lose to the Germans in Berlin before pride was restored in the final group game, when Jimmy McLaughlin netted both goals in a 2-0 home win over Greece.

Northern Ireland first entered the European Championships in 1964. Though they progressed to the second round with 2-0 victories both home and away against Poland, the team went out to Spain 2-1 on aggregate – this after a Willie Irvine goal had given them a 1-1 draw in the first leg in Bilbao!

With the 1966 World Cup Finals taking place in England, hopes were high that Northern Ireland would qualify for the tournament. The expectations were raised even further when the Irish were drawn in the same group as Holland, Switzerland and Albania. A Johnny Crossan penalty gave Ireland the points in the opening game against Switzerland in Belfast but when the sides met again a month later in Lausanne, the Swiss emerged as 2-1 winners. On St Patrick's Day 1965, goals from Crossan and Neill helped Ireland beat Holland 2-1 whilst the return in Rotterdam a few weeks later saw the sides play out a goalless draw. With Holland and Switzerland set to meet, Ireland's hopes were that the two sides would cancel each other out, allowing Northern Ireland to nip in and head the group with two victories over a currently pointless Albania. In the home game against the Albanians, a Johnny Crossan hat-trick and a fine individual goal from George Best, helped Northern Ireland to a 4-1 win. All was going to plan as the Dutch and the Swiss cancelled each other out in Amsterdam. This left Northern Ireland needing the formality of a win in Tirana and so make plans for crossing the Irish Sea. However, a 1-1 draw was all that the team could manage and with the Swiss beating the Dutch in Bern, the point gained in Albania proved to be insufficient.

After a disappointing 1968 European Championships in which Northern Ireland finished rooted to the bottom of their group, little was expected of the national side when the 1970 World Cup saw them drawn alongside Turkey and the USSR. However, qualification for the finals in Mexico got off to the most amazing start when following a 4-1 home win over Turkey, the boys in green won the return in Ankara 3-0. There followed a nine-month lay-off before Northern Ireland's next group match at home to the USSR. Despite having most of the play, the game ended goalless – it proved to be the last World Cup tie to be played on home soil for nigh on eight years! The USSR then beat Turkey to leave the Irish needing a point from their visit to Moscow to qualify for the finals, whilst the home side, who had a game in hand, needed to win to draw level on points with Northern Ireland. Despite some heroics from the Irish defence, goals from Nodija and Bishovet gave the home side a 2-0 victory.

Northern Ireland were unfortunate to be drawn against the USSR and Spain in the 1972 European Championships and though they suffered defeats in the away games, did manage draws in the

home fixtures, although the meeting with Spain was played at Hull because of the political unrest. Also in Northern Ireland's group were Cyprus and in the 5-0 win in Belfast, not only did George Best score a hat-trick but Distillery's Peter Watson's international career became the shortest ever: he won his only cap in this match after coming on as an 88th minute substitute. In May 1972, Northern Ireland's player-manager Terry Neill scored the only goal of the game as his side beat England at Wembley.

The Irish were drawn alongside Bulgaria, Portugal and whipping boys Cyprus in the 1974 World Cup qualifiers but made the most disastrous of starts. After losing 3-0 in Bulgaria, Northern Ireland unbelievably went down 1-0 in Cyprus before securing their first point with a 1-1 home draw against Portugal. This was the start of a four-game unbeaten run in the group as Cyprus were beaten 3-0 at Fulham's Craven Cottage ground and Bulgaria held to a goalless draw in Sheffield before Ireland drew 1-1 with Portugal in Lisbon.

Northern Ireland finished runners-up to Yugoslavia in the qualifying group for the 1976 European Championships with Bryan Hamilton scoring the only goal of the game against the eventual group champions. This came after a 2-0 success in Sweden and hopes were high that at last Northern Ireland would qualify for the final stages. But despite a resounding victory over Norway, who had beaten the Irish in the group's opening game, Northern Ireland went down to defeat at home to Sweden and in Yugoslavia.

Goals from Chris McGrath and Derek Spence helped Northern Ireland draw 2-2 against 1978 World Cup qualifying group favourites Holland in Rotterdam, but defeats in Belgium and Iceland left the Irish needing to win all their three home games to stand a chance of qualification. Unfortunately, sandwiched in-between victories over Iceland and Belgium, a match in which Gerry Armstrong scored twice, the Dutch won 1-0 to qualify for the finals in Argentina. They went on to reach the World Cup Final where they lost 3-1 to the host side.

Northern Ireland gave a much better showing in the 1980 European Championships, this in spite of being drawn in the same group as England, the Republic of Ireland, Bulgaria and Denmark. After a goalless draw in Dublin, Northern Ireland beat Denmark at home and Bulgaria away before losing 4-0 to England at Wembley. Goals from Chris Nicholl and Armstrong helped to complete the double over Bulgaria but there followed heavy defeats against Denmark (0-4) and England (1-5) before a Gerry Armstrong goal gave them both points in the home game against the Republic. Northern Ireland finished runners-up in the group, six points behind leaders England.

In February 1980 Billy Bingham had been appointed Northern Ireland manager. Three months later the national side won the Home International Championship outright for only the second time in their history.

For the 1982 World Cup Finals in Spain, Northern Ireland had been drawn against Scotland, Portugal, Sweden and Israel. Despite an uninspiring goalless draw against Israel in Tel Aviv just weeks after Bingham's appointment, there followed victories at Windsor Park over both Sweden and Portugal whilst the home and away games against Scotland produced draws.

However, after they had gone down to single goal defeats in the return matches with the Swedes and the Portuguese, Northern Ireland's qualification for the finals was under great threat. However, after Israel had unbelievably beaten Portugal 4-1, Northern Ireland needed just a point from their home game against Israel to qualify for their second World Cup Finals. As it transpired, a Gerry Armstrong goal clinched both points in an emotional night at Windsor Park and Northern Ireland qualified for the finals as runners-up behind Group 6 winners Scotland.

Come the summer, Northern Ireland were paired with Yugoslavia, Honduras and the hosts, Spain. Yugoslavia had to be content with a goalless draw against the admirable Northern Ireland team fielding 17-year-old Norman Whiteside but then the youngster's team had to be satisfied with a point against the so-called minnows of the group, Honduras. Northern Ireland had taken an early lead through Gerry Armstrong and threatened to take them apart. They held on, restricting the Irish to the one goal and managed an equaliser on the hour mark. The score remained 1-1. In their final game, Northern Ireland were really up against it, requiring at least a 1-1 draw against Spain in the last Group 5 game. In the sweltering Luis Casanova stadium in Valencia, Northern Ireland played perhaps their most outstanding World Cup game ever. They overcame all the odds – a weak referee, the heat, the hostile crowd, the cynical Spanish tackling – to hold on to a 0-0 half-time score. Gerry Armstrong put them ahead two minutes into the second-half but 12 minutes later, they were staring disaster in the face when Mal Donaghy was sent-off for a seemingly innocuous shove. The Northern Ireland side, with Pat Jennings outstanding, showed their determination by refusing to relinquish their lead and so qualified for the next round as top of their group!

The doughty fighters of Northern Ireland then held Austria to a 2-2 draw in the next game and met France requiring a victory to progress to the last four of the competition. The searing temperatures in Madrid's Calderon stadium left the Irish struggling and Platini, fit again after injury, directed a steady flow of French attacks on the wilting Irishmen. With a little over a quarter-of-an-hour to go, the French were 3-0 up but a Gerry Armstrong goal was not enough to revive the Irish who went out 4-1, so ending their wonderfully brave challenge.

Northern Ireland were undoubtedly the surprise packet of the 1984 European Championship qualifying stages. Their five-team group consisting of West Germany, Austria, Turkey and Albania was supposed to be a pushover for the West Germans, the World Cup runners-up and reigning European Champions. But Northern Ireland inflicted two 1-0 victories, home and away, upon West Germany to throw the group wide open. It went down to the wire with the Germans needing to beat Albania at home in their last game to qualify, which they did with only 10 minutes to spare and got through only on goal difference from Northern Ireland.

In the summer of 1984 Northern Ireland achieved a third outright win the Home International Championships. This was the final year of the competition and the trophy is now retained at the Irish FA headquarters, Windsor Avenue, Belfast.

Following these excellent performances in the European Championship and the Home Internationals, Northern Ireland hoped to be among the qualification front-runners for the 1986 World Cup Finals in Mexico. Finland, who along with England, Romania and Turkey, made up the rest of Group 3, were Northern Ireland's first opponents. Yet against a side that hadn't won any of its 22 previous internationals, Northern Ireland crashed to a 1-0 defeat! There followed two successive home victories over Romania and Finland. The next visitors to Windsor Park were England, a game that looked to be heading for a goalless draw until Mark Hateley's late strike won the points for Bobby Robson's side. Billy Bingham's side then produced two wins and a draw from their next three qualifiers, leaving them needing a point from their final match against England. A backs-to-the-wall performance from the Irish back four plus an outstanding display of goalkeeping by Pat Jennings saw the Irish hold out for a memorable goalless draw and so secure the point they so desperately required.

When the draw for the finals in Mexico was made, Northern Ireland again found themselves facing Spain, whilst other group members were Algeria and three-times world champions, Brazil. Northern Ireland's first match against Algeria was a hard, bad-tempered affair in which they failed to convert a number of chances after Norman Whiteside had scored from a free-kick in the

fifth minute. In the second-half, Algeria equalised and were then content to play out a 1-1 draw as the Irish, wilting in the heat, dropped a vital point. Having lost to Northern Ireland in the 1982 World Cup, Spain were keen to exact revenge against them this time, and took the lead through Butragueno after only one minute! Salinas scored a second after 18 minutes and although Northern Ireland managed to pull a goal back just after half-time – after a farcical sliced clearance by Zubizaretta had been headed to Clarke – Spain deserved their 2-1 victory.

Northern Ireland were outclassed in the last group game against Brazil, who had already qualified: despite a sterling performance by Pat Jennings (on his 41st birthday), they went down 3-0, so failing to reach the next stage.

Following a disappointing 1988 European Championships, when Northern Ireland's solitary victory was a 1-0 defeat of bottom-of-the-table Turkey in their last qualifying game, the Irish also failed to light up the following World Cup campaign, though they did win their first group match against Malta. Despite a draw against the Republic of Ireland, who qualified for Italia '90, Northern Ireland's only other success came in the return fixture against Malta.

The 1992 European Championship qualifiers saw Northern Ireland record their biggest-ever away win international football when Colin Clarke netted a hat-trick in a 5-0 win against the Faroe Islands, a match played in Landskrona, Sweden. Unfortunately, the Irish were outplayed by both Yugoslavia and Denmark, with the former qualifying for the finals as group winners.

The formidable task confronting Northern Ireland in qualifying for the 1994 World Cup Finals in the United States was again underlined when they only drew 2-2 with Lithuania, this after they had led the Windsor Park encounter 2-0. A valuable point was dropped and manager Bingham's hopes of accumulating a maximum eight points from his side's first four home games were dashed. The results in the remainder of the campaign were mixed but manager Bingham had produced a squad that revealed much potential. They held the Republic of Ireland to a 1-1 draw in a tension-filled match at Windsor Park, when a Jimmy Quinn goal almost ended Jack Charlton's hopes of making it to the United States. Alan McLaughlin's equaliser ten minutes from time saved the day.

Bryan Hamilton was nominated as Northern Ireland's first full-time manager to replace Billy Bingham who retired after 15 years' distinguished service and after a 2-0 win over Romania in Belfast, a 4-1 defeat of Liechtenstein in the opening European Championship Group 6 game followed. There were some excellent results in the 1996 European Championships, with wins against Austria in Vienna and Latvia in Riga whilst sandwiched in between was a 1-1 draw with the Republic of Ireland in Dublin. Then came a disastrous 2-0 defeat by Canada before a 2-1 humiliation by Latvia at Windsor Park. That scoreline proved to be a catastrophe, especially in view of the Republic being held to a scoreless draw in Liechtenstein and then losing 2-1 to Austria at Lansdowne Road. Three points against Latvia would have put Northern Ireland back into qualification for the Euro finals to be held in England. However, Hamilton's side rallied and ended the group with a stunning 5-3 home win over Austria.

Despite this, the next World Cup qualifying campaign was a complete let down, with the national side's worst moment coming in the neutral city of Zurich when Northern Ireland lost 1-0 to Albania! Prior to that there had been commendable draws with European champions Germany in Nuremberg and Portugal in Belfast, along with a 3-0 friendly win over Belgium. Also there was a scoreless draw against Thailand in the heat and humidity of Bangkok. With many of the established players unavailable, the performances of the youngsters underlined the depth in talent at Northern Ireland's disposal. However, with only seven points out of a possible 30, the national side slumped to 92nd in the FIFA world rankings. This crisis situation led to the termination of Bryan Hamilton's contract, though the Irish FA International Committee were 'conscious of the

valuable public relations work carried out by the manager as an adjunct to his main duties and responsibilities'.

His replacement was Lawrie McMenemy, former assistant to England manager Graham Taylor, with Joe Jordan, ex-Manchester United and AC Milan striker and Pat Jennings as the goalkeeping coach. What was labelled as 'The Dream management Team' had an excellent start with victories over Slovakia and Switzerland as they laid the basis for the European Championship. However, results in competitive matches were still disappointing, though the 1-0 win over the Republic of Ireland in a charity match for the Omagh Bomb Disaster Fund – the team missing 10 regulars – was a major morale boost. Elimination from the European Championship qualifiers, following one win in eight matches, heralded the departure of McMenemy and his management team, who declined to take up an extension option on their contract.

World Cup hero Sammy McIlroy who had been with Macclesfield took over, assisted by Jim Harvey who was manager of non-League Morecambe. McIlroy had an initial success against Luxembourg and Malta but there soon followed a 1-0 defeat by Hungary at Windsor Park. Bad luck, conceding late goals, elementary defensive blunders, injuries and suspensions were to beset McIlroy's team in the months ahead. For instance, he was without 10 regulars for the World Cup qualifying match against the Czech Republic in Prague, yet his makeshift team held the home side to 1-1, until the final two minutes when the Czechs struck twice! In Bulgaria, they lost 4-3, the highest number of away goals scored for a number of years but bad defending ruined the outcome.

The 4-0 defeat by Norway in a friendly international at Windsor Park in February 2001 proved disastrous in more ways than one. Celtic midfielder Neil Lennon was booed by a small number of fans every time he touched the ball – their protest at affiliation with the Parkhead club following his transfer from Leicester City. The action of the minority was totally condemned by the entire Northern Ireland sporting public and the Irish FA, who immediately drew up a Code of Conduct which operates now at all games.

Throughout his tenure as Northern Ireland manager, Sammy McIlroy, who brought pride and passion to the squad, reminiscent of the halcyon World Cup days of Sweden 1958, Spain '82 and Mexico '86, was never able to parade his original selections in any game due to withdrawals and premature retirement from players such as Lennon, Horlock and Magilton. There was depression and drama with the national team. It went 1,298 minutes and 15 matches without scoring a goal until Preston North End striker David Healy ended the drought against Norway and went on to establish a new all-time Northern Ireland scoring record of 14 – one more than that which existed for years and was held by Colin Clarke and Billy Gillespie.

Sammy McIlroy resigned as manager 24 hours after the final 2004 European Championship qualifier against Greece in Athens to join Stockport County. Jimmy Nicholl, Dunfermline Athletic's assistant-coach seemed a certainty to succeed him but the job went to Lawrie Sanchez, Wimbledon's FA Cup Final hero, who played three times for Northern Ireland under Billy Bingham.

Sanchez brought a new dimension to the management of the national side, getting the team on a winning streak – five matches undefeated. This lifted morale and at last Northern Ireland fans found themselves with a feel-good factor. There were some good wins and promising performances in friendlies and on the Caribbean tour. This resulted in an improvement in attendances and phenomenal support both home and abroad.

After a disappointing start to the 2006 World Cup qualifiers, Northern Ireland beat Azerbaijan 2-0 before a David Healy goal brought a never-to-be-forgotten 1-0 victory over England. Healy's goal lifted the morale of the entire country – a goal which is now a piece of Irish football history. It pushed Sanchez's team into a comparatively respectable FIFA ranking after years of hovering in the doldrums along with other fellow strugglers. Northern Ireland finished fourth in the World Cup Group 6 qualifying series but with a little more luck could have got third place. Following the emergence of young players like Steve Davis, Sammy Clingan and Kyle Lafferty to name but three, Sanchez will hope that the years ahead bring further joy for Northern Ireland supporters and qualification for the finals of the 2008 European Championships for the first time ever!

DID YOU KNOW?
The Irish FA is the fourth oldest international Football Association in the world

Above: A selection of NI player cards

CHAPTER TWO
THE PLAYERS

1   J HAMILTON

Position   Goalkeeper

Clubs   Knock

Caps   2

Date	Team	Result	G
18 Feb 1882	England	0-13	
25 Feb 1882	Wales	1-7	

2   J McALERY

Position   Full-back

Clubs   Cliftonville

Caps   2

Date	Team	Result	G
18 Feb 1882	England	0-13	
25 Feb 1882	Wales	1-7	

3   D RATTRAY

Position   Left-back

Clubs   Avoniel

Caps   3

Date	Team	Result	G
18 Feb 1882	England	0-13	
24 Feb 1883	England	0-7	
17 Mar 1883	Wales	1-1	

4   D C MARTIN

Position   Wing-half

Clubs   Cliftonville

Caps   3

Date	Team	Result	G
18 Feb 1882	England	0-13	
25 Feb 1882	Wales	1-7	
24 Feb 1883	England	0-7	

5   J HASTINGS

Position   Centre-half

Clubs   Knock; Ulster

Caps   7

Date	Team	Result	G
18 Feb 1882	England	0-13	
25 Feb 1882	Wales	1-7	
17 Mar 1883	Wales	1-1	
26 Jan 1884	Scotland	0-5	
23 Feb 1884	England	1-8	
12 Mar 1886	England	1-6	
20 Mar 1886	Scotland	2-7	

6   J BUCKLE

Position   Wing-half

Clubs   Cliftonville

Caps   1

Date	Team	Result	G
18 Feb 1882	England	0-13	

7   W B R McWHA

Position   Outside-right

Clubs   Knock; Cliftonville

Caps   7   Goals   1

Date	Team	Result	G
18 Feb 1882	England	0-13	
25 Feb 1882	Wales	1-7	
24 Feb 1883	England	0-7	
17 Mar 1883	Wales	1-1	
23 Feb 1884	England	1-8	1
28 Feb 1885	England	0-4	
11 Apr 1885	Wales	2-8	

8   J R DAVISON

Position   Forward

Clubs   Cliftonville

Caps   8

Date	Team	Result	G
18 Feb 1882	England	0-13	
25 Feb 1882	Wales	1-7	
24 Feb 1883	England	0-7	
17 Mar 1883	Wales	1-1	
26 Jan 1884	Scotland	0-5	
9 Feb 1884	Wales	0-6	
23 Feb 1884	England	1-8	
28 Feb 1885	England	0-4	

Date	Team	Result	G
26 Jan 1884	Scotland	0-5	
9 Feb 1884	Wales	0-6	
23 Feb 1884	England	1-8	
27 Feb 1886	Wales	0-5	
12 Mar 1886	England	1-6	
20 Mar 1886	Scotland	2-7	
5 Feb 1887	England	0-7	
3 Mar 1888	Wales	0-11	
7 Apr 1888	England	1-5	1
9 Mar 1889	Scotland	0-7	
8 Feb 1890	Wales	2-5	

9 JOHN SINCLAIR

Position   Centre-forward

Clubs   Knock

Caps   2

Date	Team	Result	G
18 Feb 1882	England	0-13	
25 Feb 1882	Wales	1-7	

10 A H DILL

Position   Wing-half/Winger

Clubs   Knock; Down Athletic; Cliftonville

Caps   9   Goals   1

Date	Team	Result	G
18 Feb 1882	England	0-13	
25 Feb 1882	Wales	1-7	
17 Mar 1883	Wales	1-1	
26 Jan 1884	Scotland	0-5	
9 Feb 1884	Wales	0-6	
23 Feb 1884	England	1-8	
28 Feb 1885	England	0-4	
14 Mar 1885	Scotland	2-8	
11 Apr 1885	Wales	2-8	1

11 D McCAW

Position   Winger

Clubs   Malone

Caps   1

Date	Team	Result	G
18 Feb 1882	England	0-13	

12 WILLIAM CRONE

Position   Full-back/Centre-half

Clubs   Distillery

Caps   12   Goals   1

Date	Team	Result	G
25 Feb 1882	Wales	1-7	

13 J CONDY

Position   Forward

Clubs   Distillery

Caps   3   Goals   1

Date	Team	Result	G
25 Feb 1882	Wales	1-7	
12 Mar 1886	England	1-6	
20 Mar 1886	Scotland	2-7	1

14 R S JOHNSTON

Position   Forward

Clubs   Distillery

Caps   4   Goals   2

Date	Team	Result	G
25 Feb 1882	Wales	1-7	1
23 Feb 1884	England	1-8	
12 Mar 1886	England	1-6	
20 Mar 1886	Scotland	2-7	1

15 J RANKINE

Position   Goalkeeper

Clubs   Alexander

Caps   2

Date	Team	Result	G
24 Feb 1883	England	0-7	
17 Mar 1883	Wales	1-1	

16 J WATSON

Position   Full-back

Clubs   Ulster

Caps   9

Date	Team	Result	G
24 Feb 1883	England	0-7	
17 Mar 1883	Wales	1-1	

Date	Team	Result	G
27 Feb 1886	Wales	0-5	
12 Mar 1886	England	1-6	
20 Mar 1886	Scotland	2-7	
19 Feb 1887	Scotland	1-4	
13 Mar 1887	Wales	4-1	
2 Mar 1889	England	1-6	
27 Apr 1889	Wales	1-3	

Date	Team	Result	G
24 Feb 1883	England	0-7	
9 Feb 1884	Wales	0-6	
19 Feb 1887	Scotland	1-4	
27 Apr 1889	Wales	1-3	
8 Feb 1890	Wales	2-5	
29 Mar 1890	Scotland	1-4	

17 T B MOLYNEUX

Position   Wing-half

Clubs   Ligoniel; Cliftonville

Caps   11   Goals   1

Date	Team	Result	G
24 Feb 1883	England	0-7	
17 Mar 1883	Wales	1-1	
26 Jan 1884	Scotland	0-5	
9 Feb 1884	Wales	0-6	
23 Feb 1884	Wales	1-8	
28 Feb 1885	England	0-4	
11 Apr 1885	Wales	2-8	1
27 Feb 1886	Wales	0-5	
12 Mar 1886	England	1-6	
20 Mar 1886	Scotland	2-7	
24 Mar 1888	Scotland	2-10	

18 W J MORROW

Position   Wing-half/Forward

Clubs   Moyola Park

Caps   3   Goals   1

Date	Team	Result	G
24 Feb 1883	England	0-7	
17 Mar 1883	Wales	1-1	1
26 Jan 1884	Scotland	0-5	

19 R M C POTTS

Position   Forward

Clubs   Cliftonville

Caps   2

Date	Team	Result	G
24 Feb 1883	England	0-7	
17 Mar 1883	Wales	1-1	

20 JACK REID

Position   Forward

Clubs   Ulster

Caps   6

21 E A SPILLER

Position   Forward

Clubs   Cliftonville

Caps   5

Date	Team	Result	G
24 Feb 1883	England	0-7	
17 Mar 1883	Wales	1-1	
26 Jan 1884	Scotland	0-5	
9 Feb 1884	Wales	0-6	
23 Feb 1884	England	1-8	

22 R J HUNTER

Position   Goalkeeper

Clubs   Cliftonville

Caps   3

Date	Team	Result	G
26 Jan 1884	Scotland	0-5	
9 Feb 1884	Wales	0-6	
23 Feb 1884	England	1-8	

23 M WILSON

Position   Right-back

Clubs   Distillery

Caps   3

Date	Team	Result	G
26 Jan 1884	Scotland	0-5	
9 Feb 1884	Wales	0-6	
23 Feb 1884	England	1-8	

24 J T GIBB

Position   Forward
Clubs   Wellington Park; Cliftonville

Caps   10   Goals   2

Date	Team	Result	G
26 Jan 1884	Scotland	0-5	
9 Feb 1884	Wales	0-6	
28 Feb 1885	England	0-4	
14 Mar 1885	Scotland	2-8	2
11 Apr 1885	Wales	2-8	

Date	Team	Result	G
20 Mar 1886	Scotland	2-7	
5 Feb 1887	England	0-7	
19 Feb 1887	Scotland	1-4	
13 Mar 1887	Wales	4-1	
9 Mar 1889	Scotland	0-7	

25 ARTHUR DAVID GAUSSEN

Position   Winger

Clubs   Moyola Park; Magherafelt

Caps   6

Date	Team	Result	G
26 Jan 1884	Scotland	0-5	
23 Feb 1884	England	1-8	
3 Mar 1888	Wales	0-11	
7 Apr 1888	England	1-5	
2 Mar 1889	England	1-6	
27 Apr 1889	Wales	1-3	

26 H LOCKHART

Position   Centre-half

Clubs   Russell School

Caps   1

Date	Team	Result	G
9 Feb 1884	Wales	0-6	

27 R REDMOND

Position   Wing-half

Clubs   Cliftonville

Caps   1

Date	Team	Result	G
9 Feb 1884	Wales	0-6	

28 A W HENDERSON

Position   Goalkeeper

Clubs   Ulster

Caps   3

Date	Team	Result	G
28 Feb 1885	England	0-4	
14 Mar 1885	Scotland	2-8	
11 Apr 1885	Wales	2-8	

29 G HEWISON

Position   Full-back

Clubs   Moyola Park

Caps   2

Date	Team	Result	G
28 Feb 1885	England	0-4	
14 Mar 1885	Scotland	2-8	

30 FREDERICK WILLIAM MOORHEAD

Position   Full-back

Clubs   Dublin University

Caps   1

Date	Team	Result	G
28 Feb 1885	England	0-4	

31 W J HOUSTON

Position   Centre-half

Clubs   Moyola Park

Caps   2

Date	Team	Result	G
28 Feb 1885	England	0-4	
14 Mar 1885	Scotland	2-8	

32 WILLIAM L'ESTRANGE EAMES

Position   Wing-half/Full-back

Born   Dublin, 18 July 1863

Clubs   Dublin University

Caps   3

Date	Team	Result	G
28 Feb 1885	England	0-4	
14 Mar 1885	Scotland	2-8	
11 Apr 1885	Wales	2-8	

33 G MAGEE

Position   Inside-forward

Clubs   Wellington Park

Caps   3

Date	Team	Result	G
28 Feb 1885	England	0-4	
14 Mar 1885	Scotland	2-8	
11 Apr 1885	Wales	2-8	

34   W JOHNSTON

Position   Full-back

Clubs   Oldpark

Caps   2

Date	Team	Result	G
14 Mar 1885	Scotland	2-8	
11 Apr 1885	Wales	2-8	

35   R MUIR

Position   Wing-half/Centre-half

Clubs   Oldpark

Caps   2

Date	Team	Result	G
14 Mar 1885	Scotland	2-8	
11 Apr 1885	Wales	2-8	

36   T L McLEAN

Position   Winger

Clubs   Limavady

Caps   1

Date	Team	Result	G
14 Mar 1885	Scotland	2-8	

37   JOSEPH SHERRARD

Position   Forward/Wing-half

Clubs   Limavady

Caps   3   Goals   1

Date	Team	Result	G
14 Mar 1885	Scotland	2-8	
13 Mar 1887	Wales	4-1	1
3 Mar 1888	Wales	0-11	

38   WILLOUGHBY JAMES HAMILTON

Position   Winger

Clubs   Dublin Association

Caps   1

Date	Team	Result	G
11 Apr 1885	Wales	2-8	

39   WILLIAM DRUMMOND HAMILTON

Position   Forward

Clubs   Dublin Association

Caps   1

Date	Team	Result	G
11 Apr 1885	Wales	2-8	

40   SHAW GILLESPIE

Position   Goalkeeper

Clubs   Hertford

Caps   6

Date	Team	Result	G
27 Feb 1886	Wales	0-5	
12 Mar 1886	England	1-6	
20 Mar 1886	Scotland	2-7	
5 Feb 1887	England	0-7	
19 Feb 1887	Scotland	1-4	
13 Mar 1887	Wales	4-1	

41   A D DEVINE

Position   Full-back/Wing-half

Clubs   Limavady

Caps   4

Date	Team	Result	G
27 Feb 1886	Wales	0-5	
12 Mar 1886	England	1-6	
13 Mar 1887	Wales	4-1	
3 Mar 1888	Wales	0-11	

42   A McARTHUR

Position   Wing-half

Clubs   Distillery

Caps   1

Date	Team	Result	G
27 Feb 1886	Wales	0-5	

43   JOHN McCLATCHEY

Position   Forward

Clubs   Distillery

Caps   3

Date	Team	Result	G
27 Feb 1886	Wales	0-5	

Date	Team	Result	G
12 Mar 1886	England	1-6	
20 Mar 1886	Scotland	2-7	

44 E R WHITFIELD

Position   Forward

Clubs   Dublin University

Caps   1

Date	Team	Result	G
27 Feb 1886	Wales	0-5	

45 R H SMYTH

Position   Centre-forward

Clubs   Dublin University

Caps   1

Date	Team	Result	G
27 Feb 1886	Wales	0-5	

46 J LEMON

Position   Forward

Born   Greyabbey, 19 May 1864
Died   3 December 1913

Clubs   Glentoran; Belfast YMCA

Caps   3   Goals   2

Date	Team	Result	G
27 Feb 1886	Wales	0-5	
24 Mar 1888	Scotland	2-10	1
27 Apr 1889	Wales	1-3	1

47 E O ROPER

Position   Outside-left

Clubs   Dublin University

Caps   1

Date	Team	Result	G
27 Feb 1886	Wales	0-5	

48 W TURNER

Position   Winger

Clubs   Cliftonville

Caps   3

Date	Team	Result	G
12 Mar 1886	England	1-6	
20 Mar 1886	Scotland	2-7	
24 Mar 1888	Scotland	2-10	

49 J R WILLIAMS

Position   Outside-left

Clubs   Ulster

Caps   2   Goals   1

Date	Team	Result	G
12 Mar 1886	England	1-6	1
20 Mar 1886	Scotland	2-7	

50 F BROWNE

Position   Full-back/Forward

Clubs   Cliftonville

Caps   5   Goals   2

Date	Team	Result	G
5 Feb 1887	England	0-7	
19 Feb 1887	Scotland	1-4	1
13 Mar 1887	Wales	4-1	1
24 Mar 1888	Scotland	2-10	
7 Apr 1888	England	1-5	

51 W T FOX

Position   Full-back

Clubs   Ulster

Caps   2

Date	Team	Result	G
5 Feb 1887	England	0-7	
19 Feb 1887	Scotland	1-4	

52 A ROSBOTHAM

Position   Centre-half

Clubs   Cliftonville

Caps   7

Date	Team	Result	G
5 Feb 1887	England	0-7	
19 Feb 1887	Scotland	1-4	
13 Mar 1887	Wales	4-1	
3 Mar 1888	Wales	0-11	
24 Mar 1888	Scotland	2-10	
7 Apr 1888	England	1-5	
2 Mar 1889	England	1-6	

53   W LESLIE

Position   Centre-half

Clubs   Belfast YMCA

Caps   1

Date	Team	Result	G
5 Feb 1887	England	0-7	

54   J ALLEN

Position   Wing-half

Clubs   Limavady

Caps   1

Date	Team	Result	G
5 Feb 1887	England	0-7	

55   O M STANFIELD

Position   Forward

Clubs   Distillery

Caps   30   Goals   11

Date	Team	Result	G
5 Feb 1887	England	0-7	
19 Feb 1887	Scotland	1-4	
13 Mar 1887	Wales	4-1	1
3 Mar 1888	Wales	0-11	
24 Mar 1888	Scotland	2-10	
7 Apr 1888	England	1-5	
2 Mar 1889	England	1-6	
9 Mar 1889	Scotland	0-7	
27 Apr 1889	Wales	1-3	
15 Mar 1890	England	1-9	
29 Mar 1890	Scotland	1-4	
7 Feb 1891	Wales	7-2	4
7 Mar 1891	England	1-6	
28 Mar 1891	Scotland	1-2	1
27 Feb 1892	Wales	1-1	1
5 Mar 1892	England	0-2	
19 Mar 1892	Scotland	2-3	
25 Feb 1893	England	1-6	
5 Apr 1893	Wales	4-3	
24 Feb 1894	Wales	1-4	1
3 Mar 1894	England	2-2	1
31 Mar 1894	Scotland	1-2	1
9 Mar 1895	England	0-9	
30 Mar 1895	Scotland	1-3	
29 Feb 1896	Wales	1-6	
7 Mar 1896	England	0-2	
28 Mar 1896	Scotland	3-3	
20 Feb 1897	England	0-6	
6 Mar 1897	Wales	4-3	1
27 Mar 1897	Scotland	1-5	

56   JAMES MARK SMALL

Position   Forward

Born: 7 July 1867
Died: 27 December 1963

Clubs   Clarence; Cliftonville

Caps   4

Date	Team	Result	G
5 Feb 1887	England	0-7	
25 Feb 1893	England	1-6	
25 Mar 1893	Scotland	1-6	
5 Apr 1893	Wales	4-3	

57   N M BROWN

Position   Winger

Clubs   Limavady

Caps   1

Date	Team	Result	G
5 Feb 1887	England	0-7	

58   R L MOORE

Position   Wing-half

Clubs   Ulster

Caps   2

Date	Team	Result	G
19 Feb 1887	Scotland	1-4	
13 Mar 1887	Wales	4-1	

59   ROBERT ANDERSON BAXTER

Position   Wing-half

Clubs   Distillery

Caps   1

Date	Team	Result	G
19 Feb 1887	Scotland	1-4	

60   J PEDEN

Position   Outside-left

Clubs   Linfield; Distillery

Caps   24   Goals   7

Date	Team	Result	G
19 Feb 1887	Scotland	1-4	
13 Mar 1887	Wales	4-1	1

3 Mar 1888	Wales	0-11	
7 Apr 1888	England	1-5	
2 Mar 1889	England	1-6	
9 Mar 1889	Scotland	0-7	
8 Feb 1890	Wales	2-5	
29 Mar 1890	Scotland	1-4	1
7 Feb 1891	Wales	7-2	
6 Mar 1891	England	1-6	
27 Feb 1892	Wales	1-1	
5 Mar 1892	England	0-2	
25 Feb 1893	England	1-6	
25 Mar 1893	Scotland	1-6	
5 Apr 1893	Wales	4-3	3
29 Feb 1896	Wales	1-6	
7 Mar 1896	England	0-2	
28 Mar 1896	Scotland	3-3	
6 Mar 1897	Wales	4-3	1
27 Mar 1897	Scotland	1-5	
19 Feb 1898	Wales	1-0	1
5 Mar 1898	England	2-3	
26 Mar 1898	Scotland	0-3	
4 Mar 1899	Wales	1-0	

61 SAMUEL NATHANIEL BAXTER

Position   Forward

Clubs   Cliftonville

Caps   1

Date	Team	Result	G
13 Mar 1887	Wales	4-1	

62 JOHN CLUGSTON

Position   Goalkeeper

Clubs   Cliftonville

Caps   14

Date	Team	Result	G
3 Mar 1888	Wales	0-11	
2 Mar 1889	England	1-6	
9 Mar 1889	Scotland	0-7	
27 Apr 1889	Wales	1-3	
15 Mar 1890	England	1-9	
29 Mar 1890	Scotland	1-4	
7 Feb 1891	Wales	7-2	
7 Mar 1891	England	1-6	
27 Feb 1892	Wales	1-1	
5 Mar 1892	England	0-2	
19 Mar 1892	Scotland	2-3	
25 Feb 1893	England	1-6	
25 Mar 1893	Scotland	1-6	
5 Apr 1893	Wales	4-3	

DID YOU KNOW?
John Clugston, who played 14 times for Ireland between 1888 and 1893 was also an international Lacrosse player.

63 G FORBES

Position   Full-back

Clubs   Limavady; Distillery

Caps   3

Date	Team	Result	G
3 Mar 1888	Wales	0-11	
7 Mar 1891	England	1-6	
28 Mar 1891	Scotland	1-2	

64 J BARRY

Position   Centre-forward

Clubs   Bohemians

Caps   3

Date	Team	Result	G
3 Mar 1888	Wales	0-11	
24 Mar 1888	Scotland	2-10	
2 Mar 1889	England	1-6	

65 JAMES McILMUNN WILTON

Position   Forward

Clubs   St Columb's Court; Cliftonville; St Columb's Court

Caps   7   Goals   2

Date	Team	Result	G
3 Mar 1888	Wales	0-11	
7 Apr 1888	England	1-5	
2 Mar 1889	England	1-6	1
9 Mar 1889	Scotland	0-7	
15 Mar 1890	England	1-9	
25 Mar 1893	Scotland	1-6	
5 Apr 1893	Wales	4-3	1

66 R LAWTHER

Position   Goalkeeper

Clubs   Distillery

Caps   2

Date	Team	Result	G
24 Mar 1888	Scotland	2-10	
7 Apr 1888	England	1-5	

67   R WILSON

Position	Right-back	
Clubs	Cliftonville	
Caps	1	

Date	Team	Result	G
24 Mar 1888	Scotland	2-10	

68   J FORSYTHE

Position	Wing-half	
Clubs	Belfast YMCA	
Caps	2	

Date	Team	Result	G
24 Mar 1888	Scotland	2-10	
7 Apr 1888	England	1-5	

69   WILLIAM DALTON

Position	Winger	
Born	Belfast, 16 March 1870	
Died	Canada, 19 May 1946	
Clubs	Belfast YMCA; Cliftonville; Linfield	
Caps	11 Goals 4	

Date	Team	Result	G
24 Mar 1888	Scotland	2-10	1
8 Feb 1890	Wales	2-5	2
29 Mar 1890	Scotland	1-4	
7 Feb 1891	Wales	7-2	1
28 Mar 1891	Scotland	1-2	
27 Feb 1892	Wales	1-1	
5 Mar 1892	England	0-2	
19 Mar 1892	Scotland	2-3	
24 Feb 1894	Wales	1-4	
3 Mar 1894	England	2-2	
31 Mar 1894	Scotland	1-2	

70   M SILO

Position	Full-back	
Clubs	Belfast YMCA	
Caps	1	

Date	Team	Result	G
7 Apr 1888	England	1-5	

71   JOHN McVICKER

Position	Centre-forward	
Born	Belfast 29 April 1868	
Clubs	Linfield; Glentoran	
Caps	2	

Date	Team	Result	G
7 Apr 1888	England	1-5	
9 Mar 1889	Scotland	0-7	

72   MANLIFFE FRANCIS GOODBODY

Position	Full-back	
Clubs	Dublin University	
Caps	2	

Date	Team	Result	G
2 Mar 1889	England	1-6	
7 Feb 1891	Wales	7-2	

73   A CRAWFORD

Position	Wing-half	
Clubs	Distillery; Cliftonville	
Caps	6	

Date	Team	Result	G
2 Mar 1889	England	1-6	
27 Apr 1889	Wales	1-3	
7 Feb 1891	Wales	7-2	
7 Mar 1891	England	1-6	
28 Mar 1891	Scotland	1-2	
5 Apr 1893	Wales	4-3	

74   S COOKE

Position	Wing-half	
Clubs	Belfast YMCA	
Caps	3	

Date	Team	Result	G
2 Mar 1889	England	1-6	
15 Mar 1890	England	1-9	
29 Mar 1890	Scotland	1-4	

75   ROBERT CRONE

Position	Full-back	
Clubs	Distillery	
Caps	4	

Date	Team	Result	G
9 Mar 1889	Scotland	0-7	
8 Feb 1890	Wales	2-5	
15 Mar 1890	England	1-9	
29 Mar 1890	Scotland	1-4	

26 Mar 1898	Scotland	0-3	
18 Feb 1899	England	2-13	
4 Mar 1899	Wales	1-0	
23 Feb 1901	Scotland	0-11	
23 Mar 1901	Wales	0-1	

76 W THOMPSON

Position   Wing-half

Clubs   Belfast Athletic

Caps   1

Date	Team	Result	G
9 Mar 1889	Scotland	0-7	

77 J CHRISTIAN

Position   Centre-half

Born   1865

Clubs   Belfast Rangers; Linfield; Glentoran

Caps   1

Date	Team	Result	G
9 Mar 1889	Scotland	0-7	

78 SAMUEL TORRANS

Position   Forward/Full-back

Born   Belfast, 27 October 1869
Died   Belfast, 8 May 1948

Clubs   Linfield

Caps   26   Goals   1

Date	Team	Result	G
9 Mar 1889	Scotland	0-7	
8 Feb 1890	Wales	2-5	
29 Mar 1890	Scotland	1-4	
7 Feb 1891	Wales	7-2	1
28 Mar 1891	Scotland	1-2	
27 Feb 1892	Wales	1-1	
5 Mar 1892	England	0-2	
19 Mar 1892	Scotland	2-3	
25 Feb 1893	England	1-6	
25 Mar 1893	Scotland	1-6	
24 Feb 1894	Wales	1-4	
3 Mar 1894	England	2-2	
31 Mar 1894	Scotland	1-2	
9 Mar 1895	England	0-9	
29 Feb 1896	Wales	1-6	
7 Mar 1896	England	0-2	
28 Mar 1896	Scotland	3-3	
20 Feb 1897	England	0-6	
6 Mar 1897	Wales	4-3	
27 Mar 1897	Scotland	1-5	
5 Mar 1898	England	2-3	

79 A R ELLEMAN

Position   Full-back/Forward

Clubs   Cliftonville

Caps   2

Date	Team	Result	G
27 Apr 1889	Wales	1-3	
15 Mar 1890	England	1-9	

80 L V BENNETT

Position   Centre-half

Clubs   Dublin University

Caps   1

Date	Team	Result	G
27 Apr 1889	Wales	1-3	

81 JAMES CAMPBELL PERCY

Position   Centre-forward

Born   15 February 1869
Died   26 October 1928

Clubs   Belfast YMCA

Caps   1

Date	Team	Result	G
27 Apr 1889	Wales	1-3	

82 JOHN GILLESPIE

Position   Outside-left

Clubs   West Down

Caps   1

Date	Team	Result	G
27 Apr 1889	Wales	1-3	

83 W GALBRAITH

Position   Goalkeeper

Clubs   Distillery

Caps   1

Date	Team	Result	G
8 Feb 1890	Wales	2-5	

R K STEWART

Position   Full-back

Clubs   St Columb's Court; Cliftonville

Caps   11

Date	Team	Result	G
8 Feb 1890	Wales	2-5	
15 Mar 1890	England	1-9	
29 Mar 1890	Scotland	1-4	
27 Feb 1892	Wales	1-1	
5 Mar 1892	England	0-2	
19 Mar 1892	Scotland	2-3	
25 Feb 1893	England	1-6	
5 Apr 1893	Wales	4-3	
24 Feb 1894	Wales	1-4	
3 Mar 1894	England	2-2	
31 Mar 1894	Scotland	1-2	

DID YOU KNOW?
John Reynolds, who played League football in Ireland, Scotland and England was only the second player to represent two different nations in international championships. He played five times for Ireland between 1890 and 1891 and eight times for England between 1892 and 1894.

85   JOHN REYNOLDS

Position   Centre-half/Winger

Born   Blackburn, 21 February 1869

Clubs   Distillery; Ulster

Caps   5   Goals   1

Date	Team	Result	G
8 Feb 1890	Wales	2-5	
15 Mar 1890	England	1-9	1
7 Feb 1891	Wales	7-2	
7 Mar 1891	England	1-6	
28 Mar 1891	Scotland	1-2	

86   G GAFFIKIN

Position   Forward

Born   17 May 1868
Died   31 December 1936

Clubs   Linfield

Caps   15   Goals   4

Date	Team	Result	G
8 Feb 1890	Wales	2-5	
29 Mar 1890	Scotland	1-4	

Date	Team	Result	G
7 Feb 1891	Wales	7-2	1
28 Mar 1891	Scotland	1-2	
27 Feb 1892	Wales	1-1	
5 Mar 1892	England	0-2	
19 Mar 1892	Scotland	2-3	1
25 Feb 1893	England	1-6	1
25 Mar 1893	Scotland	1-6	1
5 Apr 1893	Wales	4-3	
24 Feb 1894	Wales	1-4	
3 Mar 1894	England	2-2	
31 Mar 1894	Scotland	1-2	
9 Mar 1895	England	0-9	
16 Mar 1895	Wales	2-2	

DID YOU KNOW? The youngest-ever player to win a cap is Samuel Johnston of Distillery, who was just 15 years and 154 days old when he played against England in Ireland's first-ever match on 18 February 1882.

87   SAMUEL JOHNSTON

Position   Centre-forward/Wing-half

Clubs   Linfield; Distillery

Caps   4

Date	Team	Result	G
8 Feb 1890	Wales	2-5	
20 Mar 1893	Scotland	1-6	
5 Apr 1893	Wales	4-3	
3 Mar 1894	England	2-2	

88   J WILLIAMSON

Position   Wing-half/Forward

Clubs   Cliftonville

Caps   3   Goals   1

Date	Team	Result	G
15 Mar 1890	England	1-9	
19 Mar 1892	Scotland	2-3	1
25 Mar 1893	Scotland	1-6	

89   S SPENCER

Position   Centre-half

Clubs   Distillery

Caps   6

Date	Team	Result	G
15 Mar 1890	England	1-9	
29 Mar 1890	Scotland	1-4	
27 Feb 1892	Wales	1-1	
5 Mar 1892	England	0-2	
19 Mar 1892	Scotland	2-3	
25 Feb 1893	England	1-6	

90   R McILVENEY

Position   Inside-forward

Clubs   Distillery

Caps   2

Date	Team	Result	G
15 Mar 1890	England	1-9	
7 Mar 1891	England	1-6	

91   ROBERT MORRISON

Position   Left-back

Born   Scotland, 30 August 1869
Died   12 July 1891

Clubs   Linfield

Caps   2

Date	Team	Result	G
7 Feb 1891	Wales	7-2	
7 Mar 1891	England	1-6	

92   RICHARD (Dick) MOORE

Position   Wing-half

Born   Holywood 1868
Died   29 October 1918

Clubs   Linfield

Caps   3

Date	Team	Result	G
7 Feb 1891	Wales	7-2	
7 Mar 1891	England	1-6	
28 Mar 1891	Scotland	1-2	

93   T WHITESIDE

Position   Outside-right

Clubs   Distillery

Caps   1   Goals   1

Date	Team	Result	G
7 Mar 1891	England	1-6	1

94   W McCABE

Position   Centre-forward

Clubs   Ulster

Caps   1

Date	Team	Result	G
7 Mar 1891	England	1-6	

95   J LOYAL

Position   Goalkeeper

Clubs   Clarence

Caps   1

Date	Team	Result	G
28 Mar 1891	Scotland	1-2	

96   ROBERT WILLIAM GORDON

Position   Full-back

Born   Belfast, 28 February 1871
Died   Belfast, 4 May 1948

Clubs   Linfield; Belfast Celtic

Caps   7

Date	Team	Result	G
28 Mar 1891	Scotland	1-2	
27 Feb 1892	Wales	1-1	
5 Mar 1892	England	0-2	
19 Mar 1892	Scotland	2-3	
25 Feb 1893	England	1-6	
25 Mar 1893	Scotland	1-6	
5 Apr 1893	Wales	4-3	

97   D BRISBY

Position   Inside-forward

Clubs   Distillery

Caps   1

Date	Team	Result	G
28 Mar 1891	Scotland	1-2	

98   NATHANIEL McKEOWN

Position   Wing-half

Born   Lisburn, 9 April 1868
Died   Belfast, 11 June 1924

Clubs   Linfield

Caps   7

Date	Team	Result	G
27 Feb 1892	Wales	1-1	
5 Mar 1892	England	0-2	
19 Mar 1892	Scotland	2-3	
25 Feb 1893	England	1-6	
25 Mar 1893	Scotland	1-6	

Date	Team	Result
5 Apr 1893	Wales	4-3
24 Feb 1894	Wales	1-4

99 W CUNNINGHAM

Position Wing-half

Clubs Ulster

Caps 4

Date	Team	Result	G
27 Feb 1892	Wales	1-1	
5 Mar 1892	England	0-2	
19 Mar 1892	Scotland	2-3	
25 Feb 1893	England	1-6	

100 ROBERT TORRANS

Position Full-back

Born Belfast, 28 November 1866
Died Toronto, Canada, 18 March 1956

Clubs Linfield

Caps 1

Date	Team	Result	G
25 Mar 1893	Scotland	1-6	

101 THOMAS GORDON

Position Goalkeeper

Born Belfast, 24 May 1867
Died Belfast, 4 June 1916

Clubs Linfield; Belfast Celtic

Caps 2

Date	Team	Result	G
24 Feb 1894	Wales	1-4	
9 Mar 1895	England	0-9	

102 J BURNETT

Position Centre-half

Clubs Distillery; Glentoran

Caps 5

Date	Team	Result	G
24 Feb 1894	Wales	1-4	
3 Mar 1894	England	2-2	
31 Mar 1894	Scotland	1-2	
9 Mar 1895	England	0-9	
16 Mar 1895	Wales	2-2	

103 ROBERT GEORGE MILNE

Position Wing-half

Born Forfar, 1 October 1870
Died Belfast, 2 March 1953

Clubs Gordon Highlanders; Forfar; Linfield

Caps 27 Goals 2

Date	Team	Result	G
24 Feb 1894	Wales	1-4	
3 Mar 1894	England	2-2	
31 Mar 1894	Scotland	1-2	
9 Mar 1895	England	0-9	
16 Mar 1895	Wales	2-2	
29 Feb 1896	Wales	1-6	
7 Mar 1896	England	0-2	
28 Mar 1896	Scotland	3-3	1
20 Feb 1897	England	0-6	
27 Mar 1897	Scotland	1-5	
19 Feb 1898	Wales	1-0	
5 Mar 1898	England	2-3	
26 Mar 1898	Scotland	0-3	
18 Feb 1899	England	2-13	
4 Mar 1899	Wales	1-0	
23 Mar 1901	Wales	0-1	
22 Feb 1902	Wales	3-0	
1 Mar 1902	Scotland	1-5	1
22 Mar 1902	England	0-1	
14 Feb 1903	England	0-4	
21 Mar 1903	Scotland	2-0	
12 Mar 1904	England	1-3	
21 Mar 1904	Wales	1-0	
26 Mar 1904	Scotland	1-1	
17 Feb 1906	England	0-5	
17 Mar 1906	Scotland	0-1	
2 Apr 1906	Wales	4-4	

104 W K GIBSON

Position Forward

Clubs Cliftonville

Caps 13 Goals 1

Date	Team	Result	G
24 Feb 1894	Wales	1-4	
3 Mar 1894	England	2-2	1
31 Mar 1894	Scotland	1-2	
30 Mar 1895	Scotland	1-3	
6 Mar 1897	Wales	4-3	
19 Feb 1898	Wales	1-0	
5 Mar 1898	England	2-3	
26 Mar 1898	Scotland	0-3	
23 Feb 1901	Scotland	0-11	
9 Mar 1901	England	0-3	
23 Mar 1901	Wales	0-1	
22 Feb 1902	Wales	3-0	
1 Mar 1902	Scotland	1-5	

105 J H BARRON

Position   Outside-left

Clubs   Cliftonville

Caps   7   Goals   3

Date	Team	Result	G
24 Feb 1894	Wales	1-4	
3 Mar 1894	England	2-2	
31 Mar 1894	Scotland	1-2	
30 Mar 1895	Scotland	1-3	
28 Mar 1896	Scotland	3-3	2
20 Feb 1897	England	0-6	
6 Mar 1897	Wales	4-3	1

106 T SCOTT

Position   Goalkeeper

Clubs   Cliftonville

Caps   13

Date	Team	Result	G
3 Mar 1894	England	2-2	
31 Mar 1894	Scotland	1-2	
16 Mar 1895	Wales	2-2	
30 Mar 1895	Scotland	1-3	
29 Feb 1896	Wales	1-6	
7 Mar 1896	England	0-2	
28 Mar 1896	Scotland	3-3	
20 Feb 1897	England	0-6	
6 Mar 1897	Wales	4-3	
19 Feb 1898	Wales	1-0	
5 Mar 1898	England	2-3	
26 Mar 1898	Scotland	0-3	
24 Feb 1900	Wales	0-2	

107 HUGH GORDON

Position   Right-back

Born   Belfast, 17 May 1873
Died   Belfast, 3 April 1910

Clubs   Linfield; Distillery; Belfast Celtic

Caps   3

Date	Team	Result	G
9 Mar 1895	England	0-9	
7 Mar 1896	England	0-2	
28 Mar 1896	Scotland	3-3	

108 HIRIAM WALTON McKIE

Position   Wing-half

Clubs   Cliftonville

Caps   3

Date	Team	Result	G
9 Mar 1895	England	0-9	
16 Mar 1895	Wales	2-2	
30 Mar 1895	Scotland	1-3	

109 THOMAS MORRISON

Position   Winger

Born   1874

Clubs   Stormont; Glentoran; Burnley; Glentoran; Celtic; Manchester United; Colne; Burnley; Glentoran

Caps   7

Date	Team	Result	G
9 Mar 1895	England	0-9	
16 Mar 1895	Wales	2-2	
30 Mar 1895	Scotland	1-3	
4 Mar 1899	Wales	1-0	
24 Feb 1900	Wales	0-2	
1 Mar 1902	Scotland	1-5	
22 Mar 1902	England	0-1	

110 WILLIAM C SHERRARD

Position   Forward

Died: 1895

Clubs   Cliftonville

Caps   3   Goals   2

Date	Team	Result	G
9 Mar 1895	England	0-9	
16 Mar 1895	Wales	2-2	1
30 Mar 1895	Scotland	1-3	1

111 THOMAS HENRY JORDAN

Position   Outside-left

Born   Lurgan, 16 November 1872
Died   Belfast, June 1940

Clubs   Linfield; Distillery

Caps   2

Date	Team	Result	G
9 Mar 1895	England	0-9	
16 Mar 1895	Wales	2-2	

112 J PONSONBY

Position   Full-back/Centre-half

Clubs   Distillery

Caps   9

Date	Team	Result	G
16 Mar 1895	Wales	2-2	
30 Mar 1895	Scotland	1-3	
29 Feb 1896	Wales	1-6	
7 Mar 1896	England	0-2	
28 Mar 1896	Scotland	3-3	
20 Feb 1897	England	0-6	
6 Mar 1897	Wales	4-3	
27 Mar 1897	Scotland	1-5	
18 Feb 1899	England	2-13	

113   L J SCOTT

Position   Left-back

Clubs   Dublin University

Caps   2

Date	Team	Result	G
16 Mar 1895	Wales	2-2	
30 Mar 1895	Scotland	1-3	

114   GEORGE WARRINGTON GAUKRODGER

Position   Inside-forward

Born   Yorkshire, 7 December 1877
Died   Yorkshire, 4 July 1938

Clubs   Linfield

Caps   1   Goals   1

Date	Team	Result	G
16 Mar 1895	Wales	2-2	1

115   T E ALEXANDER

Position   Centre-half

Clubs   Cliftonville

Caps   1

Date	Team	Result	G
30 Mar 1895	Scotland	1-3	

116   THOMAS McCLATCHEY

Position   Wing-half

Clubs   Distillery

Caps   1

Date	Team	Result	G
30 Mar 1895	Scotland	1-3	

117   S McCOY

Position   Right-half

Clubs   Distillery

Caps   1

Date	Team	Result	G
29 Feb 1896	Wales	1-6	

118   J CAMPBELL

Position   Wing-half

Clubs   Cliftonville

Caps   1

Date	Team	Result	G
29 Feb 1896	Wales	1-6	

119   A TURNER

Position   Winger

Clubs   Cliftonville

Caps   1   Goals   1

Date	Team	Result	G
29 Feb 1896	Wales	1-6	1

120   G BAIRD

Position   Forward

Clubs   Distillery

Caps   3

Date	Team	Result	G
29 Feb 1896	Wales	1-6	
7 Mar 1896	England	0-2	
28 Mar 1896	Scotland	3-3	

121   J McCASHIN

Position   Inside-forward

Clubs   Cliftonville

Caps   4

Date	Team	Result	G
29 Feb 1896	Wales	1-6	
19 Feb 1898	Wales	1-0	
26 Mar 1898	Scotland	0-3	
25 Mar 1899	Scotland	1-9	

122   J C FITZPATRICK

Position	Right-half
Clubs	Bohemians
Caps	2

Date	Team	Result	G
7 Mar 1896	England	0-2	
28 Mar 1896	Scotland	3-3	

123   J KELLY

Position	Forward
Born	1 December 1870
Died	22 February 1935
Clubs	Glentoran
Caps	1

Date	Team	Result	G
7 Mar 1896	England	0-2	

124   E TURNER

Position	Inside-forward
Clubs	Cliftonville
Caps	1

Date	Team	Result	G
7 Mar 1896	England	0-2	

125   D MORROGH

Position	Forward
Clubs	Bohemians
Caps	1

Date	Team	Result	G
28 Mar 1896	Scotland	3-3	

126   JOHN PYPER

Position	Wing-half/Full-back
Born:	9 January 1878
Died:	6 August 1952
Clubs	Cliftonville
Caps	9 Goals 1

Date	Team	Result	G
20 Feb 1897	England	0-6	
6 Mar 1897	Wales	4-3	1
27 Mar 1897	Scotland	1-5	
18 Feb 1899	England	2-13	
4 Mar 1899	Wales	1-0	
24 Feb 1900	Wales	0-2	
3 Mar 1900	Scotland	0-2	
17 Mar 1900	England	0-2	
1 Mar 1902	Scotland	1-5	

127   GEORGE McMASTER

Position	Left-half
Clubs	Glentoran
Caps	3

Date	Team	Result	G
20 Feb 1897	England	0-6	
6 Mar 1897	Wales	4-3	
27 Mar 1897	Scotland	1-5	

128   J CAMPBELL

Position	Winger
Clubs	Cliftonville
Caps	14 Goals 1

Date	Team	Result	G
20 Feb 1897	England	0-6	
6 Mar 1897	Wales	4-3	
27 Mar 1897	Scotland	1-5	
19 Feb 1898	Wales	1-0	
5 Mar 1898	England	2-3	
26 Mar 1898	Scotland	0-3	
18 Feb 1899	England	2-13	1
3 Mar 1900	Scotland	0-2	
17 Mar 1900	England	0-2	
23 Feb 1901	Scotland	0-11	
23 Mar 1901	Wales	0-1	
1 Mar 1902	Scotland	1-5	
14 Feb 1903	England	0-4	
26 Mar 1904	Scotland	1-1	

129   G HALL

Position	Forward
Clubs	Distillery
Caps	1

Date	Team	Result	G
20 Feb 1897	England	0-6	

130   JOHN DARLING

Position	Inside-forward/Wing-half
Born	Belfast, 30 October 1877

Died   Belfast, 8 February 1946

Clubs   Linfield

Caps   21   Goals   1

Date	Team	Result	G
20 Feb 1897	England	0-6	
27 Mar 1897	Scotland	1-5	
3 Mar 1900	Scotland	0-2	
22 Feb 1902	Wales	3-0	
1 Mar 1902	Scotland	1-5	
22 Mar 1902	England	0-1	
14 Feb 1903	England	0-4	
21 Mar 1903	Scotland	2-0	
28 Mar 1903	Wales	2-0	
25 Feb 1905	England	1-1	
18 Mar 1905	Scotland	0-4	
8 Apr 1905	Wales	2-2	
17 Feb 1906	England	0-5	
17 Mar 1906	Scotland	0-1	
2 Apr 1906	Wales	4-4	
11 Apr 1908	Wales	1-0	
13 Feb 1909	England	0-4	
12 Feb 1910	England	1-1	
19 Mar 1910	Scotland	1-0	
11 Apr 1910	Wales	1-4	1
6 Mar 1912	Scotland	1-4	

131   JAMES PYPER

Position Forward

Born: 18 April 1876
Died: 5 March 1925

Clubs   Cliftonville

Caps   7   Goals   2

Date	Team	Result	G
6 Mar 1897	Wales	4-3	
27 Mar 1897	Scotland	1-5	1
19 Feb 1898	Wales	1-0	
5 Mar 1898	England	2-3	1
26 Mar 1898	Scotland	0-3	
25 Mar 1899	Scotland	1-9	
17 Mar 1900	England	0-2	

132   J THOMPSON

Position Goalkeeper

Clubs   Distillery

Caps   1

Date	Team	Result	G
27 Mar 1897	Scotland	1-5	

133   MICHAEL COCHRANE

Position Full-back

Clubs   Milltown; Distillery; Leicester Fosse;
          Middlesbrough; Distillery

Caps   8

Date	Team	Result	G
19 Feb 1898	Wales	1-0	
5 Mar 1898	England	2-3	
26 Mar 1898	Scotland	0-3	
18 Feb 1899	England	2-13	
24 Feb 1900	Wales	0-2	
3 Mar 1900	Scotland	0-2	
17 Mar 1900	England	0-2	
23 Feb 1901	Scotland	0-11	

134   WILLIAM ANDERSON

Position Wing-half

Born   Holywood, 14 February 1877
Died   Portadown, 28 April 1938

Clubs   Linfield; Cliftonville; Portadown

Caps   4

Date	Team	Result	G
19 Feb 1898	Wales	1-0	
5 Mar 1898	England	2-3	
26 Mar 1898	Scotland	0-3	
25 Mar 1899	Scotland	1-9	

135   JACK LYTTLE

Position Wing-half

Clubs   Glentoran

Caps   1

Date	Team	Result	G
19 Feb 1898	Wales	1-0	

136   JOHN THOMPSON MERCER

Position Forward

Born   Belfast, 10 March 1879
Died   15 February 1944

Clubs   Distillery; Linfield; Distillery

Caps   11   Goals   1

Date	Team	Result	G
19 Feb 1898	Wales	1-0	
5 Mar 1898	England	2-3	1
26 Mar 1898	Scotland	0-3	
18 Feb 1899	England	2-13	

Date	Team	Result	
22 Feb 1902	Wales	3-0	
22 Mar 1902	England	0-1	
21 Mar 1903	Scotland	2-0	
28 Mar 1903	Wales	2-0	
12 Mar 1904	England	1-3	
21 Mar 1904	Wales	1-0	
18 Mar 1905	Scotland	0-4	

137   JOSEPH CROFT McALLEN

Position   Winger

Born   Belfast, 11 March 1874
Died   Belfast, 9 September 1945

Clubs   Bloomfield; Linfield

Caps   9   **Goals**   1

Date	Team	Result	G
5 Mar 1898	England	2-3	
18 Feb 1899	England	2-13	1
4 Mar 1899	Wales	1-0	
25 Mar 1899	Scotland	1-9	
24 Feb 1900	Wales	0-2	
3 Mar 1900	Scotland	0-2	
17 Mar 1900	England	0-2	
23 Mar 1901	Wales	0-1	
1 Mar 1902	Scotland	1-5	

138   JAMES LEWIS

Position   Goalkeeper

Born   1874
Died   April 1957

Clubs   Glentoran

Caps   4

Date	Team	Result	G
18 Feb 1899	England	2-13	
4 Mar 1899	Wales	1-0	
25 Mar 1899	Scotland	1-9	
3 Mar 1900	Scotland	0-2	

139   J WARING

Position   Centre-forward

Clubs   Distillery

Caps   1

Date	Team	Result	G
18 Feb 1899	England	2-13	

140   J WATTIE

Position   Forward

Clubs   Distillery

Caps   1

Date	Team	Result	G
18 Feb 1899	England	2-13	

141   ARCHIBALD LEE GOODALL

Position   Centre-half/Centre-forward

Born   Belfast, 19 June 1864
Died   London, 29 November 1929

Clubs   Liverpool Stanley; Preston North End;
Aston Villa; Derby County; Plymouth
Argyle; Glossop; Wolverhampton
Wanderers

Caps   10   **Goals**   2

Date	Team	Result	G
4 Mar 1899	Wales	1-0	
25 Mar 1899	Scotland	1-9	1
24 Feb 1900	Wales	0-2	
17 Mar 1900	England	0-2	
9 Mar 1901	England	0-3	
1 Mar 1902	Scotland	1-5	
14 Feb 1903	England	0-4	
28 Mar 1903	Wales	2-0	1
12 Mar 1904	England	1-3	
21 Mar 1904	Wales	1-0	

142   JOHN (Jack) TAGGART

Position   Left-half

Born   Belfast, 3 January 1872
Died   1927

Clubs   Belfast Distillery; Middlesbrough; West
Bromwich Albion; Walsall

Caps   1

Date	Team	Result	G
4 Mar 1899	Wales	1-0	

143   P A MELDON

Position   Forward

Clubs   Dublin Freebooters

Caps   2   **Goals**   1

Date	Team	Result	G
4 Mar 1899	Wales	1-0	1
25 Mar 1899	Scotland	1-9	

144   JOHN D HANNA

Position   Centre-forward

Clubs   Royal Artillery Portsmouth

Caps   1

Date	Team	Result	G
4 Mar 1899	Wales	1-0	

145   SAMUEL SWAN

Position   Full-back

Born   Ligoniel, 3 February 1872
Died   Ligoniel, 3 April 1903

Clubs   Ligoniel; Linfield

Caps   1

Date	Team	Result	G
25 Mar 1899	Scotland	1-9	

146   T A FOREMAN

Position   Left-back

Clubs   Cliftonville

Caps   1

Date	Team	Result	G
25 Mar 1899	Scotland	1-9	

147   J McSHANE

Position   Left-half

Clubs   Cliftonville

Caps   4

Date	Team	Result	G
25 Mar 1899	Scotland	1-9	
24 Feb 1900	Wales	0-2	
3 Mar 1900	Scotland	0-2	
17 Mar 1900	England	0-2	

148   DR G SHEENAN

Position   Outside-right

Clubs   Bohemians

Caps   3

Date	Team	Result	G
25 Mar 1899	Scotland	1-9	
24 Feb 1900	Wales	0-2	
17 Mar 1900	England	0-2	

149   HUGH MAGINNIS

Position   Left-half

Born   Belfast, 1878

Clubs   Linfield; Glossop; Distillery

Caps   8

Date	Team	Result	G
24 Feb 1900	Wales	0-2	
3 Mar 1900	Scotland	0-2	
17 Mar 1900	England	0-2	
21 Mar 1903	Scotland	2-0	
28 Mar 1903	Wales	2-0	
12 Mar 1904	England	1-3	
21 Mar 1904	Wales	1-0	
26 Mar 1904	Scotland	1-1	

150   JOHN H (Jack) KIRWAN

Position   Outside-left

Born   Wicklow, 1878
Died   9 January 1959

Clubs   Southport Central; Everton; Tottenham Hotspur; Chelsea; Clyde; Leyton Orient

Caps   17   Goals   2

Date	Team	Result	G
24 Feb 1900	Wales	0-2	
22 Feb 1902	Wales	3-0	
22 Mar 1902	England	0-1	
14 Feb 1903	England	0-4	
21 Mar 1903	Scotland	2-0	1
28 Mar 1903	Wales	2-0	
12 Mar 1904	England	1-3	1
21 Mar 1904	Wales	1-0	
26 Mar 1904	Scotland	1-1	
25 Feb 1905	England	1-1	
18 Mar 1905	Scotland	0-4	
8 Apr 1905	Wales	2-2	
17 Feb 1906	England	0-5	
17 Mar 1906	Scotland	0-1	
2 Apr 1906	Wales	4-4	
23 Feb 1907	Wales	2-3	
15 Mar 1909	Scotland	0-5	

151   A KEARNS

Position   Inside-right

Clubs   Distillery; Blackpool

Caps   6

Date	Team	Result	G
24 Feb 1900	Wales	0-2	
3 Mar 1900	Scotland	0-2	
17 Mar 1900	England	0-2	
22 Feb 1902	Wales	3-0	

Date	Team	Result	G
1 Mar 1902	Scotland	1-5	
22 Mar 1902	England	0-1	

152	J BARRY		

Position   Centre-half

Clubs   Bohemians

Caps   1

Date	Team	Result	G
3 Mar 1900	Scotland	0-2	

153	P McAULEY		

Position   Centre-forward

Clubs   Belfast Celtic

Caps   1

Date	Team	Result	G
3 Mar 1900	Scotland	0-2	

154	MATTHEW MICHAEL REILLY		

Position   Goalkeeper

Born   Donnybrook, 22 March 1874
Died   Dublin, 9 December 1954

Clubs   Benburb; Royal Artillery Portsmouth;
Portsmouth; Southampton St Mary's;
Portsmouth; Dundee; Notts County;
Tottenham Hotspur; Shelbourne

Caps   2

Date	Team	Result	G
17 Mar 1900	England	0-2	
22 Mar 1902	England	0-1	

155	S McALPINE		

Position   Goalkeeper

Clubs   Cliftonville

Caps   1

Date	Team	Result	G
23 Feb 1901	Scotland	0-11	

156	PATRICK (Paddy) FARRELL		

Position   Centre-half

Born   Belfast, 3 April 1872
Died   1950

Clubs   Belfast Celtic; Distillery; Celtic; Woolwich
Arsenal; Brighton United; Distillery;
Brighton & Hove Albion

Caps   2

Date	Team	Result	G
23 Feb 1901	Scotland	0-11	
23 Mar 1901	Wales	0-1	

157	J CONNOR		

Position   Centre-half

Clubs   Glentoran; Belfast Celtic

Caps   13

Date	Team	Result	G
23 Feb 1901	Scotland	0-11	
9 Mar 1901	England	0-3	
25 Feb 1905	England	1-1	
18 Mar 1905	Scotland	0-4	
8 Apr 1905	Wales	2-2	
16 Feb 1907	England	0-1	
16 Mar 1907	Scotland	0-3	
15 Feb 1908	England	1-3	
14 Mar 1908	Scotland	0-5	
20 Mar 1909	Wales	2-3	
28 Jan 1911	Wales	1-2	
11 Feb 1911	England	1-2	
18 Mar 1911	Scotland	0-2	

158	J E SCOTT		

Position   Outside-right

Clubs   Cliftonville

Caps   1

Date	Team	Result	G
23 Feb 1901	Scotland	0-11	

159	J E SMITH		

Position   Inside-forward

Clubs   Distillery

Caps   2

Date	Team	Result	G
23 Feb 1901	Scotland	0-11	
23 Mar 1901	Wales	0-1	

160   H O'REILLY

Position   Inside-left

Clubs   Dublin Freebooters

Caps   3

Date	Team	Result	G
23 Feb 1901	Scotland	0-11	
23 Mar 1901	Wales	0-1	
26 Mar 1904	Scotland	1-1	

161   R CLARKE

Position   Outside-left

Clubs   Belfast Celtic

Caps   2

Date	Team	Result	G
23 Feb 1901	Scotland	0-11	
9 Mar 1901	England	0-3	

162   J V NOLAN-WHELAN

Position   Goalkeeper

Clubs   Dublin Freebooters

Caps   4

Date	Team	Result	G
9 Mar 1901	England	0-3	
23 Mar 1901	Wales	0-1	
22 Feb 1902	Wales	3-0	
1 Mar 1902	Scotland	1-5	

163   PETER BOYLE

Position   Left-back

Born   Carlingford

Clubs   Albion Rovers; Sunderland; Sheffield United; Motherwell; Clapton Orient

Caps   5

Date	Team	Result	G
9 Mar 1901	England	0-3	
22 Mar 1902	England	0-1	
21 Mar 1903	Scotland	2-0	
28 Mar 1903	Wales	2-0	
12 Mar 1904	England	1-3	

164   JOHN BURNISON

Position   Left-half

Clubs   Distillery; Bolton Wanderers

Caps   2

Date	Team	Result	G
9 Mar 1901	England	0-3	
23 Mar 1901	Wales	0-1	

165   T BLACK

Position   Outside-right

Clubs   Glentoran

Caps   1

Date	Team	Result	G
9 Mar 1901	England	0-3	

166   ROY REA

Position   Inside-forward

Clubs   Glentoran

Caps   1

Date	Team	Result	G
9 Mar 1901	England	0-3	

167   J MANSFIELD

Position   Centre-forward

Clubs   Dublin Freebooters

Caps   1

Date	Team	Result	G
9 Mar 1901	England	0-3	

168   I DOHERTY

Position   Inside-left

Clubs   Belfast Celtic

Caps   1

Date	Team	Result	G
9 Mar 1901	England	0-3	

169   H McKELVEY

Position   Centre-forward

Born   Comber, 9 November 1879

Died	6 May 1940
Clubs	Glentoran
Caps	1

Date	Team	Result	G
23 Mar 1901	Wales	0-1	

170   WILLIAM R (Bill) McCRACKEN

Position	Right-back
Born	Belfast, 29 January 1883
Died	Hull, 20 January 1979
Clubs	Distillery; Newcastle United
Caps	15 Goals 1

Date	Team	Result	G
22 Feb 1902	Wales	3-0	
22 Mar 1902	England	0-1	
14 Feb 1903	England	0-4	
12 Mar 1904	England	1-3	
21 Mar 1904	Wales	1-0	1
26 Mar 1904	Scotland	1-1	
25 Feb 1905	England	1-1	
18 Mar 1905	Scotland	0-4	
8 Apr 1905	Wales	2-2	
16 Feb 1907	England	0-1	
25 Oct 1919	England	1-1	
22 Oct 1921	England	1-1	
4 Mar 1922	Scotland	1-2	
1 Apr 1922	Wales	1-1	
3 Mar 1923	Scotland	0-1	

171   H NICHOLL

Position	Left-half
Clubs	Belfast Celtic
Caps	3

Date	Team	Result	G
22 Feb 1902	Wales	3-0	
22 Mar 1902	England	0-1	
25 Feb 1905	England	1-1	

172   JAMES MAXWELL

Position	Forward
Born	Belfast, 29 April 1879
Died	15 February 1944
Clubs	Linfield; Belfast Celtic; Glentoran
Caps	7 Goals 2

Date	Team	Result	G
22 Feb 1902	Wales	3-0	

Date	Team	Result	G
14 Feb 1903	England	0-4	
28 Mar 1903	Wales	2-0	
18 Mar 1905	Scotland	0-4	
8 Apr 1905	Wales	2-2	
2 Apr 1906	Wales	4-4	2
16 Mar 1907	Scotland	0-3	

173   ANDREW GARA

Position	Centre-forward
Born	1875
Clubs	Wigan County; Preston North End; Nottingham Forest; Bristol City
Caps	3 Goals 3

Date	Team	Result	G
22 Feb 1902	Wales	3-0	3
1 Mar 1902	Scotland	1-5	
22 Mar 1902	England	0-1	

174   WILLIAM (Billy) SCOTT

Position	Goalkeeper
Born	Belfast
Clubs	Cliftonville; Linfield; Everton; Leeds City
Caps	25

Date	Team	Result	G
14 Feb 1903	England	0-4	
21 Mar 1903	Scotland	2-0	
28 Mar 1903	Wales	2-0	
12 Mar 1904	England	1-3	
21 Mar 1904	Wales	1-0	
26 Mar 1904	Scotland	1-1	
25 Feb 1905	England	1-1	
18 Mar 1905	Scotland	0-4	
16 Feb 1907	England	0-1	
16 Mar 1907	Scotland	0-3	
15 Feb 1908	England	1-3	
14 Mar 1908	Scotland	0-5	
11 Apr 1908	Wales	1-0	
13 Feb 1909	England	0-4	
15 Mar 1909	Scotland	0-5	
20 Mar 1909	Wales	2-3	
12 Feb 1910	England	1-1	
19 Mar 1910	Scotland	1-0	
28 Jan 1911	Wales	1-2	
11 Feb 1911	England	1-2	
18 Mar 1911	Scotland	0-2	
10 Feb 1912	England	1-6	
18 Jan 1913	Wales	0-1	
15 Feb 1913	England	2-1	
15 Mar 1913	Scotland	1-2	

175   G McMILLAN

Position   Full-back

Clubs   Distillery

Caps   2

Date	Team	Result	G
14 Feb 1903	England	0-4	
8 Apr 1905	Wales	2-2	

176   JAMES (Paddy) SHERIDAN

Position   Inside-forward

Born   Belfast, 25 April 1884

Clubs   Cambuslang Hibernian; Everton; Stoke; New Brompton

Caps   6   Goals   2

Date	Team	Result	G
14 Feb 1903	England	0-4	
21 Mar 1903	Scotland	2-0	
28 Mar 1903	Wales	2-0	1
12 Mar 1904	England	1-3	
26 Mar 1904	Scotland	1-1	1
25 Feb 1905	England	1-1	

177   H A de B SLOAN

Position   Forward

Clubs   Bohemians

Caps   8   Goals   4

Date	Team	Result	G
14 Feb 1903	England	0-4	
26 Mar 1904	Scotland	1-1	
25 Feb 1905	England	1-1	
2 Apr 1906	Wales	4-4	2
16 Feb 1907	England	0-1	
23 Feb 1907	Wales	2-3	1
11 Apr 1908	Wales	1-0	1
15 Mar 1909	Scotland	0-5	

178   A McCARTNEY

Position   Full-back

Clubs   Ulster; Linfield; Everton; Belfast Celtic; Glentoran

Caps   15

Date	Team	Result	G
21 Mar 1903	Scotland	2-0	
28 Mar 1903	Wales	2-0	
21 Mar 1904	Wales	1-0	
26 Mar 1904	Scotland	1-1	

Date	Team	Result	G
25 Feb 1905	England	1-1	
18 Mar 1905	Scotland	0-4	
16 Feb 1907	England	0-1	
23 Feb 1907	Wales	2-3	
16 Mar 1907	Scotland	0-3	
15 Feb 1908	England	1-3	
14 Mar 1908	Scotland	0-5	
11 Apr 1908	Wales	1-0	
13 Feb 1909	England	0-4	
15 Mar 1909	Scotland	0-5	
20 Mar 1909	Wales	2-3	

179   MAURICE JOSEPH CONNOR

Position   Centre-forward

Born   Lochee, 14 July 1880
Died   August 1934

Clubs   Dundee Fereday; Glentoran; Gordon Highlanders; West Bromwich Albion; Walsall; Bristol City; Woolwich Arsenal;Brentford; New Brompton; Fulham; Blackpool; Glentoran; Treharris

Caps   3   Goals   1

Date	Team	Result	G
21 Mar 1903	Scotland	2-0	1
28 Mar 1903	Wales	2-0	
12 Mar 1904	England	1-3	

180   THOMAS SHANKS

Position   Inside-forward

Born   New Ross, Co. Wexford 1880

Clubs   Wexford; Derby West End; Derby County; Brentford; Woolwich Arsenal; Brentford; Leicester Fosse; Leyton; Clapton Orient; York City

Caps   3

Date	Team	Result	G
21 Mar 1903	Scotland	2-0	
21 Mar 1904	Wales	1-0	
25 Feb 1905	England	1-1	

181   HAROLD R (Harry) BUCKLE

Position   Outside-left

Born   Belfast 1882

Clubs   Cliftonville; Sunderland; Portsmouth; Bristol Rovers; Coventry City; Belfast Celtic; Fordsons

Caps   2

Date	Team	Result	G
12 Mar 1904	England	1-3	
11 Apr 1908	Wales	1-0	

182   ENGLISH McCONNELL

Position   Wing-half/Centre-half

Born   Larne 1881
Died   Belfast 1960

Clubs   Cliftonville; Glentoran; Sunderland;
Sheffield Wednesday; Chelsea; South
Shields; Linfield

Caps   12

Date	Team	Result	G
21 Mar 1904	Wales	1-0	
26 Mar 1904	Scotland	1-1	
18 Mar 1905	Scotland	0-4	
17 Feb 1906	England	0-5	
16 Feb 1907	England	0-1	
14 Mar 1908	Scotland	0-5	
11 Apr 1908	Wales	1-0	
15 Mar 1909	Scotland	0-5	
20 Mar 1909	Wales	2-3	
12 Feb 1910	England	1-1	
19 Mar 1910	Scotland	1-0	
11 Apr 1910	Wales	1-4	

183   H KIRKWOOD

Position   Inside-left

Clubs   Cliftonville

Caps   1

Date	Team	Result	G
21 Mar 1904	Wales	1-0	

184   NEIL MURPHY

Position   Centre-forward

Clubs   Sheffield United; Queen's Park Rangers;
Luton Town; Gainsborough Trinity

Caps   3   Goals   1

Date	Team	Result	G
25 Feb 1905	England	1-1	
18 Mar 1905	Scotland	0-4	
8 Apr 1905	Wales	2-2	1

185   CHARLES O'HAGAN

Position   Inside-left

Born   Buncrana, Co. Donegal 1882

Clubs   St Columb's College; Derry Celtic;
Old Xaverians; Everton; Tottenham
Hotspur; Middlesbrough; Aberdeen;
Greenock Morton

Caps   11   Goals   2

Date	Team	Result	G
18 Mar 1905	Scotland	0-4	
8 Apr 1905	Wales	2-2	1
17 Feb 1906	England	0-5	
17 Mar 1906	Scotland	0-1	
2 Apr 1906	Wales	4-4	
16 Feb 1907	England	0-1	
23 Feb 1907	Wales	2-3	1
16 Mar 1907	Scotland	0-3	
14 Mar 1908	Scotland	0-5	
11 Apr 1908	Wales	1-0	
13 Feb 1909	England	0-4	

186 R REYNOLDS

Position   Goalkeeper

Clubs   Bohemians

Caps   1

Date	Team	Result	G
8 Apr 1905	Wales	2-2	

187   R S JOHNSTON

Position   Left-half

Clubs   Distillery

Caps   1

Date	Team	Result	G
8 Apr 1905	Wales	2-2	

188   A HUNTER

Position   Outside-right

Clubs   Distillery; Belfast Celtic

Caps   8   Goals   1

Date	Team	Result	G
8 Apr 1905	Wales	2-2	
17 Feb 1906	England	0-5	
17 Mar 1906	Scotland	0-1	
2 Apr 1906	Wales	4-4	
11 Apr 1908	Wales	1-0	
13 Feb 1909	England	0-4	

Date	Team	Result	
15 Mar 1909	Scotland	0-5	
20 Mar 1909	Wales	2-3	1

189   J J SHERRY

Position   Goalkeeper

Clubs   Bohemians

Caps   2

Date	Team	Result	G
17 Feb 1906	England	0-5	
23 Feb 1907	Wales	2-3	

190   H McILROY

Position   Left-back

Clubs   Cliftonville

Caps   1

Date	Team	Result	G
17 Feb 1906	England	0-5	

191   J WRIGHT

Position   Right-half

Clubs   Cliftonville

Caps   6

Date	Team	Result	G
17 Feb 1906	England	0-5	
17 Mar 1906	Scotland	0-1	
2 Apr 1906	Wales	4-4	
16 Feb 1907	England	0-1	
23 Feb 1907	Wales	2-3	
16 Mar 1907	Scotland	0-3	

192   T S MULHOLLAND

Position   Inside-forward

Clubs   Belfast Celtic

Caps   2

Date	Team	Result	G
17 Feb 1906	England	0-5	
17 Mar 1906	Scotland	0-1	

193   VALENTINE (Val) HARRIS

Position   Right-half/Forward

Born   Dublin

Clubs   Shelbourne; Everton; Shelbourne

Caps   20

Date	Team	Result	G
17 Feb 1906	England	0-5	
16 Feb 1907	England	0-1	
23 Feb 1907	Wales	2-3	
15 Feb 1908	England	1-3	
14 Mar 1908	Scotland	0-5	
11 Apr 1908	Wales	1-0	
13 Feb 1909	England	0-4	
15 Mar 1909	Scotland	0-5	
20 Mar 1909	Wales	2-3	
12 Feb 1910	England	1-1	
19 Mar 1910	Scotland	1-0	
11 Apr 1910	Wales	1-4	
28 Jan 1911	Wales	1-2	
11 Feb 1911	England	1-2	
18 Mar 1911	Scotland	0-2	
10 Feb 1912	England	1-6	
15 Feb 1913	England	2-1	
15 Mar 1913	Scotland	1-2	
19 Jan 1914	Wales	2-1	
14 Mar 1914	Scotland	1-1	

194   FREDERICK W McKEE

Position   Goalkeeper

Clubs   Belfast Celtic; Cliftonville; Sunderland; Cliftonville; Bradford City; Belfast Celtic

Caps   5

Date	Team	Result	G
17 Mar 1906	Scotland	0-1	
2 Apr 1906	Wales	4-4	
19 Jan 1914	Wales	2-1	
14 Feb 1914	England	3-0	
14 Mar 1914	Scotland	1-1	

195   GEORGE V W WILLIS

Position   Right-back

Born   Belfast, 17 March 1885
Died   20 March 1925

Clubs   Linfield

Caps   4

Date	Team	Result	G
17 Mar 1906	Scotland	0-1	
2 Apr 1906	Wales	4-4	
16 Mar 1907	Scotland	0-3	
6 Mar 1912	Scotland	1-4	

196   J J LEDWIDGE

Position   Wing-half

Clubs   Shelbourne

Caps   2

Date	Team	Result	G
17 Mar 1906	Scotland	0-1	
2 Apr 1906	Wales	4-4	

197   T M R WADDELL

Position   Centre-forward

Clubs   Cliftonville

Caps   1

Date	Team	Result	G
17 Mar 1906	Scotland	0-1	

198   J BLAIR

Position   Inside-forward

Clubs   Cliftonville

Caps   5

Date	Team	Result	G
16 Feb 1907	England	0-1	
23 Feb 1907	Wales	2-3	
16 Mar 1907	Scotland	0-3	
15 Feb 1908	England	1-3	
14 Mar 1908	Scotland	0-5	

199   SAM YOUNG

Position   Outside-left

Born   Belfast, 14 February 1884
Died   Belfast, 28 November 1954

Clubs   Linfield; Airdrieonians; Linfield

Caps   9   Goals   2

Date	Team	Result	G
16 Feb 1907	England	0-1	
16 Mar 1907	Scotland	0-3	
15 Feb 1908	England	1-3	
14 Mar 1908	Scotland	0-5	
13 Feb 1909	England	0-4	
6 Mar 1912	Scotland	1-4	
19 Jan 1914	Wales	2-1	1
14 Feb 1914	England	3-0	
14 Mar 1914	Scotland	1-1	1

200   J SEYMOUR

Position   Right-back

Clubs   Cliftonville

Caps   2

Date	Team	Result	G
23 Feb 1907	Wales	2-3	
20 Mar 1909	Wales	2-3	

201   C CROTHERS

Position   Centre-half

Clubs   Distillery

Caps   1

Date	Team	Result	G
23 Feb 1907	Wales	2-3	

202   G McCLURE

Position   Wing-half

Clubs   Cliftonville; Distillery

Caps   4

Date	Team	Result	G
23 Feb 1907	Wales	2-3	
16 Mar 1907	Scotland	0-3	
15 Feb 1908	England	1-3	
13 Feb 1909	England	0-4	

203   E McGUIRE

Position   Centre-forward

Clubs   Distillery

Caps   1

Date	Team	Result	G
16 Mar 1907	Scotland	0-3	

204   A B (Sandy) CRAIG

Position   Full-back

Clubs   Glasgow Rangers; Greenock Morton

Caps   9

Date	Team	Result	G
15 Feb 1908	England	1-3	
14 Mar 1908	Scotland	0-5	
11 Apr 1908	Wales	1-0	
15 Mar 1909	Scotland	0-5	
6 Mar 1912	Scotland	1-4	
13 Apr 1912	Wales	3-2	
19 Jan 1914	Wales	2-1	
14 Feb 1914	England	3-0	
14 Mar 1914	Scotland	1-1	

205   D J HANNON

Position   Forward

Clubs   Bohemians

Caps   6   Goals   1

Date	Team	Result	G
15 Feb 1908	England	1-3	1
14 Mar 1908	Scotland	0-5	
11 Feb 1911	England	1-2	
18 Mar 1911	Scotland	0-2	
13 Apr 1912	Wales	3-2	
15 Feb 1913	England	2-1	

206   HENRY VICTOR ARTHUR MERCER

Position   Centre-forward

Born   Enniskillen, 22 April 1887
Died   6 January 1961

Clubs   St Columb's Court; Linfield; Derry Celtic

Caps   1

Date	Team	Result	G
15 Feb 1908	England	1-3	

207   SAMUEL BURNISON

Position   Right-back

Born   Belfast, 1891

Clubs   Distillery; Bradford Park Avenue; Distillery

Caps   8

Date	Team	Result	G
15 Feb 1908	England	1-3	
12 Feb 1910	England	1-1	
19 Mar 1910	Scotland	1-0	
28 Jan 1911	Wales	1-2	
11 Feb 1911	England	1-2	
18 Mar 1911	Scotland	0-2	
10 Feb 1912	England	1-6	
18 Jan 1913	Wales	0-1	

DID YOU KNOW?
Willie Andrews, who played three times for Ireland (once in 1908 and twice in 1913) had no British qualifications. Neither he nor his parents were born in the UK. He was born in Kansas City, Missouri.

208   WILLIAM (Willie) ANDREWS

Position   Right-half/Inside-right

Born   Kansas City, Missouri, United States 1886

Clubs   Glentoran; Oldham Athletic; Stockport County; Glentoran; Grimsby Town; Belfast United; Darlington

Caps   3

Date	Team	Result	G
14 Mar 1908	Scotland	0-5	
15 Feb 1913	England	2-1	
15 Mar 1913	Scotland	1-2	

209   W J HAMILTON

Position   Forward

Clubs   Distillery

Caps   1

Date	Team	Result	G
11 Apr 1908	Wales	1-0	

210   J BALFE

Position   Full-back

Clubs   Shelbourne

Caps   2

Date	Team	Result	G
13 Feb 1909	England	0-4	
11 Apr 1910	Wales	1-4	

211   WILLIAM (Bill) LACEY

Position   Winger/Right-half

Born   Wexford, 24 September 1889
Died   1969

Clubs   Shelbourne; Everton; Liverpool; New Brighton; Shelbourne; Cork Bohemians

Caps   23   Goals   3

Date	Team	Result	G
13 Feb 1909	England	0-4	
15 Mar 1909	Scotland	0-5	
20 Mar 1909	Wales	2-3	1
12 Feb 1910	England	1-1	
19 Mar 1910	Scotland	1-0	
11 Apr 1910	Wales	1-4	
28 Jan 1911	Wales	1-2	
11 Feb 1911	England	1-2	
18 Mar 1911	Scotland	0-2	
10 Feb 1912	England	1-6	

Date	Team	Result	G
18 Jan 1913	Wales	0-1	
19 Jan 1914	Wales	2-1	
14 Feb 1914	England	3-0	2
14 Mar 1914	Scotland	1-1	
25 Oct 1919	England	1-1	
14 Feb 1919	Wales	2-2	
13 Mar 1919	Scotland	0-3	
23 Oct 1920	England	0-2	
26 Feb 1921	Scotland	0-2	
9 Apr 1921	Wales	1-2	
22 Oct 1921	England	1-1	
4 Mar 1922	Scotland	1-2	
22 Oct 1924	England	1-3	

212   W GREER

Position   Centre-forward

Clubs   Queen's Park Rangers

Caps   3

Date	Team	Result	G
13 Feb 1909	England	0-4	
15 Mar 1909	Scotland	0-5	
20 Mar 1909	Wales	2-3	

213   C G WEBB

Position   Inside-left

Clubs   Brighton & Hove Albion

Caps   3

Date	Team	Result	G
15 Mar 1909	Scotland	0-5	
20 Mar 1909	Wales	2-3	
18 Mar 1911	Scotland	0-2	

214   J C SLEMIN

Position   Outside-left

Clubs   Bohemians

Caps   1

Date	Team	Result	G
20 Mar 1909	Wales	2-3	

215   P McCANN

Position   Left-back

Born: 1881
Died: 22 June 1935

Clubs   Belfast Celtic; Glentoran

Caps   7

Date	Team	Result	G
12 Feb 1910	England	1-1	
19 Mar 1910	Scotland	1-0	
11 Apr 1910	Wales	1-4	
11 Feb 1911	England	1-2	
18 Mar 1911	Scotland	0-2	
10 Feb 1912	England	1-6	
18 Jan 1913	Wales	0-1	

216   WILLIAM THOMAS JAMES (Bill) RENNEVILLE

Position   Centre-forward

Born   Mullingar, May 1888
Died   1948

Clubs   Leyton; Aston Villa; Walsall

Caps   4

Date	Team	Result	G
12 Feb 1910	England	1-1	
19 Mar 1910	Scotland	1-0	
11 Apr 1910	Wales	1-4	
28 Jan 1911	Wales	1-2	

217   JAMES M MURRAY

Position   Centre-forward

Clubs   Motherwell; Sheffield Wednesday; Derry Celtic

Caps   3

Date	Team	Result	G
12 Feb 1910	England	1-1	
19 Mar 1910	Scotland	1-0	
11 Apr 1910	Wales	1-4	

218   JOHN MURPHY

Position   Inside-right

Born   Belfast, 1886

Clubs   Shelbourne; Bradford City; Luton Town

Caps   3

Date	Team	Result	G
12 Feb 1910	England	1-1	
19 Mar 1910	Scotland	1-0	
11 Apr 1910	Wales	1-4	

219   FRANCIS W (Frank) THOMPSON

Position   Outside-left

Born   Ballynahinch

Clubs   Cliftonville; Linfield; Bradford City; Clyde

Caps 12   Goals 2

Date	Team	Result	G
12 Feb 1910	England	1-1	1
19 Mar 1910	Scotland	1-0	1
11 Apr 1910	Wales	1-4	
28 Jan 1911	Wales	1-2	
11 Feb 1911	England	1-2	
10 Feb 1912	England	1-6	
13 Apr 1912	Wales	3-2	
18 Jan 1913	Wales	0-1	
15 Feb 1913	England	2-1	
15 Mar 1913	Scotland	1-2	
14 Feb 1914	England	3-0	
14 Mar 1914	Scotland	1-1	

220   J C O'HEHIR

Position   Goalkeeper

Clubs   Bohemians

Caps   1

Date	Team	Result	G
11 Apr 1910	Wales	1-4	

221   P J THUNDER

Position   Left-back

Clubs   Bohemians

Caps   1

Date	Team	Result	G
28 Jan 1911	Wales	1-2	

222   HARRY HAMPTON

Position   Wing-half

Born   Dublin

Clubs   Dundee; Bradford City; Belfast Distillery

Caps   9

Date	Team	Result	G
28 Jan 1911	Wales	1-2	
11 Feb 1911	England	1-2	
18 Mar 1911	Scotland	0-2	
10 Feb 1912	England	1-6	
13 Apr 1912	Wales	3-2	
18 Jan 1913	Wales	0-1	
15 Feb 1913	England	2-1	
15 Mar 1913	Scotland	1-2	
14 Feb 1914	England	3-0	

223   WILLIAM (Billy) HALLIGAN

Position   Inside-forward/Centre-forward

Born   Athlone, August 1886
Died   1950

Clubs   Belfast Celtic; Belfast Distillery; Leeds City; Derby County; Wolverhampton Wanderers; Hull City; Preston North End; Oldham Athletic; Nelson; Boston Town; Wisbech Town

Caps   2   Goals   1

Date	Team	Result	G
28 Jan 1911	Wales	1-2	1
10 Feb 1912	England	1-6	

224   JAMES LOWRY McAULEY

Position   Inside-left

Born   Portarlington, 1889
Died   Preston, 8 October 1945

Clubs   Preston Rangers; Cliftonville Olympic; Brighton & Hove Albion; Huddersfield Town; Preston North End; Leicester City; Grimsby Town; Lancaster Town; Morecambe

Caps   6   Goals   1

Date	Team	Result	G
28 Jan 1911	Wales	1-2	
11 Feb 1911	England	1-2	1
10 Feb 1912	England	1-6	
6 Mar 1912	Scotland	1-4	
15 Feb 1913	England	2-1	
15 Mar 1913	Scotland	1-2	

225   J McDONNELL

Position   Centre-forward

Clubs   Bohemians

Caps   4

Date	Team	Result	G
11 Feb 1911	England	1-2	
18 Mar 1911	Scotland	0-2	
13 Apr 1912	Wales	3-2	
18 Jan 1913	Wales	0-1	

226   JOHN WALKER

Position   Outside-left

Born   Glasgow, 1890

Clubs   Belfast Celtic; Bury; Glentoran

Caps   1

Date	Team	Result	G
18 Mar 1911	Scotland	0-2	

227   MICHAEL (Mickey) HAMILL

Position   Left-half/Centre-half/Inside-right

Born   Belfast, 19 January 1885
Died   1943

Clubs   St Paul's Swifts; Belfast Rangers;
Belfast Celtic; Manchester United; Belfast
Celtic; Manchester City; Fall River
Marksmen; Boston Wonder Workers;
New York Giants; Belfast Celtic

Caps   7   Goals   1

Date	Team	Result	G
10 Feb 1912	England	1-6	1
14 Feb 1914	England	3-0	
14 Mar 1914	Scotland	1-1	
25 Oct 1919	England	1-1	
14 Feb 1919	Wales	2-2	
13 Mar 1919	Scotland	0-3	
26 Feb 1921	Scotland	0-2	

228   PATRICK (Pat) O'CONNELL

Position   Centre-half

Born   Dublin, 1887

Clubs   Belfast Celtic; Sheffield Wednesday; Hull
City; Manchester United; Dumbarton;
Rochdale; Ashington

Caps   5

Date	Team	Result	G
10 Feb 1912	England	1-6	
6 Mar 1912	Scotland	1-4	
19 Jan 1914	Wales	2-1	
14 Feb 1914	England	3-0	
14 Mar 1914	Scotland	1-1	

229   JOHN A (Jack) HANNA

Position   Goalkeeper

Born   Belfast

Clubs   Linfield; Nottingham Forest; Scunthorpe
United

Caps   2

Date	Team	Result	G
6 Mar 1912	Scotland	1-4	
13 Apr 1912	Wales	3-2	

230   JOSEPH MORAN

Position   Left-half

Born   Dublin

Clubs   Shelbourne; Leeds City

Caps   1

Date	Team	Result	G
6 Mar 1912	Scotland	1-4	

231   JOHN HOUSTON

Position   Outside-right/Centre-forward

Born   Belfast

Clubs   Linfield; Everton; Linfield

Caps   6

Date	Team	Result	G
6 Mar 1912	Scotland	1-4	
13 Apr 1912	Wales	3-2	
18 Jan 1913	Wales	0-1	
15 Feb 1913	England	2-1	
15 Mar 1913	Scotland	1-2	
14 Mar 1914	Scotland	1-1	

232   JAMES McKNIGHT

Position   Inside-forward

Born   Newtownards, 2 February 1892
Died   16 March 1920

Clubs   Glentoran; Preston North End; Glentoran;
Nottingham Forest; Belfast Celtic

Caps   2   Goals   2

Date	Team	Result	G
6 Mar 1912	Scotland	1-4	1
15 Mar 1913	Scotland	1-2	1

233   JOSEPH ENRIGHT

Position   Inside-left/Outside-right

Born   Belfast, 1890

Clubs   Shelbourne; Leeds City; Newport County;
Coventry City

Caps   1

Date	Team	Result	G
6 Mar 1912	Scotland	1-4	

234   W G McCONNELL

Position   Left-back

Clubs   Bohemians

Caps   6

Date	Team	Result	G
13 Apr 1912	Wales	3-2	
15 Feb 1913	England	2-1	
15 Mar 1913	Scotland	1-2	
19 Jan 1914	Wales	2-1	
14 Feb 1914	England	3-0	
14 Mar 1914	Scotland	1-1	

235   B BRENNAN

Position   Centre-half

Clubs   Bohemians

Caps   1   Goals   1

Date	Team	Result	G
13 Apr 1912	Wales	3-2	1

236   DAVID ROLLO

Position   Full-back

Born   Belfast, 26 August 1891
Died   Blackpool, 17 February 1963

Clubs   Distillery; Linfield; Blackburn Rovers; Port Vale

Caps   16

Date	Team	Result	G
13 Apr 1912	Wales	3-2	
18 Jan 1913	Wales	0-1	
19 Jan 1914	Wales	2-1	
14 Feb 1914	England	3-0	
14 Feb 1919	Wales	2-2	
13 Mar 1919	Scotland	0-3	
23 Oct 1920	England	0-2	
26 Feb 1921	Scotland	0-2	
9 Apr 1921	Wales	1-2	
22 Oct 1921	England	1-1	
21 Oct 1922	England	0-2	
1 Mar 1924	Scotland	0-2	
15 Mar 1924	Wales	0-1	
18 Apr 1925	Wales	0-0	
24 Oct 1925	England	0-0	
20 Oct 1926	England	3-3	

237   JOHN (Jack) McCANDLESS

Position   Winger/Inside-left

Born   Coleraine, 29 February 1892
Died   Coleraine, 12 October 1940

Clubs   Linfield; Bradford Park Avenue; Accrington Stanley; Barn; Mid-Rhondda United

Caps   5   Goals   2

Date	Team	Result	G
13 Apr 1912	Wales	3-2	2
18 Jan 1913	Wales	0-1	
14 Feb 1919	Wales	2-2	
13 Mar 1919	Scotland	0-3	
23 Oct 1920	England	0-2	

238   L DONNELLY

Position   Centre-half

Clubs   Distillery

Caps   1

Date	Team	Result	G
18 Jan 1913	Wales	0-1	

239   P WARREN

Position   Left-back

Clubs   Shelbourne

Caps   2

Date	Team	Result	G
15 Feb 1913	England	2-1	
15 Mar 1913	Scotland	1-2	

240   WILLIAM BALLINTRE (Billy) GILLESPIE

Position   Inside-forward/Centre-forward

Born   Kerrykeel, 6 August 1891
Died   Bexley, 2 July 1981

Clubs   Derry Institute; Leeds City; Sheffield United; Derry City

Caps   25   Goals   12

Date	Team	Result	G
15 Feb 1913	England	2-1	2
15 Mar 1913	Scotland	1-2	
19 Jan 1914	Wales	2-1	1
14 Feb 1914	England	3-0	1
14 Feb 1919	Wales	2-2	
13 Mar 1919	Scotland	0-3	
23 Oct 1920	England	0-2	
22 Oct 1921	England	1-1	1
4 Mar 1922	Scotland	1-2	1
1 Apr 1922	Wales	1-1	1
21 Oct 1922	England	0-2	
3 Mar 1923	Scotland	0-1	
14 Apr 1923	Wales	3-0	1
20 Oct 1923	England	2-1	1

Date	Team	Result	G
1 Mar 1924	Scotland	0-2	
15 Mar 1924	Wales	0-1	
22 Oct 1924	England	1-3	1
28 Feb 1925	Scotland	0-3	
13 Feb 1926	Wales	3-0	1
27 Feb 1926	Scotland	0-4	
20 Oct 1926	England	3-0	1
9 Apr 1927	Wales	2-2	
22 Oct 1927	England	2-0	
22 Oct 1928	England	1-2	
20 Oct 1930	England	1-5	

241   H C SEYMOUR

Position   Outside-right

Clubs   Bohemians

Caps   1

Date	Team	Result	G
19 Jan 1914	Wales	2-1	

242   LOUIS JAMES A O BOOKMAN
(born Louis Buchalter)

Position   Outside-left

Born   Zagaren, Lithuania
Died   Dublin, 10 June 1943

Clubs   Belfast Celtic; Bradford City; West Bromwich Albion; Luton Town; Port Vale; Shelbourne

Caps   4

Date	Team	Result	G
19 Jan 1914	Wales	2-1	
26 Feb 1921	Scotland	0-2	
9 Apr 1921	Wales	1-2	
22 Oct 1921	England	1-1	

243   ROBERT NIXON

Position   Inside-forward

Born   Co. Monaghan, 4 March 1892
Died   Larne, 6 November 1977

Clubs   Linfield

Caps   1

Date	Team	Result	G
14 Mar 1914	Scotland	1-1	

244   W O'HAGAN

Position   Goalkeeper

Clubs   St Mirren

Caps   2

Date	Team	Result	G
25 Oct 1919	England	1-1	
14 Feb 1920	Wales	2-2	

245   WILLIAM McCANDLESS

Position   Full-back

Born   Ballymena, 20 December 1892
Died   Swansea, 18 July 1955

Clubs   Ligoniel; Cliftonville; Linfield; Glasgow Rangers

Caps   9   Goals   1

Date	Team	Result	G
25 Oct 1919	England	1-1	
14 Feb 1920	Wales	2-2	1
23 Oct 1920	England	0-2	
9 Apr 1921	Wales	1-2	
4 Mar 1922	Scotland	1-2	
1 Mar 1924	Scotland	0-2	
15 Mar 1924	Wales	0-1	
28 Feb 1925	Scotland	0-3	
2 Feb 1929	Wales	2-2	

246   WILLIAM EMERSON

Position   Right-half

Born   Enniskillen, 16 December 1891
Died   January 1961

Clubs   Glentoran; Burnley; Glentoran

Caps   11   Goals   1

Date	Team	Result	G
25 Oct 1919	England	1-1	
14 Feb 1920	Wales	2-2	1
13 Mar 1920	Scotland	0-3	
23 Oct 1920	England	0-2	
22 Oct 1921	England	1-1	
4 Mar 1922	Scotland	1-2	
1 Apr 1922	Wales	1-1	
21 Oct 1922	England	0-2	
3 Mar 1923	Scotland	0-1	
14 Apr 1923	Wales	3-0	
20 Oct 1923	England	2-1	

247   JAMES FERRIS

Position   Inside-forward

Born   Belfast, 28 November 1894
Died   Belfast 1932

Clubs   Distillery; Belfast Celtic; Chelsea; Preston North End; Pontypridd; Belfast Celtic

Caps	5	Goals	1

Date	Team	Result	G
25 Oct 1919	England	1-1	1
14 Feb 1920	Wales	2-2	
23 Oct 1920	England	0-2	
26 Feb 1921	Scotland	0-2	
25 Feb 1928	Scotland	1-0	

248   A SNAPE

Position   Forward

Clubs   Airdrieonans

Caps   1

Date	Team	Result	G
25 Oct 1919	England	1-1	

249   JOSEPH GOWDY

Position   Centre-forward

Born   Belfast, December 1897

Clubs   Glentoran; Queen's Island; Falkirk

Caps   6

Date	Team	Result	G
25 Oct 1919	England	1-1	
15 Mar 1924	Wales	0-1	
24 Oct 1925	England	0-0	
27 Feb 1926	Scotland	0-4	
20 Oct 1926	England	3-3	
26 Feb 1927	Scotland	0-2	

250   PATRICK (Patsy) GALLAGHER

Position   Inside-right

Born   Ramelton, Co. Donegal, 16 April 1893
Died   Scotstown, 17 June 1953

Clubs   Clydebank Juniors; Glasgow Celtic;
Falkirk

Caps   11

Date	Team	Result	G
25 Oct 1919	England	1-1	
13 Mar 1920	Scotland	0-3	
4 Mar 1922	Scotland	1-2	
3 Mar 1923	Scotland	0-1	
14 Apr 1923	Wales	3-0	
1 Mar 1924	Scotland	0-2	
15 Mar 1924	Wales	0-1	
22 Oct 1924	England	1-3	
28 Feb 1925	Scotland	0-3	
18 Apr 1925	Wales	0-0	
26 Feb 1927	Scotland	0-2	

251   DAVID LYNER

Position   Winger

Born   Belfast, 9 January 1893

Clubs   Owen O'Cork; Glentoran; Belfast
Distillery; Glentoran; Manchester United;
Kilmarnock; Queen's Island; Clydebank;
Mid-Rhondda United; New Brighton;
Glentoran

Caps   6

Date	Team	Result	G
25 Oct 1919	England	1-1	
14 Feb 1920	Wales	2-2	
4 Mar 1922	Scotland	1-2	
1 Apr 1922	Wales	1-1	
21 Oct 1922	England	0-2	
14 Apr 1923	Wales	3-0	

252   ROBERT (Bert) MANDERSON

Position   Full-back

Clubs   Glasgow Rangers

Caps   5

Date	Team	Result	G
14 Feb 1920	Wales	2-2	
13 Mar 1920	Scotland	0-3	
22 Oct 1924	England	1-3	
28 Feb 1925	Scotland	0-3	
27 Feb 1926	Scotland	0-4	

DID YOU KNOW?
Elisha Scott was 42 years and 200 days old when he played
for Ireland against Wales in Belfast on 11 March 1936.

253   ELISHA SCOTT

Position   Goalkeeper

Born   Belfast, 24 June 1894
Died   1959

Clubs   Linfield; Broadway United; Liverpool;
Belfast Celtic

Caps   31

Date	Team	Result	G
13 Mar 1920	Scotland	0-3	
23 Oct 1920	England	0-2	
26 Feb 1921	Scotland	0-2	
9 Apr 1921	Wales	1-2	
22 Oct 1921	England	1-1	
18 Apr 1925	Wales	0-0	
24 Oct 1925	England	0-0	
13 Feb 1926	Wales	3-0	
27 Feb 1926	Scotland	0-4	

20 Oct 1926	England	3-3	
26 Feb 1927	Scotland	0-2	
9 Apr 1927	Wales	2-2	
22 Oct 1927	England	2-0	
4 Feb 1928	Wales	1-2	
25 Feb 1928	Scotland	1-0	
22 Oct 1928	England	1-2	
2 Feb 1929	Wales	2-2	
23 Feb 1929	Scotland	3-7	
19 Oct 1929	England	0-3	
20 Oct 1930	England	1-5	
5 Dec 1931	Wales	4-0	
17 Sep 1932	Scotland	0-4	
17 Oct 1932	England	0-1	
7 Dec 1932	Wales	1-4	
16 Sep 1933	Scotland	2-1	
14 Oct 1933	England	0-3	
4 Nov 1933	Wales	1-1	
20 Oct 1934	Scotland	2-1	
19 Oct 1935	England	1-3	
13 Nov 1935	Scotland	1-2	
11 Mar 1936	Wales	3-2	

254 PATRICK ROBINSON

Position   Outside-right

Born   Belfast, 1892

Clubs   Belfast Distillery; Blackburn Rovers;
Caerphilly; Linfield; Brooklyn Wanderers

Caps   2

Date	Team	Result	G
13 Mar 1920	Scotland	0-3	
9 Apr 1921	Wales	1-2	

255 E A BROOKES

Position   Centre-forward

Clubs   Shelbourne

Caps   1

Date	Team	Result	G
13 Mar 1920	Scotland	0-3	

256 ROBERT McCRACKEN

Position   Right-half

Born   Dromore, 25 June 1900

Clubs   Dromore United; Belfast Distillery; Crystal
Palace; Portadown

Caps   4

Date	Team	Result	G
23 Oct 1920	England	0-2	
22 Oct 1921	England	1-1	

4 Mar 1922	Scotland	1-2	
1 Apr 1922	Wales	1-1	

257 PATRICK J KELLY

Position   Outside-right

Born   Kilcoo

Clubs   Belfast Celtic; Manchester City; West
Ham United; Fordsons

Caps   1

Date	Team	Result	G
23 Oct 1920	England	0-2	

258 JOHN FRANCIS (Jack) DORAN

Position   Centre-forward/Centre-half

Born   Belfast, 3 January 1896
Died   1940

Clubs   Gillingham; Pontypridd; Newcastle
Empire; Coventry City; Norwich City;
Brighton & Hove Albion; Manchester City;
Crewe Alexandra; Mid-Rhondda United;
Shelbourne; Boston Town

Caps   3

Date	Team	Result	G
23 Oct 1920	England	0-2	
22 Oct 1921	England	1-1	
1 Apr 1922	Wales	1-1	

259 JAMES ALPHONSO (Jimmy) MULLIGAN

Position   Left-back

Born   Bessbrook, 27 April 1895
Died   1966

Clubs   Bessbrook Strollers; St David's Swifts;
Belfast Celtic; Manchester City;
Southport; Manchester North End;
Manchester Central

Caps   1

Date	Team	Result	G
26 Feb 1921	Scotland	0-2	

260 ERNEST EDWIN (Bert) SMITH

Position   Centre-half

Born   Donegal, 4 January 1890

Clubs   Cardiff City; Middlesbrough; Watford;
Emsworth

Caps   4

Date	Team	Result	G
26 Feb 1921	Scotland	0-2	
21 Oct 1922	England	0-2	
14 Apr 1923	Wales	3-0	
20 Oct 1923	England	2-1	

261   MICHAEL TERENCE O'BRIEN

Position   Centre-half/Left-half

Born   Kilcock, 10 August 1893
Died   Uxbridge, 21 September 1940

Clubs   Walker Celtic; Wallsend; Blyth Spartans;
           Newcastle East End; Celtic; Brentford;
           Norwich City; South Shields; Queen's
           Park Rangers; Leicester City; Hull City;
           Brooklyn Wanderers; Derby County;
           Walsall; Norwich City; Watford

Caps   10

Date	Team	Result	G
26 Feb 1921	Scotland	0-2	
4 Mar 1922	Scotland	1-2	
1 Apr 1922	Wales	1-1	
1 Mar 1924	Scotland	0-2	
15 Mar 1924	Wales	0-1	
22 Oct 1924	England	1-3	
28 Feb 1925	Scotland	0-3	
18 Apr 1925	Wales	0-0	
13 Feb 1926	Wales	3-0	
9 Apr 1927	Wales	2-2	

262   S McGREGOR

Position   Outside-right

Clubs   Glentoran

Caps   1

Date	Team	Result	G
26 Feb 1921	Scotland	0-2	

263   DANIEL McKINNEY

Position   Centre-forward/Inside-forward

Born   Belfast, 9 November 1898
Died   1956

Clubs   St Paul's Swifts; Belfast Celtic; Hull City;
           Bradford City; Norwich City

Caps   2

Date	Team	Result	G
26 Feb 1921	Scotland	0-2	
1 Mar 1924	Scotland	0-2	

264   M J SCRAGGS

Position   Centre-half

Clubs   Glentoran

Caps   2

Date	Team	Result	G
9 Apr 1921	Wales	1-2	
22 Oct 1921	England	1-1	

265   J HARRIS

Position   Left-half

Clubs   Cliftonville; Glenavon

Caps   1

Date	Team	Result	G
9 Apr 1921	Wales	1-2	

266   JOHN (Jack) BROWN

Position   Inside-forward

Born   Belfast, 1 September 1900

Clubs   Glenavon; Tranmere Rovers; Mid-
           Rhondda United; Merthyr Town; Crystal
           Palace; Aberdare Athletic

Caps   3

Date	Team	Result	G
9 Apr 1921	Wales	1-2	
20 Oct 1923	England	2-1	
15 Mar 1924	Wales	0-1	

267   ROBERT JAMES (Jimmy) CHAMBERS

Position   Winger

Born   Mullaghglass, 26 July 1908
Died   1977

Clubs   Newry Town; Bury; Nottingham Forest

Caps   12   Goals   3

Date	Team	Result	G
9 Apr 1921	Wales	1-2	1
22 Oct 1927	England	2-0	
4 Feb 1928	Wales	1-2	1
25 Feb 1928	Scotland	1-0	1
22 Oct 1928	England	1-2	
2 Feb 1929	Wales	2-2	
23 Feb 1929	Scotland	3-7	
1 Feb 1930	Wales	7-0	
22 Feb 1930	Scotland	1-3	
19 Sep 1931	Scotland	1-3	
17 Oct 1931	England	2-6	

Date	Team	Result	G
5 Dec 1931	Wales	4-0	

268 ALLAN MATHIESON

Position Inside-forward

Born Belfast, 1897

Clubs Glentoran; Luton Town; Exeter City; New Brighton

Caps 2

Date	Team	Result	G
9 Apr 1921	Wales	1-2	
22 Oct 1921	England	1-1	

269 FRANCIS J COLLINS

Position Goalkeeper

Born 1897

Clubs Wanderers FC; Jacobs FC; Glasgow Celtic; Jacobs FC

Caps 1

Date	Team	Result	G
4 Mar 1922	Scotland	1-2	

270 ROBERT WILLIAM (Bobby) IRVINE

Position Inside-forward/Centre-forward

Born Lisburn, 29 April 1900
Died Leicester, 1979

Clubs Dunmurry; Everton; Portsmouth; Chester; Connah's Quay; Derry City; Watford

Caps 15 Goals 3

Date	Team	Result	G
4 Mar 1922	Scotland	1-2	
21 Oct 1922	England	0-2	
14 Apr 1923	Wales	3-0	2
20 Oct 1923	England	2-1	
1 Mar 1924	Scotland	0-2	
22 Oct 1924	England	1-3	
24 Oct 1925	England	0-0	
20 Oct 1926	England	3-3	1
9 Apr 1927	Wales	2-2	
22 Oct 1927	England	2-0	
25 Feb 1928	Scotland	1-0	
22 Oct 1928	England	1-2	
22 Feb 1930	Scotland	1-3	
20 Oct 1930	England	1-5	
5 Dec 1931	Wales	4-0	

271 J A C MEHAFFEY

Position Goalkeeper

Clubs Queen's Island

Caps 1

Date	Team	Result	G
1 Apr 1922	Wales	1-1	

272 J J CURRAN

Position Left-back

Clubs Glenavon; Pontypridd

Caps 4

Date	Team	Result	G
1 Apr 1922	Wales	1-1	
21 Oct 1922	England	0-2	
3 Mar 1923	Scotland	0-1	
20 Oct 1923	England	2-1	

273 WILLIAM J (Billy) CROOKS

Position Inside-right

Born Belfast, 12 December 1900

Clubs St Galls; Glentoran; Manchester United; New Brighton; Belfast Celtic; Larne; Glentoran

Caps 1

Date	Team	Result	G
1 Apr 1922	Wales	1-1	

274 JOSEPH TONER

Position Outside-left

Born Castlewellan, 30 March 1894
Died 15 November 1954

Clubs Belfast United; Arsenal; St Johnstone; Coleraine

Caps 8

Date	Team	Result	G
1 Apr 1922	Wales	1-1	
14 Apr 1923	Wales	3-0	
20 Oct 1923	England	2-1	
15 Mar 1924	Wales	0-1	
22 Oct 1924	England	1-3	
28 Feb 1925	Scotland	0-3	
20 Oct 1926	England	3-3	
26 Feb 1927	Scotland	0-2	

ALFRED IRELAND HARLAND

Position	Goalkeeper
Born	Belfast, 26 November 1897
Died	Cheshire, 20 May 1986
Clubs	Dunmurry; Linfield; Everton
Caps	1

Date	Team	Result	G
21 Oct 1922	England	0-2	

276 **FRANCIS GERALD MORGAN**

Position	Wing-half
Born	Belfast, 25 July 1899
Died	Belfast, 3 March 1959
Clubs	Cliftonville; Linfield; Nottingham Forest; Luton Town; Grantham; Cork; Ballymena United
Caps	7

Date	Team	Result	G
21 Oct 1922	England	0-2	
1 Mar 1924	Scotland	0-2	
20 Oct 1926	England	3-3	
22 Oct 1927	England	2-0	
4 Feb 1928	Wales	1-2	
25 Feb 1928	Scotland	1-0	
22 Oct 1928	England	1-2	

277 **PATRICK NELIS**

Position	Centre-forward/Inside-forward
Born	Derry, 5 October 1898
Died	1970
Clubs	Londonderry Distillery; Accrington Stanley; Nottingham Forest; Wigan Borough; Coleraine
Caps	1

Date	Team	Result	G
21 Oct 1922	England	0-2	

278 **J BURNS**

Position	Outside-left
Clubs	Glenavon
Caps	1

Date	Team	Result	G
21 Oct 1922	England	0-2	

279 **THOMAS G FARQUHARSON**

Position	Goalkeeper
Born	Dublin, 4 December 1898
Died	1974
Clubs	Abertillery; Cardiff City
Caps	7

Date	Team	Result	G
3 Mar 1923	Scotland	0-1	
14 Apr 1923	Wales	3-0	
20 Oct 1923	England	2-1	
1 Mar 1924	Scotland	0-2	
15 Mar 1924	Wales	0-1	
22 Oct 1924	England	1-3	
28 Feb 1925	Scotland	0-3	

280 **SAMUEL JOHNSTONE IRVING**

Position	Right-half/Inside-right
Born	Belfast, 28 August 1894
Died	Dundee, December 1968
Clubs	Shildon Athletic; Newcastle United; Galashiels United; Esh Winning; Bristol City; Dundee; Blyth Spartans; Shildon Athletic; Dundee; Partick Thistle; New York Centrals; Cardiff City; Chelsea; Bristol Rovers
Caps	18

Date	Team	Result	G
3 Mar 1923	Scotland	0-1	
14 Apr 1923	Wales	3-0	
20 Oct 1923	England	2-1	
1 Mar 1924	Scotland	0-2	
15 Mar 1924	Wales	0-1	
22 Oct 1924	England	1-3	
28 Feb 1925	Scotland	0-3	
18 Apr 1925	Wales	0-0	
13 Feb 1926	Wales	3-0	
27 Feb 1926	Scotland	0-4	
20 Oct 1926	England	3-3	
26 Feb 1927	Scotland	0-2	
9 Apr 1927	Wales	2-2	
22 Oct 1927	England	2-0	
4 Feb 1928	Wales	1-2	
25 Feb 1928	Scotland	1-0	
22 Oct 1928	England	1-2	
22 Apr 1931	Wales	2-3	

281 **GEORGE HENRY MOORHEAD**

Position	Centre-half
Born	New Zealand, 27 May 1895
Died	Lurgan, 20 June 1975
Clubs	Brighton & Hove Albion; Southampton;

Glenavon; Linfield

Caps   3

Date	Team	Result	G
3 Mar 1923	Scotland	0-1	
25 Feb 1928	Scotland	1-0	
23 Feb 1929	Scotland	3-7	

282   H McKENZIE

Position   Outside-right

Clubs   Distillery

Caps   1

Date	Team	Result	G
3 Mar 1923	Scotland	0-1	

283   GEORGE HULL (Paddy) REID

Position   Centre-forward/Inside-left

Born   Belfast, January 1896

Clubs   Distillery; Blackpool; Walsall; Cardiff City; Fulham; Stockport County; Rotherham United; Mid-Rhondda United

Caps   1

Date	Team	Result	G
3 Mar 1923	Scotland	0-1	

284   W MOORE

Position   Outside-left

Clubs   Falkirk

Caps   1

Date	Team	Result	G
3 Mar 1923	Scotland	0-1	

285   JOHN ALEXANDER (Alex) MACKIE

Position   Right-back

Born   Belfast, 23 February 1903
Died   20 June 1984

Clubs   Forth River; Arsenal; Portsmouth; Northampton Town

Caps   3

Date	Team	Result	G
14 Apr 1923	Wales	3-0	
20 Oct 1934	Scotland	2-1	
27 Mar 1935	Wales	1-3	

286   ANDREW LYND KENNEDY

Position   Left-back/Centre-half

Born   Belfast, 1 September 1897
Died   December 1963

Clubs   Belfast Celtic; Glentoran; Crystal Palace; Arsenal; Everton; Tranmere Rovers

Caps   2

Date	Team	Result	G
14 Apr 1923	Wales	3-0	
22 Oct 1924	England	1-3	

287   ANDREW McCLUGGAGE

Position   Full-back

Born   Larne, 1 September 1900
Died   1954

Clubs   Invervale; Cliftonville; Bradford Park Avenue; Burnley; Dundalk; Preston North End; Morecambe ; Larne

Caps   12   Goals   2

Date	Team	Result	G
20 Oct 1923	England	2-1	
26 Feb 1927	Scotland	0-2	
9 Apr 1927	Wales	2-2	
22 Oct 1927	England	2-0	
4 Feb 1928	Wales	1-2	
25 Feb 1928	Scotland	1-0	
22 Oct 1928	England	1-2	
2 Feb 1929	Wales	2-2	1
23 Feb 1929	Scotland	3-7	
1 Feb 1930	Wales	7-0	1
20 Oct 1930	England	1-5	
22 Apr 1931	Wales	2-3	

288   THOMAS CROFT

Position   Inside-forward

Clubs   Queen's Island

Caps   1   Goals   1

Date	Team	Result	G
20 Oct 1923	England	2-1	1

289   JOHN McGRILLEN

Position   Outside-left

Clubs   Clyde; Belfast Celtic

Caps   2

Date	Team	Result	G
1 Mar 1924	Scotland	0-2	
26 Feb 1927	Scotland	0-2	

290   PATRICK McILVENNY

Position   Centre-forward

Clubs   Distillery

Caps   1

Date	Team	Result	G
15 Mar 1924	Wales	0-1	

291   H A CHATTON

Position   Right-half/Centre-half

Clubs   Partick Thistle

Caps   3

Date	Team	Result	G
22 Oct 1924	England	1-3	
28 Feb 1925	Scotland	0-3	
24 Oct 1925	England	0-0	

292   C MARTIN

Position   Outside-right

Clubs   Bo'ness

Caps   1

Date	Team	Result	G
28 Feb 1925	Scotland	0-3	

293   E CARROLL

Position   Centre-forward

Clubs   Glenavon

Caps   1

Date	Team	Result	G
28 Feb 1925	Scotland	0-3	

294   WILLIAM HENRY (Billy) McCONNELL

Position   Left-back

Born   Corbolis, 2 September 1898

Clubs   Slough Town; Arsenal; Slough Town; Reading; Slough Town

Caps   8

Date	Team	Result	G
18 Apr 1925	Wales	0-0	
24 Oct 1925	England	0-0	
13 Feb 1926	Wales	3-0	
20 Oct 1926	England	3-3	
26 Feb 1927	Scotland	0-2	
9 Apr 1927	Wales	2-2	
22 Oct 1927	England	2-0	
4 Feb 1928	Wales	1-2	

295   J GARRATT

Position   Right-half

Clubs   Distillery

Caps   1

Date	Team	Result	G
18 Apr 1925	Wales	0-0	

296   THOMAS S COWAN

Position   Outside-right

Clubs   Queen's Island

Caps   1

Date	Team	Result	G
18 Apr 1925	Wales	0-0	

297   A S SLOAN

Position   Centre-forward

Clubs   London Caledonians

Caps   1

Date	Team	Result	G
18 Apr 1925	Wales	0-0	

298   HUGH L MEEK

Position   Inside-left

Clubs   Glentoran

Caps   1

Date	Team	Result	G
18 Apr 1925	Wales	0-0	

299   HENRY WILSON

Position   Outside-left

Born   Belfast, 10 August 1891

Clubs	Dunmurry; Glenavon; Hull City; Charlton Athletic; Linfield
Caps	1

Date	Team	Result	G
18 Apr 1925	Wales	0-0	

Position	Outside-right
Clubs	Ards
Caps	5

Date	Team	Result	G
24 Oct 1925	England	0-0	
13 Feb 1926	Wales	3-0	
27 Feb 1926	Scotland	0-4	
20 Oct 1926	England	3-3	
9 Apr 1927	Wales	2-2	

301   THOMAS MILLEN SLOAN

Position	Centre-half
Born	Belfast, 23 September 1898
Died	2 June 1973
Clubs	Crusaders; Linfield; Cardiff City; Linfield
Caps	11

Date	Team	Result	G
24 Oct 1925	England	0-0	
13 Feb 1926	Wales	3-0	
27 Feb 1926	Scotland	0-4	
26 Feb 1927	Scotland	0-2	
9 Apr 1927	Wales	2-2	
22 Oct 1927	England	2-0	
4 Feb 1928	Wales	1-2	
22 Oct 1928	England	1-2	
1 Feb 1930	Wales	7-0	
22 Feb 1930	Scotland	1-3	
21 Feb 1931	Scotland	0-0	

302   HUGH H DAVEY

Position	Centre-forward/Inside-left
Born	Belfast, 14 June 1898
Clubs	Glentoran; Blackburn Rovers; Bournemouth; Reading; Portsmouth; Belfast Celtic
Caps	5 Goals 1

Date	Team	Result	G
24 Oct 1925	England	0-0	
20 Oct 1926	England	3-3	1
26 Feb 1927	Scotland	0-2	

22 Oct 1927	England	2-0
4 Feb 1928	Wales	1-2

303   JAMES (Jimmy) HOPKINS

Position	Inside-left
Born	Ballymoney, 12 July 1901
Died	1943
Clubs	Willowfield United; Belfast United; Arsenal; Brighton & Hove Albion; Aldershot
Caps	1

Date	Team	Result	G
24 Oct 1925	England	0-0	

304   DAVID McMULLAN

Position	Outside-left/Left-half
Born	Belfast
Clubs	Belfast Distillery; Liverpool; New York Giants; Belfast Celtic; Exeter City; Belfast Distillery
Caps	3

Date	Team	Result	G
24 Oct 1925	England	0-0	
13 Feb 1926	Wales	3-0	
26 Feb 1927	Scotland	0-2	

305   WILLIAM G BROWN

Position	Right-back
Clubs	Glenavon
Caps	1

Date	Team	Result	G
13 Feb 1926	Wales	3-0	

306   ALEXANDER STEELE

Position	Left-half/Inside-forward
Born	Belfast, 19 March 1899
Died	1980
Clubs	Barnville; Dunmurry; Glenavon; Charlton Athletic; Swansea Town; Fulham
Caps	4

Date	Team	Result	G
13 Feb 1926	Wales	3-0	
27 Feb 1926	Scotland	0-4	

2 Feb 1929	Wales	2-2	
23 Feb 1929	Scotland	3-7	

307　S CURRAN

Position　Centre-forward

Clubs　Belfast Celtic

Caps　3　Goals　2

Date	Team	Result	G
13 Feb 1926	Wales	3-0	2
27 Feb 1926	Scotland	0-4	
25 Feb 1928	Scotland	1-0	

308　THOMAS WATSON

Position　Left-back

Born　Belfast, 4 October 1902
Clubs　Crusaders; Cardiff City; Linfield

Caps　1

Date	Team	Result	G
27 Feb 1926	Scotland	0-4	

309　J MAHOOD

Position　Outside-left

Clubs　Belfast Celtic; Ballymena

Caps　9　Goals　2

Date	Team	Result	G
27 Feb 1926	Scotland	0-4	
22 Oct 1927	England	2-0	1
4 Feb 1928	Wales	1-2	
25 Feb 1928	Scotland	1-0	
22 Oct 1928	England	1-2	
2 Feb 1929	Wales	2-2	1
23 Feb 1929	Scotland	3-7	
1 Feb 1930	Wales	7-0	
16 Sep 1933	Scotland	2-1	

310　H JOHNSTON

Position　Centre-forward

Clubs　Portadown

Caps　1　Goals　2

Date	Team	Result	G
9 Apr 1927	Wales	2-2	2

311　JOHN HAROLD McCAW

Position　Outside-left

Born　Belfast, 17 March 1906
Died　Belfast, 13 August 1982

Clubs　Brentwood; Glentoran; Linfield; Stockport County; Newry Town

Caps　5　Goals　1

Date	Team	Result	G
9 Apr 1927	Wales	2-2	
22 Feb 1930	Scotland	1-3	1
20 Oct 1930	England	1-5	
21 Feb 1931	Scotland	0-0	
22 Apr 1931	Wales	2-3	

312　JAMES (Jimmy) DUNNE

Position　Centre-forward

Born　Ringsend, 3 September 1905
Died　December 1949

Clubs　Shamrock Rovers; New Brighton; Sheffield United; Arsenal; Southampton; Shamrock Rovers

Caps　7　Goals　4

Date	Team	Result	G
4 Feb 1928	Wales	1-2	
20 Oct 1930	England	1-5	1
22 Apr 1931	Wales	2-3	1
19 Sep 1931	Scotland	1-3	1
17 Oct 1931	England	2-6	1
17 Oct 1932	England	0-1	
7 Dec 1932	Wales	1-4	

313　PATRICK (Paddy) McCONNELL

Position　Inside-forward

Born　Rasharkin, 5 February 1900
Died　1971

Clubs　Belshill Athletic; Larkhall Thistle; Bathgate; Bradford City; Doncaster Rovers; Southport; Shelbourne; Boston United; Grantham Town; Hibernian

Caps　2

Date	Team	Result	G
4 Feb 1928	Wales	1-2	
17 Oct 1931	England	2-6	

314   ROBERT HAMILTON

Position   Left-back

Clubs   Glasgow Rangers

Caps   5

Date	Team	Result	G
25 Feb 1928	Scotland	1-0	
22 Oct 1928	England	1-2	
19 Oct 1929	England	0-3	
22 Feb 1930	Scotland	1-3	
19 Sep 1931	Scotland	1-3	

315   JAMES (Joe) BAMBRICK

Position   Centre-forward

Born   Belfast, 3 November 1905
Died   Belfast, 27 November 1983

Clubs   Ulster Rangers; Glentoran; Linfield; Chelsea; Walsall

Caps   11   Goals   12

Date	Team	Result	G
22 Oct 1928	England	1-2	1
2 Feb 1929	Wales	2-2	
23 Feb 1929	Scotland	3-7	2
19 Oct 1929	England	0-3	
1 Feb 1930	Wales	7-0	6
22 Feb 1930	Scotland	1-3	
5 Dec 1931	Wales	4-0	1
27 Mar 1935	Wales	1-3	1
19 Oct 1935	England	1-3	
13 Nov 1935	Scotland	1-2	
16 Mar 1938	Wales	1-0	1

316   JOSEPH MILLER

Position   Right-half

Born   Belfast, 27 April 1900

Clubs   Morton; Johnstone; Nuneaton Town; Aberdare Athletic; Middlesbrough; Hibernian; Bournemouth; Ballymena

Caps   3

Date	Team	Result	G
2 Feb 1929	Wales	2-2	
23 Feb 1929	Scotland	3-7	
19 Oct 1929	England	0-3	

317   JAMES H (Jimmy) ELWOOD

Position   Centre-half

Born   Belfast, 12 June 1901
Died   1937

Clubs   Glentoran; Manchester City; Chesterfield; Bradford Park Avenue; Derry City

Caps   2

Date	Team	Result	G
2 Feb 1929	Wales	2-2	
19 Oct 1929	England	0-3	

318   RICHARD WILLIAM MORRIS (Dick) ROWLEY

Position   Inside-forward/Centre-forward

Born   Enniskillen, 13 January 1904
Died   Southampton, 18 April 1984

Clubs   Andover; Swindon Town; London Casuals; Southampton; Tottenham Hotspur; Preston North End

Caps   6   Goals   1

Date	Team	Result	G
2 Feb 1929	Wales	2-2	
23 Feb 1929	Scotland	3-7	1
19 Oct 1929	England	0-3	
1 Feb 1930	Wales	7-0	
22 Apr 1931	Wales	2-3	
19 Sep 1931	Scotland	1-3	

319   LAWRENCE (Lawrie) CUMMING

Position   Inside-forward

Born   Derry, 1907

Clubs   Alloa Athletic; Huddersfield Town; Oldham Athletic; Southampton; Queen of the South; Alloa Athletic; St Mirren

Caps   3

Date	Team	Result	G
2 Feb 1929	Wales	2-2	
23 Feb 1929	Scotland	3-7	
19 Oct 1929	England	0-3	

320   HUGH FLACK

Position   Right-back

Born   Belfast, 1903

Clubs   Crusaders; Burnley; Swansea Town; Distillery; Halifax Town

Caps   1

Date	Team	Result	G
23 Feb 1929	Scotland	3-7	

321   SAMUEL R RUSSELL

Position   Right-back

Born   Downpatrick, 2 January 1900

Clubs   Belfast Distillery; Newcastle United; Shelbourne; Bradford City; Derry City

Caps   3

Date	Team	Result	G
19 Oct 1929	England	0-3	
22 Feb 1930	Scotland	1-3	
17 Oct 1931	England	2-6	

322   WILLIAM McCLEERY

Position   Inside-forward

Born   Belfast

Clubs   Cliftonville; Queen's Island; Blackburn Rovers; Queen's Island; Shelbourne; Linfield

Caps   9

Date	Team	Result	G
19 Oct 1929	England	0-3	
1 Feb 1930	Wales	7-0	
20 Oct 1930	England	1-5	
21 Feb 1931	Scotland	0-0	
22 Apr 1931	Wales	2-3	
19 Sep 1931	Scotland	1-3	
5 Dec 1931	Wales	4-0	
17 Oct 1932	England	0-1	
7 Dec 1932	Wales	1-4	

323   HENRY ANTHONY (Harry) DUGGAN

Position   Forward

Born   Dublin, 8 June 1903
Died   Leeds, September 1968

Clubs   Richmond United; Leeds United; Newport County

Caps   8

Date	Team	Result	G
19 Oct 1929	England	0-3	
20 Oct 1930	England	1-5	
22 Apr 1931	Wales	2-3	
17 Oct 1932	England	0-1	
14 Oct 1933	England	0-3	
20 Oct 1934	Scotland	2-1	
27 Mar 1935	Wales	1-3	
13 Nov 1935	Scotland	1-2	

324   PETER J KAVANAGH

Position   Outside-left

Born   Dublin, 1910
Died   Glasgow, 15 February 1993

Clubs   Drumcondra; Bohemians; Glasgow Celtic; Northampton Town; Guildford City; Hibernian; Stranraer; Waterford

Caps   1

Date	Team	Result	G
19 Oct 1929	England	0-3	

325   A GARDINER

Position   Goalkeeper

Clubs   Cliftonville

Caps   5

Date	Team	Result	G
1 Feb 1930	Wales	7-0	
22 Feb 1930	Scotland	1-3	
21 Feb 1931	Scotland	0-0	
19 Sep 1931	Scotland	1-3	
17 Oct 1931	England	2-6	

326   R P FULTON

Position   Left-back

Clubs   Belfast Celtic

Caps   20

Date	Team	Result	G
1 Feb 1930	Wales	7-0	
20 Oct 1930	England	1-5	
21 Feb 1931	Scotland	0-0	
22 Apr 1931	Wales	2-3	
17 Oct 1931	England	2-6	
5 Dec 1931	Wales	4-0	
17 Sep 1932	Scotland	0-4	
17 Oct 1932	England	0-1	
16 Sep 1933	Scotland	2-1	
14 Oct 1933	England	0-3	
4 Nov 1933	Wales	1-1	
20 Oct 1934	Scotland	2-1	
6 Feb 1935	England	1-2	
27 Mar 1935	Wales	1-3	
13 Nov 1935	Scotland	1-2	
11 Mar 1936	Wales	3-2	
31 Oct 1936	Scotland	1-3	
18 Nov 1936	England	1-3	
17 Mar 1937	Wales	1-4	
16 Mar 1938	Wales	1-0	

327 JACK JONES

Position	Centre-half
Born	Lurgan, 3 April 1907
Died	Lurgan, 20 March 1986
Clubs	Linfield; Hibernian
Caps	23

Date	Team	Result	G
1 Feb 1930	Wales	7-0	
22 Feb 1930	Scotland	1-3	
20 Oct 1930	England	1-5	
21 Feb 1931	Scotland	0-0	
22 Apr 1931	Wales	2-3	
19 Sep 1931	Scotland	1-3	
17 Oct 1931	England	2-6	
17 Sep 1932	Scotland	0-4	
17 Oct 1932	England	0-1	
7 Dec 1932	Wales	1-4	
16 Sep 1933	Scotland	2-1	
14 Oct 1933	England	0-3	
4 Nov 1933	Wales	1-1	
20 Oct 1934	Scotland	2-1	
6 Feb 1935	England	1-2	
27 Mar 1935	Wales	1-3	
19 Oct 1935	England	1-3	
13 Nov 1935	Scotland	1-2	
11 Mar 1936	Wales	3-2	
31 Oct 1936	Scotland	1-3	
18 Nov 1936	England	1-3	
17 Mar 1937	Wales	1-4	
23 Oct 1937	England	1-5	

328 JAMES McCAMBRIDGE

Position	Forward
Born	Larne, September 1905
Clubs	Larne; Ballymena United; Everton; Cardiff City; Ballymena United; Bristol Rovers; Exeter City; Sheffield Wednesday; Hartlepool United; Cheltenham Town
Caps	4

Date	Team	Result	G
1 Feb 1930	Wales	7-0	
22 Feb 1930	Scotland	1-3	
22 Apr 1931	Wales	2-3	
17 Oct 1931	England	2-6	

329 R McDONALD

Position	Wing-half
Clubs	Glasgow Rangers
Caps	2

Date	Team	Result	G
22 Feb 1930	Scotland	1-3	
17 Oct 1931	England	2-6	

330 W REID

Position	Centre-half
Clubs	Heart of Midlothian
Caps	1

Date	Team	Result	G
20 Oct 1930	England	1-5	

331 J McNINCH

Position	Full-back
Clubs	Ballymena
Caps	3

Date	Team	Result	G
21 Feb 1931	Scotland	0-0	
19 Sep 1931	Scotland	1-3	
5 Dec 1931	Wales	4-0	

332 HUGH BLAIR

Position	Outside-right
Born	Belfast, 21 May 1909
Clubs	Portadown; Swansea Town; Millwall
Caps	3

Date	Team	Result	G
21 Feb 1931	Scotland	0-0	
19 Sep 1931	Scotland	1-3	
16 Sep 1933	Scotland	2-1	

333 E FALLOON

Position	Forward
Clubs	Aberdeen
Caps	2

Date	Team	Result	G
21 Feb 1931	Scotland	0-0	
17 Sep 1932	Scotland	0-4	

334 F C ROBERTS

Position	Centre-forward
Clubs	Glentoran

Caps   1

Date	Team	Result	G
21 Feb 1931	Scotland	0-0	

335   JOHN GEARY

Position   Forward

Clubs   Glentoran

Caps   2

Date	Team	Result	G
21 Feb 1931	Scotland	0-0	
19 Sep 1931	Scotland	1-3	

336   W DIFFIN

Position   Goalkeeper

Clubs   Belfast Celtic

Caps   1

Date	Team	Result	G
22 Apr 1931	Wales	2-3	

337   WILLIAM ALEXANDER (Bill) GOWDY

Position   Left-half

Born   Belfast, 24 December 1903
Died   Larne, 16 March 1958

Clubs   Cliftonville; Ards; Hull City; Sheffield Wednesday; Gateshead; Linfield; Hibernian; Altrincham; Aldershot

Caps   6

Date	Team	Result	G
19 Sep 1931	Scotland	1-3	
17 Sep 1932	Scotland	0-4	
20 Oct 1934	Scotland	2-1	
6 Feb 1935	England	1-2	
27 Mar 1935	Wales	1-3	
11 Mar 1936	Wales	3-2	

338   WILLIAM (Billy) MITCHELL

Position   Right-half

Born   Lurgan, 22 November 1910
Died   Belfast, 1978

Clubs   Cliftonville; Distillery; Chelsea; Bath City

Caps   15

Date	Team	Result	G
17 Oct 1931	England	2-6	

Date	Team	Result	G
5 Dec 1931	Wales	4-0	
17 Oct 1932	England	0-1	
7 Dec 1932	Wales	1-4	
16 Sep 1933	Scotland	2-1	
4 Nov 1933	Wales	1-1	
20 Oct 1934	Scotland	2-1	
6 Feb 1935	England	1-2	
19 Oct 1935	England	1-3	
13 Nov 1935	Scotland	1-2	
31 Oct 1936	Scotland	1-3	
18 Nov 1936	England	1-3	
17 Mar 1937	Wales	1-4	
23 Oct 1937	England	1-5	
10 Nov 1937	Scotland	1-1	

339   J KELLY

Position   Outside-left

Clubs   Derry City

Caps   11   Goals   4

Date	Team	Result	G
17 Oct 1931	England	2-6	1
5 Dec 1931	Wales	4-0	2
17 Sep 1932	Scotland	0-4	
17 Oct 1932	England	0-1	
7 Dec 1932	Wales	1-4	
4 Nov 1933	Wales	1-1	
19 Oct 1935	England	1-3	
13 Nov 1935	Scotland	1-2	1
11 Mar 1936	Wales	3-2	
31 Oct 1936	Scotland	1-3	
18 Nov 1936	England	1-3	

340   MAURICE ARCHIBALD PYPER

Position   Centre-half

Born   Limavady, 4 September 1904
Died   Belfast, 1 March 1990

Clubs   Linfield

Caps   1

Date	Team	Result	G
5 Dec 1931	Wales	4-0	

341   WILLIAM T (Billy) MILLAR

Position   Forward

Born   Ballymena, 21 June 1903

Clubs   Lochgelly United; Linfield; Liverpool; Barrow; Newport County; Carlisle United; Sligo Rovers; Cork City; Drumcondra

Caps   2   Goals   1

Date	Team	Result	G
5 Dec 1931	Wales	4-0	1
17 Sep 1932	Scotland	0-4	

342   WILLIAM (Billy) COOK

Position   Full-back

Born   Coleraine, 20 January 1909
Died   Liverpool, December 1992

Clubs   Port Glasgow Athletic; Glasgow Celtic; Everton; Ellesmere Port Town; Wrexham; Rhyl

Caps   15

Date	Team	Result	G
17 Sep 1932	Scotland	0-4	
17 Oct 1932	England	0-1	
7 Dec 1932	Wales	1-4	
6 Feb 1935	England	1-2	
13 Nov 1935	Scotland	1-2	
11 Mar 1936	Wales	3-2	
31 Oct 1936	Scotland	1-3	
18 Nov 1936	England	1-3	
17 Mar 1937	Wales	1-4	
23 Oct 1937	England	1-5	
10 Nov 1937	Scotland	1-1	
16 Mar 1938	Wales	1-0	
8 Oct 1938	Scotland	0-2	
16 Nov 1938	England	0-7	
15 Mar 1939	Wales	1-3	

343   EDDIE MITCHELL

Position   Outside-right

Born   Whitehouse, 26 September 1912
Died   10 January 1964

Clubs   Cliftonville; Glentoran

Caps   2

Date	Team	Result	G
17 Sep 1932	Scotland	0-4	
4 Nov 1933	Wales	1-1	

344   THOMAS J M PRIESTLEY

Position   Inside-right

Born   Belfast, March 1911
Died   Belfast, December 1985

Clubs   Coleraine; Linfield; Chelsea

Caps   2

Date	Team	Result	G
17 Sep 1932	Scotland	0-4	
14 Oct 1933	England	0-3	

345   S ENGLISH

Position   Inside-forward

Clubs   Glasgow Rangers

Caps   2   Goals   1

Date	Team	Result	G
17 Sep 1932	Scotland	0-4	
7 Dec 1932	Wales	1-4	1

346   P MOORE

Position   Inside-forward

Clubs   Aberdeen

Caps   1

Date	Team	Result	G
17 Oct 1932	England	0-1	

347   JOHN DOHERTY

Position   Inside-left

Clubs   Cliftonville

Caps   1

Date	Team	Result	G
17 Oct 1932	England	0-1	
7 Dec 1932	Wales	1-4	

348   THOMAS WILLIGHAN

Position   Full-back

Born   Belfast
Clubs   Willowfield; Burnley

Caps   2

Date	Team	Result	G
7 Dec 1932	Wales	1-4	
16 Sep 1933	Scotland	2-1	

349   WILLIAM HOUSTON

Position   Outside-right

Born   Ballymena, 5 October 1906
Died   Larne, 2 October 1992

Clubs   Summerfield; Barn FC; Linfield

Caps   1

Date	Team	Result	G
7 Dec 1932	Wales	1-4	

350   JOHN McMAHON

Position   Right-half

Clubs   Bohemians

Caps   1

Date	Team	Result	G
16 Sep 1933	Scotland	2-1	

351   ALEXANDER ERNEST (Alex) STEVENSON

Position   Inside-left

Born   Dublin, 19 August 1912
Died   1985

Clubs   Dolphin; Glasgow Rangers; Everton; Bootle

Caps   17   Goals   5

Date	Team	Result	G
16 Sep 1933	Scotland	2-1	
14 Oct 1933	England	0-3	
4 Nov 1933	Wales	1-1	
20 Oct 1934	Scotland	2-1	
6 Feb 1935	England	1-2	1
13 Nov 1935	Scotland	1-2	
11 Mar 1936	Wales	3-2	1
18 Nov 1936	England	1-3	
17 Mar 1937	Wales	1-4	1
23 Oct 1937	England	1-5	1
16 Mar 1938	Wales	1-0	
8 Oct 1938	Scotland	0-2	
16 Nov 1938	England	0-7	
15 Mar 1939	Wales	1-3	
27 Nov 1946	Scotland	0-0	
16 Apr 1947	Wales	2-1	1
4 Oct 1947	Scotland	2-0	

352   DAVID KIRKER (Davy) MARTIN

Position   Centre-forward

Born   Belfast, 1 February 1914
Died   1991

Clubs   Royal Ulster Rifles; Cliftonville; Belfast Celtic; Wolverhampton Wanderers; Nottingham Forest; Notts County; Glentoran

Caps   10   Goals   3

Date	Team	Result	G
16 Sep 1933	Scotland	2-1	2
14 Oct 1933	England	0-3	
4 Nov 1933	Wales	1-1	
20 Oct 1934	Scotland	2-1	1
6 Feb 1935	England	1-2	
11 Mar 1936	Wales	3-2	
31 Oct 1936	Scotland	1-3	

Date	Team	Result	G
23 Oct 1937	England	1-5	
10 Nov 1937	Scotland	1-1	
8 Oct 1938	Scotland	0-2	

353   JOHN (Jackie) COULTER

Position   Outside-left

Born   Whiteabbey 1912
Died   1981

Clubs   Carrickfergus; Brantwood; Dunmurry; Cliftonville; Belfast Celtic; Everton; Grimsby Town; Chester; Chelmsford City; Swansea Town

Caps   11   Goals   1

Date	Team	Result	G
16 Sep 1933	Scotland	2-1	
14 Oct 1933	England	0-3	
4 Nov 1933	Wales	1-1	
20 Oct 1934	Scotland	2-1	1
6 Feb 1935	England	1-2	
27 Mar 1935	Wales	1-3	
31 Oct 1936	Scotland	1-3	
17 Mar 1937	Wales	1-4	
10 Nov 1937	Scotland	1-1	
16 Mar 1938	Wales	1-0	
8 Oct 1938	Scotland	0-2	

354   SIDNEY EDWARD (Sid) REID

Position   Full-back

Born   Belfast

Clubs   Cliftonville Strollers; Belfast Distillery; Derby County; Reading

Caps   3

Date	Team	Result	G
14 Oct 1933	England	0-3	
4 Nov 1933	Wales	1-1	
19 Oct 1935	England	1-3	

355   WALTER S McMILLAN

Position   Centre-half/Right-half

Born   Belfast, 24 November 1913

Clubs   Carrickfergus; Cliftonville; Arsenal; Manchester United; Chesterfield; Millwall; Tonbridge

Caps   7

Date	Team	Result	G
14 Oct 1933	England	0-3	
20 Oct 1934	Scotland	2-1	
31 Oct 1936	Scotland	1-3	

10 Nov 1937	Scotland	1-1	
16 Mar 1938	Wales	1-0	
8 Oct 1938	Scotland	0-2	
16 Nov 1938	England	0-7	

16 Mar 1938	Wales	1-0	
8 Oct 1938	Scotland	0-2	
16 Nov 1938	England	0-7	
15 Mar 1939	Wales	1-3	

356   SAMUEL JONES

Position   Left-half

Born   Lurgan, 14 September 1911
Died   1993

Clubs   Distillery; Blackpool

Caps   2

Date	Team	Result	G
14 Oct 1933	England	0-3	
4 Nov 1933	Wales	1-1	

357   THOMAS BREEN

Position   Goalkeeper

Born   Drogheda, 27 April 1917
Died   1988

Clubs   Newry Town; Belfast Celtic; Manchester
United; Belfast Celtic; Linfield; Shamrock
Rovers; Glentoran

Caps   9

Date	Team	Result	G
6 Feb 1935	England	1-2	
27 Mar 1935	Wales	1-3	
31 Oct 1936	Scotland	1-3	
18 Nov 1936	England	1-3	
17 Mar 1937	Wales	1-4	
23 Oct 1937	England	1-5	
10 Nov 1937	Scotland	1-1	
8 Oct 1938	Scotland	0-2	
15 Mar 1939	Wales	1-3	

358   JOHN (Jackie) BROWN

Position   Winger

Born   Belfast, 8 November 1914

Clubs   Belfast Celtic; Wolverhampton
Wanderers; Coventry City; Birmingham;
Barry Town; Ipswich Town

Caps   10   Goals   1

Date	Team	Result	G
6 Feb 1935	England	1-2	
27 Mar 1935	Wales	1-3	
19 Oct 1935	England	1-3	1
18 Nov 1936	England	1-3	
17 Mar 1937	Wales	1-4	
10 Nov 1937	Scotland	1-1	

359   PETER DESMOND DOHERTY

Position   Inside-forward/Outside-right

Born   Magherafelt, 5 June 1913
Died   Fleetwood, 6 April 1990

Clubs   Coleraine; Glentoran; Blackpool;
Manchester City; Derby County;
Huddersfield Town; Doncaster Rovers

Caps   16   Goals   3

Date	Team	Result	G
6 Feb 1935	England	1-2	
27 Mar 1935	Wales	1-3	
19 Oct 1935	England	1-3	
13 Nov 1935	Scotland	1-2	
18 Nov 1936	England	1-3	
17 Mar 1937	Wales	1-4	
23 Oct 1937	England	1-5	
10 Nov 1937	Scotland	1-1	1
16 Nov 1938	England	0-7	
15 Mar 1939	Wales	1-3	
28 Sep 1946	England	2-7	
16 Apr 1947	Wales	2-1	1
5 Nov 1947	England	2-2	1
10 Mar 1948	Wales	0-2	
17 Nov 1948	Scotland	2-3	
1 Nov 1950	Scotland	1-6	

360   KEILLOR McCULLOUGH

Position   Right-back/Right-half/Inside-right

Born   Larne

Clubs   Newington Rangers; Belfast Celtic;
Manchester City; Northampton Town

Caps   5

Date	Team	Result	G
27 Mar 1935	Wales	1-3	
19 Oct 1935	England	1-3	
13 Nov 1935	Scotland	1-2	
31 Oct 1936	Scotland	1-3	
18 Nov 1936	England	1-3	

361   C ALLAN

Position   Left-back

Clubs   Cliftonville

Caps   1

Date	Team	Result	G
19 Oct 1935	England	1-3	

Date	Team	Result	G
18 Nov 1936	England	1-3	1

362 ROBERT JAMES (Bobby) BROWNE

Position   Left-half

Born   Derry, 9 February 1912
Died   1994

Clubs   Maleven; Clooney Rovers; Derry City;
           Leeds United; York City; Thorne Colliery

Caps   6

Date	Team	Result	G
19 Oct 1935	England	1-3	
11 Mar 1936	Wales	3-2	
23 Oct 1937	England	1-5	
16 Mar 1938	Wales	1-0	
8 Oct 1938	Scotland	0-2	
16 Nov 1938	England	0-7	

363 NORMAN KERNAGHAN

Position   Outside-right

Clubs   Belfast Celtic

Caps   3   Goals   2

Date	Team	Result	G
11 Mar 1936	Wales	3-2	1
31 Oct 1936	Scotland	1-3	1
23 Oct 1937	England	1-5	

364 T J GIBB

Position   Inside-forward

Clubs   Cliftonville

Caps   1   Goals   1

Date	Team	Result	G
11 Mar 1936	Wales	3-2	1

365 THOMAS LAWRENCE DAVIS

Position   Centre-forward/Inside-right

Born   Dublin, 1911

Clubs   Midland Athletic; Cork; Shelbourne;
           Exeter City; Boston Town; Torquay
           United; New Brighton; FC de Metz;
           Oldham Athletic; Tranmere Rovers; York
           City; Workington; Belfast Distillery

Caps   1   Goals   1

366 THOMAS HENRY BROLLY

Position   Wing-half/Centre-half

Born   Belfast, 1 June 1912
Died   1986

Clubs   Crusaders; Glenavon; Sheffield
           Wednesday; Millwall

Caps   4

Date	Team	Result	G
17 Mar 1937	Wales	1-4	
16 Mar 1938	Wales	1-0	
16 Nov 1938	England	0-7	
15 Mar 1939	Wales	1-3	

367 S J BANKS

Position   Centre-forward

Clubs   Cliftonville

Caps   1

Date	Team	Result	G
17 Mar 1937	Wales	1-4	

368 WILLIAM EDWARD (Bill) HAYES

Position   Full-back

Born   Cork, 7 November 1915

Clubs   St Vincents (Sheffield); Huddersfield
           Town; Burnley

Caps   4

Date	Team	Result	G
23 Oct 1937	England	1-5	
10 Nov 1937	Scotland	1-1	
8 Oct 1938	Scotland	0-2	
16 Nov 1938	England	0-7	

369 OWEN MADDEN

Position   Outside-left/Inside-left

Born   Cork, 5 December 1916
Died   1991

Clubs   Cork Southern Rovers; Cork; Norwich
           City; Birmingham; Sligo Rovers; Cork
           City; Cork United; Cork Athletic

Caps   1

Date	Team	Result	G
23 Oct 1937	England	1-5	

370   M DOHERTY

Position   Right-half

Clubs   Derry City

Caps   1

Date	Team	Result	G
10 Nov 1937	Scotland	1-1	

371   JAMES (Jimmy) McALINDEN

Position   Inside-forward

Born   Belfast, 31 December 1917
Died   Belfast, November 1993

Clubs   Glentoran; Belfast Celtic; Portsmouth; Stoke City; Southend United; Glenavon

Caps   4

Date	Team	Result	G
10 Nov 1937	Scotland	1-1	
8 Oct 1938	Scotland	0-2	
28 Sep 1946	England	2-7	
9 Oct 1948	England	2-6	

372   JAMES FRANCIS (Jim) TWOMEY

Position   Goalkeeper

Born   Newry, 13 April 1914
Died   9 November, 1984

Clubs   Newry Town; Leeds United; Halifax Town

Caps   2

Date	Team	Result	G
16 Mar 1938	Wales	1-0	
16 Nov 1938	England	0-7	

373   P FARRELL

Position   Inside-right

Clubs   Hibernian

Caps   1

Date	Team	Result	G
16 Mar 1938	Wales	1-0	

374   MATTHEW AUGUSTINE O'MAHONEY

Position   Centre-half

Born   Mullinavat, 9 January 1913
Died   1992

Clubs   Liverpool; New Brighton; Hoylake; Southport; Wolverhampton Wanderers; Newport County; Bristol Rovers; Ipswich Town; Yarmouth Town

Caps   1

Date	Team	Result	G
8 Oct 1938	Scotland	0-2	

375   DAVID COCHRANE

Position   Outside-right

Born   Portadown, 14 August 1920

Clubs   Leeds United; Linfield; Shamrock Rovers; Leeds United

Caps   12

Date	Team	Result	G
16 Nov 1938	England	0-7	
15 Mar 1939	Wales	1-3	
28 Sep 1946	England	2-7	
27 Nov 1946	Scotland	0-0	
16 Apr 1947	Wales	2-1	
4 Oct 1947	Scotland	2-0	
5 Nov 1947	England	2-2	
10 Mar 1948	Wales	0-2	
17 Nov 1948	Scotland	2-3	
9 Mar 1949	Wales	0-2	
1 Oct 1949	Scotland	2-8	
16 Nov 1949	England	2-9	

376   HENRY (Harry) BAIRD

Position   Wing-half

Born   Belfast, 17 August 1913
Died   1973

Clubs   Linfield; Manchester United; Huddersfield Town; Ipswich Town

Caps   1

Date	Team	Result	G
16 Nov 1938	England	0-7	

377   MALCOLM PARTRIDGE BUTLER

Position   Full-back/Centre-forward

Born   Belfast, 6 August 1913
Died   1987

Clubs   Elmgrove; Belfast Celtic; Bangor; Blackpool; Accrington Stanley

Caps   1

Date	Team	Result	G
15 Mar 1939	Wales	1-3	

Position   Centre-half
Clubs   Belfast Celtic

Caps   1

Date	Team	Result	G
15 Mar 1939	Wales	1-3	

379   E WEIR

Position   Left-half

Clubs   Clyde

Caps   1

Date	Team	Result	G
15 Mar 1939	Wales	1-3	

380   DUDLEY MILLIGAN

Position   Centre-forward

Born   Johannesburg, South Africa, 7 November 1916

Clubs   Clyde (Cape Town); Chesterfield; Bournemouth; Walsall

Caps   1   Goals   1

Date	Team	Result	G
15 Mar 1939	Wales	1-3	1

381   ALEX RUSSELL

Position   Goalkeeper

Born   Ballymena, 18 January 1923
Clubs   Cliftonville; Linfield

Caps   1

Date	Team	Result	G
28 Sep 1946	England	2-7	

382   WILLIAM CHARLES (Bill) GORMAN

Position   Full-back

Born   Sligo, 13 July 1911
Died   1978

Clubs   Shettleston Juniors; Bury; Brentford

Caps   4

Date	Team	Result	G
28 Sep 1946	England	2-7	
27 Nov 1946	Scotland	0-0	
16 Apr 1947	Wales	2-1	
10 Mar 1948	Wales	0-2	

383   THOMAS (Bud) AHERNE

Position   Full-back

Born   Limerick, 26 January 1919
Died   January 2000

Clubs   Limerick; Belfast Celtic; Luton Town

Caps   4

Date	Team	Result	G
28 Sep 1946	England	2-7	
4 Oct 1947	Scotland	2-0	
9 Mar 1949	Wales	0-2	
8 Mar 1950	Wales	0-0	

384   JOHN JAMES CAREY

Position   Full-back

Born   Dublin, 23 February 1919
Died   27 August 1995

Clubs   St James' Gate; Manchester United

Caps   7

Date	Team	Result	G
28 Sep 1946	England	2-7	
27 Nov 1946	Scotland	0-0	
16 Apr 1947	Wales	2-1	
5 Nov 1947	England	2-2	
9 Oct 1948	England	2-6	
17 Nov 1948	Scotland	2-3	
9 Mar 1949	Wales	0-2	

DID YOU KNOW?
On 28 September 1946, Johnny Carey played for Northern Ireland and then played for the Republic of Ireland only two days later. Both appearances were made against England.

385   JOHN JOSEPH (Jack) VERNON

Position   Centre-half

Born   Belfast, 26 September 1918
Died   1981

Clubs   Belfast Celtic; West Bromwich Albion; Crusaders

Caps   17

Date	Team	Result	G
28 Sep 1946	England	2-7	
27 Nov 1946	Scotland	0-0	
16 Apr 1947	Wales	2-1	
4 Oct 1947	Scotland	2-0	
5 Nov 1947	England	2-2	
10 Mar 1948	Wales	0-2	
9 Oct 1948	England	2-6	
17 Nov 1948	Scotland	2-3	
9 Mar 1949	Wales	0-2	
1 Oct 1949	Scotland	2-8	
16 Nov 1949	England	2-9	
7 Oct 1950	England	1-4	
1 Nov 1950	Scotland	1-6	
7 Mar 1951	Wales	1-2	
12 May 1951	France	2-2	
6 Oct 1951	Scotland	0-2	
14 Nov 1951	England	0-2	

386   J P DOUGLAS

Position   Left-half

Clubs   Belfast Celtic

Caps   1

Date	Team	Result	G
28 Sep 1946	England	2-7	

387   EDWARD JAMES McMORRAN

Position   Inside-forward

Born   Larne, 2 September 1923
Died   Larne, 27 January 1984

Clubs   Belfast Celtic; Manchester City; Leeds
United; Barnsley; Doncaster Rovers;
Crewe Alexandra

Caps   15   Goals   4

Date	Team	Result	G
28 Sep 1946	England	2-7	
7 Oct 1950	England	1-4	1
1 Nov 1950	Scotland	1-6	
7 Mar 1951	Wales	1-2	
6 Oct 1951	Scotland	0-2	
14 Nov 1951	England	0-2	
19 Mar 1952	Wales	0-3	
4 Oct 1952	England	2-2	
5 Nov 1952	Scotland	1-1	
11 Nov 1952	France	1-3	
15 Apr 1953	Wales	2-3	2
11 Nov 1953	England	1-3	1
11 Apr 1956	Wales	1-1	
25 Apr 1957	Italy	0-1	
1 May 1957	Portugal	3-0	

388   NORMAN H LOCKHART

Position   Outside-left

Born   Belfast, 4 March 1924
Died   Belfast, 19 August 1993

Clubs   Distillery; Linfield; Swansea Town;
Coventry City; Aston Villa;
Bury; Ards

Caps   8   Goals   3

Date	Team	Result	G
28 Sep 1946	England	2-7	2
8 Mar 1950	Wales	0-0	
7 Mar 1951	Wales	1-2	
19 Mar 1952	Wales	0-3	
3 Oct 1953	Scotland	1-3	1
11 Nov 1953	England	1-3	
20 Apr 1955	Wales	2-3	
11 Apr 1956	Wales	1-1	

389   EDWARD (Ted) HINTON

Position   Goalkeeper

Born   Belfast, 20 May 1922
Died   1988

Clubs   Distillery; Fulham; Millwall

Caps   7

Date	Team	Result	G
27 Nov 1946	Scotland	0-0	
16 Apr 1947	Wales	2-1	
4 Oct 1947	Scotland	2-0	
5 Nov 1947	England	2-2	
10 Mar 1948	Wales	0-2	
7 Mar 1951	Wales	1-2	
12 May 1951	France	2-2	

390   JAMES McBURNEY FEENEY

Position   Full-back

Born   Ligoniel, 23 June 1921
Died   Belfast, 17 March 1985

Clubs   Crusaders; Ards; Linfield; Swansea Town;
Ipswich Town; Ards

Caps   2

Date	Team	Result	G
27 Nov 1946	Scotland	0-0	
16 Nov 1949	England	2-9	

391   CORNELIUS JOSEPH (Con) MARTIN

Position   Centre-half/Goalkeeper

Born   Dublin, 20 March 1923

Clubs   Drumcondra; Glentoran; Leeds United;
Aston Villa

Caps   6

Date	Team	Result	G
27 Nov 1946	Scotland	0-0	
4 Oct 1947	Scotland	2-0	
5 Nov 1947	England	2-2	
10 Mar 1948	Wales	0-2	
9 Oct 1948	England	2-6	
8 Mar 1950	Wales	0-0	

392   PETER DESMOND FARRELL

Position   Wing-half

Born   Dublin, 16 August 1922
Died   16 March 1999

Clubs   Shamrock Rovers; Everton; Tranmere
Rovers; Holyhist Town

Caps   7

Date	Team	Result	G
27 Nov 1946	Scotland	0-0	
16 Apr 1947	Wales	2-1	
4 Oct 1947	Scotland	2-0	
5 Nov 1947	England	2-2	
10 Mar 1948	Wales	0-2	
9 Oct 1948	England	2-6	
9 Mar 1949	Wales	0-2	

393   DAVID JOHN WALSH

Position   Centre-forward

Born   Waterford, 28 April 1923

Clubs   Linfield; West Bromwich Albion; Aston
Villa; Walsall

Caps   9   Goals   5

Date	Team	Result	G
27 Nov 1946	Scotland	0-0	
16 Apr 1947	Wales	2-1	
4 Oct 1947	Scotland	2-0	
5 Nov 1947	England	2-2	1
10 Mar 1948	Wales	0-2	
9 Oct 1948	England	2-6	2
17 Nov 1948	Scotland	2-3	2
9 Mar 1949	Wales	0-2	
8 Mar 1950	Wales	0-0	

DID YOU KNOW?
Davy Walsh is the only player to have represented both
Northern Ireland and the Republic of Ireland in World Cup
matches – in 1950 for Northern Ireland, and 1949 and 1953
for the Republic.

394   THOMAS JOSEPH EGLINGTON

Position   Forward

Born   Dublin, 15 January 1923
Died   18 February 2004

Clubs   Shamrock Rovers; Everton; Tranmere
Rovers

Caps   6

Date	Team	Result	G
27 Nov 1946	Scotland	0-0	
16 Apr 1947	Wales	2-1	
4 Oct 1947	Scotland	2-0	
5 Nov 1947	England	2-2	
10 Mar 1948	Wales	0-2	
9 Oct 1948	England	2-6	

395   JOSEPH WALTER (Paddy) SLOAN

Position   Wing-half

Born   Lurgan, 30 April 1921
Died   1993

Clubs   Glenavon; Manchester United; Tranmere
Rovers; Arsenal; Sheffield United; Brescia
(Italy); Norwich City

Caps   1

Date	Team	Result	G
16 Apr 1947	Wales	2-1	

396   WILLIAM WALSH

Position   Wing-half

Born   Dublin, 31 May 1921

Clubs   Manchester United; Manchester City

Caps   5

Date	Team	Result	G
4 Oct 1947	Scotland	2-0	
5 Nov 1947	England	2-2	
10 Mar 1948	Wales	0-2	
9 Oct 1948	England	2-6	
17 Nov 1948	Scotland	2-3	

397   SAMUEL SMYTH

Position   Inside-forward

Born   Belfast, 25 February 1925

Clubs   Linfield; Wolverhampton Wanderers;
Stoke City; Liverpool

Caps   9   Goals   5

Date	Team	Result	G
4 Oct 1947	Scotland	2-0	2
5 Nov 1947	England	2-2	

Date	Team	Result	G
10 Mar 1948	Wales	0-2	
17 Nov 1948	Scotland	2-3	
9 Mar 1949	Wales	0-2	
1 Oct 1949	Scotland	2-8	2
16 Nov 1949	England	2-9	1
8 Mar 1950	Wales	0-0	
14 Nov 1951	England	0-2	

398   W SMYTH

Position   Goalkeeper

Clubs   Distillery

Caps   4

Date	Team	Result	G
9 Oct 1948	England	2-6	
17 Nov 1948	Scotland	2-3	
3 Oct 1953	Scotland	1-3	
11 Nov 1953	England	1-3	

399   JOHN FRANCIS O'DRISCOLL

Position   Winger

Born   Cork, 20 September 1921
Died   1988

Clubs   Cork; Swansea Town

Caps   3

Date	Team	Result	G
9 Oct 1948	England	2-6	
17 Nov 1948	Scotland	2-3	
9 Mar 1949	Wales	0-2	

400   CHARLES PATRICK TULLY

Position   Inside-left

Born   Belfast, 11 July 1924
Died   Belfast, 27 July 1971

Clubs   Belfast Celtic; Glasgow Celtic; Cork Hibernians

Caps   10   Goals   3

Date	Team	Result	G
9 Oct 1948	England	2-6	
16 Nov 1949	England	2-9	
6 Oct 1951	Scotland	0-2	
4 Oct 1952	England	2-2	2
5 Nov 1952	Scotland	1-1	
11 Nov 1952	France	1-3	1
15 Apr 1953	Wales	2-3	
3 Oct 1953	Scotland	1-3	
2 Nov 1955	England	0-3	
15 Oct 1958	Spain	2-6	

401   THOMAS RODERICK (Rory) KEANE

Position   Full-back

Born   Limerick, 31 August 1922
Clubs   Limerick; Swansea Town

Caps   1

Date	Team	Result	G
17 Nov 1948	Scotland	2-3	

402   JAMES JOSEPH McCABE

Position   Wing-half

Born   Derry, 17 September 1918
Died   1989

Clubs   South Bank; Middlesbrough; Leeds United

Caps   6

Date	Team	Result	G
17 Nov 1948	Scotland	2-3	
9 Mar 1949	Wales	0-2	
16 Nov 1949	England	2-9	
7 Mar 1951	Wales	1-2	
15 Apr 1953	Wales	2-3	
3 Oct 1953	Scotland	1-3	

403   C MOORE

Position   Goalkeeper

Clubs   Glentoran

Caps   1

Date	Team	Result	G
9 Mar 1949	Wales	0-2	

404   ROBERT ANDERSON BRENNAN

Position   Inside-forward

Born   Belfast, 14 March 1925

Clubs   Distillery; Luton Town; Birmingham City; Fulham; Norwich City

Caps   5   Goals   1

Date	Team	Result	G
9 Mar 1949	Wales	0-2	
1 Oct 1949	Scotland	2-8	
16 Nov 1949	England	2-9	1
8 Mar 1950	Wales	0-0	
7 Oct 1950	England	1-4	

| 405 | PATRICK KELLY |

Position Goalkeeper

Born South Africa, 9 April 1918
Died 1985

Clubs Aberdeen; Barnsley; Crewe Alexandra

Caps 1

Date	Team	Result	G
1 Oct 1949	Scotland	2-8	

| 406 | GERALD COLUMBA BOWLER |

Position Centre-half

Born Derry, 8 June 1919

Clubs Distillery; Portsmouth; Hull City; Millwall

Caps 3

Date	Team	Result	G
1 Oct 1949	Scotland	2-8	
16 Nov 1949	England	2-9	
8 Mar 1950	Wales	0-0	

| 407 | ALFRED McMICHAEL |

Position Full-back

Born Belfast, 1 October 1927

Clubs Linfield; Newcastle United

Caps 40

Date	Team	Result	G
1 Oct 1949	Scotland	2-8	
16 Nov 1949	England	2-9	
7 Oct 1950	England	1-4	
1 Nov 1950	Scotland	1-6	
12 May 1951	France	2-2	
8 Oct 1951	Scotland	0-2	
14 Nov 1951	England	0-2	
19 Mar 1952	Wales	0-3	
4 Oct 1952	England	2-2	
5 Nov 1952	Scotland	1-1	
11 Nov 1952	France	1-3	
15 Apr 1953	Wales	2-3	
3 Oct 1953	Scotland	1-3	
11 Nov 1953	England	1-3	
21 Mar 1954	Wales	2-1	
2 Oct 1954	England	0-2	
20 Apr 1955	Wales	2-3	
11 Apr 1956	Wales	1-1	
6 Oct 1956	England	1-1	
7 Nov 1956	Scotland	0-1	
18 Jan 1957	Portugal	1-1	
10 Apr 1957	Wales	0-0	
25 Apr 1957	Italy	0-1	
1 May 1957	Portugal	3-0	
5 Oct 1957	Scotland	1-1	
6 Nov 1957	England	3-2	
4 Dec 1957	Italy	2-2	
15 Jan 1958	Italy	1-3	
16 Apr 1958	Wales	1-1	
8 Jun 1958	Czechoslovakia	1-0	
11 Jun 1958	Argentina	1-3	
15 Jun 1958	West Germany	2-2	
17 Jun 1958	Czechoslovakia	2-1	
19 Jun 1958	France	0-4	
15 Oct 1958	Spain	2-6	
5 Nov 1958	Scotland	2-2	
22 Apr 1959	Wales	4-1	
3 Oct 1959	Scotland	0-4	
18 Nov 1959	England	1-2	
6 Apr 1960	Wales	2-3	

| 408 | ROBERT DENNIS (Danny) BLANCHFLOWER |

Position Wing-half

Born Belfast, 10 February 1926
Died 9 December 1993

Clubs Glentoran; Barnsley; Aston Villa; Tottenham Hotspur

Caps 56 **Goals** 2

Date	Team	Result	G
1 Oct 1949	Scotland	2-8	
8 Mar 1950	Wales	0-0	
7 Oct 1950	England	1-4	
1 Nov 1950	Scotland	1-6	
12 May 1951	France	2-2	
19 Mar 1952	Wales	0-3	
4 Oct 1952	England	2-2	
5 Nov 1952	Scotland	1-1	
11 Nov 1952	France	1-3	
15 Apr 1953	Wales	2-3	
3 Oct 1953	Scotland	1-3	
11 Nov 1953	England	1-3	
21 Mar 1954	Wales	2-1	
2 Oct 1954	England	0-2	
3 Nov 1954	Scotland	2-2	
20 Apr 1955	Wales	2-3	
8 Oct 1955	Scotland	2-1	
2 Nov 1955	England	0-3	
11 Apr 1956	Wales	1-1	
6 Oct 1956	England	1-1	
7 Nov 1956	Scotland	0-1	
16 Jan 1957	Portugal	1-1	
10 Apr 1957	Wales	0-0	
25 Apr 1957	Italy	0-1	
1 May 1957	Portugal	3-0	
5 Oct 1957	Scotland	1-1	
6 Nov 1957	England	3-2	
4 Dec 1957	Italy	2-2	
15 Jan 1958	Italy	1-3	
16 Apr 1958	Wales	1-1	
8 Jun 1958	Czechoslovakia	1-0	
11 Jun 1958	Argentina	1-3	
15 Jun 1958	West Germany	2-2	
17 Jun 1958	Czechoslovakia	2-1	
19 Jun 1958	France	0-4	

Date	Team	Result	G
4 Oct 1958	England	3-3	
15 Oct 1958	Spain	2-6	
5 Nov 1958	Scotland	2-2	
22 Apr 1959	Wales	4-1	
3 Oct 1959	Scotland	0-4	
18 Nov 1959	England	1-2	
6 Apr 1960	Wales	2-3	1
8 Oct 1960	England	2-5	
26 Oct 1960	West Germany	3-4	
9 Nov 1960	Scotland	2-5	1
12 Apr 1961	Wales	1-5	
10 May 1961	West Germany	1-2	
7 Oct 1961	Scotland	1-6	
17 Oct 1961	Greece	2-0	
22 Nov 1961	England	1-1	
11 Apr 1962	Wales	0-4	
9 May 1962	Holland	0-4	
10 Oct 1962	Poland	2-0	
20 Oct 1962	England	1-3	
7 Nov 1962	Scotland	1-5	
28 Nov 1962	Poland	2-0	

409   RAYMOND OSBORN FERRIS

Position   Wing-half

Born   Newry, 22 September 1920
Died   1994

Clubs   Cambridge Town; Crewe Alexandra;
Birmingham City

Caps   3   Goals   1

Date	Team	Result	G
1 Oct 1949	Scotland	2-8	
12 May 1951	France	2-2	1
6 Oct 1951	Scotland	0-2	

410   EDWARD CROSSAN

Position   Inside-forward

Born   Derry, 17 November 1925

Clubs   Derry City; Blackburn Rovers; Tranmere
Rovers

Caps   3   Goals   1

Date	Team	Result	G
1 Oct 1949	Scotland	2-8	
7 Oct 1950	England	1-4	
20 Apr 1955	Wales	2-3	1

411   JOHN McKENNA

Position   Outside-right

Born   Belfast, 6 June 1926
Died   1980

Clubs   Linfield; Huddersfield Town; Blackpool;
Southport

Caps   7

Date	Team	Result	G
1 Oct 1949	Scotland	2-8	
16 Nov 1949	England	2-9	
8 Mar 1950	Wales	0-0	
7 Oct 1950	England	1-4	
1 Nov 1950	Scotland	1-6	
12 May 1951	France	2-2	
14 Nov 1951	England	0-2	

412   HUGH REDMOND KELLY

Position   Goalkeeper

Born   Lurgan, 17 August 1919
Died   1977

Clubs   Belfast Celtic; Fulham; Southampton;
Exeter City

Caps   4

Date	Team	Result	G
16 Nov 1949	England	2-9	
8 Mar 1950	Wales	0-0	
7 Oct 1950	England	1-4	
1 Nov 1950	Scotland	1-6	

413   REGINALD ALPHONSO RYAN

Position   Inside-forward

Born   Dublin, 30 October 1925
Died   Birmingham, 13 February 1997

Clubs   Nuneaton Borough; West Bromwich
Albion; Derby County; Coventry City

Caps   1

Date	Team	Result	G
8 Mar 1950	Wales	0-0	

414   CHARLES GALLOGLY

Position   Full-back

Born   Banbridge, 16 June 1925

Clubs   Glenavon; Huddersfield Town; Watford;
Bournemouth

Caps   2

Date	Team	Result	G
7 Oct 1950	England	1-4	
1 Nov 1950	Scotland	1-6	

415 WILBUR CUSH

Position Wing-half/Inside-forward

Born Lurgan, 10 June 1928
Died 28 July 1981

Clubs Glenavon; Leeds United; Portadown

Caps 26 Goals 5

Date	Team	Result	G
7 Oct 1950	England	1-4	
1 Nov 1950	Scotland	1-6	
3 Oct 1953	Scotland	1-3	
11 Nov 1953	England	1-3	
16 Jan 1957	Portugal	1-1	
10 Apr 1957	Wales	0-0	
25 Apr 1957	Italy	0-1	
1 May 1957	Portugal	3-0	
4 Dec 1957	Italy	2-2	2
15 Jan 1958	Italy	1-3	
16 Apr 1958	Wales	1-1	
8 Jun 1958	Czechoslovakia	1-0	1
11 Jun 1958	Argentina	1-3	
15 Jun 1958	West Germany	2-2	
17 Jun 1958	Czechoslovakia	2-1	
19 Jun 1958	France	0-4	
4 Oct 1958	England	3-3	1
15 Oct 1958	Spain	2-6	1
5 Nov 1958	Scotland	2-2	
22 Apr 1959	Wales	4-1	
3 Oct 1959	Scotland	0-4	
18 Nov 1959	England	1-2	
6 Apr 1960	Wales	2-3	
3 May 1961	Greece	1-2	
10 May 1961	West Germany	1-2	
17 Oct 1961	Greece	2-0	

416 JOHN PETER CAMPBELL

Position Outside-left

Born Derry, 28 June 1923
Died 1968

Clubs Belfast Celtic; Fulham

Caps 2

Date	Team	Result	G
7 Oct 1950	England	1-4	
1 Nov 1950	Scotland	1-6	

417 J KEVIN McGARRY

Position Inside-forward

Clubs Cliftonville

Caps 3 Goals 1

Date	Team	Result	G
1 Nov 1950	Scotland	1-6	1

Date	Team	Result	
7 Mar 1951	Wales	1-2	
12 May 1951	France	2-2	

418 WILLIAM GEORGE LEONARD GRAHAM

Position Full-back

Born Belfast, 17 October 1925

Clubs Brantwood; Doncaster Rovers; Torquay United

Caps 14

Date	Team	Result	G
7 Mar 1951	Wales	1-2	
12 May 1951	France	2-2	
6 Oct 1951	Scotland	0-2	
14 Nov 1951	England	0-2	
19 Mar 1952	Wales	0-3	
5 Nov 1952	Scotland	1-1	
11 Nov 1952	France	1-3	
11 Nov 1953	England	1-3	
21 Mar 1954	Wales	2-1	
3 Nov 1954	Scotland	2-2	
20 Apr 1955	Wales	2-3	
8 Oct 1955	Scotland	2-1	
2 Nov 1955	England	0-3	
4 Oct 1958	England	3-3	

419 WILLIAM EDWARD CUNNINGHAM

Position Full-back

Born Belfast, 20 February 1930

Clubs St Mirren; Leicester City; Dunfermline Athletic

Caps 30

Date	Team	Result	G
7 Mar 1951	Wales	1-2	
4 Oct 1952	England	2-2	
3 Oct 1953	Scotland	1-3	
3 Nov 1954	Scotland	2-2	
8 Oct 1955	Scotland	2-1	
2 Nov 1955	England	0-3	
11 Apr 1956	Wales	1-1	
6 Oct 1956	England	1-1	
7 Nov 1956	Scotland	0-1	
16 Jan 1957	Portugal	1-1	
10 Apr 1957	Wales	0-0	
25 Apr 1957	Italy	0-1	
1 May 1957	Portugal	3-0	
5 Oct 1957	Scotland	1-1	
15 Jan 1958	Italy	1-3	
16 Apr 1958	Wales	1-1	
8 Jun 1958	Czechoslovakia	1-0	
11 Jun 1958	Argentina	1-3	
15 Jun 1958	West Germany	2-2	
17 Jun 1958	Czechoslovakia	2-1	
19 Jun 1958	France	0-4	
4 Oct 1958	England	3-3	

Date	Team	Result	G
5 Nov 1958	Scotland	2-2	
22 Apr 1959	Wales	4-1	
3 Oct 1959	Scotland	0-4	
18 Nov 1959	England	1-2	
6 Apr 1960	Wales	2-3	
12 Apr 1961	Wales	1-5	
11 Apr 1962	Wales	0-4	
9 May 1962	Holland	0-4	

420 WILLIAM DICKSON

Position Wing-half

Born Lurgan, 15 April 1923

Clubs Glenavon; Notts County; Chelsea; Arsenal; Mansfield Town

Caps 12

Date	Team	Result	G
7 Mar 1951	Wales	1-2	
12 May 1951	France	2-2	
6 Oct 1951	Scotland	0-2	
14 Nov 1951	England	0-2	
19 Mar 1952	Wales	0-3	
4 Oct 1952	England	2-2	
5 Nov 1952	Scotland	1-1	
11 Nov 1952	France	1-3	
15 Apr 1953	Wales	2-3	
11 Nov 1953	England	1-3	
21 Mar 1954	Wales	2-1	
2 Oct 1954	England	0-2	

421 WILLIAM HUGHES

Position Outside-right

Born Ballymena, 9 May 1929

Clubs Larne Town; Bolton Wanderers; Bournemouth

Caps 1

Date	Team	Result	G
7 Mar 1951	Wales	1-2	

422 WILLIAM J (Billy) SIMPSON

Position Centre-forward

Clubs Glasgow Rangers

Caps 12   Goals 5

Date	Team	Result	G
7 Mar 1951	Wales	1-2	1
12 May 1951	France	2-2	1
3 Oct 1953	Scotland	1-3	
11 Nov 1953	England	1-3	
2 Oct 1954	England	0-2	
25 Apr 1957	Italy	0-1	

Date	Team	Result	G
1 May 1957	Portugal	3-0	1
5 Oct 1957	Scotland	1-1	
6 Nov 1957	England	3-2	1
15 Jan 1958	Italy	1-3	
16 Apr 1958	Wales	1-1	1
5 Nov 1958	Scotland	2-2	

423 WILLIAM LAURENCE (Billy) BINGHAM

Position Outside-right

Born Belfast, 5 August 1931

Clubs Glentoran; Sunderland; Luton Town; Everton; Port Vale

Caps 56   Goals 9

Date	Team	Result	G
12 May 1951	France	2-2	
6 Oct 1951	Scotland	0-2	
14 Nov 1951	England	0-2	
19 Mar 1952	Wales	0-3	
4 Oct 1952	England	2-2	
5 Nov 1952	Scotland	1-1	
11 Nov 1952	France	1-3	
15 Apr 1953	Wales	2-3	
3 Oct 1953	Scotland	1-3	
11 Nov 1953	England	1-3	
21 Mar 1954	Wales	2-1	
2 Oct 1954	England	0-2	
3 Nov 1954	Scotland	2-2	1
20 Apr 1955	Wales	2-3	
8 Oct 1955	Scotland	2-1	1
2 Nov 1955	England	0-3	
11 Apr 1956	Wales	1-1	
6 Oct 1956	England	1-1	
7 Nov 1956	Scotland	0-1	
16 Jan 1957	Portugal	1-1	1
10 Apr 1957	Wales	0-0	
25 Apr 1957	Italy	0-1	
1 May 1957	Portugal	3-0	
5 Oct 1957	Scotland	1-1	1
6 Nov 1957	England	3-2	
4 Dec 1957	Italy	2-2	
15 Jan 1958	Italy	1-3	
16 Apr 1958	Wales	1-1	
8 Jun 1958	Czechoslovakia	1-0	
11 Jun 1958	Argentina	1-3	
15 Jun 1958	West Germany	2-2	
17 Jun 1958	Czechoslovakia	2-1	
19 Jun 1958	France	0-4	
4 Oct 1958	England	3-3	
15 Oct 1958	Spain	2-6	
5 Nov 1958	Scotland	2-2	
22 Apr 1959	Wales	4-1	
3 Oct 1959	Scotland	0-4	
18 Nov 1959	England	1-2	1
6 Apr 1960	Wales	2-3	1
8 Oct 1960	England	2-5	
26 Oct 1960	West Germany	3-4	
9 Nov 1960	Scotland	2-5	
25 Apr 1961	Italy	2-3	
3 May 1961	Greece	1-2	
10 May 1961	West Germany	1-2	

Date	Team	Result	G
17 Oct 1961	Greece	2-0	
22 Nov 1961	England	1-1	
10 Oct 1962	Poland	2-0	
20 Oct 1962	England	1-3	
7 Nov 1962	Scotland	1-5	1
28 Nov 1962	Poland	2-0	1
30 May 1963	Spain	1-1	
12 Oct 1963	Scotland	2-1	1
30 Oct 1963	Spain	0-1	
20 Nov 1963	England	3-8	

Above: Jimmy McIlroy

424 WILLIAM NORMAN McCOURT UPRICHARD

Position Goalkeeper

Born Portadown, 20 April 1928

Clubs Distillery; Arsenal; Swindon Town; Portsmouth; Southend United

Caps 18

Date	Team	Result	G
6 Oct 1951	Scotland	0-2	
14 Nov 1951	England	0-2	
19 Mar 1952	Wales	0-3	
4 Oct 1952	England	2-2	
5 Nov 1952	Scotland	1-1	
11 Nov 1952	France	1-3	
15 Apr 1953	Wales	2-3	
2 Oct 1954	England	0-2	
3 Nov 1954	Scotland	2-2	
20 Apr 1955	Wales	2-3	
8 Oct 1955	Scotland	2-1	
2 Nov 1955	England	0-3	
11 Apr 1956	Wales	1-1	
5 Oct 1957	Scotland	1-1	
15 Jan 1958	Italy	1-3	
17 Jun 1958	Czechoslovakia	2-1	
15 Oct 1958	Spain	2-6	
5 Nov 1958	Scotland	2-2	

425 JAMES (Jimmy) McILROY

Position Inside-forward

Born Lambeg, 25 October 1931

Clubs Glentoran; Burnley; Stoke City; Oldham Athletic

Caps 55 Goals 9

Date	Team	Result	G
6 Oct 1951	Scotland	0-2	
14 Nov 1951	England	0-2	
19 Mar 1952	Wales	0-3	
4 Oct 1952	England	2-2	
5 Nov 1952	Scotland	1-1	
15 Apr 1953	Wales	2-3	
3 Oct 1953	Scotland	1-3	
11 Nov 1953	England	1-3	
21 Mar 1954	Wales	2-1	
2 Oct 1954	England	0-2	
3 Nov 1954	Scotland	2-2	
20 Apr 1955	Wales	2-3	
8 Oct 1955	Scotland	2-1	
2 Nov 1955	England	0-3	
11 Apr 1956	Wales	1-1	
6 Oct 1956	England	1-1	1
7 Nov 1956	Scotland	0-1	
16 Jan 1957	Portugal	1-1	
10 Apr 1957	Wales	0-0	
25 Apr 1957	Italy	0-1	
1 May 1957	Portugal	3-0	1
5 Oct 1957	Scotland	1-1	
6 Nov 1957	England	3-2	1
4 Dec 1957	Italy	2-2	
15 Jan 1958	Italy	1-3	
16 Apr 1958	Wales	1-1	
8 Jun 1958	Czechoslovakia	1-0	
11 Jun 1958	Argentina	1-3	
15 Jun 1958	West Germany	2-2	
17 Jun 1958	Czechoslovakia	2-1	
19 Jun 1958	France	0-4	
4 Oct 1958	England	3-3	
15 Oct 1958	Spain	2-6	1
5 Nov 1958	Scotland	2-2	1
22 Apr 1959	Wales	4-1	1
3 Oct 1959	Scotland	0-4	
18 Nov 1959	England	1-2	

Date	Team	Result	G
6 Apr 1960	Wales	2-3	
8 Oct 1960	England	2-5	
26 Oct 1960	West Germany	3-4	
12 Apr 1961	Wales	1-5	
3 May 1961	Greece	1-2	1
10 May 1961	West Germany	1-2	1
7 Oct 1961	Scotland	1-6	
17 Oct 1961	Greece	2-0	
22 Nov 1961	England	1-1	1
9 May 1962	Holland	0-4	
10 Oct 1962	Poland	2-0	
20 Oct 1962	England	1-3	
7 Nov 1962	Scotland	1-5	
28 Nov 1962	Poland	2-0	
3 Apr 1963	Wales	1-4	
2 Oct 1965	Scotland	3-2	
10 Nov 1965	England	1-2	
24 Nov 1965	Albania	1-1	

426   ROBERT (Bertie) PEACOCK

Position   Left-half

Born   Coleraine, 29 September 1928
Died   22 July 2004

Clubs   Coleraine; Glentoran; Glasgow Celtic;
            Coleraine; Morton (loan); Hamilton
            Steelers (Canada)

Caps   31   Goals   2

Date	Team	Result	G
6 Oct 1951	Scotland	0-2	
11 Nov 1952	France	1-3	
21 Mar 1954	Wales	2-1	
2 Oct 1954	England	0-2	
3 Nov 1954	Scotland	2-2	
8 Oct 1955	Scotland	2-1	
2 Nov 1955	England	0-3	
10 Apr 1957	Wales	0-0	
25 Apr 1957	Italy	0-1	
1 May 1957	Portugal	3-0	
5 Oct 1957	Scotland	1-1	
6 Nov 1957	England	3-2	
4 Dec 1957	Italy	2-2	
15 Jan 1958	Italy	1-3	
16 Apr 1958	Wales	1-1	
8 Jun 1958	Czechoslovakia	1-0	
11 Jun 1958	Argentina	1-3	
15 Jun 1958	West Germany	2-2	
17 Jun 1958	Czechoslovakia	2-1	
4 Oct 1958	England	3-3	1
5 Nov 1958	Scotland	2-2	
22 Apr 1959	Wales	4-1	1
3 Oct 1959	Scotland	0-4	
18 Nov 1959	England	1-2	
8 Oct 1960	England	2-5	
26 Oct 1960	West Germany	3-4	
9 Nov 1960	Scotland	2-5	
25 Apr 1961	Italy	2-3	
3 May 1961	Greece	1-2	
10 May 1961	West Germany	1-2	
7 Oct 1961	Scotland	1-6	

427   FRANCIS JOSEPH McCOURT

Position   Wing-half

Born   Portadown, 9 December 1925

Clubs   Shamrock Rovers; Bristol Rovers;
            Shamrock Rovers; Bristol Rovers;
            Manchester City; Colchester United

Caps   6

Date	Team	Result	G
14 Nov 1951	England	0-2	
19 Mar 1952	Wales	0-3	
4 Oct 1952	England	2-2	
5 Nov 1952	Scotland	1-1	
11 Nov 1952	France	1-3	
15 Apr 1953	Wales	2-3	

428   SEAMUS DONAL (Jimmy) D'ARCY

Position   Inside-forward

Born   Newry, 14 December 1921
Died   22 February 1985

Clubs   Waterford; Limerick; Ballymena; Charlton
            Athletic; Chelsea; Brentford

Caps   5   Goals   1

Date	Team	Result	G
19 Mar 1952	Wales	0-3	
4 Oct 1952	England	2-2	
5 Nov 1952	Scotland	1-1	1
11 Nov 1952	France	1-3	
15 Apr 1953	Wales	2-3	

429   HENRY (Harry) GREGG

Position   Goalkeeper

Born   Derry, 27 October 1932

Clubs   Dundalk; Linfield; Coleraine; Doncaster
            Rovers; Manchester United; Stoke City

Caps   25

Date	Team	Result	G
21 Mar 1954	Wales	2-1	
6 Oct 1956	England	1-1	
7 Nov 1956	Scotland	0-1	
16 Jan 1957	Portugal	1-1	
10 Apr 1957	Wales	0-0	
25 Apr 1957	Italy	0-1	
1 May 1957	Portugal	3-0	
6 Nov 1957	England	3-2	
4 Dec 1957	Italy	2-2	
16 Apr 1958	Wales	1-1	
8 Jun 1958	Czechoslovakia	1-0	
11 Jun 1958	Argentina	1-3	
15 Jun 1958	West Germany	2-2	

Date	Team	Result	G
19 Jun 1958	France	0-4	
4 Oct 1958	England	3-3	
22 Apr 1959	Wales	4-1	
3 Oct 1959	Scotland	0-4	
18 Nov 1959	England	1-2	
6 Apr 1960	Wales	2-3	
8 Oct 1960	England	2-5	
9 Nov 1960	Scotland	2-5	
7 Oct 1961	Scotland	1-6	
17 Oct 1961	Greece	2-0	
12 Oct 1963	Scotland	2-1	
20 Nov 1963	England	3-8	

430   JOHN (Jackie) BLANCHFLOWER

Position   Centre-half

Born   Belfast, 7 March 1933
Died   2 September 1998

Clubs   Manchester United

Caps   12   Goals   1

Date	Team	Result	G
21 Mar 1954	Wales	2-1	
2 Oct 1954	England	0-2	
3 Nov 1954	Scotland	2-2	
8 Oct 1955	Scotland	2-1	1
11 Apr 1956	Wales	1-1	
6 Oct 1956	England	1-1	
7 Nov 1956	Scotland	0-1	
16 Jan 1957	Portugal	1-1	
5 Oct 1957	Scotland	1-1	
6 Nov 1957	England	3-2	
4 Dec 1957	Italy	2-2	
15 Jan 1958	Italy	1-3	

431   WILLIAM JOHN McADAMS

Position   Centre-forward

Born   Belfast, 20 January 1934
Died   13 October 2002

Clubs   Glenavon; Distillery; Manchester City;
Bolton Wanderers; Leeds United;
Brentford; Queen's Park Rangers; Barrow

Caps   15   Goals   7

Date	Team	Result	G
21 Mar 1954	Wales	2-1	
3 Nov 1954	Scotland	2-2	1
6 Oct 1956	England	1-1	
5 Oct 1957	Scotland	1-1	
4 Dec 1957	Italy	2-2	
8 Oct 1960	England	2-5	2
26 Oct 1960	West Germany	3-4	3
9 Nov 1960	Scotland	2-5	
12 Apr 1961	Wales	1-5	
25 Apr 1961	Italy	2-3	1
3 May 1961	Greece	1-2	
10 May 1961	West Germany	1-2	

Date	Team	Result	G
17 Oct 1961	Greece	2-0	
22 Nov 1961	England	1-1	
9 May 1962	Holland	0-4	

432   PETER JAMES McPARLAND

Position   Outside-left

Born   Newry 25 April 1934

Clubs   Dundalk; Aston Villa; Wolverhampton
Wanderers; Plymouth Argyle; Worcester
City

Caps   34   Goals   11

Date	Team	Result	G
21 Mar 1954	Wales	2-1	2
2 Oct 1954	England	0-2	
3 Nov 1954	Scotland	2-2	
8 Oct 1955	Scotland	2-1	
2 Nov 1955	England	0-3	
6 Oct 1956	England	1-1	
7 Nov 1956	Scotland	0-1	
16 Jan 1957	Portugal	1-1	
10 Apr 1957	Wales	0-0	
5 Oct 1957	Scotland	1-1	
6 Nov 1957	England	3-2	
4 Dec 1957	Italy	2-2	
15 Jan 1958	Italy	1-3	1
16 Apr 1958	Wales	1-1	
8 Jun 1958	Czechoslovakia	1-0	
11 Jun 1958	Argentina	1-3	1
15 Jun 1958	West Germany	2-2	2
17 Jun 1958	Czechoslovakia	2-1	2
19 Jun 1958	France	0-4	
4 Oct 1958	England	3-3	
15 Oct 1958	Spain	2-6	
5 Nov 1958	Scotland	2-2	
22 Apr 1959	Wales	4-1	2
3 Oct 1959	Scotland	0-4	
18 Nov 1959	England	1-2	
6 Apr 1960	Wales	2-3	
8 Oct 1960	England	2-5	
26 Oct 1960	West Germany	3-4	
9 Nov 1960	Scotland	2-5	1
12 Apr 1961	Wales	1-5	
25 Apr 1961	Italy	2-3	
3 May 1961	Greece	1-2	
10 May 1961	West Germany	1-2	
9 May 1962	Holland	0-4	

433   F J MONTGOMERY

Position   Full-back

Clubs   Coleraine

Caps   1

Date	Team	Result	G
2 Oct 1954	England	0-2	

434   W T McCAVANA

Position   Centre-half

Clubs   Coleraine

Caps   3

Date	Team	Result	G
3 Nov 1954	Scotland	2-2	
8 Oct 1955	Scotland	2-1	
2 Nov 1955	England	0-3	

435   J W McCLEARY

Position   Centre-half

Clubs   Cliftonville

Caps   1

Date	Team	Result	G
20 Apr 1955	Wales	2-3	

436   THOMAS CASEY

Position   Wing-half

Born   Comber, 11 March 1930

Clubs   Bangor; Leeds United; Bournemouth; Newcastle United; Portsmouth; Bristol City; Gloucester City

Caps   12   Goals   2

Date	Team	Result	G
20 Apr 1955	Wales	2-3	
11 Apr 1956	Wales	1-1	
6 Oct 1956	England	1-1	
7 Nov 1956	Scotland	0-1	
16 Jan 1957	Portugal	1-1	
10 Apr 1957	Wales	0-0	
25 Apr 1957	Italy	0-1	
1 May 1957	Portugal	3-0	1
15 Jun 1958	West Germany	2-2	
19 Jun 1958	France	0-4	
4 Oct 1958	England	3-3	1
15 Oct 1958	Spain	2-6	

437   JAMES WALKER

Position   Centre-forward

Born   Belfast, 29 March 1932

Clubs   Linfield; Doncaster Rovers

Caps   1   Goals   1

Date	Team	Result	G
20 Apr 1955	Wales	2-3	1

438   FRANCIS (Fay) COYLE

Position   Centre-forward

Born   Derry, 1 April 1924

Clubs   Coleraine; Nottingham Forest

Caps   4

Date	Team	Result	G
8 Oct 1955	Scotland	2-1	
2 Nov 1955	England	0-3	
16 Jan 1957	Portugal	1-1	
1 Jun 1958	Argentina	1-3	

439   J JONES

Position   Centre-forward

Clubs   Glenavon

Caps   3   Goals   1

Date	Team	Result	G
11 Apr 1956	Wales	1-1	1
6 Oct 1956	England	1-1	
10 Apr 1957	Wales	0-0	

440   ROBERT JAMES SHIELDS

Position   Centre-forward

Born   Derry, 26 September 1931

Clubs   Crusaders; Sunderland; Southampton

Caps   1

Date	Team	Result	G
7 Nov 1956	Scotland	0-1	

441   THOMAS A DICKSON

Position   Inside-forward

Born   Belfast, 16 July 1929

Clubs   Brantwood; Linfield; Glentoran

Caps   1

Date	Team	Result	G
7 Nov 1956	Scotland	0-1	

442   RICHARD MATTHEWSON (Dick) KEITH

Position   Right-back

Born   Belfast, 15 May 1933
Died   28 February 1967

Clubs   Linfield; Newcastle United; Bournemouth;

Weymouth

Caps   23

Date	Team	Result	G
6 Nov 1957	England	3-2	
4 Dec 1957	Italy	2-2	
16 Apr 1958	Wales	1-1	
8 Jun 1958	Czechoslovakia	1-0	
11 Jun 1958	Argentina	1-3	
15 Jun 1958	West Germany	2-2	
17 Jun 1958	Czechoslovakia	2-1	
19 Jun 1958	France	0-4	
4 Oct 1958	England	3-3	
15 Oct 1958	Spain	2-6	
5 Nov 1958	Scotland	2-2	
22 Apr 1959	Wales	4-1	
3 Oct 1959	Scotland	0-4	
18 Nov 1959	England	1-2	
8 Oct 1960	England	2-5	
26 Oct 1960	West Germany	3-4	
9 Nov 1960	Scotland	2-5	
12 Apr 1961	Wales	1-5	
25 Apr 1961	Italy	2-3	
3 May 1961	Greece	1-2	
10 May 1961	West Germany	1-2	
11 Apr 1962	Wales	0-4	
9 May 1962	Holland	0-4	

443   SAMUEL McKEE McCRORY

Position   Inside-forward

Born   Belfast, 11 October 1924

Clubs   Linfield; Swansea Town; Ipswich Town; Plymouth Argyle; Southend United

Caps   1   Goals   1

Date	Team	Result	G
6 Nov 1957	England	3-2	1

DID YOU KNOW?
Northern Ireland forward Derek Dougan got a nasty shock when he scored a last-minute equaliser for Wolves against Millwall in their Second Division match in April 1967. Dougan turned to celebrate with a fan who had rushed on to the pitch only to discover it was a Millwall supporter who promptly punched him in the face!

444   ALEXANDER DEREK DOUGAN

Position   Centre-forward

Born   Belfast, 20 January 1938

Clubs   Distillery; Portsmouth; Blackburn Rovers; Aston Villa; Peterborough United; Leicester City; Wolverhampton Wanderers

Caps   43   Goals   8

Date	Team	Result	G
8 Jun 1958	Czechoslovakia	1-0	
3 Oct 1959	Scotland	0-4	
8 Oct 1960	England	2-5	
12 Apr 1961	Wales	1-5	1
25 Apr 1961	Italy	2-3	1
3 May 1961	Greece	1-2	
10 Oct 1962	Poland	2-0	1
7 Nov 1962	Scotland	1-5	
28 Nov 1962	Poland	2-0	
2 Oct 1965	Scotland	3-2	1
10 Nov 1965	England	1-2	
24 Nov 1965	Albania	1-1	
30 Mar 1966	Wales	4-1	
7 May 1966	West Germany	0-2	
22 Jun 1966	Mexico	4-1	
22 Oct 1966	England	0-2	
16 Nov 1966	Scotland	1-2	
12 Apr 1957	Wales	0-0	
21 Oct 1967	Scotland	1-0	
28 Feb 1968	Wales	0-2	
10 Sep 1968	Israel	3-2	1
23 Oct 1968	Turkey	4-1	1
11 Dec 1968	Turkey	3-0	
3 May 1969	England	1-3	
6 May 1969	Scotland	1-1	
19 May 1969	Wales	0-0	
10 Sep 1969	USSR	0-0	
22 Oct 1969	USSR	0-2	
18 Apr 1970	Scotland	0-1	
21 Apr 1970	England	1-3	
11 Nov 1970	Spain	0-3	
3 Feb 1971	Cyprus	3-0	1
21 Apr 1971	Cyprus	5-0	1
15 May 1971	England	0-1	
18 May 1971	Scotland	1-0	
22 May 1971	Wales	1-0	
22 Sep 1971	USSR	0-1	
13 Oct 1971	USSR	1-1	
20 May 1972	Scotland	0-2	
23 May 1972	England	1-0	
27 May 1972	Wales	0-0	
18 Oct 1972	Bulgaria	0-3	
14 Feb 1973	Cyprus	0-1	

445   JOHN SCOTT

Position   Outside-right

Born   Belfast, 22 December 1933
Died   1978

Clubs   Ormond Star; Manchester United; Grimsby Town; York City

Caps   2

Date	Team	Result	G
17 Jun 1958	Czechoslovakia	2-1	
19 Jun 1958	France	0-4	

Position   Centre-half

Clubs   Ards

Caps   4

Date	Team	Result	G
15 Oct 1958	Spain	2-6	
8 Oct 1960	England	2-5	
26 Oct 1960	West Germany	3-4	
9 Nov 1960	Scotland	2-5	

447   MATTHEW JAMES HILL

Position   Inside-forward

Born   Carrickfergus, 31 October 1935

Clubs   Linfield; Newcastle United; Norwich City; Everton; Port Vale

Caps   7

Date	Team	Result	G
22 Apr 1959	Wales	4-1	
6 Apr 1960	Wales	2-3	
26 Oct 1960	West Germany	3-4	
7 Oct 1961	Scotland	1-6	
12 Oct 1963	Scotland	2-1	
30 Oct 1963	Spain	0-1	
20 Nov 1963	England	3-8	

448   JOHN ANDREW CROSSAN

Position   Inside-forward

Born   Derry, 29 November 1938

Clubs   Coleraine; Sparta Rotterdam; Standard Liège; Sunderland; Manchester City; Middlesbrough; Tongeren (Belgium)

Caps   24   Goals   10

Date	Team	Result	G
18 Nov 1959	England	1-2	
28 Nov 1962	Poland	2-0	1
3 Apr 1963	Wales	1-4	
30 May 1963	Spain	1-1	
12 Oct 1963	Scotland	2-1	
30 Oct 1963	Spain	0-1	
20 Nov 1963	England	3-8	1
15 Apr 1964	Wales	3-2	
29 Apr 1964	Uruguay	3-0	2
3 Oct 1964	England	3-4	
14 Oct 1964	Switzerland	1-0	1
14 Nov 1964	Switzerland	1-2	
25 Nov 1964	Scotland	2-3	
17 Mar 1965	Holland	2-1	1
31 Mar 1965	Wales	0-5	
7 Apr 1965	Holland	0-0	
7 May 1965	Albania	4-1	3

2 Oct 1965	Scotland	3-2	1
10 Nov 1965	England	1-2	
24 Nov 1965	Albania	1-1	
7 May 1966	West Germany	0-2	
22 Oct 1966	England	0-2	
16 Nov 1966	Scotland	1-2	
21 Oct 1967	Scotland	1-0	

449   ALEXANDER RUSSELL ELDER

Position   Left-back

Born   Lisburn, 25 April 1941

Clubs   Altona; Glentoran; Burnley; Stoke City; Leek Town

Caps   40   Goals   1

Date	Team	Result	G
6 Apr 1960	Wales	2-3	
8 Oct 1960	England	2-5	
26 Oct 1960	West Germany	3-4	
9 Nov 1960	Scotland	2-5	
12 Apr 1961	Wales	1-5	
3 May 1961	Greece	1-2	
10 May 1961	West Germany	1-2	
7 Oct 1961	Scotland	1-6	
17 Oct 1961	Greece	2-0	
22 Nov 1961	England	1-1	
10 Oct 1962	Poland	2-0	
20 Oct 1962	England	1-3	
7 Nov 1962	Scotland	1-5	
28 Nov 1962	Poland	2-0	
3 Apr 1963	Wales	1-4	
30 May 1963	Spain	1-1	
15 Apr 1964	Wales	3-2	
29 Apr 1964	Uruguay	3-0	
3 Oct 1964	England	3-4	
14 Oct 1964	Switzerland	1-0	
14 Nov 1964	Switzerland	1-2	
25 Nov 1964	Scotland	2-3	
17 Mar 1965	Holland	2-1	
31 Mar 1965	Wales	0-5	
7 Apr 1965	Holland	0-0	
7 May 1965	Albania	4-1	
2 Oct 1965	Scotland	3-2	
10 Nov 1965	England	1-2	
24 Nov 1965	Albania	1-1	
30 Mar 1966	Wales	4-1	
22 Jun 1966	Mexico	4-1	1
22 Oct 1966	England	0-2	
16 Nov 1966	Scotland	1-2	
12 Apr 1967	Wales	0-0	
22 Nov 1967	England	0-2	
28 Feb 1968	Wales	0-2	
3 May 1969	England	1-3	
6 May 1969	Scotland	1-1	
19 May 1969	Wales	0-0	
10 Sep 1969	USSR	0-0	

450   WILLIAM IAN LAWTHER

Position	Centre-forward
Born	Belfast, 20 October 1939
Clubs	Crusaders; Sunderland; Blackburn Rovers; Scunthorpe United; Brentford; Halifax Town; Stockport County
Caps	4

Date	Team	Result	G
6 Apr 1960	Wales	2-3	
25 Apr 1961	Italy	2-3	
7 Oct 1961	Scotland	1-6	
9 May 1962	Holland	0-4	

451   JOHN (Jack) McCLELLAND

Position	Goalkeeper
Born	Lurgan, 19 May 1940
Died	March 1976
Clubs	Glenavon; Arsenal; Fulham; Lincoln City
Caps	6

Date	Team	Result	G
26 Oct 1960	West Germany	3-4	
12 Apr 1961	Wales	1-5	
25 Apr 1961	Italy	2-3	
3 May 1961	Greece	1-2	
10 May 1961	West Germany	1-2	
22 Jun 1966	Mexico	4-1	

452   WALTER BRUCE

Position	Inside-right
Clubs	Glentoran
Caps	2

Date	Team	Result	G
9 Nov 1960	Scotland	2-5	
12 Apr 1967	Wales	0-0	

453   JAMES JOSEPH NICHOLSON

Position	Midfield		
Born	Belfast, 27 February 1943		
Clubs	Manchester United; Huddersfield Town; Bury		
Caps	41	Goals	6

Date	Team	Result	G
9 Nov 1960	Scotland	2-5	
12 Apr 1961	Wales	1-5	

Date	Team	Result	G
17 Oct 1961	Greece	2-0	
22 Nov 1961	England	1-1	
11 Apr 1962	Wales	0-4	
9 May 1962	Holland	0-4	
10 Oct 1962	Poland	2-0	
20 Oct 1962	England	1-3	
7 Nov 1962	Scotland	1-5	
28 Nov 1962	Poland	2-0	
17 Mar 1965	Holland	2-1	
31 Mar 1965	Wales	0-5	
7 Apr 1965	Holland	0-0	
7 May 1965	Albania	4-1	
2 Oct 1965	Scotland	3-2	
10 Nov 1965	England	1-2	
24 Nov 1965	Albania	1-1	
30 Mar 1966	Wales	4-1	
22 Jun 1966	Mexico	4-1	1
16 Nov 1966	Scotland	1-2	1
12 Apr 1967	Wales	0-0	
21 Oct 1967	Scotland	1-0	
22 Nov 1967	England	0-2	
28 Feb 1968	Wales	0-2	
23 Oct 1968	Turkey	4-1	
11 Dec 1968	Turkey	3-0	1
3 May 1969	England	1-3	
6 May 1969	Scotland	1-1	
19 May 1969	Wales	0-0	
10 Sep 1969	USSR	0-0	
22 Oct 1969	USSR	0-2	
18 Apr 1970	Scotland	0-1	
21 Apr 1970	England	1-3	
25 Apr 1970	Wales	0-1	
3 Feb 1971	Cyprus	3-0	1

Above: Jimmy Nicholson

Date	Team	Result	G
21 Apr 1971	Cyprus	5-0	1
15 May 1971	England	0-1	
18 May 1971	Scotland	1-0	
22 May 1971	Wales	1-0	
22 Sep 1971	USSR	0-1	
13 Oct 1971	USSR	1-1	1

454   THOMAS C STEWART

Position   Outside-right

Born   Belfast, 16 August 1935

Clubs   Ballymena United; Linfield

Caps   1

Date	Team	Result	G
12 Apr 1961	Wales	1-5	

455   WILLIAM JAMES McCULLOUGH

Position   Left-back

Born   Larne, 27 July 1935

Clubs   Portadown; Arsenal; Millwall

Caps   10

Date	Team	Result	G
25 Apr 1961	Italy	2-3	
30 May 1963	Spain	1-1	
12 Oct 1963	Scotland	2-1	
30 Oct 1963	Spain	0-1	
20 Nov 1963	England	3-8	
15 Apr 1964	Wales	3-2	
29 Apr 1964	Uruguay	3-0	
3 Oct 1964	England	3-4	
14 Oct 1964	Switzerland	1-0	
22 Oct 1966	England	0-2	

456   MARTIN HARVEY

Position   Wing-half

Born   Belfast, 19 September 1941

Clubs   Sunderland

Caps   34   Goals   2

Date	Team	Result	G
25 Apr 1961	Italy	2-3	
9 May 1962	Holland	0-4	
3 Apr 1963	Wales	1-4	1
30 May 1963	Spain	1-1	
12 Oct 1963	Scotland	2-1	
30 Oct 1963	Spain	0-1	
20 Nov 1963	England	3-8	
15 Apr 1964	Wales	3-2	
29 Apr 1964	Uruguay	3-0	
3 Oct 1964	England	3-4	

Date	Team	Result	G
14 Oct 1964	Switzerland	1-0	
14 Nov 1964	Switzerland	1-2	
25 Nov 1964	Scotland	2-3	
17 Mar 1965	Holland	2-1	
31 Mar 1965	Wales	0-5	
7 Apr 1965	Holland	0-0	
7 May 1965	Albania	4-1	
2 Oct 1965	Scotland	3-2	
10 Nov 1965	England	1-2	
24 Nov 1965	Albania	1-1	
30 Mar 1966	Wales	4-1	1
7 May 1966	West Germany	0-2	
22 Jun 1966	Mexico	4-1	
22 Oct 1966	England	0-2	
16 Nov 1966	Scotland	1-2	
22 Nov 1967	England	0-2	
28 Feb 1968	Wales	0-2	
10 Sep 1968	Israel	3-2	
23 Oct 1968	Turkey	4-1	
11 Dec 1968	Turkey	3-0	
3 May 1969	England	1-3	
22 Oct 1969	USSR	0-2	
21 Apr 1971	Cyprus	5-0	
22 May 1971	Wales	1-0	

457   WILLIAM JOHN TERENCE (TERRY) NEILL

Position   Centre-half

Born   Belfast, 8 May 1942

Clubs   Bangor; Arsenal; Hull City

Caps   59   Goals   2

Date	Team	Result	G
25 Apr 1961	Italy	2-3	
3 May 1961	Greece	1-2	
10 May 1961	West Germany	1-2	
7 Oct 1961	Scotland	1-6	
17 Oct 1961	Greece	2-0	
22 Nov 1961	England	1-1	
11 Apr 1962	Wales	0-4	
20 Oct 1962	England	1-3	
28 Nov 1962	Poland	2-0	
3 Apr 1963	Wales	1-4	
30 May 1963	Spain	1-1	
12 Oct 1963	Scotland	2-1	
30 Oct 1963	Spain	0-1	
20 Nov 1963	England	3-8	
15 Apr 1964	Wales	3-2	
29 Apr 1964	Uruguay	3-0	
3 Oct 1964	England	3-4	
14 Oct 1964	Switzerland	1-0	
25 Nov 1964	Scotland	2-3	
17 Mar 1965	Holland	2-1	1
31 Mar 1965	Wales	0-5	
7 Apr 1965	Holland	0-0	
7 May 1965	Albania	4-1	
2 Oct 1965	Scotland	3-2	
10 Nov 1965	England	1-2	
24 Nov 1965	Albania	1-1	
30 Mar 1966	Wales	4-1	
7 May 1966	West Germany	0-2	
22 Jun 1966	Mexico	4-1	

Date	Team	Result	G
16 Nov 1966	Scotland	1-2	
12 Apr 1967	Wales	0-0	
21 Oct 1967	Scotland	1-0	
22 Nov 1967	England	0-2	
10 Sep 1968	Israel	3-2	
23 Oct 1968	Turkey	4-1	
11 Dec 1968	Turkey	3-0	
3 May 1969	England	1-3	
6 May 1969	Scotland	1-1	
19 May 1969	Wales	0-0	
10 Sep 1969	USSR	0-0	
22 Oct 1969	USSR	0-2	
18 Apr 1970	Scotland	0-1	
21 Apr 1970	England	1-3	
25 Apr 1970	Wales	0-1	
11 Nov 1970	Spain	0-3	
3 Feb 1971	Cyprus	3-0	
22 Sep 1971	USSR	0-1	
13 Oct 1971	USSR	1-1	
16 Feb 1972	Spain	1-1	
20 May 1972	Scotland	0-2	
23 May 1972	England	1-0	1
27 May 1972	Wales	0-0	
18 Oct 1972	Bulgaria	0-3	
14 Feb 1973	Cyprus	0-1	
28 Mar 1973	Portugal	1-1	
8 May 1973	Cyprus	3-0	
12 May 1973	England	1-2	
16 May 1973	Scotland	2-1	
19 May 1973	Wales	1-0	

458 EDWARD JAMES (JIMMY) MAGILL

Position   Full-back

Born   Lurgan, 17 May 1939

Clubs   Portadown; Arsenal; Brighton & Hove Albion

Caps   26

Date	Team	Result	G
7 Oct 1961	Scotland	1-6	
17 Oct 1961	Greece	2-0	
22 Nov 1961	England	1-1	
10 Oct 1962	Poland	2-0	
20 Oct 1962	England	1-3	
7 Nov 1962	Scotland	1-5	
28 Nov 1962	Poland	2-0	
3 Apr 1963	Wales	1-4	
30 May 1963	Spain	1-1	
12 Oct 1963	Scotland	2-1	
30 Oct 1963	Spain	0-1	
20 Nov 1963	England	3-8	
15 Apr 1964	Wales	3-2	
29 Apr 1964	Uruguay	3-0	
3 Oct 1964	England	3-4	
14 Oct 1964	Switzerland	1-0	
14 Nov 1964	Switzerland	1-2	
25 Nov 1964	Scotland	2-3	
7 Apr 1965	Holland	0-0	
7 May 1965	Albania	4-1	
2 Oct 1965	Scotland	3-2	
10 Nov 1965	England	1-2	
24 Nov 1965	Albania	1-1	
30 Mar 1966	Wales	4-1	
7 May 1966	West Germany	0-2	
22 Jun 1966	Mexico	4-1	

459 SAMUEL J WILSON

Position   Forward

Clubs   Glenavon; Falkirk; Dundee

Caps   12   Goals   7

Date	Team	Result	G
7 Oct 1961	Scotland	1-6	
12 Oct 1963	Scotland	2-1	1
30 Oct 1963	Spain	0-1	
20 Nov 1963	England	3-8	2
15 Apr 1964	Wales	3-2	1
29 Apr 1964	Uruguay	3-0	1
3 Oct 1964	England	3-4	1
14 Oct 1964	Switzerland	1-0	
30 Mar 1966	Wales	4-1	1
7 May 1966	West Germany	0-2	
16 Nov 1966	Scotland	1-2	
22 Nov 1967	England	0-2	

460 JAMES CHRISTOPHER McLAUGHLIN

Position   Winger

Born   Derry, 22 December 1940

Clubs   Derry City; Birmingham City; Shrewsbury Town; Swansea City; Peterborough United; Shrewsbury Town; Swansea City

Caps   12   Goals   6

Date	Team	Result	G
7 Oct 1961	Scotland	1-6	1
17 Oct 1961	Greece	2-0	2
22 Nov 1961	England	1-1	
11 Apr 1962	Wales	0-4	
3 Apr 1963	Wales	1-4	
15 Apr 1964	Wales	3-2	1
29 Apr 1964	Uruguay	3-0	
3 Oct 1964	England	3-4	2
14 Oct 1964	Switzerland	1-0	
14 Nov 1964	Switzerland	1-2	
31 Mar 1965	Wales	0-5	
30 Mar 1966	Wales	4-1	

461 VICTOR HUNTER

Position   Goalkeeper

Clubs   Coleraine

Caps   2

Date	Team	Result	G
22 Nov 1961	England	1-1	
30 Oct 1963	Spain	0-1	

462   HUGH HENRY BARR

Position   Inside-forward

Born   Ballymena, 17 May 1935

Clubs   Cliftonville; Ballymena United; Linfield; Coventry City; Ely Town

Caps   3   Goals   1

Date	Team	Result	G
22 Nov 1961	England	1-1	
10 Oct 1962	Poland	2-0	
20 Oct 1962	England	1-3	1

463   WILLIAM RONALD BRIGGS

Position   Goalkeeper

Born   Belfast, 29 March 1943

Clubs   Manchester United; Swansea City; Bristol Rovers

Caps   2

Date	Team	Result	G
11 Apr 1962	Wales	0-4	
17 Mar 1965	Holland	2-1	

464   WILLIAM McCAULEY HUMPHRIES

Position   Outside-right

Born   Belfast, 8 June 1936

Clubs   Ards; Leeds United; Ards; Coventry City; Swansea City

Caps   14   Goals   1

Date	Team	Result	G
11 Apr 1962	Wales	0-4	
9 May 1962	Holland	0-4	
10 Oct 1962	Poland	2-0	1
20 Oct 1962	England	1-3	
7 Nov 1962	Scotland	1-5	
3 Apr 1963	Wales	1-4	
30 May 1963	Spain	1-1	
12 Oct 1963	Scotland	2-1	
30 Oct 1963	Spain	0-1	
20 Nov 1963	England	3-8	
25 Nov 1964	Scotland	2-3	
17 Mar 1965	Holland	2-1	
31 Mar 1965	Wales	0-5	
7 May 1965	Albania	4-1	

465   WILLIAM CECIL JOHNSTON

Position   Inside-forward

Born   Dungannon, 21 May 1942

Clubs   Glenavon; Oldham Athletic

Caps   2   Goals   1

Date	Team	Result	G
11 Apr 1962	Wales	0-4	
22 Jun 1966	Mexico	4-1	1

466   JAMES O'NEILL

Position   Centre-forward

Born   Larne, 24 November 1941

Clubs   Sunderland; Walsall; Hakoah (Australia); Darlington

Caps   1

Date	Team	Result	G
11 Apr 1962	Wales	0-4	

467   ROBERT MUNN (Bobby) BRAITHWAITE

Position   Winger

Born   Belfast, 24 February 1937

Clubs   Crusaders; Linfield; Middlesbrough; Durban (South Africa)

Caps   10

Date	Team	Result	G
11 Apr 1962	Wales	0-4	
28 Nov 1962	Poland	2-0	
30 May 1963	Spain	1-1	
15 Apr 1964	Wales	3-2	
29 Apr 1964	Uruguay	3-0	
3 Oct 1964	England	3-4	
14 Oct 1964	Switzerland	1-0	
14 Nov 1964	Switzerland	1-2	
25 Nov 1964	Scotland	2-3	
7 Apr 1965	Holland	0-0	

468   ROBERT JAMES IRVINE

Position   Goalkeeper

Born   Carrickfergus, 17 January 1942

Clubs   Linfield; Stoke City; Altrincham; Telford United

Caps   8

Date	Team	Result	G
9 May 1962	Holland	0-4	
10 Oct 1962	Poland	2-0	
20 Oct 1962	England	1-3	
7 Nov 1962	Scotland	1-5	
28 Nov 1962	Poland	2-0	
3 Apr 1963	Wales	1-4	
30 May 1963	Spain	1-1	
31 Mar 1965	Wales	0-5	

469 SAMUEL HATTON

Position Centre-half

Born Belfast, 28 February 1936
Died Belfast, 30 March 1995

Clubs Ards; Linfield

Caps 2

Date	Team	Result	G
10 Oct 1962	Poland	2-0	
7 Nov 1962	Scotland	1-5	

470 SAMUEL THOMAS McMILLAN

Position Inside-forward

Born Belfast 29 September 1941

Clubs Boyland YC; Manchester United;
Wrexham; Southend United; Chester City;
Stockport County

Caps 2

Date	Team	Result	G
20 Oct 1962	England	1-3	
7 Nov 1962	Scotland	1-5	

471 A C CAMPBELL

Position Centre-half

Clubs Crusaders

Caps 2

Date	Team	Result	G
3 April 1963	Wales	1-4	
14 Nov 1964	Switzerland	1-2	

472 WILLIAM JOHN IRVINE

Position Centre-forward

Born Carrickfergus, 18 June 1943

Clubs Burnley; Preston North End; Brighton &
Hove Albion; Halifax Town

Caps 23 Goals 9

Date	Team	Result	G
3 Apr 1963	Wales	1-4	
30 May 1963	Spain	1-1	1
14 Nov 1964	Switzerland	1-2	
25 Nov 1964	Scotland	2-3	1
17 Mar 1965	Holland	2-1	
31 Mar 1965	Wales	0-5	
7 Apr 1965	Holland	0-0	
7 May 1965	Albania	4-1	1
2 Oct 1965	Scotland	3-2	1
10 Nov 1965	England	1-2	1
24 Nov 1965	Albania	1-1	1
30 Mar 1966	Wales	4-1	1
22 Jun 1966	Mexico	4-1	
22 Oct 1966	England	0-2	
16 Nov 1966	Scotland	1-2	
22 Nov 1967	England	0-2	
28 Feb 1968	Wales	0-2	
10 Sep 1968	Israel	3-2	2
23 Oct 1968	Turkey	4-1	
3 May 1969	England	1-3	
20 May 1972	Scotland	0-2	
23 May 1972	England	1-0	
27 May 1972	Wales	0-0	

473 JOHN PARKE

Position Full-back

Born Bangor, 6 August 1937

Clubs Cliftonville; Linfield; Hibernian;
Sunderland; Mechelen (Belgium)

Caps 14

Date	Team	Result	G
12 Oct 1963	Scotland	2-1	
30 Oct 1963	Spain	0-1	
20 Nov 1963	England	3-8	
14 Nov 1964	Switzerland	1-2	
25 Nov 1964	Scotland	2-3	
17 Mar 1965	Holland	2-1	
31 Mar 1965	Wales	0-5	
7 Apr 1965	Holland	0-0	
7 May 1965	Albania	4-1	
7 May 1966	West Germany	0-2	
22 Oct 1966	England	0-2	
16 Nov 1966	Scotland	1-2	
21 Oct 1967	Scotland	1-0	
22 Nov 1967	England	0-2	

DID YOU KNOW?
Pat Jennings made his 100th appearance for Northern Ireland against Austria on 21 September 1983.

Above: Pat Jennings

PATRICK ANTHONY JENNINGS

Position   Goalkeeper

Born   Newry, 12 June 1945

Clubs   Newry Town; Watford; Tottenham
           Hotspur; Arsenal

Caps   119

Date	Team	Result	G
15 Apr 1964	Wales	3-2	
29 Apr 1964	Uruguay	3-0	
3 Oct 1964	England	3-4	
14 Oct 1964	Switzerland	1-0	
14 Nov 1964	Switzerland	1-2	
25 Nov 1964	Scotland	2-3	
7 Apr 1965	Holland	0-0	
7 May 1965	Albania	4-1	
21 Oct 1965	Scotland	3-2	
10 Nov 1965	England	1-2	
24 Nov 1965	Albania	1-1	
30 Mar 1966	Wales	4-1	
7 May 1966	West Germany	0-2	
22 Oct 1966	England	0-2	
16 Nov 1966	Scotland	1-2	
21 Oct 1967	Scotland	1-0	
22 Nov 1967	England	0-2	
28 Feb 1968	Wales	0-2	
10 Sep 1968	Israel	3-2	
23 Oct 1968	Turkey	4-1	
11 Dec 1968	Turkey	3-0	

Date	Team	Result	G
3 May 1969	England	1-3	
6 May 1969	Scotland	1-1	
19 May 1969	Wales	0-0	
10 Sep 1969	USSR	0-0	
22 Oct 1969	USSR	0-2	
18 Apr 1970	Scotland	0-1	
21 Apr 1970	England	1-3	
3 Feb 1971	Cyprus	3-0	
21 Apr 1971	Cyprus	5-0	
15 May 1971	England	0-1	
18 May 1971	Scotland	1-0	
22 May 1971	Wales	1-0	
13 Oct 1971	USSR	1-1	
16 Feb 1972	Spain	1-1	
20 May 1972	Scotland	0-2	
23 May 1972	England	1-0	
27 May 1972	Wales	0-0	
18 Oct 1972	Bulgaria	0-3	
14 Feb 1973	Cyprus	0-1	
28 Mar 1973	Portugal	1-1	
12 May 1973	England	1-2	
16 May 1973	Scotland	2-1	
19 May 1973	Wales	1-0	
14 Nov 1973	Portugal	1-1	
11 May 1974	Scotland	1-0	
15 May 1974	England	0-1	
18 May 1974	Wales	0-1	
4 Sep 1974	Norway	1-2	
30 Oct 1974	Sweden	2-0	
16 Apr 1975	Yugoslavia	1-0	
17 May 1975	England	0-0	
20 May 1975	Scotland	0-3	
23 May 1975	Wales	1-0	
3 Sep 1975	Sweden	1-2	
29 Oct 1975	Norway	3-0	
19 Nov 1975	Yugoslavia	0-1	

Date	Team	Result
3 Mar 1976	Israel	1-1
8 May 1976	Scotland	0-3
11 May 1976	England	0-4
14 May 1976	Wales	0-1
13 Oct 1976	Holland	2-2
10 Nov 1976	Belgium	0-2
27 Apr 1977	West Germany	0-5
28 May 1977	England	1-2
1 Jun 1977	Scotland	0-3
3 Jun 1977	Wales	1-1
11 Jun 1977	Iceland	0-1
14 Sep 1977	Iceland	2-0
13 Oct 1977	Holland	0-1
16 Nov 1977	Belgium	3-0
20 Sep 1978	Republic of Ireland	0-0
25 Oct 1978	Denmark	2-1
29 Nov 1978	Bulgaria	2-0
7 Feb 1979	England	0-4
2 May 1979	Bulgaria	2-0
19 May 1979	England	0-2
22 May 1979	Scotland	0-1
25 May 1979	Wales	1-1
6 Jun 1979	Denmark	0-4
17 Oct 1979	England	1-5
21 Nov 1979	Republic of Ireland	1-0
26 Mar 1980	Israel	0-0
25 Mar 1981	Scotland	1-1
29 Apr 1981	Portugal	1-0
19 May 1981	Scotland	0-2
3 Jun 1981	Sweden	0-1
14 Oct 1981	Scotland	0-0
18 Nov 1981	Israel	1-0
23 Feb 1982	England	0-4
28 May 1982	Wales	0-3
17 Jun 1982	Yugoslavia	0-0
21 Jun 1982	Honduras	1-1
25 Jun 1982	Spain	1-0
4 Jul 1982	France	1-4
27 Apr 1983	Albania	1-0
24 May 1983	Scotland	0-0
28 May 1983	England	0-0
31 May 1983	Wales	0-1
21 Sep 1983	Austria	3-1
12 Oct 1983	Turkey	0-1
16 Nov 1983	West Germany	1-0
13 Dec 1983	Scotland	2-0
22 May 1984	Wales	1-1
27 May 1984	Finland	0-1
12 Sep 1984	Romania	2-2
14 Nov 1984	Finland	2-1
27 Feb 1985	England	0-1
27 Mar 1985	Spain	0-0
1 May 1985	Turkey	2-0
11 Sep 1985	Turkey	0-0
16 Oct 1985	Romania	1-0
13 Nov 1985	England	0-0
26 Feb 1986	France	0-0
26 Mar 1986	Denmark	1-1
23 Apr 1986	Morocco	2-1
3 Jun 1986	Algeria	1-1
7 Jun 1986	Spain	1-2
12 Jun 1986	Brazil	0-3

Above: Pat Jennings Figure

475   GEORGE BEST

Position	Forward
Born	Belfast, 22 May 1946
Died	25 November 2005
Clubs	Manchester United; Dunstable Town; Stockport County; Cork Celtic; Los Angeles Aztecs; Fulham; Fort Lauderdale Strikers; Hibernian; San Jose Earthquakes; Bournemouth; Brisbane Lions; Tobermore United
Caps	37 Goals 9

Date	Team	Result	G
15 Apr 1964	Wales	3-2	
29 Apr 1964	Uruguay	3-0	
3 Oct 1964	England	3-4	
14 Oct 1964	Switzerland	1-0	
14 Nov 1964	Switzerland	1-2	1
25 Nov 1964	Scotland	2-3	1
17 Mar 1965	Holland	2-1	
7 Apr 1965	Holland	0-0	
7 May 1965	Albania	4-1	1
2 Oct 1965	Scotland	3-2	
10 Nov 1965	England	1-2	
24 Nov 1965	Albania	1-1	
22 Oct 1966	England	0-2	
21 Oct 1967	Scotland	1-0	
23 Oct 1968	Turkey	4-1	1

Above: George Best

3 May 1969	England	1-3	
6 May 1969	Scotland	1-1	
19 May 1969	Wales	0-0	
10 Sep 1969	USSR	0-0	
18 Apr 1970	Scotland	0-1	
21 Apr 1970	England	1-3	1
25 Apr 1970	Wales	0-1	
11 Nov 1970	Spain	0-3	
3 Feb 1971	Cyprus	3-0	1
21 Apr 1971	Cyprus	5-0	3
15 May 1971	England	0-1	
18 May 1971	Scotland	1-0	
22 May 1971	Wales	1-0	
22 Sep 1971	USSR	0-1	
16 Feb 1972	Spain	1-1	
18 Oct 1972	Bulgaria	0-3	
14 Nov 1973	Portugal	1-1	
13 Oct 1976	Holland	2-2	
10 Nov 1976	Belgium	0-2	
27 Apr 1977	West Germany	0-5	
14 Sep 1977	Iceland	2-0	
13 Oct 1977	Holland	0-1	

DID YOU KNOW?
George Best's mum was an international hockey player!

476	DAVID CLEMENTS

Position   Left-back/Left-half/Outside-left

Born   Larne, 15 September 1945

Clubs   Portadown; Wolverhampton Wanderers; Coventry City; Sheffield Wednesday; Everton; New York Cosmos

Caps   48   Goals   2

Date	Team	Result	G
17 Mar 1965	Holland	2-1	
31 Mar 1965	Wales	0-5	
22 Jun 1966	Mexico	4-1	
16 Nov 1966	Scotland	1-2	
12 Apr 1967	Wales	0-0	
21 Oct 1967	Scotland	1-0	1
22 Nov 1967	England	0-2	
23 Oct 1968	Turkey	4-1	
11 Dec 1968	Turkey	3-0	
6 May 1969	Scotland	1-1	
19 May 1969	Wales	0-0	
10 Sep 1969	USSR	0-0	
22 Oct 1969	USSR	0-2	
18 Apr 1970	Scotland	0-1	
21 Apr 1970	England	1-3	
25 Apr 1970	Wales	0-1	
11 Nov 1970	Spain	0-3	
21 Apr 1971	Cyprus	5-0	
15 May 1971	England	0-1	
18 May 1971	Scotland	1-0	
22 May 1971	Wales	1-0	
22 Sep 1971	USSR	0-1	
13 Oct 1971	USSR	1-1	
16 Feb 1972	Spain	1-1	
20 May 1972	Scotland	0-2	
23 May 1972	England	1-0	
27 May 1972	Wales	0-0	
18 Oct 1972	Bulgaria	0-1	
14 Feb 1973	Cyprus	0-1	

28 Mar 1973	Portugal	1-1	
8 May 1973	Cyprus	3-0	
12 May 1973	England	1-2	1
16 May 1973	Scotland	2-1	
19 May 1973	Wales	1-0	
26 Sep 1973	Bulgaria	0-0	
14 Nov 1973	Portugal	1-1	
11 May 1974	Scotland	1-0	
15 May 1974	England	0-1	
18 May 1974	Wales	0-1	
4 Sep 1974	Norway	1-2	
16 Apr 1975	Yugoslavia	1-0	
17 May 1975	England	0-0	
20 May 1975	Scotland	0-3	
23 May 1975	Wales	1-0	
3 Sep 1975	Sweden	1-2	
19 Nov 1975	Yugoslavia	0-1	
11 May 1976	England	0-4	
14 May 1976	Wales	0-1	

477   ERIC WELSH

Position   Outside-right

Born   Belfast, 1 May 1942

Clubs   Distillery; Exeter City; Carlisle United; Torquay United; Hartlepool United

Caps   4   Goals   1

Date	Team	Result	G
30 Mar 1966	Wales	4-1	1
7 May 1966	West Germany	0-2	
22 Jun 1966	Mexico	4-1	
12 Apr 1967	Wales	0-0	

478   ROBERT JOHN NAPIER

Position   Central defender

Born   Lurgan, 23 September 1946

Clubs   Bolton Wanderers; Brighton & Hove Albion; Bradford City

Caps   1

Date	Team	Result	G
7 May 1966	West Germany	0-2	

479   V J McKINNEY

Position   Outside-left

Clubs   Falkirk

Caps   1

Date	Team	Result	G
7 May 1966	West Germany	0-2	

480   WILLIAM FERGUSON

Position   Inside-forward

Born   Belfast, 28 May 1938
Died   Belfast, 6 November 1998

Clubs   Glentoran; Linfield

Caps   2   Goals   1

Date	Team	Result	G
22 Jun 1966	Mexico	4-1	1
22 Oct 1966	England	0-2	

481   SAMUEL JOHN TODD

Position   Defender

Born   Belfast, 22 September 1945

Clubs   Glentoran; Burnley; Sheffield Wednesday; Mansfield Town

Caps   11

Date	Team	Result	G
22 Jun 1966	Mexico	4-1	
22 Oct 1966	England	0-2	
28 Feb 1968	Wales	0-2	
3 May 1969	England	1-3	
6 May 1969	Scotland	1-1	
19 May 1969	Wales	0-0	
10 Sep 1969	USSR	0-0	
18 Apr 1970	Scotland	0-1	
11 Nov 1970	Spain	0-3	
3 Feb 1971	Cyprus	3-0	
21 Apr 1971	Cyprus	5-0	

482   WILLIAM (Iam) STEWART McFAUL

Position   Goalkeeper

Born   Coleraine, 1 October 1943

Clubs   Coleraine; Linfield; Newcastle United

Caps   6

Date	Team	Result	G
22 Oct 1966	England	0-2	
25 Apr 1970	Wales	0-1	
11 Nov 1970	Spain	0-3	
22 Sep 1971	USSR	0-1	
8 May 1973	Cyprus	3-0	
26 Sep 1973	Bulgaria	0-0	

483   R McKENZIE

Position   Goalkeeper

Clubs   Airdrieonians

Caps   1

Date	Team	Result	G
12 Apr 1967	Wales	0-0	

484   DAVID JAMES CRAIG

Position   Right-back

Born   Belfast, 8 June 1944

Clubs   Newcastle United

Caps   25

Date	Team	Result	G
12 Apr 1967	Wales	0-0	
28 Feb 1968	Wales	0-2	
23 Oct 1968	Turkey	4-1	
11 Dec 1968	Turkey	3-0	
3 May 1969	England	1-3	
6 May 1969	Scotland	1-1	
19 May 1969	Wales	0-0	
22 Oct 1969	USSR	0-2	
18 Apr 1970	Scotland	0-1	
21 Apr 1970	England	1-3	
25 Apr 1970	Wales	0-1	
11 Nov 1970	Spain	0-3	
3 Feb 1971	Cyprus	3-0	
21 Apr 1971	Cyprus	5-0	
18 May 1971	Scotland	1-0	
22 Sep 1971	USSR	0-1	
20 May 1972	Scotland	0-2	
14 Feb 1973	Cyprus	0-1	
8 May 1973	Cyprus	3-0	
12 May 1973	England	1-2	
16 May 1973	Scotland	2-1	
19 May 1973	Wales	1-0	
26 Sep 1973	Bulgaria	0-0	
14 Nov 1973	Portugal	1-1	
4 Sep 1974	Norway	1-2	

485   ARTHUR STEWART

Position   Wing-half

Born   Ballymena, 13 January 1942

Clubs   Ballymena; Glentoran; Derby County; Ballymena

Caps   7

Date	Team	Result	G
12 Apr 1967	Wales	0-0	
21 Oct 1967	Scotland	1-0	
22 Nov 1967	England	0-2	
28 Feb 1968	Wales	0-2	
10 Sep 1968	Israel	3-2	
23 Oct 1968	Turkey	4-1	
11 Dec 1968	Turkey	3-0	

486   D TRAINOR

Position   Forward

Clubs   Glentoran

Caps   1

Date	Team	Result	G
12 Apr 1967	Wales	0-0	

487   WILLIAM C McKEAG

Position   Right-back

Clubs   Glentoran

Caps   2

Date	Team	Result	G
21 Oct 1967	Scotland	1-0	
28 Feb 1968	Wales	0-2	

488   W G CAMPBELL

Position   Outside-right

Clubs   Dundee

Caps   6   Goals   1

Date	Team	Result	G
21 Oct 1967	Scotland	1-0	
22 Nov 1967	England	0-2	
23 Oct 1968	Turkey	4-1	1
10 Sep 1969	USSR	0-0	
18 Apr 1970	Scotland	0-1	
25 Apr 1970	Wales	0-1	

489   JOHN TERENCE HARKIN

Position   Centre-forward

Born   Derry, 14 September 1941

Clubs   Coleraine; Port Vale; Crewe Alexandra; Cardiff City; Notts County; Southport; Shrewsbury Town

Caps   5   Goals   2

Date	Team	Result	G
28 Feb 1968	Wales	0-2	
11 Dec 1968	Turkey	3-0	2
19 May 1969	Wales	0-0	
22 Oct 1969	USSR	0-2	
11 Nov 1970	Spain	0-3	

490   PATRICK JAMES RICE

Position	Right-back
Born	Belfast, 17 March 1949
Clubs	Arsenal; Watford
Caps	49

Date	Team	Result	G
10 Sep 1968	Israel	3-2	
10 Sep 1969	USSR	0-0	
15 May 1971	England	0-1	
18 May 1971	Scotland	1-0	
22 May 1971	Wales	1-0	
13 Oct 1971	USSR	1-1	
16 Feb 1972	Spain	1-1	
20 May 1972	Scotland	0-2	
23 May 1972	England	1-0	
27 May 1972	Wales	0-0	
18 Oct 1972	Bulgaria	0-3	
14 Feb 1973	Cyprus	0-1	
12 May 1973	England	1-2	
16 May 1973	Scotland	2-1	
19 May 1973	Wales	1-0	
26 Sep 1973	Bulgaria	0-0	
14 Nov 1973	Portugal	1-1	
11 May 1974	Scotland	1-0	
15 May 1974	England	0-1	
18 May 1974	Wales	0-1	
4 Sep 1974	Norway	1-2	
16 Apr 1975	Yugoslavia	1-0	
17 May 1975	England	0-0	
20 May 1975	Scotland	0-3	
23 May 1975	Wales	1-0	
3 Sep 1975	Sweden	1-2	
29 Oct 1975	Norway	3-0	
19 Nov 1975	Yugoslavia	0-1	
3 Mar 1976	Israel	1-1	
8 May 1976	Scotland	0-3	
11 May 1976	England	0-4	
14 May 1976	Wales	0-1	
13 Oct 1976	Holland	2-2	
10 Nov 1976	Belgium	0-2	
27 Apr 1977	West Germany	0-5	
28 May 1977	England	1-2	
1 Jun 1977	Scotland	0-3	
11 Jun 1977	Iceland	0-1	
14 Sep 1977	Iceland	2-0	
13 Oct 1977	Holland	0-1	
16 Nov 1977	Belgium	3-0	
20 Sep 1978	Republic of Ireland	0-0	
25 Oct 1978	Denmark	2-1	
7 Feb 1979	England	0-4	
19 May 1979	England	0-2	
22 May 1979	Scotland	0-1	
25 May 1979	Wales	1-1	
6 Jun 1979	Denmark	0-4	
17 Oct 1979	England	1-5	

491   THOMAS JACKSON

Position	Midfield
Born	Belfast, 3 November 1946
Clubs	Glentoran; Everton; Nottingham Forest; Manchester United
Caps	35

Date	Team	Result	G
10 Sep 1968	Israel	3-2	
3 May 1969	England	1-3	
6 May 1969	Scotland	1-1	
19 May 1969	Wales	0-0	
10 Sep 1969	USSR	0-0	
22 Oct 1969	USSR	0-2	
11 Nov 1970	Spain	0-3	
20 May 1972	Scotland	0-2	
23 May 1972	England	1-0	
27 May 1972	Wales	0-0	
8 May 1973	Cyprus	3-0	
12 May 1973	England	1-2	
16 May 1973	Scotland	2-1	
19 May 1973	Wales	1-0	
26 Sep 1973	Bulgaria	0-0	
14 Nov 1973	Portugal	1-1	
11 May 1974	Scotland	1-0	
15 May 1974	England	0-1	
18 May 1974	Wales	0-1	
4 Sep 1974	Norway	1-2	
30 Oct 1974	Sweden	2-0	
16 Apr 1975	Yugoslavia	1-0	
17 May 1975	England	0-0	
20 May 1975	Scotland	0-3	
23 May 1975	Wales	1-0	
3 Sep 1975	Sweden	1-2	
29 Oct 1975	Norway	3-0	
19 Nov 1975	Yugoslavia	0-1	
13 Oct 1976	Holland	2-2	
10 Nov 1976	Belgium	0-2	
27 Apr 1977	West Germany	0-5	
28 May 1977	England	1-2	
1 Jun 1977	Scotland	0-3	
3 Jun 1977	Wales	1-1	
11 Jun 1977	Iceland	0-1	

492   DAVID SLOAN

Position	Winger
Born	Lisburn, 28 October 1941
Clubs	Bangor; Scunthorpe United; Oxford United; Walsall
Caps	2

Date	Team	Result	G
10 Sep 1968	Israel	3-2	
11 Nov 1970	Spain	0-3	

Position   Midfield

Born   Belfast, 12 August 1946

Clubs   Dundela; Middlesbrough; Sheffield
Wednesday (loan); York City; Hartlepool
United

Caps   21   Goals   3

Date	Team	Result	G
10 Sep 1968	Israel	3-2	
23 Oct 1968	Turkey	4-1	1
11 Dec 1968	Turkey	3-0	
3 May 1969	England	1-3	1
6 May 1969	Scotland	1-1	1
19 May 1969	Wales	0-0	
10 Sep 1969	USSR	0-0	
18 Apr 1970	Scotland	0-1	
21 Apr 1970	England	1-3	
25 Apr 1970	Wales	0-1	
3 Feb 1971	Cyprus	3-0	
21 Apr 1971	Cyprus	5-0	
15 May 1971	England	0-1	
18 May 1971	Scotland	1-0	
22 May 1971	Wales	1-0	
13 Oct 1971	USSR	1-1	
16 Feb 1972	Spain	1-1	
20 May 1972	Scotland	0-2	
23 May 1972	England	1-0	
27 May 1972	Wales	0-0	
18 Oct 1972	Bulgaria	0-3	

Position   Midfield

Born   Belfast, 19 September 1944

Clubs   Glentoran; Newcastle United;
Northampton Town; Hartlepool United
(loan)

Caps   1

Date	Team	Result	G
10 Sep 1968	Israel	3-2	

Position   Centre-forward

Born   Belfast, 22 December 1946

Clubs   Coleraine; Wolverhampton Wanderers;
Coleraine; Oxford United; Lincoln City
(loan)

Caps   1

Date	Team	Result	G
10 Sep 1968	Israel	3-2	

Above: Bryan Hamilton

Position   Midfield

Born   Belfast, 21 December 1946

Clubs   Linfield; Ipswich Town; Everton; Millwall;
Swindon Town; Tranmere Rovers

Caps   50   Goals   4

Date	Team	Result	G
11 Dec 1968	Turkey	3-0	
3 Feb 1971	Cyprus	3-0	
21 Apr 1971	Cyprus	5-0	
15 May 1971	England	0-1	
18 May 1971	Scotland	1-0	
22 May 1971	Wales	1-0	1
22 Sep 1971	USSR	0-1	
13 Oct 1971	USSR	1-1	
16 Feb 1972	Spain	1-1	
18 Oct 1972	Bulgaria	0-3	
14 Feb 1973	Cyprus	0-1	
28 Mar 1973	Portugal	1-1	
8 May 1973	Cyprus	3-0	
12 May 1973	England	1-2	
16 May 1973	Scotland	2-1	
19 May 1973	Wales	1-0	1
26 Sep 1973	Bulgaria	0-0	
11 May 1974	Scotland	1-0	
15 May 1974	England	0-1	
18 May 1974	Wales	0-1	
4 Sep 1974	Norway	1-2	

Date	Team	Result	G
30 Oct 1974	Sweden	2-0	
16 Apr 1975	Yugoslavia	1-0	1
17 May 1975	England	0-0	
3 Sep 1975	Sweden	1-2	
29 Oct 1975	Norway	3-0	1
19 Nov 1975	Yugoslavia	0-1	
3 Mar 1976	Israel	1-1	
8 May 1976	Scotland	0-3	
11 May 1976	England	0-4	
14 May 1976	Wales	0-1	
13 Oct 1976	Holland	2-2	
10 Nov 1976	Belgium	0-2	
27 Apr 1977	West Germany	0-5	
28 May 1977	England	1-2	
1 Jun 1977	Scotland	0-3	
3 Jun 1977	Wales	1-1	
11 Jun 1977	Iceland	0-1	
13 May 1978	Scotland	1-1	
16 May 1978	England	0-1	
19 May 1978	Wales	0-1	
20 Sep 1978	Republic of Ireland	0-0	
29 Nov 1978	Bulgaria	2-0	
2 May 1979	Bulgaria	2-0	
19 May 1979	England	0-2	
22 May 1979	Scotland	0-1	
25 May 1979	Wales	1-1	
6 Jun 1979	Denmark	0-4	
11 Jun 1980	Australia	2-1	
18 Jun 1980	Australia	2-1	

Date	Team	Result	G
4 Sep 1974	Norway	1-2	
30 Oct 1974	Sweden	2-0	
16 Apr 1975	Yugoslavia	1-0	
17 May 1975	England	0-0	
20 May 1975	Scotland	0-3	
23 May 1975	Wales	1-0	
3 Sep 1975	Sweden	1-2	1
29 Oct 1975	Norway	3-0	
19 Nov 1975	Yugoslavia	0-1	
3 Mar 1976	Israel	1-1	
8 May 1976	Scotland	0-3	
11 May 1976	England	0-4	
14 May 1976	Wales	0-1	
13 Oct 1976	Holland	2-2	
10 Nov 1976	Belgium	0-2	
27 Apr 1977	West Germany	0-5	
28 May 1977	England	1-2	
1 Jun 1977	Scotland	0-3	
3 Jun 1977	Wales	1-1	
11 Jun 1977	Iceland	0-1	
14 Sep 1977	Iceland	2-0	
13 Oct 1977	Holland	0-1	
16 Nov 1977	Belgium	3-0	
20 Sep 1978	Republic of Ireland	0-0	
25 Oct 1978	Denmark	2-1	
22 May 1979	Scotland	0-1	
25 May 1979	Wales	1-1	
6 Jun 1979	Denmark	0-4	
17 Oct 1979	England	1-5	
21 Nov 1979	Republic of Ireland	1-0	

497 ALLAN HUNTER

Position   Central defender

Born   Sion Mills, 30 June 1946

Clubs   Coleraine; Oldham Athletic; Blackburn Rovers; Ipswich Town; Colchester United

Caps   53   Goals   1

Date	Team	Result	G
22 Oct 1969	USSR	0-2	
3 Feb 1971	Cyprus	3-0	
21 Apr 1971	Cyprus	5-0	
15 May 1971	England	0-1	
18 May 1971	Scotland	1-0	
22 May 1971	Wales	1-0	
22 Sep 1971	USSR	0-1	
13 Oct 1971	USSR	1-1	
16 Feb 1972	Spain	1-1	
20 May 1972	Scotland	0-2	
23 May 1972	England	1-0	
27 May 1972	Wales	0-0	
18 Oct 1972	Bulgaria	0-3	
14 Feb 1973	Cyprus	0-1	
28 Mar 1973	Portugal	1-1	
8 May 1973	Cyprus	3-0	
12 May 1973	England	1-2	
16 May 1973	Scotland	2-1	
19 May 1973	Wales	1-0	
26 Sep 1973	Bulgaria	0-0	
11 May 1974	Scotland	1-0	
15 May 1974	England	0-1	
18 May 1974	Wales	0-1	

498 DANIEL HEGAN

Position   Midfield

Born   Coatbridge, 14 June 1943

Clubs   Albion Rovers; Sunderland; Ipswich Town; West Bromwich Albion; Wolverhampton Wanderers; Sunderland

Caps   7

Date	Team	Result	G
22 Oct 1969	USSR	0-2	
22 Sep 1971	USSR	0-1	
20 May 1972	Scotland	0-2	
23 May 1972	England	1-0	
27 May 1972	Wales	0-0	
18 Oct 1972	Bulgaria	0-3	
14 Feb 1973	Cyprus	0-1	

499 ROBERT JOHN (Bert) LUTTON

Position   Winger

Born   Banbridge, 13 July 1950

Clubs   Wolverhampton Wanderers; Brighton & Hove Albion; West Ham United

Caps   6

Date	Team	Result	G
18 Apr 1970	Scotland	0-1	
21 Apr 1970	England	1-3	
8 May 1973	Cyprus	3-0	
16 May 1973	Scotland	2-1	
19 May 1973	Wales	1-0	
14 Nov 1973	Portugal	1-1	

500   WILLIAM JAMES (Liam) O'KANE

Position   Central defender

Born   Derry, 17 June 1948

Clubs   Derry City; Nottingham Forest

Caps   20   Goals   1

Date	Team	Result	G
18 Apr 1970	Scotland	0-1	
21 Apr 1970	England	1-3	
25 Apr 1970	Wales	0-1	
11 Nov 1970	Spain	0-3	
15 May 1971	England	0-1	
18 May 1971	Scotland	1-0	
22 May 1971	Wales	1-0	
22 Sep 1971	USSR	0-1	
13 Oct 1971	USSR	1-1	
28 Mar 1973	Portugal	1-1	
8 May 1973	Cyprus	3-0	
26 Sep 1973	Bulgaria	0-0	
14 Nov 1973	Portugal	1-1	1
1 May 1974	Scotland	1-0	
15 May 1974	England	0-1	
18 May 1974	Wales	0-1	
4 Sep 1974	Norway	1-2	
30 Oct 1974	Sweden	2-0	
17 May 1975	England	0-0	
20 May 1975	Scotland	0-3	

501   D DICKSON

Position   Centre-forward

Clubs   Coleraine

Caps   4

Date	Team	Result	G
18 Apr 1970	Scotland	0-1	
25 Apr 1970	Wales	0-1	
14 Feb 1973	Cyprus	0-1	
28 Mar 1973	Portugal	1-1	

502   A O'DOHERTY

Position   Inside-forward

Clubs   Coleraine

Caps   2

Date	Team	Result	G
21 Apr 1970	England	1-3	
25 Apr 1970	Wales	0-1	

503   JOHN COWAN

Position   Midfield

Born   Belfast, 8 January 1949

Clubs   Crusaders; Newcastle United; Drogheda United; Darlington

Caps   1

Date	Team	Result	G
21 Apr 1970	England	1-3	

504   SAMUEL NELSON

Position   Left-back

Born   Belfast, 1 April 1949

Clubs   Arsenal; Brighton & Hove Albion

Caps   51   Goals   1

Date	Team	Result	G
21 Apr 1970	England	1-3	
25 Apr 1970	Wales	0-1	
11 Nov 1970	Spain	0-3	
3 Feb 1971	Cyprus	3-0	
15 May 1971	England	0-1	
18 May 1971	Scotland	1-0	
22 May 1971	Wales	1-0	
22 Sep 1971	USSR	0-1	
13 Oct 1971	USSR	1-1	
16 Feb 1972	Spain	1-1	
20 May 1972	Scotland	0-2	
23 May 1972	England	1-0	
27 May 1972	Wales	0-0	
18 Oct 1972	Bulgaria	0-3	
14 Feb 1973	Cyprus	0-1	
28 Mar 1973	Portugal	1-1	
11 May 1974	Scotland	1-0	
15 May 1974	England	0-1	
30 Oct 1974	Sweden	2-0	
16 Apr 1975	Yugoslavia	1-0	
3 Sep 1975	Sweden	1-2	
29 Oct 1975	Norway	3-0	
3 Mar 1976	Israel	1-1	
11 May 1976	England	0-4	
10 Nov 1976	Belgium	0-2	
27 Apr 1977	West Germany	0-5	
3 Jun 1977	Wales	1-1	1
11 Jun 1977	Iceland	0-1	
14 Sep 1977	Iceland	2-0	
13 Oct 1977	Holland	0-1	
16 Nov 1977	Belgium	3-0	
20 Sep 1978	Republic of Ireland	0-0	
25 Oct 1978	Denmark	2-1	
29 Nov 1978	Bulgaria	2-0	
7 Feb 1979	England	0-4	

Date	Team	Result
2 May 1979	Bulgaria	2-0
19 May 1979	England	0-2
22 May 1979	Scotland	0-1
25 May 1979	Wales	1-1
6 Jun 1979	Denmark	0-4
17 Oct 1979	England	1-5
21 Nov 1979	Republic of Ireland	1-0
26 Mar 1980	Israel	0-0
25 Mar 1981	Scotland	1-1
29 Apr 1981	Portugal	1-0
19 May 1981	Scotland	0-2
3 Jun 1981	Sweden	0-1
23 Feb 1982	England	0-4
28 Apr 1982	Scotland	1-1
25 Jun 1982	Spain	1-0
1 Jul 1982	Austria	2-2

DID YOU KNOW?
The shortest-ever international career is that of Distillery's Peter Watson, who won his only cap as an 88th minute substitute in Northern Ireland's 5-0 win over Cyprus in April 1971.

505   PETER WATSON

Position   Midfield

Clubs   Distillery

Caps   1

Date	Team	Result	G
21 Apr 1971	Cyprus	5-0	

506   THOMAS CASSIDY

Position   Midfield

Born   Belfast, 18 November 1950

Clubs   Coleraine; Newcastle United; Burnley

Caps   24   Goals   1

Date	Team	Result	G
15 May 1971	England	0-1	
13 Oct 1971	USSR	1-1	
26 Sep 1973	Bulgaria	0-0	
11 May 1974	Scotland	1-0	1
15 May 1974	England	0-1	
18 May 1974	Wales	0-1	
4 Sep 1974	Norway	1-2	
8 May 1976	Scotland	0-3	
11 May 1976	England	0-4	
14 May 1976	Wales	0-1	
27 Apr 1977	West Germany	0-5	
17 Oct 1979	England	1-5	
21 Nov 1979	Republic of Ireland	1-0	
26 Mar 1980	Israel	0-0	
16 May 1980	Scotland	1-0	
20 May 1980	England	1-1	
23 May 1980	Wales	1-0	
11 Jun 1980	Australia	2-1	
15 Jun 1980	Australia	1-1	
18 Jun 1980	Australia	2-1	
15 Oct 1980	Sweden	3-0	
19 Nov 1980	Portugal	0-1	
18 Nov 1981	Israel	1-0	
25 Jun 1982	Spain	1-0	

507   MARTIN HUGH MICHAEL O'NEILL

Position   Midfield

Born   Coleraine, 1 March 1952

Clubs   Derry City; Nottingham Forest; Norwich City; Manchester City; Norwich City; Notts County

Caps   64   Goals   8

Date	Team	Result	G
13 Oct 1971	USSR	1-1	
16 Feb 1972	Spain	1-1	
27 May 1972	Wales	0-0	
28 Mar 1973	Portugal	1-1	1
8 May 1973	Cyprus	3-0	
12 May 1973	England	1-2	
16 May 1973	Scotland	2-1	1
19 May 1973	Wales	1-0	
26 Sep 1973	Bulgaria	0-0	
14 Nov 1973	Portugal	1-1	
15 May 1974	England	0-1	
18 May 1974	Wales	0-1	
30 Oct 1974	Sweden	2-0	1
16 Apr 1975	Yugoslavia	1-0	
17 May 1975	England	0-0	
20 May 1975	Scotland	0-3	
19 Nov 1975	Yugoslavia	0-1	
28 May 1977	England	1-2	
1 Jun 1977	Scotland	0-3	
14 Sep 1977	Iceland	2-0	
13 Oct 1977	Holland	0-1	
13 May 1978	Scotland	1-1	1
16 May 1978	England	0-1	
19 May 1978	Wales	0-1	
20 Sep 1978	Republic of Ireland	0-0	
25 Oct 1978	Denmark	2-1	
29 Nov 1978	Bulgaria	2-0	
7 Feb 1979	England	0-4	
2 May 1979	Bulgaria	2-0	
6 Jun 1979	Denmark	0-4	
21 Nov 1979	Republic of Ireland	1-0	
26 Mar 1980	Israel	0-0	
11 Jun 1980	Australia	2-1	
15 Jun 1980	Australia	1-1	1
18 Jun 1980	Australia	2-1	
15 Oct 1980	Sweden	3-0	
19 Nov 1980	Portugal	0-1	
29 Apr 1981	Portugal	1-0	
19 May 1981	Scotland	0-2	
3 Jun 1981	Sweden	0-1	
14 Oct 1981	Scotland	0-0	
23 Feb 1982	England	0-4	
24 Mar 1982	France	0-4	
28 Apr 1982	Scotland	1-1	
17 Jun 1982	Yugoslavia	0-0	

21 Jun 1982	Honduras	1-1	
25 Jun 1982	Spain	1-0	
1 Jul 1982	Austria	2-2	
4 Jul 1982	France	1-4	
13 Oct 1982	Austria	0-2	
17 Nov 1982	West Germany	1-0	
15 Dec 1982	Albania	0-0	
30 Mar 1983	Turkey	2-1	1
27 Apr 1983	Albania	1-0	
24 May 1983	Scotland	0-0	
28 May 1983	England	0-0	
21 Sep 1983	Austria	3-1	1
12 Oct 1983	Turkey	0-1	
16 Nov 1983	West Germany	1-0	
4 Apr 1984	England	0-1	
22 May 1984	Wales	1-1	
27 May 1984	Finland	0-1	
12 Sep 1904	Romania	3-2	1
14 Nov 1984	Finland	2-1	

508   SAMUEL JOHN MORGAN

Position   Forward

Born   Belfast, 3 December 1946

Clubs   Gorleston; Port Vale; Aston Villa; Brighton & Hove Albion; Cambridge United; Sparta Rotterdam

Caps   18   Goals   3

Above: Sammy McIlroy

Date	Team	Result	G
16 Feb 1972	Spain	1-1	1
18 Oct 1972	Bulgaria	0-3	
28 Mar 1973	Portugal	1-1	
8 May 1973	Cyprus	3-0	1
12 May 1973	England	1-2	
16 May 1973	Scotland	2-1	
19 May 1973	Wales	1-0	
26 Sep 1973	Bulgaria	0-0	
14 Nov 1973	Portugal	1-1	
11 May 1974	Scotland	1-0	
15 May 1974	England	0-1	
30 Oct 1974	Sweden	2-0	
3 Sep 1975	Sweden	1-2	
29 Oct 1975	Norway	3-0	1
19 Nov 1975	Yugoslavia	0-1	
8 May 1976	Scotland	0-3	
14 May 1976	Wales	0-1	
25 Oct 1978	Denmark	2-1	

509   SAMUEL BAXTER McILROY

Position   Midfield

Born   Belfast, 2 August 1954

Clubs   Manchester United; Stoke City; Manchester City; Orgryte (Sweden); Manchester City; Bury; VFB Mödling (Austria); Bury; Preston North End

Caps   88   Goals   5

Date	Team	Result	G
18 Feb 1972	Spain	1-1	
20 May 1972	Scotland	0-2	
11 May 1974	Scotland	1-0	
15 May 1974	England	0-1	
18 May 1974	Wales	0-1	
4 Sep 1974	Norway	1-2	
30 Oct 1974	Sweden	2-0	
16 Apr 1975	Yugoslavia	1-0	
17 May 1975	England	0-0	
20 May 1975	Scotland	0-3	
23 May 1975	Wales	1-0	
3 Sep 1975	Sweden	1-2	
29 Oct 1975	Norway	3-0	1
19 Nov 1975	Yugoslavia	0-1	
8 May 1976	Scotland	0-3	
11 May 1976	England	0-4	
14 May 1976	Wales	0-1	
13 Oct 1976	Holland	2-2	
10 Nov 1976	Belgium	0-2	
28 May 1977	England	1-2	
1 Jun 1977	Scotland	0-3	
3 Jun 1977	Wales	1-1	
11 Jun 1977	Iceland	0-1	
14 Sep 1977	Iceland	2-0	1
13 Oct 1977	Holland	0-1	
16 Nov 1977	Belgium	3-0	
13 May 1978	Scotland	1-1	
16 May 1978	England	0-1	
19 May 1978	Wales	0-1	
20 Sep 1978	Republic of Ireland	0-0	
25 Oct 1978	Denmark	2-1	
29 Nov 1978	Bulgaria	2-0	

Date	Team	Result	G
7 Feb 1979	England	0-4	
2 May 1979	Bulgaria	2-0	
19 May 1979	England	0-2	
22 May 1979	Scotland	0-1	
25 May 1979	Wales	1-1	
6 Jun 1979	Denmark	0-4	
17 Oct 1979	England	1-5	
21 Nov 1979	Republic of Ireland	1-0	
26 Mar 1980	Israel	0-0	
16 May 1980	Scotland	1-0	
20 May 1980	England	1-1	
23 May 1980	Wales	1-0	
15 Oct 1980	Sweden	3-0	1
19 Nov 1980	Portugal	0-1	
25 Mar 1981	Scotland	1-1	
29 Apr 1981	Portugal	1-0	
19 May 1981	Scotland	0-2	
3 Jun 1981	Sweden	0-1	
14 Oct 1981	Scotland	0-0	
18 Nov 1981	Israel	1-0	
23 Feb 1982	England	0-4	
24 Mar 1982	France	0-4	
28 Apr 1982	Scotland	1-1	1
28 May 1982	Wales	0-3	
17 Jun 1982	Yugoslavia	0-0	
21 Jun 1982	Honduras	1-1	
25 Jun 1982	Spain	1-0	
1 Jul 1982	Austria	2-2	
4 Jul 1982	France	1-4	
13 Oct 1982	Austria	0-2	
17 Nov 1982	West Germany	1-0	
15 Dec 1982	Albania	0-0	
30 Mar 1983	Turkey	2-1	
27 Apr 1983	Albania	1-0	
24 May 1983	Scotland	0-0	
28 May 1983	England	0-0	
31 May 1983	Wales	0-1	
21 Sep 1983	Austria	3-1	
12 Oct 1983	Turkey	0-1	
13 Dec 1983	Scotland	2-0	1
4 Apr 1984	England	0-1	
22 May 1984	Wales	1-1	
27 May 1984	Finland	0-1	
14 Nov 1984	Finland	2-1	
27 Feb 1985	England	0-1	
1 May 1985	Turkey	2-0	
11 Sep 1985	Turkey	0-0	
16 Oct 1985	Romania	1-0	
13 Nov 1985	England	0-0	
26 Feb 1986	France	0-0	
26 Mar 1986	Denmark	1-1	
23 Apr 1986	Morocco	2-1	
3 Jun 1986	Algeria	1-1	
7 Jun 1986	Spain	1-2	
12 Jun 1986	Brazil	0-3	
15 Oct 1986	England	0-3	

510   ROBERT IRVINE COYLE

Position   Midfield

Born   Belfast, 31 January 1948

Clubs   Glentoran; Sheffield Wednesday; Grimsby Town

Caps   5

Date	Team	Result	G
28 Mar 1973	Portugal	1-1	
8 May 1973	Cyprus	3-0	
19 May 1973	Wales	1-0	
26 Sep 1973	Bulgaria	0-0	
14 Nov 1973	Portugal	1-1	

511   TREVOR ANDERSON

Position   Winger

Born   Belfast, 3 March 1951

Clubs   Portadown; Manchester United; Swindon Town; Peterborough United

Caps   22   Goals   4

Date	Team	Result	G
8 May 1973	Cyprus	3-0	2
12 May 1973	England	1-2	
16 May 1973	Scotland	2-1	1
19 May 1973	Wales	1-0	
26 Sep 1973	Bulgaria	0-0	
14 Nov 1973	Portugal	1-1	
20 May 1975	Scotland	0-3	
3 Mar 1976	Israel	1-1	
13 Oct 1976	Holland	2-2	
10 Nov 1976	Belgium	0-2	
27 Apr 1977	West Germany	0-5	
28 May 1977	England	1-2	
1 Jun 1977	Scotland	0-3	
3 Jun 1977	Wales	1-1	
11 Jun 1977	Iceland	0-1	
14 Sep 1977	Iceland	2-0	
13 Oct 1977	Holland	0-1	
16 Nov 1977	Belgium	3-0	
13 May 1978	Scotland	1-1	
16 May 1978	England	0-1	
19 May 1978	Wales	0-1	
25 Oct 1978	Denmark	2-1	1

DID YOU KNOW?
Northern Ireland winger Trevor Anderson scored a hat-trick of penalties for Swindon town against Walsall on 24 April 1976.

512   ROLAND CHRISTOPHER McGRATH

Position   Winger

Born   Belfast, 29 November 1954

Clubs   Tottenham Hotspur; Millwall (loan); Manchester United; Tulsa Roughnecks

Caps   21   Goals   4

Date	Team	Result	G
11 May 1974	Scotland	1-0	
15 May 1974	England	0-1	

Date	Team	Result	G
18 May 1974	Wales	0-1	
4 Sep 1974	Norway	1-2	
3 Mar 1976	Israel	1-1	
13 Oct 1976	Holland	2-2	1
10 Nov 1976	Belgium	0-2	
27 Apr 1977	West Germany	0-5	
28 May 1977	England	1-2	1
1 Jun 1977	Scotland	0-3	
3 Jun 1977	Wales	1-1	
11 Jun 1977	Iceland	0-1	
14 Sep 1977	Iceland	2-0	1
13 Oct 1977	Holland	0-1	
16 Nov 1977	Belgium	3-0	1
13 May 1978	Scotland	1-1	
16 May 1978	England	0-1	
19 May 1978	Wales	0-1	
29 Nov 1978	Bulgaria	2-0	
7 Feb 1979	England	0-4	
19 May 1979	England	0-2	

513   HUGH OLIVER DOWD

Position   Central defender

Born   Lurgan, 19 May 1951

Clubs   Glenavon; Sheffield Wednesday; Doncaster Rovers

Caps   3

Date	Team	Result	G
18 May 1974	Wales	0-1	
4 Sep 1974	Norway	1-2	
30 Oct 1974	Sweden	2-0	

514   THOMAS FINNEY

Position   Midfield

Born   Belfast, 6 November 1952

Clubs   Crusaders; Luton Town; Sunderland; Cambridge United; Brentford; Cambridge United

Caps   14   Goals   2

Date	Team	Result	G
4 Sep 1974	Norway	1-2	1
17 May 1975	England	0-0	
20 May 1975	Scotland	0-3	
23 May 1975	Wales	1-0	1
29 Oct 1975	Norway	3-0	
19 Nov 1975	Yugoslavia	0-1	
8 May 1976	Scotland	0-3	
17 Oct 1979	England	1-5	
26 Mar 1980	Israel	0-0	
16 May 1980	Scotland	1-0	
20 May 1980	England	1-1	
23 May 1980	Wales	1-0	
11 Jun 1980	Australia	2-1	
15 Jun 1980	Australia	1-1	

515   CHRISTOPHER JOHN NICHOLL

Position   Central defender

Born   Macclesfield, 12 October 1946

Clubs   Burnley; Witton Albion; Halifax Town; Luton Town; Aston Villa; Southampton; Grimsby Town

Caps   51   Goals   3

Date	Team	Result	G
30 Oct 1974	Sweden	2-0	1
16 Apr 1975	Yugoslavia	1-0	
17 May 1975	England	0-0	
20 May 1975	Scotland	0-3	
23 May 1975	Wales	1-0	
3 Sep 1975	Sweden	1-2	
29 Oct 1975	Norway	3-0	
19 Nov 1975	Yugoslavia	0-1	
8 May 1976	Scotland	0-3	
11 May 1976	England	0-4	
14 May 1976	Wales	0-1	
3 Jun 1977	Wales	1-1	
16 Nov 1977	Belgium	3-0	
13 May 1978	Scotland	1-1	
16 May 1978	England	0-1	
19 May 1978	Wales	0-1	
20 Sep 1978	Republic of Ireland	0-0	
29 Nov 1978	Bulgaria	2-0	
7 Feb 1979	England	0-4	
2 May 1979	Bulgaria	2-0	1
19 May 1979	England	0-2	
25 May 1979	Wales	1-1	
21 Nov 1979	Republic of Ireland	1-0	
26 Mar 1980	Israel	0-0	
16 May 1980	Scotland	1-0	
20 May 1980	England	1-1	
23 May 1980	Wales	1-0	
11 Jun 1980	Australia	2-1	1
15 Jun 1980	Australia	1-1	
18 Jun 1980	Australia	2-1	
15 Oct 1980	Sweden	3-0	
19 Nov 1980	Portugal	0-1	
25 Mar 1981	Scotland	1-1	
29 Apr 1981	Portugal	1-0	
19 May 1981	Scotland	0-2	
3 Jun 1981	Sweden	0-1	
14 Oct 1981	Scotland	0-0	
18 Nov 1981	Israel	1-0	
23 Feb 1982	England	0-4	
24 Mar 1982	France	0-4	
28 May 1982	Wales	0-3	
17 Jun 1982	Yugoslavia	0-0	
21 Jun 1982	Honduras	1-1	
25 Jun 1982	Spain	1-0	
1 Jul 1982	Austria	2-2	
4 Jul 1982	France	1-4	
24 May 1983	Scotland	0-0	
28 May 1983	England	0-0	
31 May 1983	Wales	0-1	
21 Sep 1983	Austria	3-1	
12 Oct 1983	Turkey	0-1	

516   RONALD VICTOR BLAIR

Position   Defender

Born   Coleraine, 26 September 1949

Clubs   Coleraine; Oldham Athletic; Rochdale; Oldham Athletic; Blackpool; Rochdale

Caps   5

Date	Team	Result	G
30 Oct 1974	Sweden	2-0	
20 May 1975	Scotland	0-3	
23 May 1975	Wales	1-0	
3 Sep 1975	Sweden	1-2	
3 Mar 1976	Israel	1-1	

517   DEREK WILLIAM SPENCE

Position   Forward

Born   Belfast, 18 January 1952

Clubs   Crusaders; Oldham Athletic; Bury; Blackpool; Olympiakos (Greece); Blackpool; Southend United; See Bee (Hong Kong); Bury

Caps   29   Goals   3

Date	Team	Result	G
16 Apr 1975	Yugoslavia	1-0	
17 May 1975	England	0-0	
20 May 1975	Scotland	0-3	
23 May 1975	Wales	1-0	
3 Sep 1975	Sweden	1-2	
3 Mar 1976	Israel	1-1	
8 May 1976	Scotland	0-3	
11 May 1976	England	0-4	
14 May 1976	Wales	0-1	
13 Oct 1976	Holland	2-2	1
27 Apr 1977	West Germany	0-5	
28 May 1977	England	1-2	
1 Jun 1977	Scotland	0-3	
3 Jun 1977	Wales	1-1	
11 Jun 1977	Iceland	0-1	
20 Sep 1978	Republic of Ireland	0-0	
25 Oct 1978	Denmark	2-1	1
7 Feb 1979	England	0-4	
2 May 1979	Bulgaria	2-0	
19 May 1979	England	0-2	
22 May 1979	Scotland	0-1	
25 May 1979	Wales	1-1	1
6 Jun 1979	Denmark	0-4	
21 Nov 1979	Republic of Ireland	1-0	
26 Mar 1980	Israel	0-0	
11 Jun 1980	Australia	2-1	
25 Mar 1981	Scotland	1-1	
3 Jun 1981	Sweden	0-1	
24 Mar 1982	France	0-4	

518   PETER WILLIAM SCOTT

Position   Full-back

Born   Liverpool, 19 September 1952

Clubs   Everton; Southport; York City; Aldershot

Caps   10

Date	Team	Result	G
23 May 1975	Wales	1-0	
19 Nov 1975	Yugoslavia	0-1	
3 Mar 1976	Israel	1-1	
8 May 1976	Scotland	0-3	
11 May 1976	England	0-4	
14 May 1976	Wales	0-1	
13 May 1978	Scotland	1-1	
16 May 1978	England	0-1	
19 May 1978	Wales	0-1	
22 May 1979	Scotland	0-1	

519   GEORGE TERENCE (TERRY) COCHRANE

Position   Winger

Born   Killyleagh, 23 January 1953

Clubs   Coleraine; Burnley; Middlesbrough; Gillingham; Millwall; Dallas; Hartlepool United

Caps   26   Goals   1

Date	Team	Result	G
29 Oct 1975	Norway	3-0	
13 May 1978	Scotland	1-1	
16 May 1978	England	0-1	
19 May 1978	Wales	0-1	
20 Sep 1978	Republic of Ireland	0-0	
25 Oct 1978	Denmark	2-1	
29 Nov 1978	Bulgaria	2-0	
7 Feb 1979	England	0-4	
2 May 1979	Bulgaria	2-0	
19 May 1979	England	0-2	
26 Mar 1980	Israel	0-0	
20 May 1980	England	1-1	1
23 May 1980	Wales	1-0	
11 Jun 1980	Australia	2-1	
15 Jun 1980	Australia	1-1	
18 Jun 1980	Australia	2-1	
15 Oct 1980	Sweden	3-0	
19 Nov 1980	Portugal	0-1	
25 Mar 1981	Scotland	1-1	
29 Apr 1981	Portugal	1-0	
19 May 1981	Scotland	0-2	
3 Jun 1981	Sweden	0-1	
23 Feb 1982	England	0-4	

24 Mar 1982	France	0-4
13 Dec 1983	Scotland	2-0
27 May 1984	Finland	0-1

Above: Terry Cochrane

520   JOHN JAMISON

Position	Inside-forward
Born	11 March 1958
Clubs	Glentoran
Caps	1

Date	Team	Result	G
29 Oct 1975	Norway	3-0	

521   JAMES ARCHIBALD PLATT

Position	Goalkeeper
Born	Ballymoney, 26 January 1952
Clubs	Ballymena; Middlesbrough; Hartlepool United (loan); Cardiff City (loan)
Caps	23

Date	Team	Result	G
3 Mar 1976	Israel	1-1	

13 May 1978	Scotland	1-1
16 May 1978	England	0-1
19 May 1978	Wales	0-1
16 May 1980	Scotland	1-0
20 May 1980	England	1-1
23 May 1980	Wales	1-0
11 Jun 1980	Australia	2-1
15 Jun 1980	Australia	1-1
18 Jun 1980	Australia	2-1
15 Oct 1980	Sweden	3-0
19 Nov 1980	Portugal	0-1
24 Mar 1982	France	0-4
28 Apr 1982	Scotland	1-1
28 May 1982	Wales	0-3
1 Jul 1982	Austria	2-2
13 Oct 1982	Austria	0-2
17 Nov 1982	West Germany	1-0
15 Dec 1982	Albania	0-0
30 Mar 1983	Turkey	2-1
4 Apr 1984	England	0-1
22 May 1984	Wales	1-1
23 Apr 1986	Morocco	2-1

522   JAMES MICHAEL NICHOLL

Position	Right-back
Born	Canada, 28 December 1956
Clubs	Manchester United; Sunderland; Toronto; Sunderland; Toronto; West Bromwich Albion
Caps	73 Goals 1

Date	Team	Result	G
3 Mar 1976	Israel	1-1	
14 May 1976	Wales	0-1	
13 Oct 1976	Holland	2-2	
10 Nov 1976	Belgium	0-2	
28 May 1977	England	1-2	
1 Jun 1977	Scotland	0-3	
3 Jun 1977	Wales	1-1	
11 Jun 1977	Iceland	0-1	
14 Sep 1977	Iceland	2-0	
13 Oct 1977	Holland	0-1	
16 Nov 1977	Belgium	3-0	
13 May 1978	Scotland	1-1	
16 May 1978	England	0-1	
19 May 1978	Wales	0-1	
20 Sep 1978	Republic of Ireland	0-0	
25 Oct 1978	Denmark	2-1	
29 Nov 1978	Bulgaria	2-0	
7 Feb 1979	England	0-4	
2 May 1979	Bulgaria	2-0	
19 May 1979	England	0-2	
22 May 1979	Scotland	0-1	
25 May 1979	Wales	1-1	
6 Jun 1979	Denmark	0-4	
17 Oct 1979	England	1-5	
21 Nov 1979	Republic of Ireland	1-0	
26 Mar 1980	Israel	0-0	
16 May 1980	Scotland	1-0	
20 May 1980	England	1-1	
23 May 1980	Wales	1-0	

Date	Team	Result	G
11 Jun 1980	Australia	2-1	
15 Jun 1980	Australia	1-1	
18 Jun 1980	Australia	2-1	
15 Oct 1980	Sweden	3-0	1
19 Nov 1980	Portugal	0-1	
25 Mar 1981	Scotland	1-1	
29 Apr 1981	Portugal	1-0	
19 May 1981	Scotland	0-2	
3 Jun 1981	Sweden	0-1	
14 Oct 1981	Scotland	0-0	
18 Nov 1981	Israel	1-0	
23 Feb 1982	England	0-4	
24 Mar 1982	France	0-4	
28 May 1982	Wales	0-3	
17 Jun 1982	Yugoslavia	0-0	
21 Jun 1982	Honduras	1-1	
25 Jun 1982	Spain	1-0	
1 Jul 1982	Austria	2-2	
4 Jul 1982	France	1-4	
13 Oct 1982	Austria	0-2	
17 Nov 1982	West Germany	1-0	
15 Dec 1982	Albania	0-0	
30 Mar 1983	Turkey	2-1	
27 Apr 1983	Albania	1-0	
24 May 1983	Scotland	0-0	
28 May 1983	England	0-0	
31 May 1983	Wales	0-1	
12 Oct 1983	Turkey	0-1	
16 Nov 1983	West Germany	1-0	
13 Dec 1983	Scotland	2-0	
4 Apr 1984	England	0-1	
27 May 1984	Finland	0-1	
12 Sep 1984	Romania	3-2	
14 Nov 1984	Finland	2-1	
27 Feb 1985	England	0-1	
27 Mar 1985	Spain	0-0	
1 May 1985	Turkey	2-0	
11 Sep 1985	Turkey	0-0	
16 Oct 1985	Romania	1-0	
13 Nov 1985	England	0-0	
26 Feb 1986	France	0-0	
3 Jun 1986	Algeria	1-1	
7 Jun 1986	Spain	1-2	
12 Jun 1986	Brazil	0-3	

523 WARREN FEENEY

Position   Outside-left

Clubs   Glentoran

Caps   1

Date	Team	Result	G
3 Mar 1976	Israel	1-1	1

524 PATRICK GERALD SHARP SHARKEY

Position   Midfield

Born   Omagh, 26 August 1953

Clubs   Portadown; Ipswich Town; Millwall (loan); Mansfield Town; Colchester United; Peterborough United

Caps   1

Date	Team	Result	G
8 May 1976	Scotland	0-3	

525 DAVID McCREERY

Position   Midfield

Born   Belfast, 16 September 1957

Clubs   Manchester United; Queen's Park Rangers; Tulsa Roughnecks; Newcastle United; Heart of Midlothian; Hartlepool United; Carlisle United; Hartlepool United

Caps   67

Date	Team	Result	G
8 May 1976	Scotland	0-3	
11 May 1976	England	0-4	
14 May 1976	Wales	0-1	
13 Oct 1976	Holland	2-2	
10 Nov 1976	Belgium	0-2	
27 Apr 1977	West Germany	0-5	
28 May 1977	England	1-2	
1 Jun 1977	Scotland	0-3	
3 Jun 1977	Wales	1-1	
11 Jun 1977	Iceland	0-1	
14 Sep 1977	Iceland	2-0	
13 Oct 1977	Holland	0-1	
16 Nov 1977	Belgium	3-0	
13 May 1978	Scotland	1-1	
16 May 1978	England	0-1	
19 May 1978	Wales	0-1	
20 Sep 1978	Republic of Ireland	0-0	
25 Oct 1978	Denmark	2-1	
29 Nov 1978	Bulgaria	2-0	
7 Feb 1979	England	0-4	
2 May 1979	Bulgaria	2-0	
25 May 1979	Wales	1-1	
6 Jun 1979	Denmark	0-4	
17 Oct 1979	England	1-5	
21 Nov 1979	Republic of Ireland	1-0	
16 May 1980	Scotland	1-0	
20 May 1980	England	1-1	
23 May 1980	Wales	1-0	
11 Jun 1980	Australia	2-1	
15 Jun 1980	Australia	1-1	
15 Oct 1980	Sweden	3-0	
19 Nov 1980	Portugal	0-1	
25 Mar 1981	Scotland	1-1	
29 Apr 1981	Portugal	1-0	
3 Jun 1981	Sweden	0-1	
14 Oct 1981	Scotland	0-0	
18 Nov 1981	Israel	1-0	
23 Feb 1982	England	0-4	
24 Mar 1982	France	0-4	
17 Jun 1982	Yugoslavia	0-0	
21 Jun 1982	Honduras	1-1	
25 Jun 1982	Spain	1-0	
1 Jul 1982	Austria	2-2	
4 Jul 1982	France	1-4	

Above: David McCreery

Above: Gerry Armstrong

13 Oct 1982	Austria	0-2
12 Oct 1983	Turkey	0-1
12 Sep 1984	Romania	3-2
27 Mar 1985	Spain	0-0
11 Sep 1985	Turkey	0-0
16 Oct 1985	Romania	1-0
13 Nov 1985	England	0-0
26 Feb 1986	France	0-0
26 Mar 1986	Denmark	1-1
3 Jun 1986	Algeria	1-1
7 Jun 1986	Spain	1-2
12 Jun 1986	Brazil	0-3
12 Nov 1986	Turkey	0-0
1 Apr 1987	England	0-2
29 Apr 1987	Yugoslavia	1-2
14 Oct 1987	Yugoslavia	0-3
21 Dec 1988	Spain	0-4
26 Apr 1989	Malta	2-0
26 May 1989	Chile	0-1
6 Sep 1989	Hungary	1-2
11 Oct 1989	Republic of Ireland	0-3
27 Mar 1990	Norway	2-3
18 May 1990	Uruguay	1-0

DID YOU KNOW?
The 1982 World Cup tournament saw the Irish beat hosts Spain 1-0 in Valencia to record their greatest moment in recent memory. Gerry Armstrong scored for the Irish to put them into the second round of the competition.

526   GERARD JOSEPH (GERRY) ARMSTRONG

Position   Forward

Born   Belfast, 23 May 1954

Clubs   Bangor; Tottenham Hotspur; Watford; Real Mallorca; West Bromwich Albion; Chesterfield (loan); Brighton & Hove Albion; Millwall (loan)

Caps   63   Goals   12

Date	Team	Result	G
27 Apr 1977	West Germany	0-5	
28 May 1977	England	1-2	
3 Jun 1977	Wales	1-1	
11 Jun 1977	Iceland	0-1	
16 Nov 1977	Belgium	3-0	2
13 May 1978	Scotland	1-1	
16 May 1978	England	0-1	
19 May 1978	Wales	0-1	
20 Sep 1978	Republic of Ireland	0-0	
25 Oct 1978	Denmark	2-1	
29 Nov 1978	Bulgaria	2-0	1
7 Feb 1979	England	0-4	
2 May 1979	Bulgaria	2-0	1
19 May 1979	England	0-2	
22 May 1979	Scotland	0-1	
25 May 1979	Wales	1-1	
6 Jun 1979	Denmark	0-4	
17 Oct 1979	England	1-5	

Date	Team	Result	G
21 Nov 1979	Republic of Ireland	1-0	1
26 Mar 1980	Israel	0-0	
16 May 1980	Scotland	1-0	
20 May 1980	England	1-1	
23 May 1980	Wales	1-0	
11 Jun 1980	Australia	2-1	
15 Jun 1980	Australia	1-1	
18 Jun 1980	Australia	2-1	
15 Oct 1980	Sweden	3-0	
19 Nov 1980	Portugal	0-1	
25 Mar 1981	Scotland	1-1	
29 Apr 1981	Portugal	1-0	1
19 May 1981	Scotland	0-2	
3 Jun 1981	Sweden	0-1	
14 Oct 1981	Scotland	0-0	
18 Nov 1981	Israel	1-0	1
23 Feb 1982	England	0-4	
24 May 1982	France	0-4	
28 May 1982	Wales	0-3	
17 Jun 1982	Yugoslavia	0-0	
21 Jun 1982	Honduras	1-1	1
25 Jun 1982	Spain	1-0	1
1 Jul 1982	Austria	2-2	
4 Jul 1982	France	1-4	1
13 Oct 1982	Austria	0-2	
30 Mar 1983	Turkey	2-1	
27 Apr 1983	Albania	1-0	
24 May 1983	Scotland	0-0	
28 May 1983	England	0-0	
31 May 1983	Wales	0-1	
21 Sep 1983	Austria	3-1	
16 Nov 1983	West Germany	1-0	
4 Apr 1984	England	0-1	
22 May 1984	Wales	1-1	1
27 May 1984	Finland	0-1	
12 Sep 1984	Romania	3-2	
14 Nov 1984	Finland	2-1	1
27 Feb 1985	England	0-1	
27 Mar 1985	Spain	0-0	
11 Sep 1985	Turkey	0-0	
16 Oct 1985	Romania	1-0	
13 Nov 1985	England	0-0	
26 Feb 1986	France	0-0	
26 Mar 1986	Denmark	1-1	
12 Jun 1986	Brazil	0-3	

527   CHARLES DAVID STEWART

Position	Winger
Born	Belfast, 20 May 1958
Clubs	Hull City; Chelsea; Scunthorpe United; Goole Town; Hartlepool United
Caps	1

Date	Team	Result	G
16 Nov 1977	Belgium	3-0	

528   WILLIAM ROBERT HAMILTON

Position   Forward

Born	Belfast, 9 May 1957
Clubs	Linfield; Queen's Park Rangers; Burnley; Oxford United
Caps	41 Goals 5

Date	Team	Result	G
13 May 1978	Scotland	1-1	
16 May 1980	Scotland	1-0	1
20 May 1980	England	1-1	
23 May 1980	Wales	1-0	
11 Jun 1980	Australia	2-1	
15 Jun 1980	Australia	1-1	
18 Jun 1980	Australia	2-1	
15 Oct 1980	Sweden	3-0	
19 Nov 1980	Portugal	0-1	
25 Mar 1981	Scotland	1-1	1
29 Apr 1981	Portugal	1-0	
19 May 1981	Scotland	0-2	
3 Jun 1981	Sweden	0-1	
14 Oct 1981	Scotland	0-0	
18 Nov 1981	Israel	1-0	
23 Feb 1982	England	0-4	
28 May 1982	Wales	0-3	
17 Jun 1982	Yugoslavia	0-0	
21 Jun 1982	Honduras	1-1	
25 Jun 1982	Spain	1-0	
1 Jul 1982	Austria	2-2	2
4 Jul 1982	France	1-4	
13 Oct 1982	Austria	0-2	
17 Nov 1982	West Germany	1-0	
15 Dec 1982	Albania	0-0	
27 Apr 1983	Albania	1-0	
24 May 1983	Scotland	0-0	
28 May 1983	England	0-0	
31 May 1983	Wales	0-1	
21 Sep 1983	Austria	3-1	1
12 Oct 1983	Turkey	0-1	
16 Nov 1983	West Germany	1-0	
13 Dec 1983	Scotland	2-0	
4 Apr 1984	England	0-1	
22 May 1984	Wales	1-1	
27 May 1984	Finland	0-1	
12 Sep 1984	Romania	3-2	
27 Mar 1985	Spain	0-0	
23 Apr 1986	Morocco	2-1	
3 Jun 1986	Algeria	1-1	
7 Jun 1986	Spain	1-2	

529   THOMAS E CONNELL

Position	Midfield
Clubs	Coleraine
Caps	1

Date	Team	Result	G
19 May 1978	Wales	0-1	

530   WILLIAM THOMAS CASKEY

Position   Forward

Born	Belfast, 12 October 1953

Clubs	Glentoran; Derby County; Tulsa Roughnecks; Dallas Sidekicks; Glentoran

Caps	8	Goals	1

Date	Team	Result	G
29 Nov 1978	Bulgaria	2-0	1
7 Feb 1979	England	0-4	
2 May 1979	Bulgaria	2-0	
19 May 1979	England	0-2	
22 May 1979	Scotland	0-1	
6 Jun 1979	Denmark	0-4	
17 Oct 1979	England	1-5	
24 Mar 1982	France	0-4	

531   VICTOR MORELAND

Position	Midfield

Born	Belfast, 15 June 1957

Clubs	Glentoran; Derby County; Tulsa Roughnecks; Dallas Sidekicks; Wichita Wings

Caps	6	Goals	1

Date	Team	Result	G
29 Nov 1978	Bulgaria	2-0	
2 May 1979	Bulgaria	2-0	
19 May 1979	England	0-2	
22 May 1979	Scotland	0-1	
17 Oct 1979	England	1-5	1
21 Nov 1979	Republic of Ireland	1-0	

532   THOMAS SLOAN

Position	Midfield

Born	Ballymena, 10 July 1959

Clubs	Ballymena; Manchester United; Chester City

Caps	3

Date	Team	Result	G
22 May 1979	Scotland	0-1	
25 May 1979	Wales	1-1	
6 Jun 1979	Denmark	0-4	

533   PETER C RAFFERTY

Position	Midfield

Born	Belfast, 7 November 1948

Clubs	Distillery; Linfield; Ards

Caps	1

Date	Team	Result	G
17 Oct 1979	England	1-5	

534   NOEL BROTHERSTON

Position	Winger

Born	Dundonald, 18 November 1956
Died	6 May 1995

Clubs	Tottenham Hotspur; Blackburn Rovers; Bury; Scarborough (loan); Motala (Sweden); Chorley

Caps	27	Goals	3

Date	Team	Result	G
16 May 1980	Scotland	1-0	
20 May 1980	England	1-1	
23 May 1980	Wales	1-0	1
11 Jun 1980	Australia	2-1	
15 Jun 1980	Australia	1-1	
18 Jun 1980	Australia	2-1	1
15 Oct 1980	Sweden	3-0	1
19 Nov 1980	Portugal	0-1	
14 Oct 1981	Scotland	0-0	
18 Nov 1981	Israel	1-0	
23 Feb 1982	England	0-4	
24 Mar 1982	France	0-4	
28 Apr 1982	Scotland	1-1	
28 May 1982	Wales	0-3	
21 Jun 1982	Honduras	1-1	

Above: Noel Brotherston

1 Jul 1982	Austria	2-2
13 Oct 1982	Austria	0-2
17 Nov 1982	West Germany	1-0
15 Dec 1982	Albania	0-0
30 Mar 1983	Turkey	2-1
27 Apr 1983	Albania	1-0
24 May 1983	Scotland	0-0
28 May 1983	England	0-0
31 May 1983	Wales	0-1
12 Oct 1983	Turkey	0-1
16 Oct 1984	Israel	3-0
1 May 1985	Turkey	2-0

535   MALACHY MARTIN (Mal) DONAGHY

Position   Defender

Born   Belfast, 13 September 1957

Clubs   Larne Town; Luton Town; Manchester United; Chelsea

Caps   91

Above: Mal Donaghy

Date	Team	Result	G
16 May 1980	Scotland	1-0	
20 May 1980	England	1-1	
23 May 1980	Wales	1-0	
15 Oct 1980	Sweden	3-0	
19 Nov 1980	Portugal	0-1	
19 May 1981	Scotland	0-2	
14 Oct 1981	Scotland	0-0	
18 Nov 1981	Israel	1-0	
23 Feb 1982	England	0-4	
24 Mar 1982	France	0-4	
28 Apr 1982	Scotland	1-1	
28 May 1982	Wales	0-3	
17 Jun 1982	Yugoslavia	0-0	
21 Jun 1982	Honduras	1-1	
25 Jun 1982	Spain	1-0	
4 Jul 1982	France	1-4	
13 Oct 1982	Austria	0-2	
17 Nov 1982	West Germany	1-0	
15 Dec 1982	Albania	0-0	
30 Mar 1983	Turkey	2-1	
27 Apr 1983	Albania	1-0	
24 May 1983	Scotland	0-0	
28 May 1983	England	0-0	
31 May 1983	Wales	0-1	
21 Sep 1983	Austria	3-1	
12 Oct 1983	Turkey	0-1	
16 Nov 1983	West Germany	1-0	
13 Dec 1983	Scotland	2-0	
4 Apr 1984	England	0-1	
22 May 1984	Wales	1-1	
27 May 1984	Finland	0-1	
12 Sep 1984	Romania	3-2	
14 Nov 1984	Finland	2-1	
27 Feb 1985	England	0-1	
27 Mar 1985	Spain	0-0	
1 May 1985	Turkey	2-0	
11 Sep 1985	Turkey	0-0	
16 Oct 1985	Romania	1-0	
13 Nov 1985	England	0-0	
26 Feb 1986	France	0-0	
26 Mar 1986	Denmark	1-1	
23 Apr 1986	Morocco	2-1	
3 Jun 1986	Algeria	1-1	
7 Jun 1986	Spain	1-2	
12 Jun 1986	Brazil	0-3	
15 Oct 1986	England	0-3	
12 Nov 1986	Turkey	0-0	
17 Feb 1987	Israel	1-1	
1 Apr 1987	England	0-2	
29 Apr 1987	Yugoslavia	1-2	
14 Oct 1987	Yugoslavia	0-3	
11 Nov 1987	Turkey	1-0	
17 Feb 1988	Greece	2-3	
23 Mar 1988	Poland	1-1	
28 Apr 1988	France	0-0	
21 May 1988	Malta	3-0	
14 Sep 1988	Republic of Ireland	0-0	
19 Oct 1988	Hungary	0-1	
21 Dec 1988	Spain	0-4	
8 Feb 1989	Spain	0-2	
26 Apr 1989	Malta	2-0	
26 May 1989	Chile	0-1	
11 Oct 1989	Republic of Ireland	0-3	
27 Mar 1990	Norway	2-3	
12 Sep 1990	Yugoslavia	0-2	
17 Oct 1990	Denmark	1-1	
14 Nov 1990	Austria	0-0	
5 Feb 1991	Poland	3-1	
27 Mar 1991	Yugoslavia	1-4	
1 May 1991	Faroe Islands	1-1	
11 Sep 1991	Faroe Islands	5-0	
16 Oct 1991	Austria	2-1	
13 Nov 1991	Denmark	1-2	

19 Feb 1992	Scotland	0-1
28 Apr 1992	Lithuania	2-2
2 Jun 1992	Germany	1-1
9 Sep 1992	Albania	3-0
14 Oct 1992	Spain	0-0
18 Nov 1992	Denmark	0-1
17 Feb 1993	Albania	2-1
31 Mar 1993	Republic of Ireland	0-3
28 Apr 1993	Spain	1-3
25 May 1993	Lithuania	1-0
2 Jun 1993	Latvia	2-1
8 Sep 1993	Latvia	2-0
13 Oct 1993	Denmark	0-1
17 Nov 1993	Republic of Ireland	1-1
23 Mar 1994	Romania	2-0
20 Apr 1994	Liechtenstein	4-1
3 Jun 1994	Colombia	0-2
11 Jun 1994	Mexico	0-3

536   JOHN McCLELLAND

Position   Central defender

Born   Belfast, 7 December 1955

Clubs   Portadown; Cardiff City; Bangor;
Mansfield Town; Glasgow Rangers;
Watford; Leeds United; Watford (loan);
Notts County loan); St Johnstone; Carrick
Rangers; Arbroath; Wycombe Wanderers;
Yeovil Town; Darlington

Above: John McClelland

Caps   53   Goals   1

Date	Team	Result	G
16 May 1980	Scotland	1-0	
11 Jun 1980	Australia	2-1	
15 Jun 1980	Australia	1-1	
18 Jun 1980	Australia	2-1	
15 Oct 1980	Sweden	3-0	
25 Mar 1981	Scotland	1-1	
19 May 1981	Scotland	0-2	
3 Jun 1981	Sweden	0-1	
28 Apr 1982	Scotland	1-1	
28 May 1982	Wales	0-3	
17 Jun 1982	Yugoslavia	0-0	
21 Jun 1982	Honduras	1-1	
25 Jun 1982	Spain	1-0	
1 Jul 1982	Austria	2-2	
4 Jul 1982	France	1-4	
13 Oct 1982	Austria	0-2	
17 Nov 1982	West Germany	1-0	
15 Dec 1982	Albania	0-0	
30 Mar 1983	Turkey	2-1	1
27 Apr 1983	Albania	1-0	
24 May 1983	Scotland	0-0	
28 May 1983	England	0-0	
31 May 1983	Wales	0-1	
21 Sep 1983	Austria	3-1	
12 Oct 1983	Turkey	0-1	
16 Nov 1983	West Germany	1-0	
13 Dec 1983	Scotland	2-0	
4 Apr 1984	England	0-1	
22 May 1984	Wales	1-1	
27 May 1984	Finland	0-1	
12 Sep 1984	Romania	3-2	
16 Oct 1984	Israel	3-0	
14 Nov 1984	Finland	2-1	
27 Feb 1985	England	0-1	
27 Mar 1985	Spain	0-0	
1 May 1985	Turkey	2-0	
11 Sep 1985	Turkey	0-0	
26 Feb 1986	France	0-0	
15 Oct 1986	England	0-3	
12 Nov 1986	Turkey	0-0	
17 Feb 1987	Israel	1-1	
1 Apr 1987	England	0-2	
29 Apr 1987	Yugoslavia	1-2	
1 Nov 1987	Turkey	1-0	
17 Feb 1988	Greece	2-3	
28 Apr 1988	France	0-0	
21 May 1988	Malta	3-0	
14 Sep 1988	Republic of Ireland	0-0	
19 Oct 1988	Hungary	0-1	
21 Dec 1988	Spain	0-4	
8 Feb 1989	Spain	0-2	
26 Apr 1989	Malta	2-0	
27 Mar 1990	Norway	2-3	

537   JOHN PATRICK O'NEILL

Position   Central defender

Born   Derry, 11 March 1958

Clubs   Derry BC; Leicester City; Queen's Park
Rangers; Norwich City

Caps   39   Goals   2

Date	Team	Result	G
26 Mar 1980	Israel	0-0	
16 May 1980	Scotland	1-0	
20 May 1980	England	1-1	
23 May 1980	Wales	1-0	
11 Jun 1980	Australia	2-1	1
15 Jun 1980	Australia	1-1	
18 Jun 1980	Australia	2-1	
19 Nov 1980	Portugal	0-1	
25 Mar 1981	Scotland	1-1	
29 Apr 1981	Portugal	1-0	
19 May 1981	Scotland	0-2	
3 Jun 1981	Sweden	0-1	
14 Oct 1981	Scotland	0-0	
18 Nov 1981	Israel	1-0	
23 Feb 1982	England	0-4	
24 Mar 1982	France	0-4	
28 Apr 1982	Scotland	1-1	
4 Jul 1982	France	1-4	
13 Oct 1982	Austria	0-2	
17 Nov 1982	West Germany	1-0	
15 Dec 1982	Albania	0-0	
30 Mar 1983	Turkey	2-1	
27 Apr 1983	Albania	1-0	
24 May 1983	Scotland	0-0	
13 Dec 1983	Scotland	2-0	
16 Oct 1984	Israel	3-0	
14 Nov 1984	Finland	2-1	1
27 Feb 1985	England	0-1	
27 Mar 1985	Spain	0-0	
1 May 1985	Turkey	2-0	
11 Sep 1985	Turkey	0-0	
16 Oct 1985	Romania	1-0	
13 Nov 1985	England	0-0	
26 Feb 1986	France	0-0	
26 Mar 1986	Denmark	1-1	
23 Apr 1986	Morocco	2-1	
3 Jun 1986	Algeria	1-1	
7 Jun 1986	Spain	1-2	
12 Jun 1986	Brazil	0-3	

538   COLIN CHARLES McCURDY

Position   Forward

Born   Belfast, 18 July 1954

Clubs   Linfield; Philadelphia Furies; Larne; Crusaders

Caps   1   Goals   1

Date	Team	Result	G
18 Jun 1980	Australia	2-1	1

539   ROBERT McFAUL CAMPBELL

Position   Forward

Born   Belfast, 13 September 1956

Clubs   Aston Villa; Halifax Town (loan);

Huddersfield Town; Sheffield United; Vancouver Whitecaps; Huddersfield Town; Halifax Town; Brisbane City; Bradford City; Derby County; Bradford City; Wigan Athletic; Guiseley

Caps   2

Date	Team	Result	G
28 Apr 1982	Scotland	1-1	
28 May 1982	Wales	0-3	

540   JIM CLEARY

Position   Wing-half

Clubs   Glentoran

Caps   5

Date	Team	Result	G
28 Apr 1982	Scotland	1-1	
28 May 1982	Wales	0-3	
31 May 1983	Wales	0-1	
12 Oct 1983	Turkey	0-1	
16 Oct 1984	Israel	3-0	

541   P J HEALY

Position   Forward

Clubs   Coleraine; Glentoran

Caps   4

Date	Team	Result	G
28 Apr 1982	Scotland	1-1	
28 May 1982	Wales	0-3	
21 Jun 1982	Honduras	1-1	
13 Oct 1982	Austria	0-2	

542   NORMAN WHITESIDE

Position   Midfield/Forward

Born   Belfast, 7 May 1965

Clubs   Manchester United; Everton

Caps   38   Goals   9

Date	Team	Result	G
17 Jun 1982	Yugoslavia	0-0	
21 Jun 1982	Honduras	1-1	
25 Jun 1982	Spain	1-0	
1 Jul 1982	Austria	2-2	
4 Jul 1982	France	1-4	
17 Nov 1982	West Germany	1-0	
15 Dec 1982	Albania	0-0	
30 Mar 1983	Turkey	2-1	
21 Sep 1983	Austria	3-1	1
12 Oct 1983	Turkey	0-1	
16 Nov 1983	West Germany	1-0	1

Above: Norman Whiteside

Above: Ian Stewart

Date	Team	Result	G
13 Dec 1983	Denmark	2-0	1
4 Apr 1984	England	0-1	
22 May 1984	Wales	1-1	
27 May 1984	Finland	0-1	
12 Sep 1984	Romania	3-2	1
16 Oct 1984	Israel	3-0	1
14 Nov 1984	Finland	2-1	
27 Feb 1985	England	0-1	
27 Mar 1985	Spain	0-0	
1 May 1995	Turkey	2-0	2
16 Oct 1985	Romania	1-0	
13 Nov 1985	England	0-0	
26 Feb 1986	France	0-0	
26 Mar 1986	Denmark	1-1	
23 Apr 1986	Morocco	2-1	
3 Jun 1986	Algeria	1-1	1
7 Jun 1986	Spain	1-2	
12 Jun 1986	Brazil	0-3	
15 Oct 1986	England	0-3	
17 Feb 1987	Israel	1-1	
1 Apr 1987	England	0-2	
29 Apr 1987	Yugoslavia	1-2	
11 Nov 1987	Turkey	1-0	
23 Mar 1988	Poland	1-1	
28 Apr 1988	France	0-0	
6 Sep 1989	Hungary	1-2	1
11 Oct 1989	Republic of Ireland	0-3	

543	IAN EDWIN STEWART		

Position   Left-winger

Born   Belfast, 10 September 1961

Clubs   Queen's Park Rangers; Millwall (loan); Newcastle United; Portsmouth; Brentford (loan); Aldershot

Caps   31   Goals   2

Date	Team	Result	G
24 Mar 1982	France	0-4	
13 Oct 1982	Austria	0-2	
17 Nov 1982	West Germany	1-0	1
15 Dec 1982	Albania	0-0	
3 Mar 1983	Turkey	2-1	
27 Apr 1983	Albania	1-0	1
24 May 1983	Scotland	0-0	
28 May 1983	England	0-0	
31 May 1983	Wales	0-1	
21 Sep 1983	Austria	3-1	
12 Oct 1983	Turkey	0-1	
16 Nov 1983	West Germany	1-0	
13 Dec 1983	Scotland	2-0	
4 Apr 1984	England	0-1	
22 May 1984	Wales	1-1	
27 May 1984	Finland	0-1	
12 Sep 1984	Romania	3-2	
16 Oct 1984	Israel	3-0	
14 Nov 1984	Finland	2-1	
27 Feb 1985	England	0-1	

27 Mar 1985	Spain	0-0	
1 May 1985	Turkey	2-0	
16 Oct 1985	Romania	1-0	
13 Nov 1985	England	0-0	
26 Mar 1986	Denmark	1-1	
23 Apr 1986	Morocco	2-1	
3 Jun 1986	Algeria	1-1	
7 Jun 1986	Spain	1-2	
12 Jun 1986	Brazil	0-3	
15 Oct 1986	England	0-3	
17 Feb 1987	Israel	1-1	

DID YOU KNOW?

When Ian Stewart scored the only goal for Northern Ireland against West Germany on 17 November 1982 at Windsor Park, it was his first in senior soccer. At one time on the dole in his younger days, he had played the guitar to earn a living.

544   GERRY MULLAN

Position   Winger

Clubs   Glentoran

Caps   4

Date	Team	Result	G
27 Apr 1983	Albania	1-0	
24 May 1983	Scotland	0-0	
28 May 1983	England	0-0	
31 May 1983	Wales	0-1	

545   PAUL CHRISTOPHER RAMSEY

Position   Midfield/Right-back

Born   Derry, 3 September 1962

Clubs   Leicester City; Cardiff City; St Johnstone; Cardiff City (loan); Telford United; Torquay United

Caps   14

Date	Team	Result	G
21 Sep 1983	Austria	3-1	
16 Nov 1983	West Germany	1-0	
13 Dec 1983	Scotland	2-0	
16 Oct 1984	Israel	3-0	
27 Feb 1985	England	0-1	
27 Mar 1985	Spain	0-0	
1 May 1985	Turkey	2-0	
11 Sep 1985	Turkey	0-0	
23 Apr 1986	Morocco	2-1	
17 Feb 1987	Israel	1-1	
1 Apr 1987	England	0-2	
29 Apr 1987	Yugoslavia	1-2	
14 Oct 1987	Yugoslavia	0-3	
8 Feb 1989	Spain	0-2	

546   GERARD McELHINNEY

Position   Central defender

Born   Derry, 19 September 1956

Clubs   Distillery; Bolton Wanderers; Rochdale (loan); Plymouth Argyle; Peterborough United

Caps   6

Date	Team	Result	G
16 Nov 1983	West Germany	1-0	
13 Dec 1983	Scotland	2-0	
4 Apr 1984	England	0-1	
22 May 1984	Wales	1-1	
27 May 1984	Finland	0-1	
12 Sep 1984	Romania	3-2	

547   NIGEL WORTHINGTON

Position   Left-back/Midfield

Born   Ballymena, 4 November 1961

Clubs   Ballymena United; Notts County; Sheffield Wednesday; Leeds United; Stoke City; Blackpool

Caps   66

Above: Nigel Worthington

Date	Team	Result	G
22 May 1984	Wales	1-1	
27 May 1984	Finland	0-1	
16 Oct 1984	Israel	3-0	
27 Mar 1985	Spain	0-0	
11 Sep 1985	Turkey	0-0	
16 Oct 1985	Romania	1-0	
13 Nov 1985	England	0-0	
26 Mar 1986	Denmark	1-1	
3 Jun 1986	Algeria	1-1	
7 Jun 1986	Spain	1-2	
15 Oct 1986	England	0-3	
12 Nov 1986	Turkey	0-0	
17 Feb 1987	Israel	1-1	
1 Apr 1987	England	0-2	
29 Apr 1987	Yugoslavia	1-2	
14 Oct 1987	Yugoslavia	0-3	
11 Nov 1987	Turkey	1-0	
17 Feb 1988	Greece	2-3	
23 Mar 1988	Poland	1-1	
28 Apr 1988	France	0-0	
21 May 1988	Malta	3-0	
14 Sep 1988	Republic of Ireland	0-0	
19 Oct 1998	Hungary	0-1	
21 Dec 1988	Spain	0-4	
26 Apr 1989	Malta	2-0	
6 Sep 1989	Hungary	1-2	
11 Oct 1989	Republic of Ireland	0-3	
18 May 1990	Uruguay	1-0	
12 Sep 1990	Yugoslavia	0-2	
17 Oct 1990	Denmark	1-1	
14 Nov 1990	Austria	0-0	
1 May 1991	Faroe Islands	1-1	
16 Oct 1991	Austria	2-1	
13 Nov 1991	Denmark	1-2	
19 Feb 1992	Scotland	0-1	
28 Apr 1992	Lithuania	2-2	
2 Jun 1992	Germany	1-1	
9 Sep 1992	Albania	3-0	
14 Oct 1992	Spain	0-0	
18 Nov 1992	Denmark	0-1	
31 Mar 1993	Republic of Ireland	0-3	
28 Apr 1993	Spain	1-3	
25 May 1993	Lithuania	1-0	
2 Jun 1993	Latvia	2-1	
8 Sep 1993	Latvia	2-0	
13 Oct 1993	Denmark	0-1	
17 Nov 1993	Republic of Ireland	1-1	
20 Apr 1994	Liechtenstein	4-1	
3 Jun 1994	Colombia	0-2	
11 Jun 1994	Mexico	0-3	
7 Sep 1994	Portugal	1-2	
12 Oct 1994	Austria	2-1	
16 Nov 1994	Republic of Ireland	0-4	
29 Mar 1995	Republic of Ireland	1-1	
26 Apr 1995	Latvia	1-0	
22 May 1995	Canada	0-2	
25 May 1995	Chile	1-2	
7 Jun 1995	Latvia	1-2	
3 Sep 1995	Portugal	1-1	
11 Oct 1995	Liechtenstein	4-0	
15 Nov 1995	Austria	5-3	
27 Mar 1996	Norway	0-2	
24 Apr 1996	Sweden	1-2	
29 May 1996	Germany	1-1	
22 Jan 1997	Italy	0-2	

11 Feb 1997	Belgium	3-0	

548   GEORGE THOMAS DUNLOP

Position   Goalkeeper

Born   Belfast, 16 January 1956

Clubs   Manchester City; Ballymena; Glentoran; Linfield

Caps   4

Date	Team	Result	G
16 Oct 1984	Israel	3-0	
1 Apr 1987	England	0-2	
29 Apr 1987	Yugoslavia	1-2	
11 Oct 1989	Republic of Ireland	0-3	

549   LEE DOHERTY

Position   Forward

Born   Belfast, 31 March 1963

Clubs   Linfield; Glenavon; Bangor

Caps   2   Goals   1

Date	Team	Result	G
16 Oct 1984	Israel	3-0	1
11 Nov 1987	Turkey	1-0	

550   STEVEN ALEXANDER PENNEY

Position   Winger

Born   Ballymena, 6 January 1964

Clubs   Ballymena United; Brighton & Hove Albion; Heart of Midlothian; Burnley

Caps   17   Goals   2

Date	Team	Result	G
16 Oct 1984	Israel	3-0	
11 Sep 1985	Turkey	0-0	
16 Oct 1985	Romania	1-0	
13 Nov 1985	England	0-0	
26 Feb 1986	France	0-0	
26 Mar 1986	Denmark	1-1	
23 Apr 1986	Morocco	2-1	
3 Jun 1986	Algeria	1-1	
7 Jun 1986	Spain	1-2	
15 Oct 1986	England	0-3	
12 Nov 1986	Turkey	0-0	
17 Feb 1987	Israel	1-1	1
23 Mar 1988	Poland	1-1	
28 Apr 1988	France	0-0	
21 May 1988	Malta	3-0	1
14 Sep 1988	Republic of Ireland	0-0	
21 Dec 1988	Spain	0-4	

Above: Jimmy Quinn

Date	Team	Result	G
28 Apr 1988	France	0-0	
21 May 1988	Malta	3-0	1
14 Sep 1988	Republic of Ireland	0-0	
19 Oct 1988	Hungary	0-1	
21 Dec 1988	Spain	0-4	
8 Feb 1989	Spain	0-2	
26 Apr 1989	Malta	2-0	
26 May 1989	Chile	0-1	
6 Sep 1989	Hungary	1-2	
27 Mar 1990	Norway	2-3	1
27 Mar 1991	Yugoslavia	1-4	
28 Apr 1992	Lithuania	2-2	
14 Oct 1992	Spain	0-0	
18 Nov 1992	Denmark	0-1	
17 Feb 1993	Albania	2-1	
31 Mar 1993	Republic of Ireland	0-3	
2 Jun 1993	Latvia	2-1	
8 Sep 1993	Latvia	2-0	1
13 Oct 1993	Denmark	0-1	
17 Nov 1993	Republic of Ireland	1-1	1
23 Mar 1994	Romania	2-0	
20 Apr 1994	Liechtenstein	4-1	2
3 Jun 1994	Colombia	0-2	
11 Jun 1994	Mexico	0-3	
7 Sep 1994	Portugal	1-2	1
12 Oct 1994	Austria	2-1	
26 Apr 1995	Latvia	1-0	
11 Oct 1995	Liechtenstein	4-0	1
15 Nov 1995	Austria	5-3	

552   MARTIN McGAUGHEY

Position   Forward

Clubs   Linfield

Caps   1

Date	Team	Result	G
16 Oct 1984	Israel	3-0	

553   ALAN McDONALD

Position   Central defender

Born   Belfast, 12 October 1963

Clubs   Queen's Park Rangers; Charlton Athletic; Swindon Town

Caps   52   Goals   3

Date	Team	Result	G
16 Oct 1985	Romania	1-0	
13 Nov 1985	England	0-0	
26 Feb 1986	France	0-0	
26 Mar 1986	Denmark	1-1	1
23 Apr 1986	Morocco	2-1	
3 Jun 1986	Algeria	1-1	
7 Jun 1986	Spain	1-2	
12 Jun 1986	Brazil	0-3	
15 Oct 1986	England	0-3	
12 Nov 1986	Turkey	0-0	
17 Feb 1987	Israel	1-1	

551   JAMES MARTIN (JIMMY) QUINN

Position   Forward

Born   Belfast, 18 November 1959

Clubs   Oswestry Town; Swindon Town; Blackburn Rovers; Swindon Town; Leicester City; Bradford City; West Ham United; Bournemouth; Reading; Peterborough United

Caps   46   Goals   12

Date	Team	Result	G
16 Oct 1984	Israel	3-0	1
14 Nov 1984	Finland	2-1	
27 Feb 1985	England	0-1	
27 Mar 1985	Spain	0-0	
1 May 1985	Turkey	2-0	
11 Sep 1985	Turkey	0-0	
16 Oct 1985	Romania	1-0	1
13 Nov 1985	England	0-0	
26 Feb 1986	France	0-0	
26 Mar 1986	Denmark	1-1	
23 Apr 1986	Morocco	2-1	1
15 Oct 1986	England	0-3	
12 Nov 1986	Turkey	0-0	
14 Oct 1987	Yugoslavia	0-3	
11 Nov 1987	Turkey	1-0	1
17 Feb 1988	Greece	2-3	
23 Mar 1988	Poland	1-1	

1 Apr 1987	England	0-2	
29 Apr 1987	Yugoslavia	1-2	
14 Oct 1987	Yugoslavia	0-3	
11 Nov 1987	Turkey	1-0	
23 Mar 1988	Poland	1-1	
28 Apr 1988	France	0-0	
21 May 1988	Malta	3-0	
14 Sep 1988	Republic of Ireland	0-0	
19 Oct 1988	Hungary	0-1	
21 Dec 1988	Spain	0-4	
26 May 1989	Chile	0-1	
6 Sep 1989	Hungary	1-2	
11 Oct 1989	Republic of Ireland	0-3	
18 May 1990	Uruguay	1-0	
12 Sep 1990	Yugoslavia	0-2	
17 Oct 1990	Denmark	1-1	
14 Nov 1990	Austria	0-0	
1 May 1991	Faroe Islands	1-1	
11 Sep 1991	Faroe Islands	5-0	1
19 Feb 1992	Scotland	0-1	
28 Apr 1992	Lithuania	2-2	
2 Jun 1992	Germany	1-1	
9 Sep 1992	Albania	3-0	
14 Oct 1992	Spain	0-0	
18 Nov 1992	Denmark	0-1	
17 Feb 1993	Albania	2-1	1
31 Mar 1993	Republic of Ireland	0-3	
28 Apr 1993	Spain	1-3	
25 May 1993	Lithuania	1-0	
2 Jun 1993	Latvia	2-1	
13 Oct 1993	Denmark	0-1	
17 Nov 1993	Republic of Ireland	1-1	
7 Sep 1994	Portugal	1-2	

12 Oct 1994	Austria	2-1	
29 Mar 1995	Republic of Ireland	1-1	
26 Apr 1995	Latvia	1-0	
22 May 1995	Canada	0-2	
25 May 1995	Chile	1-2	
7 Jun 1995	Latvia	1-2	
15 Nov 1995	Austria	5-3	
27 Mar 1996	Norway	0-2	

554	COLIN JOHN CLARKE

Position   Forward

Born   Newry, 30 October 1962

Clubs   Ipswich Town; Peterborough United;
            Gillingham (loan); Tranmere Rovers;
            Bournemouth; Southampton; Queen's
            Park Rangers; Portsmouth

Caps   38   Goals   13

Date	Team	Result	G
26 Feb 1986	France	0-0	
26 Mar 1986	Denmark	1-1	
23 Apr 1986	Morocco	2-1	1
3 Jun 1986	Algeria	1-1	
7 Jun 1986	Spain	1-2	1
12 Jun 1986	Brazil	0-3	
15 Oct 1986	England	0-3	
12 Nov 1986	Turkey	0-0	
29 Apr 1987	Yugoslavia	1-2	1

Above: Alan McDonald

Above: Colin Clarke

Date	Team	Result	G
14 Oct 1987	Yugoslavia	0-3	
11 Nov 1987	Turkey	1-0	
17 Feb 1988	Greece	2-3	2
23 Mar 1988	Poland	1-1	
28 Apr 1988	France	0-0	
21 May 1988	Malta	3-0	1
14 Sep 1988	Republic of Ireland	0-0	
19 Oct 1988	Hungary	0-1	
21 Dec 1988	Spain	0-4	
8 Feb 1989	Spain	0-2	
26 Apr 1989	Malta	2-0	1
26 May 1989	Chile	0-1	
6 Sep 1989	Hungary	1-2	
11 Oct 1989	Republic of Ireland	0-3	
27 Mar 1990	Norway	2-3	
12 Sep 1990	Yugoslavia	0-2	
17 Oct 1990	Denmark	1-1	1
14 Nov 1990	Austria	0-0	
5 Feb 1991	Poland	3-1	
27 Mar 1991	Yugoslavia	1-4	
1 May 1991	Faroe Islands	1-1	1
11 Sep 1991	Faroe Islands	5-0	3
16 Oct 1991	Austria	2-1	
13 Nov 1991	Denmark	1-2	
19 Feb 1992	Scotland	0-1	
2 Jun 1992	Germany	1-1	
9 Sep 1992	Albania	3-0	1
14 Oct 1992	Spain	0-0	
18 Nov 1992	Denmark	0-1	

555   MARK CAUGHEY

Position   Forward

Born   Belfast, 27 August 1960

Clubs   RUC; Linfield; Hibernian; Glentoran; Bangor

Caps   2

Date	Team	Result	G
26 Feb 1986	France	0-0	
26 Mar 1986	Denmark	1-1	

556   BERNARD ANTHONY McNALLY

Position   Midfield

Born   Shrewsbury, 17 February 1963

Clubs   Shrewsbury Town; West Bromwich Albion

Caps   5

Date	Team	Result	G
23 Apr 1986	Morocco	2-1	
12 Nov 1986	Turkey	0-0	
14 Oct 1987	Yugoslavia	0-3	
17 Feb 1988	Greece	2-3	
21 May 1988	Malta	3-0	

557   DAVID ANTHONY CAMPBELL

Position   Midfield

Born   Derry, 2 June 1965

Clubs   Nottingham Forest; Notts County (loan); Charlton Athletic; Plymouth Argyle (loan) Bradford City; Shamrock Rovers; Rotherham United; Burnley; Lincoln City; Wigan Athletic; Cambridge United

Caps   10

Date	Team	Result	G
23 Apr 1986	Morocco	2-1	
12 Jun 1986	Brazil	0-3	
15 Oct 1986	England	0-3	
12 Nov 1986	Turkey	0-0	
1 Apr 1987	England	0-2	
29 Apr 1987	Yugoslavia	1-2	
14 Oct 1987	Yugoslavia	0-3	
11 Nov 1987	Turkey	1-0	
17 Feb 1988	Greece	2-3	
23 Mar 1988	Poland	1-1	

558   GARY JAMES FLEMING

Position   Full-back

Born   Derry, 17 February 1967

Clubs   Nottingham Forest; Manchester City; Notts County (loan); Barnsley

Caps   31

Date	Team	Result	G
15 Oct 1986	England	0-3	
17 Feb 1987	Israel	1-1	
1 Apr 1987	England	0-2	
29 Apr 1987	Yugoslavia	1-2	
11 Nov 1987	Turkey	1-0	
17 Feb 1988	Greece	2-3	
23 Mar 1988	Poland	1-1	
26 Apr 1989	Malta	2-0	
26 May 1989	Chile	0-1	
6 Sep 1989	Hungary	1-2	
11 Oct 1989	Republic of Ireland	0-3	
27 Mar 1991	Yugoslavia	1-4	
28 Apr 1992	Lithuania	2-2	
2 Jun 1992	Germany	1-1	
9 Sep 1992	Albania	3-0	
14 Oct 1992	Spain	0-0	
18 Nov 1992	Denmark	0-1	
17 Feb 1993	Albania	2-1	
28 Apr 1993	Spain	1-3	
25 May 1993	Lithuania	1-0	
2 Jun 1993	Latvia	2-1	
8 Sep 1993	Latvia	2-0	
13 Oct 1993	Denmark	0-1	
17 Nov 1993	Republic of Ireland	1-1	
23 Mar 1994	Romania	2-0	
20 Apr 1994	Liechtenstein	4-1	
3 Jun 1994	Colombia	0-2	

Date	Team	Result
11 Jun 1994	Mexico	0-3
7 Sep 1994	Portugal	1-2
12 Oct 1994	Austria	2-1
16 Nov 1994	Republic of Ireland 0-4

559   PHILIP ANTHONY HUGHES

Position   Goalkeeper

Born   Belfast, 19 November 1964

Clubs   Manchester United; Leeds United; Bury; Wigan Athletic; Rochdale; Scarborough

Caps   3

Date	Team	Result	G
15 Oct 1986	England	0-3	
12 Nov 1986	Turkey	0-0	
17 Feb 1987	Israel	1-1	

560   DANIEL JOSEPH WILSON

Position   Midfield

Born   Wigan, 1 January 1960

Clubs   Wigan Athletic; Bury; Chesterfield; Nottingham Forest; Scunthorpe United; Brighton & Hove Albion; Luton Town; Sheffield Wednesday; Barnsley

Caps   24   Goals   1

Date	Team	Result	G
12 Nov 1986	Turkey	0-0	
17 Feb 1987	Israel	1-1	
1 Apr 1987	England	0-2	
14 Oct 1987	Yugoslavia	0-3	
11 Nov 1987	Turkey	1-0	
17 Feb 1988	Greece	2-3	
23 Mar 1988	Poland	1-1	1
28 Apr 1988	France	0-0	
21 May 1988	Malta	3-0	
14 Sep 1988	Republic of Ireland 0-0		
19 Oct 1988	Hungary	0-1	
8 Feb 1989	Spain	0-2	
26 Apr 1989	Malta	2-0	
26 May 1989	Chile	0-1	
6 Sep 1989	Hungary	1-2	
11 Oct 1989	Republic of Ireland 0-3		
27 Mar 1990	Norway	2-3	
18 May 1990	Uruguay	1-0	
12 Sep 1990	Yugoslavia	0-2	
17 Oct 1990	Denmark	1-1	
14 Nov 1990	Austria	0-0	
1 May 1991	Faroe Islands	1-1	
16 Oct 1991	Austria	2-1	
19 Feb 1992	Scotland	0-1	

Above: Lawrie Sanchez

561   LAWRENCE PHILLIP (LAWRIE) SANCHEZ

Position   Midfield

Born   Lambeth, 22 October 1959

Clubs   Thatcham Town; Reading; Wimbledon; Swindon Town

Caps   3

Date	Team	Result	G
12 Nov 1986	Turkey	0-0	
8 Feb 1989	Spain	0-2	
26 Apr 1989	Malta	2-0	

562   KEVIN JAMES WILSON

Position   Forward

Born   Banbury, 18 April 1961

Clubs   Banbury United; Derby County; Ipswich Town; Chelsea; Notts County; Bradford City (loan); Walsall; Northampton Town

Caps   42   Goals   6

Date	Team	Result	G
17 Feb 1987	Israel	1-1	
1 Apr 1987	England	0-2	
29 Apr 1987	Yugoslavia	1-2	

Date	Team	Result	G
14 Oct 1987	Yugoslavia	0-3	
11 Nov 1987	Turkey	1-0	
17 Feb 1988	Greece	2-3	
23 Mar 1988	Poland	1-1	
28 Apr 1988	France	0-0	
19 Oct 1988	Hungary	0-1	
21 Dec 1988	Spain	0-4	
8 Feb 1989	Spain	0-2	
26 Apr 1989	Malta	2-0	
26 May 1989	Chile	0-1	
11 Oct 1989	Republic of Ireland	0-3	
27 Mar 1990	Norway	2-3	1
18 May 1990	Uruguay	1-0	1
12 Sep 1990	Yugoslavia	0-2	
14 Nov 1990	Austria	0-0	
5 Feb 1991	Poland	3-1	
27 Mar 1991	Yugoslavia	1-4	
1 May 1991	Faroe Islands	1-1	
11 Sep 1991	Faroe Islands	5-0	1
16 Oct 1991	Austria	2-1	
13 Nov 1991	Denmark	1-2	
19 Feb 1992	Scotland	0-1	
28 Apr 1992	Lithuania	2-2	1
2 Jun 1992	Germany	1-1	
9 Sep 1992	Albania	3-0	1
14 Oct 1992	Spain	0-0	
18 Nov 1992	Denmark	0-1	
28 Apr 1993	Spain	1-3	1
25 May 1993	Lithuania	1-0	
2 Jun 1993	Latvia	2-1	
8 Sep 1993	Latvia	2-0	
13 Oct 1993	Denmark	0-1	
17 Nov 1993	Republic of Ireland	1-1	
23 Mar 1994	Romania	2-0	
20 Apr 1994	Liechtenstein	4-1	
3 Jun 1994	Colombia	0-2	
11 Jun 1994	Mexico	0-3	
16 Nov 1994	Republic of Ireland	0-4	
26 Apr 1995	Latvia	1-0	

563 RAYMOND K McCOY

Position   Midfield

Clubs   Coleraine

Caps   1

Date	Team	Result	G
29 Apr 1987	Yugoslavia	1-2	

564 ALLEN DARRELL McKNIGHT

Position   Goalkeeper

Born   Antrim, 27 January 1964

Clubs   Distillery; Glasgow Celtic; Albion Rovers; West Ham United; Airdrieonians; Rotherham United; Walsall; South China (Hong Kong); Exeter City

Caps   10

Date	Team	Result	G
14 Oct 1987	Yugoslavia	0-3	
11 Nov 1987	Turkey	1-0	
17 Feb 1988	Greece	2-3	
23 Mar 1988	Poland	1-1	
28 Apr 1988	France	0-0	
21 May 1988	Malta	3-0	
14 Sep 1988	Republic of Ireland	0-0	
19 Oct 1988	Hungary	0-1	
21 Dec 1988	Spain	0-4	
8 Feb 1989	Spain	0-2	

565 ANTON GERARD PATRICK ROGAN

Position   Defender

Born   Belfast, 25 March 1966

Clubs   Glasgow Celtic; Sunderland; Oxford United; Millwall; Blackpool

Caps   18

Date	Team	Result	G
14 Oct 1987	Yugoslavia	0-3	
17 Feb 1988	Greece	2-3	
23 Mar 1988	Poland	1-1	
14 Sep 1988	Republic of Ireland	0-0	
19 Oct 1988	Hungary	0-1	
21 Dec 1988	Spain	0-4	
8 Feb 1989	Spain	0-2	
26 Apr 1989	Malta	2-0	
26 May 1989	Chile	0-1	
6 Sep 1989	Hungary	1-2	
27 Mar 1990	Norway	2-3	
18 May 1992	Uruguay	1-0	
12 Sep 1990	Yugoslavia	0-2	
17 Oct 1990	Denmark	1-1	
14 Nov 1990	Austria	0-0	
27 Mar 1991	Yugoslavia	1-4	
28 Apr 1992	Lithuania	2-2	
9 Nov 1996	Germany	1-1	

566 MICHAEL ANDREW MARTIN O'NEILL

Position   Forward

Born   Portadown, 5 July 1969

Clubs   Coleraine; Newcastle United; Dundee United; Hibernian; Coventry City; Aberdeen (loan); Reading (loan); Wigan Athletic; St Johnstone

Caps   31   Goals   4

Date	Team	Result	G
17 Feb 1988	Greece	2-3	
23 Mar 1988	Poland	1-1	
28 Apr 1988	France	0-0	
21 May 1988	Malta	3-0	
14 Sep 1988	Republic of Ireland	0-0	
19 Oct 1988	Hungary	0-1	
21 Dec 1988	Spain	0-4	

8 Feb 1989	Spain	0-2	
26 Apr 1989	Malta	2-0	1
26 May 1989	Chile	0-1	
6 Sep 1989	Hungary	1-2	
11 Oct 1989	Republic of Ireland	0-3	
5 Feb 1991	Poland	3-1	
11 Sep 1991	Faroe Islands	5-0	
19 Feb 1992	Scotland	0-1	
2 Jun 1992	Germany	1-1	
9 Sep 1992	Albania	3-0	
17 Feb 1993	Albania	2-1	
31 Mar 1993	Republic of Ireland	0-3	
28 Apr 1993	Spain	1-3	
25 May 1993	Lithuania	1-0	
2 Jun 1993	Latvia	2-1	
20 Apr 1994	Liechtenstein	4-1	
12 Oct 1994	Austria	2-1	
16 Nov 1994	Republic of Ireland	0-4	
11 Oct 1995	Liechtenstein	4-0	1
15 Nov 1995	Austria	5-3	2
27 Mar 1996	Norway	0-2	
24 Apr 1996	Sweden	1-2	
31 Aug 1996	Ukraine	0-1	
5 Oct 1996	Armenia	1-1	

Above: Kingsley Black

567   ROBERT (Robbie) DENNISON

Position   Winger

Born   Banbridge, 30 April 1963

Clubs   Glenavon; West Bromwich Albion;
Wolverhampton Wanderers; Swansea City
(loan)

Caps   18

Date	Team	Result	G
28 Apr 1988	France	0-0	
21 May 1988	Malta	3-0	
19 Oct 1988	Hungary	0-1	
8 Feb 1989	Spain	0-2	
26 May 1989	Chile	0-1	
11 Oct 1989	Republic of Ireland	0-3	
18 May 1990	Uruguay	1-0	
12 Sep 1990	Yugoslavia	0-2	
14 Nov 1990	Austria	0-0	
5 Feb 1991	Poland	3-1	
27 Mar 1991	Yugoslavia	1-4	
1 May 1991	Faroe Islands	1-1	
11 Sep 1991	Faroe Islands	5-0	
16 Oct 1991	Austria	2-1	
13 Nov 1991	Denmark	1-2	
28 Apr 1993	Spain	1-3	
3 Jun 1994	Colombia	0-2	
22 Jan 1997	Italy	0-2	

568   KINGSLEY TERENCE BLACK

Position   Left winger

Born   Luton, 22 June 1968

Clubs   Luton Town; Nottingham Forest; Sheffield
United (loan); Millwall (loan); Grimsby
Town; Lincoln City

Caps   30   Goals   1

Date	Team	Result	G
28 Apr 1988	France	0-0	
21 May 1988	Malta	3-0	
14 Sep 1988	Republic of Ireland	0-0	
19 Oct 1988	Hungary	0-1	
21 Dec 1988	Spain	0-4	
8 Feb 1989	Spain	0-2	
26 May 1989	Chile	0-1	
6 Sept 1989	Hungary	1-2	
27 Mar 1990	Norway	2-3	
18 May 1990	Uruguay	1-0	
12 Sep 1990	Yugoslavia	0-2	
17 Oct 1990	Denmark	1-1	
14 Nov 1990	Austria	0-0	
5 Feb 1991	Poland	3-1	
27 Mar 1991	Yugoslavia	1-4	
1 May 1991	Faroe Islands	1-1	
11 Sep 1991	Faroe Islands	5-0	
16 Oct 1991	Austria	2-1	1
13 Nov 1991	Denmark	1-2	
19 Feb 1992	Scotland	0-1	

Date	Team	Result	G
28 Apr 1992	Lithuania	2-2	
2 Jun 1992	Germany	1-1	
14 Oct 1992	Spain	0-0	
18 Nov 1992	Denmark	0-1	
17 Feb 1993	Albania	2-1	
31 Mar 1993	Republic of Ireland	0-3	
28 Apr 1993	Spain	1-3	
13 Oct 1993	Denmark	0-1	
17 Nov 1993	Republic of Ireland	1-1	
23 Mar 1994	Romania	2-0	

569 THOMAS JAMES WRIGHT

Position   Goalkeeper

Born   Belfast, 29 August 1963

Clubs   Linfield; Newcastle United; Hull City (loan); Nottingham Forest; Reading (loan); Manchester City; Wrexham (loan); Newcastle United (loan); Bolton Wanderers (loan); Ballymena United

Caps   31

Date	Team	Result	G
26 Apr 1989	Malta	2-0	
26 May 1989	Chile	0-1	
6 Sep 1989	Hungary	1-2	
18 May 1990	Uruguay	1-0	
11 Sep 1991	Faroe Islands	5-0	
16 Oct 1991	Austria	2-1	
19 Feb 1992	Scotland	0-1	
2 Jun 1992	Germany	1-1	
9 Sep 1992	Albania	3-0	
14 Oct 1992	Spain	0-0	
17 Feb 1993	Albania	2-1	
31 Mar 1993	Republic of Ireland	0-3	
28 Apr 1993	Spain	1-3	
25 May 1993	Lithuania	1-0	
2 Jun 1993	Latvia	2-1	
8 Sep 1993	Latvia	2-0	
13 Oct 1993	Denmark	0-1	
17 Nov 1993	Republic of Ireland	1-1	
23 Mar 1994	Romania	2-0	
20 Apr 1994	Liechtenstein	4-1	
3 Jun 1994	Colombia	0-2	
11 Jun 1994	Mexico	0-3	
9 Nov 1996	Germany	1-1	
14 Dec 1996	Albania	2-0	
22 Jan 1997	Italy	0-2	
11 Feb 1997	Belgium	3-0	
29 Mar 1997	Portugal	0-0	
2 Apr 1997	Ukraine	1-2	
10 Sep 1997	Albania	0-1	
27 Apr 1999	Canada	1-1	
18 Aug 1999	France	0-1	

570 LIAM COYLE

Position   Midfield

Clubs   Derry City

Caps   1

Date	Team	Result	G
26 May 1989	Chile	0-1	

571 COLIN O'NEILL

Position   Midfield

Clubs   Ards; Larne; Ballymena; Portadown; Motherwell

Caps   3

Date	Team	Result	G
26 May 1989	Chile	0-1	
11 Oct 1989	Republic of Ireland	0-3	
17 Oct 1990	Denmark	1-1	

572 COLIN FREDERICK HILL

Position   Central defender

Born   Uxbridge, 12 November 1963

Clubs   Arsenal; Maritimo (Portugal); Colchester United; Sheffield United; Leicester City; Trelleborg (Sweden); Northampton Town

Caps   27   Goals   1

Date	Team	Result	G
27 Mar 1990	Norway	2-3	
18 May 1990	Uruguay	1-0	
5 Feb 1991	Poland	3-1	
27 Mar 1991	Yugoslavia	1-4	1
16 Oct 1991	Austria	2-1	
13 Nov 1991	Denmark	1-2	
29 Mar 1995	Republic of Ireland	1-1	
26 Apr 1995	Latvia	1-0	
3 Sep 1995	Portugal	1-1	
11 Oct 1995	Liechtenstein	4-0	
15 Nov 1995	Austria	5-3	
27 Mar 1996	Norway	0-2	
24 Apr 1996	Sweden	1-2	
29 May 1996	Germany	1-1	
31 Aug 1996	Ukraine	0-1	
5 Oct 1996	Armenia	1-1	
9 Nov 1996	Germany	1-1	
14 Dec 1996	Albania	2-0	
29 Mar 1997	Portugal	0-0	
2 Apr 1997	Ukraine	1-2	
30 Apr 1997	Armenia	0-0	
21 May 1997	Thailand	0-0	
20 Aug 1997	Germany	1-3	
10 Sep 1997	Albania	0-1	
11 Oct 1997	Portugal	0-1	
25 Mar 1998	Slovakia	1-0	

| 5 Sep 1998 | Turkey | 0-3 | | Caps | 51 | Goals | 7 |

Date	Team	Result	G
27 Mar 1990	Norway	2-3	
18 May 1990	Uruguay	1-0	
12 Sep 1990	Yugoslavia	0-2	
17 Oct 1990	Denmark	1-1	
14 Nov 1990	Austria	0-0	
5 Feb 1991	Poland	3-1	2
1 May 1991	Faroe Islands	1-1	
11 Sep 1991	Faroe Islands	5-0	
16 Oct 1991	Austria	2-1	
13 Nov 1991	Denmark	1-2	1
19 Feb 1992	Scotland	0-1	
28 Apr 1992	Lithuania	2-2	1
2 Jun 1992	Germany	1-1	
9 Sep 1992	Albania	3-0	
14 Oct 1992	Spain	0-0	
18 Nov 1992	Denmark	0-1	
17 Feb 1993	Albania	2-1	
31 Mar 1993	Republic of Ireland	0-3	
28 Apr 1993	Spain	1-3	
25 May 1993	Lithuania	1-0	
2 Jun 1993	Latvia	2-1	1
8 Sep 1993	Latvia	2-0	
13 Oct 1993	Denmark	0-1	
17 Nov 1993	Republic of Ireland	1-1	
23 Mar 1994	Romania	2-0	
20 Apr 1994	Liechtenstein	4-1	
3 Jun 1994	Colombia	0-2	
11 Jun 1994	Mexico	0-3	
7 Sep 1994	Portugal	1-2	
12 Oct 1994	Austria	2-1	
16 Nov 1994	Republic of Ireland	0-4	
29 Mar 1995	Republic of Ireland	1-1	
22 May 1995	Canada	0-2	
25 May 1995	Chile	1-2	
7 Jun 1995	Latvia	1-2	
9 Nov 1996	Germany	1-1	1
14 Dec 1996	Albania	2-0	
22 Jan 1997	Italy	0-2	
11 Feb 1997	Belgium	3-0	
29 Mar 1997	Portugal	0-0	
2 Apr 1997	Ukraine	1-2	
30 Apr 1997	Armenia	0-0	
20 Aug 1997	Germany	1-3	
11 Oct 1997	Portugal	0-1	
3 Jun 1998	Spain	1-4	1
26 Apr 2000	Hungary	0-1	
2 Sep 2000	Malta	1-0	
7 Oct 2000	Denmark	1-1	
11 Oct 2000	Iceland	0-1	
28 Feb 2001	Norway	0-4	
12 Oct 2002	Spain	0-3	

573   PAUL VICTOR KEE

Position   Goalkeeper

Born   Belfast, 8 November 1969

Clubs   Ards; Oxford United; Ards

Caps   9

Date	Team	Result	G
27 Mar 1990	Norway	2-3	
12 Sep 1990	Yugoslavia	0-2	
17 Oct 1990	Denmark	1-1	
14 Nov 1990	Austria	0-0	
5 Feb 1991	Poland	3-1	
27 Mar 1991	Yugoslavia	1-4	
1 May 1991	Faroe Islands	1-1	
12 Oct 1994	Austria	2-1	
16 Nov 1994	Republic of Ireland	0-4	

574   GERALD PAUL (GERRY) TAGGART

Position   Central defender

Born   Belfast, 18 October 1970

Clubs   Manchester City; Barnsley; Bolton
Wanderers; Leicester City; Stoke City

Above: Gerry Taggart

575   IAIN DOWIE

Position   Forward

Born   Hatfield, 9 January 1965

Clubs   St Albans; Wealdstone; Hendon;
Luton Town; Fulham (loan); West Ham
United; Southampton; Crystal Palace;
Queen's Park Rangers

Caps   59   Goals   12

Date	Team	Result	G
27 Mar 1990	Norway	2-3	
18 May 1990	Uruguay	1-0	
12 Sep 1990	Yugoslavia	0-2	
17 Oct 1990	Denmark	1-1	
14 Nov 1990	Austria	0-0	
27 Mar 1991	Yugoslavia	1-4	
1 May 1991	Faroe Islands	1-1	
11 Sep 1991	Faroe Islands	5-0	
16 Oct 1991	Austria	2-1	1
13 Nov 1991	Denmark	1-2	
19 Feb 1992	Scotland	0-1	
28 Apr 1992	Lithuania	2-2	
9 Sep 1992	Albania	3-0	
17 Feb 1993	Albania	2-1	
31 Mar 1993	Republic of Ireland	0-3	
28 Apr 1993	Spain	1-3	
25 May 1993	Lithuania	1-0	1
2 Jun 1993	Latvia	2-1	
8 Sep 1993	Latvia	2-0	
13 Oct 1993	Denmark	0-1	
17 Nov 1993	Republic of Ireland	1-1	
23 Mar 1994	Romania	2-0	
20 Apr 1994	Liechtenstein	4-1	1
3 Jun 1994	Colombia	0-2	
11 Jun 1994	Mexico	0-3	
12 Oct 1994	Austria	2-1	
16 Nov 1994	Republic of Ireland	0-4	
29 Mar 1995	Republic of Ireland	1-1	1
26 Apr 1995	Latvia	1-0	1
22 May 1995	Canada	0-2	

Above: Iain Dowie

Date	Team	Result	G
25 May 1995	Chile	1-2	1
7 Jun 1995	Latvia	1-2	1
3 Sep 1995	Portugal	1-1	
15 Nov 1995	Austria	5-3	1
27 Mar 1996	Norway	0-2	
29 May 1996	Germany	1-1	
31 Aug 1996	Ukraine	0-1	
5 Oct 1996	Armenia	1-1	
9 Nov 1996	Germany	1-1	
14 Dec 1996	Albania	2-0	2
29 Mar 1997	Portugal	0-0	
2 Apr 1997	Ukraine	1-2	1
30 Apr 1997	Armenia	0-0	
21 May 1997	Thailand	0-0	
10 Sep 1997	Albania	0-1	
11 Oct 1997	Portugal	0-1	
25 Mar 1998	Slovakia	1-0	
22 Apr 1995	Switzerland	1-0	
3 Jun 1998	Spain	1-4	
5 Sep 1998	Turkey	0-3	
10 Oct 1998	Finland	1-0	
18 Nov 1998	Moldova	2-2	1
27 Mar 1999	Germany	0-3	
31 Mar 1999	Moldova	0-0	
27 Apr 1999	Canada	1-1	
29 May 1999	Republic of Ireland	1-0	
18 Aug 1999	France	0-1	
4 Sep 1999	Turkey	0-3	
8 Sep 1999	Germany	0-4	

576   JOHN DEVINE

Position   Full-back

Clubs   Glentoran

Caps   1

Date	Team	Result	G
18 May 1990	Uruguay	1-0	

577   STEPHEN JOSEPH (STEVE) MORROW

Position   Midfield/Defender

Born   Bangor, 2 July 1970

Clubs   Bangor; Arsenal; Reading (loan); Watford (loan); Reading (loan); Barnet (loan);Q.P.R.; Peterborough Utd (loan)

Caps   39   Goals   1

Date	Team	Result	G
18 May 1990	Uruguay	1-0	
14 Nov 1990	Austria	0-0	
5 Feb 1991	Poland	3-1	
27 Mar 1991	Yugoslavia	1-4	
11 Sep 1991	Faroe Islands	5-0	
19 Feb 1992	Scotland	0-1	
2 Jun 1992	Germany	1-1	
14 Oct 1992	Spain	0-0	
17 Feb 1993	Albania	2-1	
31 Mar 1993	Republic of Ireland	0-3	

23 Mar 1994	Romania	2-0	1
3 Jun 1994	Colombia	0-2	
11 Jun 1994	Mexico	0-3	
7 Sep 1994	Portugal	1-2	
16 Nov 1994	Republic of Ireland	0-4	
29 Mar 1995	Republic of Ireland	1-1	
7 Jun 1995	Latvia	1-2	
3 Sep 1995	Portugal	1-1	
24 Apr 1996	Sweden	1-2	
31 Aug 1996	Ukraine	0-1	
9 Nov 1996	Germany	1-1	
14 Dec 1996	Albania	2-0	
22 Jan 1997	Italy	0-2	
11 Feb 1997	Belgium	3-0	
29 Mar 1997	Portugal	0-0	
2 Apr 1997	Ukraine	1-2	
30 Apr 1997	Armenia	0-0	
20 Aug 1997	Germany	1-3	
11 Oct 1997	Portugal	0-1	
25 Mar 1998	Slovakia	1-0	
22 Apr 1998	Switzerland	1-0	
3 Jun 1998	Spain	1-4	
5 Sep 1998	Turkey	0-3	
10 Oct 1998	Finland	1-0	
18 Nov 1998	Moldova	2-2	
27 Mar 1999	Germany	0-3	
31 Mar 1999	Moldova	0-0	
8 Sep 1999	Germany	0-4	
9 Oct 1999	Finland	1-4	

578   S D McBRIDE

Position   Outside-right

Clubs   Glenavon

Caps   4

Date	Team	Result	G
17 Oct 1990	Denmark	1-1	
5 Feb 1991	Poland	3-1	
11 Sep 1991	Faroe Islands	5-0	
13 Nov 1991	Denmark	1-2	

579   JAMES (JIM) MAGILTON

Position   Midfield

Born   Belfast, 6 May 1969

Clubs   Liverpool; Oxford United; Southampton; Sheffield Wednesday; Ipswich Town

Caps   52   Goals   5

Date	Team	Result	G
5 Feb 1991	Poland	3-1	1
27 Mar 1991	Yugoslavia	1-4	

1 May 1991	Faroe Islands	1-1	
11 Sep 1991	Faroe Islands	5-0	
16 Oct 1991	Austria	2-1	
13 Nov 1991	Denmark	1-2	
19 Feb 1992	Scotland	0-1	
28 Apr 1992	Lithuania	2-2	
2 Jun 1992	Germany	1-1	
9 Sep 1992	Albania	3-0	1
18 Nov 1992	Denmark	0-1	
17 Feb 1993	Albania	2-1	1
31 Mar 1993	Republic of Ireland	0-3	
25 May 1993	Lithuania	1-0	
2 Jun 1993	Latvia	2-1	1
8 Sep 1993	Latvia	2-0	
13 Oct 1993	Denmark	0-1	
17 Nov 1993	Republic of Ireland	1-1	
23 Mar 1994	Romania	2-0	
20 Apr 1994	Liechtenstein	4-1	
3 Jun 1994	Colombia	0-2	
11 Jun 1994	Mexico	0-3	
7 Sep 1994	Portugal	1-2	
12 Oct 1994	Austria	2-1	
16 Nov 1994	Republic of Ireland	0-4	
29 Mar 1995	Republic of Ireland	1-1	
22 May 1995	Canada	0-2	
25 May 1995	Chile	1-2	
7 Jun 1995	Latvia	1-2	
3 Sep 1995	Portugal	1-1	
27 Mar 1996	Norway	0-2	
29 May 1996	Germany	1-1	
31 Aug 1996	Ukraine	0-1	
5 Oct 1996	Armenia	1-1	
11 Feb 1997	Belgium	3-0	1

Above: Jim Magilton

Date	Team	Result	
29 Mar 1997	Portugal	0-0	
20 Aug 1997	Germany	1-3	
11 Oct 1997	Portugal	0-1	
3 Jun 1998	Spain	1-4	
23 Feb 2000	Luxembourg	3-1	
16 Aug 2000	Yugoslavia	1-2	
2 Sep 2000	Malta	1-0	
7 Oct 2000	Denmark	1-1	
11 Oct 2000	Iceland	0-1	
28 Feb 2001	Norway	0-4	
24 Mar 2001	Czech Republic	0-1	
28 Mar 2001	Bulgaria	3-4	
1 Sep 2001	Denmark	1-1	
5 Sep 2001	Iceland	3-0	
6 Oct 2001	Malta	1-0	
13 Feb 2002	Poland	1-4	
27 Mar 2002	Liechtenstein	0-0	

580   PAUL ANDREW WILLIAMS

Position   Central defender/Forward

Born   Sheffield, 8 September 1963

Clubs   Nuneaton Borough; Preston North End;
Newport County; Sheffield United;
Hartlepool United; Stockport County;
West Bromwich Albion; Coventry City
(loan); Stockport County; Rochdale;
Doncaster Rovers (loan)

Caps   1

Date	Team	Result	G
1 May 1991	Faroe Islands	1-1	

581   ALAN WILLIAM FETTIS

Position   Goalkeeper

Born   Belfast, 1 February 1971

Clubs   Ards; Hull City; West Bromwich Albion
(loan); Nottingham Forest; Blackburn
Rovers; York City; Sheffield United (loan);
Grimsby Town; Hull City

Caps   25

Date	Team	Result	G
13 Nov 1991	Denmark	1-2	
28 Apr 1992	Lithuania	2-2	
18 Nov 1992	Denmark	0-1	
11 Jun 1994	Mexico	0-3	
7 Sep 1994	Portugal	1-2	
29 Mar 1995	Republic of Ireland	1-1	
26 Apr 1995	Latvia	1-0	
22 May 1995	Canada	0-2	
25 May 1995	Chile	1-2	
7 Jun 1995	Latvia	1-2	
3 Sep 1995	Portugal	1-1	
11 Oct 1995	Liechtenstein	4-0	
15 Nov 1995	Austria	5-3	
27 Mar 1996	Norway	0-2	

Date	Team	Result	
29 May 1996	Germany	1-1	
31 Aug 1996	Ukraine	0-1	
5 Oct 1996	Armenia	1-1	
30 Apr 1997	Armenia	0-0	
11 Oct 1997	Portugal	0-1	
25 Mar 1998	Slovakia	1-0	
22 Apr 1998	Switzerland	1-0	
3 Jun 1998	Spain	1-4	
5 Sep 1998	Turkey	0-3	
10 Oct 1998	Finland	0-1	
18 Nov 1998	Moldova	2-2	

582   MICHAEL EAMONN HUGHES

Position   Midfield

Born   Larne, 2 August 1971

Clubs   Carrick Rangers; Manchester City; RS
Strasbourg (France); West Ham United;
Wimbledon; Birmingham City (loan);
Crystal Palace

Caps   71   Goals   5

Date	Team	Result	G
13 Nov 1991	Denmark	1-2	
19 Feb 1992	Scotland	0-1	
28 Apr 1992	Lithuania	2-2	
2 Jun 1992	Germany	1-1	1
9 Sep 1992	Albania	3-0	
14 Oct 1992	Spain	0-0	

Above: Micheal Hughes

Date	Team	Result	G
18 Nov 1992	Denmark	0-1	
31 Mar 1993	Republic of Ireland	0-3	
28 Apr 1993	Spain	1-3	
25 May 1993	Lithuania	1-0	
2 Jun 1993	Latvia	2-1	
8 Sep 1993	Latvia	2-0	
13 Oct 1993	Denmark	0-1	
17 Nov 1993	Republic of Ireland	1-1	
23 Mar 1994	Romania	2-0	
20 Apr 1994	Liechtenstein	4-1	
3 Jun 1994	Colombia	0-2	
11 Jun 1994	Mexico	0-3	
7 Sep 1994	Portugal	1-2	
12 Oct 1994	Austria	2-1	
16 Nov 1994	Republic of Ireland	0-4	
29 Mar 1995	Republic of Ireland	1-1	
26 Apr 1995	Latvia	1-0	
22 May 1995	Canada	0 2	
25 May 1995	Chile	1-2	
7 Jun 1995	Latvia	1-2	
3 Sep 1995	Portugal	1-1	1
11 Oct 1995	Liechtenstein	4-0	
15 Nov 1995	Austria	5-3	
27 Mar 1996	Norway	0-2	
29 May 1996	Germany	1-1	
31 Aug 1996	Ukraine	0-1	
5 Oct 1996	Armenia	1-1	
9 Nov 1996	Germany	1-1	
14 Dec 1996	Albania	2-0	
22 Jan 1997	Italy	0-2	
2 Apr 1997	Ukraine	1-2	
20 Aug 1997	Germany	1-3	1
11 Oct 1997	Portugal	0-1	
25 Mar 1998	Slovakia	1-0	
22 Apr 1998	Switzerland	1-0	
3 Jun 1998	Spain	1-4	
5 Sep 1998	Turkey	0-3	
10 Oct 1998	Finland	1-0	
18 Nov 1998	Moldova	2-2	
27 Mar 1999	Germany	0-3	
31 Mar 1999	Moldova	0-0	
18 Aug 1999	France	0-1	
4 Sep 1999	Turkey	0-3	
8 Sep 1999	Germany	0-4	
9 Oct 1999	Finland	1-4	
23 Feb 2000	Luxembourg	3-1	
28 Mar 2000	Malta	3-0	1
26 Apr 2000	Hungary	0-1	
24 Mar 2001	Czech Republic	0-1	
28 Mar 2001	Bulgaria	3-4	
2 Jun 2001	Bulgaria	0-1	
6 Jun 2001	Czech Republic	1-3	
1 Sep 2001	Denmark	1-1	
5 Sep 2001	Iceland	3-0	1
6 Oct 2001	Malta	1-0	
13 Feb 2002	Poland	1-4	
27 Mar 2002	Liechtenstein	0-0	
12 Oct 2002	Spain	0-3	
16 Oct 2002	Ukraine	0-0	
6 Sep 2003	Ukraine	0-0	
11 Oct 2003	Greece	0-1	
18 Feb 2004	Norway	1-4	
28 April 2004	Serbia	1-1	
4 Sep 2004	Poland	0-3	
8 Sep 2004	Wales	2-2	

583   PHILIP GRAY

Position	Forward
Born	Belfast, 2 October 1968
Clubs	Tottenham Hotspur; Barnsley (loan); Fulham (loan); Luton Town; Sunderland; Nancy (France); Fortuna Sittard (Holland); Burnley; Oxford United; Boston United; Chelmsford City
Caps	26 Goals 5

Date	Team	Result	G
18 Nov 1992	Denmark	0-1	
17 Feb 1993	Albania	2-1	
31 Mar 1993	Republic of Ireland	0-3	
28 Apr 1993	Spain	1-3	
8 Sep 1993	Latvia	2-0	1
13 Oct 1993	Denmark	0-1	
17 Nov 1993	Republic of Ireland	1-1	
23 Mar 1994	Romania	2-0	1
20 Apr 1994	Liechtenstein	4-1	
7 Sep 1994	Portugal	1-2	
12 Oct 1994	Austria	2-1	
10 Nov 1994	Republic of Ireland	0-4	
22 May 1995	Canada	0-2	
25 May 1995	Chile	1-2	
3 Sep 1995	Portugal	1-1	
11 Oct 1995	Liechtenstein	4-0	1
15 Nov 1995	Austria	5-3	1
31 Aug 1996	Ukraine	0-1	
5 Oct 1996	Armenia	1-1	
9 Nov 1996	Germany	1-1	
18 Nov 1998	Moldova	2-2	
2 Sep 2000	Malta	1-0	1
7 Oct 2000	Denmark	1-1	
11 Oct 2000	Iceland	0-1	
28 Feb 2001	Norway	0-4	
24 Mar 2001	Czech Republic	0-1	

584   KEITH ROWLAND

Position	Left-back/Midfield
Born	Portadown, 1 September 1971
Clubs	Bournemouth; Coventry City (loan); West Ham United; Queen's Park Rangers
Caps	19 Goals 1

Date	Team	Result	G
8 Sep 1993	Latvia	2-0	
22 May 1995	Canada	0-2	
25 May 1995	Chile	1-2	
7 Jun 1995	Latvia	1-2	
3 Sep 1995	Portugal	1-1	
11 Oct 1995	Liechtenstein	4-0	
27 Mar 1996	Norway	0-2	
24 Apr 1996	Sweden	1-2	
29 May 1996	Germany	1-1	
31 Aug 1996	Ukraine	0-1	
5 Oct 1996	Armenia	1-1	

Date	Team	Result	G
22 Jan 1997	Italy	0-2	
10 Sep 1997	Albania	0-1	
5 Sep 1998	Turkey	0-3	
10 Oct 1998	Finland	1-0	1
18 Nov 1998	Moldova	2-2	
27 Mar 1999	Germany	0-3	
27 Apr 1999	Canada	1-1	
29 May 1999	Republic of Ireland	1-0	

585   STEPHEN MARTIN (STEVE) LOMAS

Position   Midfield

Born   Hanover, Germany, 18 January 1974

Clubs   Manchester City; West Ham United

Caps   45   Goals   3

Date	Team	Result	G
23 Mar 1994	Romania	2-0	
20 Apr 1994	Liechtenstein	4-1	1
3 Jun 1994	Colombia	0-2	
11 Jun 1994	Mexico	0-3	
7 Sep 1994	Portugal	1-2	
12 Oct 1994	Austria	2-1	
3 Sep 1995	Portugal	1-1	
11 Oct 1995	Liechtenstein	4-0	
15 Nov 1995	Austria	5-3	
27 Mar 1996	Norway	0-2	
24 Apr 1996	Sweden	1-2	
29 May 1996	Germany	1-1	
31 Aug 1996	Ukraine	0-1	
5 Oct 1996	Armenia	1-1	
9 Nov 1996	Germany	1-1	
14 Dec 1996	Albania	2-0	
22 Jan 1997	Italy	0-2	
11 Feb 1997	Belgium	3-0	
29 Mar 1997	Portugal	0-0	
2 Apr 1997	Ukraine	1-2	
30 Apr 1997	Armenia	0-0	
21 May 1997	Thailand	0-0	
10 Sep 1997	Albania	0-1	
11 Oct 1997	Portugal	0-1	
25 Mar 1998	Slovakia	1-0	1
22 Apr 1998	Switzerland	1-0	
18 Nov 1998	Moldova	2-2	
27 Mar 1999	Germany	0-3	
31 Mar 1999	Moldova	0-0	
27 Apr 1999	Canada	1-1	
18 Aug 1999	France	0-1	
4 Sep 1999	Turkey	0-3	
8 Sep 1999	Germany	0-4	
23 Feb 2000	Luxembourg	3-1	
28 Mar 2000	Malta	3-0	
2 Sep 2000	Malta	1-0	
7 Oct 2000	Denmark	1-1	
11 Oct 2000	Iceland	0-1	
13 Feb 2002	Poland	1-4	1
27 Mar 2002	Liechtenstein	0-0	
12 Oct 2002	Spain	0-3	
16 Oct 2002	Ukraine	0-0	
12 Feb 2003	Finland	0-1	
29 Mar 2003	Armenia	0-1	
2 Apr 2003	Greece	0-2	

Above: Steve Lomas

586   GEORGE O'BOYLE

Position   Forward

Born   Belfast, 14 December 1967

Clubs   Dunfermline Athletic; St Johnstone

Caps   13   Goals   1

Date	Team	Result	G
3 Jun 1994	Colombia	0-2	
11 Jun 1994	Mexico	0-3	
7 Sep 1994	Portugal	1-2	
26 Apr 1995	Latvia	1-0	
22 May 1995	Canada	0-2	
25 May 1995	Chile	1-2	
24 Apr 1996	Sweden	1-2	
29 May 1996	Germany	1-1	1
22 Jan 1997	Italy	0-2	
11 Feb 1997	Belgium	3-0	
25 Mar 1998	Slovakia	1-0	
22 Apr 1998	Switzerland	1-0	
10 Oct 1998	Finland	1-0	

587   DARREN JAMES PATTERSON

Position   Defender

Born   Belfast, 15 October 1969

Clubs	West Bromwich Albion; Wigan Athletic; Crystal Palace; Luton Town; Preston North End (loan); Dundee United; York City; Oxford United

Caps	17	Goals	1

Date	Team	Result	G
3 Jun 1994	Colombia	0-2	
11 Jun 1994	Mexico	0-3	
16 Nov 1994	Republic of Ireland	0-4	
29 Mar 1995	Republic of Ireland	1-1	
26 Apr 1995	Latvia	1-0	
22 May 1995	Canada	0-2	
25 May 1995	Chile	1-2	
7 Jun 1995	Latvia	1-2	
27 Mar 1996	Norway	0-2	
24 Apr 1996	Swedon	1-2	
22 Apr 1998	Switzerland	1-0	1
3 Jun 1998	Spain	1-4	
10 Oct 1998	Finland	1-0	
18 Nov 1998	Moldova	2-2	
27 Mar 1999	Germany	0-3	
31 Mar 1999	Moldova	0-0	
29 May 1999	Republic of Ireland	1-0	

Above: Neil Lennon

588	NEIL FRANCIS LENNON

Position	Midfield

Born	Lurgan, 25 June 1971

Clubs	Manchester City; Crewe Alexandra; Leicester City; Glasgow Celtic

Caps	40	Goals	2

Date	Team	Result	G
11 Jun 1994	Mexico	0-3	
25 May 1995	Chile	1-2	
3 Sep 1995	Portugal	1-1	
11 Oct 1995	Liechtenstein	4-0	
15 Nov 1995	Austria	5-3	
27 Mar 1996	Norway	0-2	
31 Aug 1996	Ukraine	0-1	
5 Oct 1996	Armenia	1-1	1
9 Nov 1996	Germany	1-1	
14 Dec 1996	Albania	2-0	
11 Feb 1997	Belgium	3-0	
29 Mar 1997	Portugal	0-0	
2 Apr 1997	Ukraine	1-2	
30 Apr 1997	Armenia	0-0	
21 May 1997	Thailand	0-0	
20 Aug 1997	Germany	1-3	
10 Sep 1997	Albania	0-1	
11 Oct 1997	Portugal	0-1	
25 Mar 1998	Slovakia	1-0	
22 Apr 1998	Switzerland	1-0	
3 Jun 1998	Spain	1-4	
5 Sep 1998	Turkey	0-3	
10 Oct 1998	Finland	1-0	
18 Nov 1998	Moldova	2-2	1
27 Mar 1999	Germany	0-3	
31 Mar 1999	Moldova	0-0	
29 May 1999	Republic of Ireland	1-0	
18 Aug 1999	France	0-1	
4 Sep 1999	Turkey	0-3	
8 Sep 1999	Germany	0-4	
9 Oct 1999	Finland	1-4	
28 Mar 2000	Malta	3-0	
26 Apr 2000	Hungary	0-1	
7 Oct 2000	Denmark	1-1	
11 Oct 2000	Iceland	0-1	
28 Feb 2001	Norway	0-4	
24 Mar 2001	Czech Republic	0-1	
28 Mar 2001	Bulgaria	3-4	
2 Jun 2001	Bulgaria	0-1	
13 Feb 2002	Poland	1-4	

589	KEITH ROBERT GILLESPIE

Position	Winger

Born	Larne, 18 February 1975

Clubs	Manchester United; Wigan Athletic; Newcastle United; Blackburn Rovers; Leicester City; Sheffield United

Caps	68	Goals	2

Date	Team	Result	G
7 Sep 1994	Portugal	1-2	
12 Oct 1994	Austria	2-1	1
16 Nov 1994	Republic of Ireland	0-4	
29 Mar 1995	Republic of Ireland	1-1	
26 Apr 1995	Latvia	1-0	

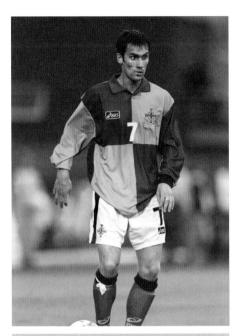

Above: Keith Gillespie

Date	Team	Result	G
13 Feb 2002	Poland	1-4	
27 Mar 2002	Liechtenstein	0-0	
17 Apr 2002	Spain	0-5	
21 Aug 2002	Cyprus	0-0	
12 Oct 2002	Spain	0-3	
16 Oct 2002	Ukraine	0-0	
12 Feb 2003	Finland	0-1	
29 Mar 2003	Armenia	0-1	
2 Apr 2003	Greece	0-2	
6 Sep 2003	Ukraine	0-0	
10 Sep 2003	Armenia	0-1	
11 Oct 2003	Greece	0-1	
18 Feb 2004	Norway	1-4	
28 Apr 2004	Serbia	1-1	
30 May 2004	Barbados	1-1	
2 Jun 2004	St Kitts & Nevis	2-0	
6 Jun 2004	Trinidad & Tobago	3-0	
18 Aug 2004	Switzerland	0-0	
9 Oct 2004	Azerbaijan	0-0	
13 Oct 2004	Austria	3-3	
9 Feb 2005	Canada	0-1	
26 Mar 2005	England	0-4	
30 Mar 2005	Poland	0-1	
4 Jun 2005	Germany	1-4	
17 Aug 2005	Malta	1-1	
3 Sep 2005	Azerbaijan	2-0	
7 Sep 2005	England	1-0	
8 Oct 2005	Wales	2-3	1
12 Oct 2005	Austria	0-2	
15 Nov 2005	Portugal	1-1	

Date	Team	Result	G
22 May 1995	Canada	0-2	
25 May 1995	Chile	1-2	
7 Jun 1995	Latvia	1-2	
3 Sep 1995	Portugal	1-1	
15 Nov 1995	Austria	5-3	
27 Mar 1996	Norway	0-2	
29 May 1996	Germany	1-1	
31 Aug 1996	Ukraine	0-1	
5 Oct 1996	Armenia	1-1	
11 Feb 1997	Belgium	3-0	
29 Mar 1997	Portugal	0-0	
2 Apr 1997	Ukraine	1-2	
20 Aug 1997	Germany	1-3	
10 Sep 1997	Albania	0-1	
25 Mar 1998	Slovakia	1-0	
22 Apr 1998	Switzerland	1-0	
5 Sep 1998	Turkey	0-3	
10 Oct 1998	Finland	1-0	
18 Nov 1998	Moldova	2-2	
27 Mar 1999	Germany	0-3	
31 Mar 1999	Moldova	0-0	
18 Aug 1999	France	0-1	
4 Sep 1999	Turkey	0-3	
8 Sep 1999	Germany	0-4	
23 Feb 2000	Luxembourg	3-1	
28 Mar 2000	Malta	3-0	
26 Apr 2000	Hungary	0-1	
16 Aug 2000	Yugoslavia	1-2	
24 Mar 2001	Czech Republic	0-1	
28 Mar 2001	Bulgaria	3-4	
2 Jun 2001	Bulgaria	0-1	
1 Sep 2001	Denmark	1-1	
5 Sep 2001	Iceland	3-0	

590   KEVIN HORLOCK

Position   Midfield

Born   Erith, 1 November 1972

Clubs   West Ham United; Swindon Town;
Manchester City; West Ham United

Caps   32

Date	Team	Result	G
26 Apr 1995	Latvia	1-0	
22 May 1995	Canada	0-2	
9 Nov 1996	Germany	1-1	
14 Dec 1996	Albania	2-0	
22 Jan 1997	Italy	0-2	
11 Feb 1997	Belgium	3-0	
2 Apr 1997	Ukraine	1-2	
30 Apr 1997	Armenia	0-0	
21 May 1997	Thailand	0-0	
20 Aug 1997	Germany	1-3	
10 Sep 1997	Albania	0-1	
11 Oct 1997	Portugal	0-1	
5 Sep 1998	Turkey	0-3	
10 Oct 1998	Finland	1-0	
27 Mar 1999	Germany	0-3	
31 Mar 1999	Moldova	0-0	
27 Apr 1999	Canada	1-1	
18 Aug 1999	France	0-1	
4 Sep 1999	Turkey	0-3	
8 Sep 1999	Germany	0-4	
28 Mar 2000	Malta	3-0	
16 Aug 2000	Yugoslavia	1-2	

Above: Kevin Horlock

Date	Team	Result	G
22 Jan 1997	Italy	0-2	
11 Feb 1997	Belgium	3-0	
27 Apr 1999	Canada	1-1	
29 May 1999	Republic of Ireland	1-0	
18 Aug 1999	France	0-1	
4 Sep 1999	Turkey	0-3	

Position   Central defender

Born   Lurgan, 6 September 1973

Clubs   Portadown; Manchester United; Swansea
City; Wigan Athletic; Scunthorpe
United (loan); Tranmere Rovers;
Portadown

Caps   7

Date	Team	Result	G
22 May 1995	Canada	0-2	
25 May 1995	Chile	1-2	
7 Jun 1995	Latvia	1-2	
11 Oct 1995	Liechtenstein	4-0	
21 May 1997	Thailand	0-0	
10 Sep 1997	Albania	0-1	
23 Feb 2000	Luxembourg	3-1	

Position   Winger

Born   Belfast, 29 December 1973

Clubs   Glenavon; Tottenham Hotspur; Barnet
(loan); Stoke City; St Johnstone

Caps   17   Goals   2

Date	Team	Result	G
22 May 1995	Canada	0-2	
25 May 1995	Chile	1-2	
7 Jun 1995	Latvia	1-2	
11 Oct 1995	Liechtenstein	4-0	1
27 Mar 1996	Norway	0-2	
24 Apr 1996	Sweden	1-2	1
29 May 1996	Germany	1-1	
5 Oct 1996	Armenia	1-1	
14 Dec 1996	Albania	2-0	
11 Feb 1997	Belgium	3-0	
29 Mar 1997	Portugal	0-0	
2 Apr 1997	Ukraine	1-2	
30 Apr 1997	Armenia	0-0	
21 May 1997	Thailand	0-0	
20 Aug 1997	Germany	1-3	
10 Sep 1997	Albania	0-1	
11 Oct 1997	Portugal	0-1	

Date	Team	Result	
2 Sep 2000	Malta	1-0	
7 Oct 2000	Denmark	1-1	
11 Oct 2000	Iceland	0-1	
1 Sep 2001	Denmark	1-1	
5 Sep 2001	Iceland	3-0	
6 Oct 2001	Malta	1-0	
17 Apr 2002	Spain	0-5	
21 Aug 2002	Cyprus	0-0	
12 Oct 2002	Spain	0-3	
16 Oct 2002	Ukraine	0-0	

Position   Central defender

Born   Coleraine, 18 November 1968

Clubs   Coleraine; Newcastle United; Crusaders;
Wrexham; Reading

Caps   15

Date	Team	Result	G
26 Apr 1995	Latvia	1-0	
3 Sep 1995	Portugal	1-1	
11 Oct 1995	Liechtenstein	4-0	
15 Nov 1995	Austria	5-3	
24 Apr 1996	Sweden	1-2	
29 May 1996	Germany	1-1	
5 Oct 1996	Armenia	1-1	
9 Nov 1996	Germany	1-1	
14 Dec 1996	Albania	2-0	

28 Feb 2001	Norway	0-4	
28 Mar 2001	Bulgaria	3-4	

594   TREVOR JOHN WOOD

Position   Goalkeeper

Born   Jersey, 3 November 1968

Clubs   Brighton & Hove Albion; Port Vale; Walsall; Hereford United

Caps   1

Date	Team	Result	G
11 Oct 1995	Liechtenstein	4-0	

595   AIDAN JOHN DAVISON

Position   Goalkeeper

Born   Sedgefield, 11 May 1968

Clubs   Billingham; Notts County; Bury; Millwall; Bolton Wanderers; Hull City; Bradford City; Grimsby Town; Sheffield United; Bradford City; Grimsby Town; Colchester United

Caps   3

Date	Team	Result	G
24 Apr 1996	Sweden	1-2	
21 May 1997	Thailand	0-0	
20 Aug 1997	Germany	1-3	

596   JONATHAN DAVID McCARTHY

Position   Midfield

Born   Middlesbrough, 18 August 1970

Clubs   Hartlepool United; Shepshed Charterhouse; York City; Port Vale; Birmingham City; Sheffield Wednesday (loan); Port Vale; York City; Carlisle United; Hucknall Town

Caps   18

Date	Team	Result	G
24 Apr 1996	Sweden	1-2	
22 Jan 1997	Italy	0-2	
30 Apr 1997	Armenia	0-0	
21 May 1997	Thailand	0-0	
11 Oct 1997	Portugal	0-1	
25 Mar 1998	Slovakia	1-0	
3 Jun 1998	Spain	1-4	
10 Oct 1998	Finland	1-0	
18 Nov 1998	Moldova	2-2	
27 Mar 1999	Germany	0-3	
27 Apr 1999	Canada	1-1	
29 May 1999	Republic of Ireland	1-0	
18 Aug 1999	France	0-1	
4 Sep 1999	Turkey	0-3	
8 Sep 1999	Germany	0-4	
9 Oct 1999	Finland	1-4	

597   STEPHEN JAMES QUINN

Position   Forward

Born   Coventry, 15 December 1974

Clubs   Birmingham City; Blackpool; Stockport County (loan); West Bromwich Albion; Notts County (Loan); Bristol Rovers (loan); Willem II (Holland)

Caps   46   Goals   4

Date	Team	Result	G
24 Apr 1996	Sweden	1-2	
14 Dec 1996	Albania	2-0	
22 Jan 1997	Italy	0-2	
11 Feb 1997	Belgium	3-0	1
29 Mar 1997	Portugal	0-0	
2 Apr 1997	Ukraine	1-2	
30 Apr 1997	Armenia	0-0	
21 May 1997	Thailand	0-0	
20 Aug 1997	Germany	1-3	
10 Sep 1997	Albania	0-1	
25 Mar 1998	Slovakia	1-0	
22 Apr 1998	Switzerland	1-0	
5 Sep 1998	Turkey	0-3	
10 Oct 1998	Finland	1-0	
29 May 1999	Republic of Ireland	1-0	

Above: James Quinn

Date	Team	Result	G
18 Aug 1999	France	0-1	
4 Sep 1999	Turkey	0-3	
8 Sep 1999	Germany	0-4	
9 Oct 1999	Finland	1-4	
23 Feb 2000	Luxembourg	3-1	1
28 Mar 2000	Malta	3-0	1
16 Aug 2000	Yugoslavia	1-2	
2 Jun 2001	Bulgaria	0-1	
6 Jun 2001	Czech Republic	1-3	
6 Oct 2001	Malta	1-0	
21 Aug 2002	Cyprus	0-0	
12 Feb 2003	Finland	0-1	
29 Mar 2003	Armenia	0-1	
2 Apr 2003	Greece	0-2	
28 Apr 2004	Serbia	1-1	1
30 May 2004	Barbados	1-1	
6 Jun 2004	Trinidad & Tobago	3-0	
4 Sep 2004	Poland	0-3	
8 Sep 2004	Wales	2-2	
9 Oct 2004	Azerbaijan	0-0	
13 Oct 2004	Austria	3-3	
30 Mar 2005	Poland	0-1	
17 Aug 2005	Malta	1-1	
3 Sep 2005	Azerbaijan	2-0	
7 Sep 2005	England	1-0	
8 Oct 2005	Wales	2-3	
12 Oct 2005	Austria	0-2	
15 Nov 2005	Portugal	1-1	
1 Mar 2006	Estonia	1-0	
21 May 2006	Uruguay	0-1	
26 May 2006	Romania	0-2	

598   DANIEL JOSEPH GRIFFIN

Position   Central defender

Born   Belfast, 19 August 1977

Clubs   St Andrew's BC; St Johnstone; Dundee United; Stockport County

Caps   29   Goals   1

Date	Team	Result	G
29 May 1996	Germany	1-1	
31 Aug 1996	Ukraine	0-1	
22 Jan 1997	Italy	0-2	
11 Feb 1997	Belgium	3-0	
21 May 1997	Thailand	0-0	
20 Aug 1997	Germany	1-3	
10 Sep 1997	Albania	0-1	
18 Nov 1998	Moldova	2-2	
29 May 1999	Republic of Ireland	1-0	1
23 Feb 2000	Luxembourg	3-1	
28 Mar 2000	Malta	3-0	
26 Apr 2000	Hungary	0-1	
16 Aug 2000	Yugoslavia	1-2	
28 Feb 2001	Norway	0-4	
24 Mar 2001	Czech Republic	0-1	
28 Mar 2001	Bulgaria	3-4	
2 Jun 2001	Bulgaria	0-1	
6 Jun 2001	Czech Republic	1-3	
1 Sep 2001	Denmark	1-1	
5 Sep 2001	Iceland	3-0	
6 Oct 2001	Malta	1-0	

Date	Team	Result	G
13 Feb 2002	Poland	1-4	
21 Aug 2002	Cyprus	0-0	
3 Jun 2003	Italy	0-2	
11 Jun 2003	Spain	0-0	
6 Sep 2003	Ukraine	0-0	
10 Sep 2003	Armenia	0-1	
11 Oct 2003	Greece	0-1	
18 Feb 2004	Norway	1-4	

599   IAN ROBERT NOLAN

Position   Left-back

Born   Liverpool, 9 July 1970

Clubs   Preston North End; Marine; Tranmere Rovers; Sheffield Wednesday; Bradford City; Wigan Athletic; Southport

Caps   18

Date	Team	Result	G
5 Oct 1996	Armenia	1-1	
9 Nov 1996	Germany	1-1	
14 Dec 1996	Albania	2-0	
29 Mar 1997	Portugal	0-0	
2 Apr 1997	Ukraine	1-2	
20 Aug 1997	Germany	1-3	
11 Oct 1997	Portugal	0-1	
8 Sep 1999	Germany	0-4	
9 Oct 1999	Finland	1-4	
23 Feb 2000	Luxembourg	3-1	
28 Mar 2000	Malta	3-0	
26 Apr 2000	Hungary	0-1	
16 Aug 2000	Yugoslavia	1-2	
2 Sep 2000	Malta	1-0	
28 Mar 2001	Bulgaria	3-4	
2 Jun 2001	Bulgaria	0-1	
6 Jun 2001	Czech Republic	1-3	
17 Apr 2002	Spain	0-5	

600   PHILIP PATRICK MULRYNE

Position   Midfield

Born   Belfast, 1 January 1978

Clubs   Manchester United; Norwich City; Cardiff City

Caps   27   Goals   3

Date	Team	Result	G
11 Feb 1997	Belgium	3-0	1
30 Apr 1997	Armenia	0-0	
21 May 1997	Thailand	0-0	
10 Sep 1997	Albania	0-1	
3 Jun 1998	Spain	1-4	
5 Sep 1998	Turkey	0-3	
10 Oct 1998	Finland	1-0	
27 Apr 1999	Canada	1-1	
16 Aug 2000	Yugoslavia	1-2	
7 Oct 2000	Denmark	1-1	
2 Jun 2001	Bulgaria	0-1	

Date	Team	Result	G
6 Jun 2001	Czech Republic	1-3	1
1 Sep 2001	Denmark	1-1	1
5 Sep 2001	Iceland	3-0	
13 Feb 2002	Poland	1-4	
27 Mar 2002	Liechtenstein	0-0	
12 Oct 2002	Spain	0-3	
16 Oct 2002	Ukraine	0-0	
6 Sep 2003	Ukraine	0-0	
10 Sep 2003	Armenia	0-1	
31 Mar 2004	Estonia	1-0	
28 Apr 2004	Serbia	1-1	
30 May 2004	Barbados	1-1	
2 Jun 2004	St Kitts & Nevis	2-0	
6 Jun 2004	Trinidad & Tobago	3-0	
9 Feb 2005	Canada	0-1	
17 Aug 2005	Malta	1-1	

601   JEFFREY WHITLEY

Position   Midfield

Born   Zambia, 28 January 1979

Clubs   Manchester City; Wrexham (loan); Notts County (loan); Sunderland

Caps   20   Goals   1

Date	Team	Result	G
11 Feb 1997	Belgium	3-0	
21 May 1997	Thailand	0-0	
3 Jun 1998	Spain	1-4	
9 Oct 1999	Finland	1-4	
16 Aug 2000	Yugoslavia	1-2	
7 Oct 2000	Denmark	1-1	
28 Feb 2001	Norway	0-4	
11 Oct 2003	Greece	0-1	
31 Mar 2004	Estonia	1-0	
28 Apr 2004	Serbia	1-1	
2 Jun 2004	St Kitts & Nevis	2-0	
6 Jun 2004	Trinidad & Tobago	3-0	
4 Sep 2004	Poland	0-3	
8 Sep 2004	Wales	2-2	1
9 Oct 2004	Azerbaijan	0-0	
13 Oct 2004	Austria	3-3	
9 Feb 2005	Canada	0-1	
26 Mar 2005	England	0-4	
30 Mar 2005	Poland	0-1	
17 Aug 2005	Malta	1-1	

DID YOU KNOW?
Manchester City's Jeff Whitley became the first black player to play for Northern Ireland in a full international match when he came off the bench for the last three minutes in the 3-0 win over Belgium on 11 February 1997.

602   IAIN JENKINS

Position   Defender

Born   Prescot, 24 November 1972

Clubs   Everton; Bradford City (loan); Chester City

Caps   6

Date	Team	Result	G
30 Apr 1997	Armenia	0-0	
21 May 1997	Thailand	0-0	
25 Mar 1998	Slovakia	1-0	
22 Apr 1998	Switzerland	1-0	
3 Jun 1998	Spain	1-4	
9 Oct 1999	Finland	1-4	

603   ROY ERIC CARROLL

Position   Goalkeeper

Born   Enniskillen, 30 September 1977

Clubs   Hull City; Wigan Athletic; Manchester United; West Ham United

Caps   17

Date	Team	Result	G
21 May 1997	Thailand	0-0	
29 May 1999	Republic of Ireland	1-0	
23 Feb 2000	Luxembourg	3-1	
28 Mar 2000	Malta	3-0	
2 Sep 2000	Malta	1-0	
7 Oct 2000	Denmark	1-1	
1 Oct 2000	Iceland	0-1	
24 Mar 2001	Czech Republic	0-1	
28 Mar 2001	Bulgaria	3-4	
27 Mar 2002	Liechtenstein	0-0	
17 Apr 2002	Spain	0-5	
12 Feb 2003	Finland	0-1	
3 Jun 2003	Italy	0-2	
28 Apr 2004	Serbia	1-1	
18 Aug 2004	Switzerland	0-0	
13 Oct 2004	Austria	3-3	
9 Feb 2005	Canada	0-1	

604   STEPHEN ROBINSON

Position   Midfield

Born   Lisburn, 10 December 1974

Clubs   Tottenham Hotspur; Bournemouth; Preston North End; Bristol City; Luton Town

Caps   5

Date	Team	Result	G
21 May 1997	Thailand	0-0	
31 Mar 1999	Moldova	0-0	
29 May 1999	Republic of Ireland	1-0	
23 Feb 2000	Luxembourg	3-1	
26 Apr 2000	Hungary	0-1	

605   DANIEL JAMES SONNER

Position   Midfield

Born	Wigan, 9 January 1972	
Clubs	Burnley; Bury; Ipswich Town; Sheffield Wednesday; Birmingham City; Walsall; Nottingham Forest; Peterborough United; Port Vale (loan)	
Caps	13	

Date	Team	Result	G
10 Sep 1997	Albania	0-1	
27 Mar 1999	Germany	0-3	
27 Apr 1999	Canada	1-1	
23 Feb 2000	Luxembourg	3-1	
28 Mar 2000	Malta	3-0	
26 Apr 2000	Hungary	0-1	
28 Feb 2001	Norway	0-4	
31 Mar 2004	Estonia	1-0	
28 Apr 2004	Serbia	1-1	
30 May 2004	Barbados	1-1	
2 Jun 2004	St Kitts & Nevis	2-0	
6 Jun 2004	Trinidad & Tobago	3-0	
18 Aug 2004	Switzerland	0-0	

606 AARON WILLIAM HUGHES

Position	Defender
Born	Cookstown, 8 November 1979
Clubs	Newcastle United; Aston Villa
Caps	46

Above: Aaron Hughes

Date	Team	Result	G
25 Mar 1998	Slovakia	1-0	
22 Apr 1998	Switzerland	1-0	
3 Jun 1998	Spain	1-4	
5 Sep 1998	Turkey	0-3	
10 Oct 1998	Finland	1-0	
31 Mar 1999	Moldova	0-0	
27 Apr 1999	Canada	1-1	
29 May 1999	Republic of Ireland	1-0	
18 Aug 1999	France	0-1	
4 Sep 1999	Turkey	0-3	
23 Feb 2000	Luxembourg	3-1	
26 Apr 2000	Hungary	0-1	
16 Aug 2000	Yugoslavia	1-2	
2 Sep 2000	Malta	1-0	
7 Oct 2000	Denmark	1-1	
11 Oct 2000	Iceland	0-1	
28 Feb 2001	Norway	0-4	
24 Mar 2001	Czech Republic	0-1	
2 Jun 2001	Bulgaria	0-1	
6 Jun 2001	Czech Republic	1-3	
1 Sep 2001	Denmark	1-1	
5 Sep 2001	Iceland	3-0	
13 Feb 2002	Poland	1-4	
17 Apr 2002	Spain	0-5	
12 Oct 2002	Spain	0-3	
16 Oct 2002	Ukraine	0-0	
12 Feb 2003	Finland	0-1	
29 Mar 2003	Armenia	0-1	
2 Apr 2003	Greece	0-2	
3 Jun 2003	Italy	0-2	
11 Jun 2003	Spain	0-0	
6 Sep 2003	Ukraine	0-0	
10 Sep 2003	Armenia	0-1	
11 Oct 2003	Greece	0-1	
18 Feb 2004	Norway	1-4	
18 Aug 2004	Switzerland	0-0	
4 Sep 2004	Poland	0-3	
8 Sep 2004	Wales	2-2	
9 Oct 2004	Azerbaijan	0-0	
13 Oct 2004	Austria	3-3	
9 Feb 2005	Canada	0-1	
26 Mar 2005	England	0-4	
30 Mar 2005	Poland	0-1	
17 Aug 2005	Malta	1-1	
3 Sep 2005	Azerbaijan	2-0	
7 Sep 2005	England	1-0	

607 JAMES WHITLEY

Position	Midfield
Born	Zambia, 14 April 1975
Clubs	Manchester City; Blackpool (loan); Norwich City (loan); Swindon Town (loan); Northampton Town (loan); Wrexham
Caps	3

Date	Team	Result	G
3 Jun 1998	Spain	1-4	
5 Sep 1998	Turkey	0-3	

9 Oct 1999	Finland	1-4

Position   Goalkeeper

Born   Hildshein, Germany, 4 September 1971

Clubs   Farnborough Town; Barnet; Southampton; Fulham; Birmingham City

Caps   52

Date	Team	Result	G
27 Mar 1999	Germany	0-3	
31 Mar 1999	Moldova	0-0	
27 Apr 1999	Canada	1-1	
29 May 1999	Republic of Ireland	1-0	
18 Aug 1999	France	0-1	
4 Sep 1999	Turkey	0-3	
8 Sep 1999	Germany	0-4	
9 Oct 1999	Finland	1-4	
23 Feb 2000	Luxembourg	3-1	
28 Mar 2000	Malta	3-0	
26 Apr 2000	Hungary	0-1	
16 Aug 2000	Yugoslavia	1-2	
28 Feb 2001	Norway	0-4	
2 Jun 2001	Bulgaria	0-1	
6 Jun 2001	Czech Republic	1-3	
1 Sep 2001	Denmark	1-1	
5 Sep 2001	Iceland	3-0	
6 Oct 2001	Malta	1-0	

13 Feb 2002	Poland	1-4
27 Mar 2002	Liechtenstein	0-0
17 Apr 2002	Spain	0-5
21 Aug 2002	Cyprus	0-0
12 Oct 2002	Spain	0-3
16 Oct 2002	Ukraine	0-0
12 Feb 2003	Finland	0-1
29 Mar 2003	Armenia	0-1
2 Apr 2003	Greece	0-2
3 Jun 2003	Italy	0-2
11 Jun 2003	Spain	0-0
6 Sep 2003	Ukraine	0-0
10 Sep 2003	Armenia	0-1
11 Oct 2003	Greece	0-1
18 Feb 2004	Norway	1-4
31 Mar 2004	Estonia	1-0
28 Apr 2004	Serbia	1-1
30 May 2004	Barbados	1-1
2 Jun 2004	St Kitts & Nevis	2-0
6 Jun 2004	Trinidad & Tobago	3-0
4 Sep 2004	Poland	0-3
8 Sep 2004	Wales	2-2
9 Oct 2004	Azerbaijan	0-0
9 Feb 2005	Canada	0-1
26 Mar 2005	England	0-4
30 Mar 2005	Poland	0-1
4 Jun 2005	Germany	1-4
17 Aug 2005	Malta	1-1
3 Sep 2005	Azerbaijan	2-0
7 Sep 2005	England	1-0
8 Oct 2005	Wales	2-3
12 Oct 2005	Austria	0-2
15 Nov 2005	Portugal	1-1
1 Mar 2006	Estonia	1-0

Above: Maik Taylor

Position   Winger

Born   Lurgan, 10 September 1973

Clubs   Portadown; Notts County; Watford; Wigan Athletic; Derby County (loan); Peterborough United

Caps   20

Date	Team	Result	G
18 Nov 1998	Moldova	2-2	
27 Mar 1999	Germany	0-3	
18 Aug 1999	France	0-1	
4 Sep 1999	Turkey	0-3	
8 Sep 1999	Germany	0-4	
9 Oct 1999	Finland	1-4	
28 Feb 2001	Norway	0-4	
28 Mar 2001	Bulgaria	3-4	
6 Jun 2001	Czech Republic	1-3	
1 Sep 2001	Denmark	1-1	
5 Sep 2001	Iceland	3-0	
6 Oct 2001	Malta	1-0	
13 Feb 2002	Poland	1-4	
21 Aug 2002	Cyprus	0-0	
12 Feb 2003	Finland	0-1	
3 Jun 2003	Italy	0-2	
11 Jun 2003	Spain	0-0	

6 Sep 2003	Ukraine	0-0	
11 Oct 2003	Greece	0-1	
18 Feb 2004	Norway	1-4	

610   MARK STUART WILLIAMS

Position   Central defender

Born   Stalybridge, 28 September 1970

Clubs   Newtown; Shrewsbury Town;
Chesterfield; Watford; Wimbledon; Stoke
City; MK Dons; Rushden & Diamonds

Caps   36

Date	Team	Result	G
27 Mar 1999	Germany	0-3	
31 Mar 1999	Moldova	0-0	
27 Apr 1999	Canada	1-1	
29 May 1999	Republic of Ireland	1-0	
18 Aug 1999	France	0-1	
4 Sep 1999	Turkey	0-3	
8 Sep 1999	Germany	0-4	
9 Oct 1999	Finland	1-4	
23 Feb 2000	Luxembourg	3-1	
28 Mar 2000	Malta	3-0	
26 Apr 2000	Hungary	0-1	
16 Aug 2000	Yugoslavia	1-2	
11 Oct 2000	Iceland	0-1	
28 Feb 2001	Norway	0-4	
24 Mar 2001	Czech Republic	0-1	
28 Mar 2001	Bulgaria	3-4	
6 Jun 2001	Czech Republic	1-3	
27 Mar 2002	Liechtenstein	0-0	
17 Apr 2002	Spain	0-5	
21 Aug 2002	Cyprus	0-0	
12 Feb 2003	Finland	0-1	
29 Mar 2003	Armenia	0-1	
2 Apr 2003	Greece	0-2	
3 Jun 2003	Italy	0-2	
11 Jun 2003	Spain	0-0	
18 Feb 2004	Norway	1-4	
31 Mar 2004	Estonia	1-0	
28 Apr 2004	Serbia	1-1	
30 May 2004	Barbados	1-1	
6 Jun 2004	Trinidad & Tobago	3-0	
18 Aug 2004	Switzerland	0-0	
4 Sep 2004	Poland	0-3	
8 Sep 2004	Wales	2-2	
9 Oct 2004	Azerbaijan	0-0	
13 Oct 2004	Austria	3-3	
30 Mar 2005	Poland	0-1	

611   ADRIAN COOTE

Position   Forward

Born   Great Yarmouth, 13 September 1978

Clubs   Norwich City; Colchester United; Bristol
Rovers (loan); Wivenhoe Town

Caps   6

Date	Team	Result	G
27 Apr 1999	Canada	1-1	
29 May 1999	Republic of Ireland	1-0	
9 Oct 1999	Finland	1-4	
23 Feb 2000	Luxembourg	3-1	
28 Mar 2000	Malta	3-0	
26 Apr 2000	Hungary	0-1	

612   GLENN FERGUSON

Position   Forward

Born   Belfast, 10 July 1969

Clubs   Glenavon; Linfield

Caps   5

Date	Team	Result	G
27 Apr 1999	Canada	1-1	
28 Feb 2001	Norway	0-4	
24 Mar 2001	Czech Republic	0-1	
2 Jun 2001	Bulgaria	0-1	
6 Jun 2001	Czech Republic	1-3	

613   RORY HAMILL

Position   Left winger

Born   Coleraine, 4 May 1976

Clubs   Portstewart; Fulham; Glentoran

Caps   1

Date	Team	Result	G
27 Apr 1999	Canada	1-1	

614   PAUL FRANCIS McVEIGH

Position   Midfield/Forward

Born   Belfast, 6 December 1977

Clubs   Tottenham Hotspur; Norwich City

Caps   20

Date	Team	Result	G
27 Apr 1999	Canada	1-1	
5 Sep 2001	Iceland	3-0	
13 Feb 2002	Poland	1-4	
12 Oct 2002	Spain	0-3	
16 Oct 2002	Ukraine	0-0	
12 Feb 2003	Finland	0-1	
29 Mar 2003	Armenia	0-1	
2 Apr 2003	Greece	0-2	
3 Jun 2003	Italy	0-2	
11 Jun 2003	Spain	0-0	
10 Sep 2003	Armenia	0-1	
18 Feb 2004	Norway	1-4	
28 Apr 2004	Serbia	1-1	
30 May 2004	Barbados	1-1	

Date	Team	Result
2 Jun 2004	St Kitts & Nevis	2-0
6 Jun 2004	Trinidad & Tobago	3-0
18 Aug 2004	Switzerland	0-0
4 Sep 2004	Poland	0-3
8 Sep 2004	Wales	2-2
13 Oct 2004	Austria	3-3

615   DAMIEN MICHAEL JOHNSON

Position   Midfield

Born   Lisburn, 18 November 1978

Clubs   Blackburn Rovers; Nottingham Forest (loan); Birmingham City

Caps   42

Date	Team	Result	G
29 May 1999	Republic of Ireland	1-0	
9 Oct 1999	Finland	1-4	
23 Feb 2000	Luxembourg	3-1	
28 Mar 2000	Malta	3-0	
26 Apr 2000	Hungary	0-1	
16 Aug 2000	Yugoslavia	1-2	
2 Sep 2000	Malta	1-0	
11 Oct 2000	Iceland	0-1	
28 Feb 2001	Norway	1-4	
28 Mar 2001	Bulgaria	3-4	
2 Jun 2001	Bulgaria	0-1	
6 Jun 2001	Czech Republic	1-3	
6 Oct 2001	Malta	1-0	

Above: Damien Johnson

Date	Team	Result
13 Feb 2002	Poland	1-4
27 Mar 2002	Liechtenstein	0-0
17 Apr 2002	Spain	0-5
21 Aug 2002	Cyprus	0-0
12 Oct 2002	Spain	0-3
16 Oct 2002	Ukraine	0-0
12 Feb 2003	Finland	0-1
29 Mar 2003	Armenia	0-1
2 Apr 2003	Greece	0-2
3 Jun 2003	Italy	0-2
11 Jun 2003	Spain	0-0
6 Sep 2003	Ukraine	0-0
10 Sep 2003	Armenia	0-1
18 Feb 2004	Norway	1-4
30 May 2004	Barbados	1-1
2 Jun 2004	St Kitts & Nevis	2-0
6 Jun 2004	Trinidad & Tobago	3-0
18 Aug 2004	Switzerland	0-0
4 Sep 2004	Poland	0-3
8 Sep 2004	Wales	2-2
9 Oct 2004	Azerbaijan	0-0
13 Oct 2004	Austria	3-3
26 Mar 2005	England	0-4
4 Jun 2005	Germany	1-4
17 Aug 2005	Malta	1-1
3 Sep 2005	Azerbaijan	2-0
7 Sep 2005	England	1-0
8 Oct 2005	Wales	2-3
12 Oct 2005	Austria	0-2

616   DAVID JONATHAN HEALY

Position   Forward

Born   Downpatrick, 5 August 1979

Clubs   Manchester United; Port Vale (loan); Preston North End; Norwich City (loan); Leeds United

Caps   49   Goals   19

Date	Team	Result	G
23 Feb 2000	Luxembourg	3-1	2
28 Mar 2000	Malta	3-0	1
26 Apr 2000	Hungary	0-1	
16 Aug 2000	Yugoslavia	1-2	1
2 Sep 2000	Malta	1-0	
7 Oct 2000	Denmark	1-1	1
11 Oct 2000	Iceland	0-1	
28 Feb 2001	Norway	0-4	
24 Mar 2001	Czech Republic	0-1	
28 Mar 2001	Bulgaria	3-4	2
2 Jun 2001	Bulgaria	0-1	
6 Jun 2001	Czech Republic	1-3	
1 Sep 2001	Denmark	1-1	
5 Sep 2001	Iceland	3-0	1
6 Oct 2001	Malta	1-0	1
13 Feb 2002	Poland	1-4	
27 Mar 2002	Liechtenstein	0-0	
17 Apr 2002	Spain	0-5	
21 Aug 2002	Cyprus	0-0	
12 Oct 2002	Spain	0-3	
16 Oct 2002	Ukraine	0-0	
12 Feb 2003	Finland	0-1	

Above: David Healy

Above: Colin Murdock

29 Mar 2003	Armenia	0-1	
2 Apr 2003	Greece	0-2	
3 Jun 2003	Italy	0-2	
11 Jun 2003	Spain	0-0	
6 Sep 2003	Ukraine	0-0	
10 Sep 2003	Armenia	0-1	
11 Oct 2003	Greece	0-1	
18 Feb 2004	Norway	1-4	1
31 Mar 2004	Estonia	1-0	
28 Apr 2004	Serbia	1-1	
30 May 2004	Barbados	1-1	1
2 Jun 2004	St Kitts & Nevis	2-0	1
6 Jun 2004	Trinidad & Tobago	3-0	2
18 Aug 2004	Switzerland	0-0	
4 Sep 2004	Poland	0-3	
8 Sep 2004	Wales	2-2	1
13 Oct 2004	Austria	3-3	1
9 Feb 2005	Canada	0-1	
26 Mar 2005	England	0-4	
30 Mar 2005	Poland	0-1	
4 Jun 2005	Germany	1-4	1
17 Aug 2005	Malta	1-1	1
3 Sep 2005	Azerbaijan	2-0	
7 Sep 2005	England	1-0	1
8 Oct 2005	Wales	2-3	
12 Oct 2005	Austria	0-2	
1 Mar 2006	Estonia	1-0	

617   COLIN JAMES MURDOCK

Position	Central defender
Born	Ballymena, 2 July 1975
Clubs	Manchester United; Preston North End; Hibernian; Crewe Alexandra; Rotherham United
Caps	33 Goals 1

Date	Team	Result	G
23 Feb 2000	Luxembourg	3-1	
28 Mar 2000	Malta	3-0	
16 Aug 2000	Yugoslavia	1-2	
2 Sep 2000	Malta	1-0	
7 Oct 2000	Denmark	1-1	
11 Oct 2000	Iceland	0-1	
28 Feb 2001	Norway	0-4	
24 Mar 2001	Czech Republic	0-1	
28 Mar 2001	Bulgaria	3-4	
2 Jun 2001	Bulgaria	0-1	
6 Jun 2001	Czech Republic	1-3	
1 Sep 2001	Denmark	1-1	
6 Oct 2001	Malta	1-0	
21 Aug 2002	Cyprus	0-0	
12 Oct 2002	Spain	0-3	
16 Oct 2002	Ukraine	0-0	
11 Oct 2003	Greece	0-1	
30 May 2004	Barbados	1-1	
2 Jun 2004	St Kitts & Nevis	2-0	
6 Jun 2004	Trinidad & Tobago	3-0	

18 Aug 2004	Switzerland	0-0	
8 Sep 2004	Wales	2-2	
9 Oct 2004	Azerbaijan	0-0	
13 Oct 2004	Austria	3-3	1
9 Feb 2005	Canada	0-1	
26 Mar 2005	England	0-4	
30 Mar 2005	Poland	0-1	
17 Aug 2005	Malta	1-1	
8 Oct 2005	Wales	2-3	
12 Oct 2005	Austria	0-2	
15 Nov 2005	Portugal	1-1	
21 May 2006	Uruguay	0-1	
26 May 2006	Romania	0-2	

618   ANDREW ROBERT KIRK

Position   Forward

Born   Belfast, 29 May 1979

Clubs   Glentoran; Heart of Midlothian; Boston United; Northampton Town

Caps   8

Date	Team	Result	G
26 Apr 2001	Hungary	0-1	
28 Feb 2001	Norway	0-4	
16 Oct 2002	Ukraine	0-0	
12 Feb 2003	Finland	0-1	
2 Apr 2003	Greece	0-2	
9 Feb 2005	Canada	0-1	
26 Mar 2005	England	0-4	
4 Jun 2005	Germany	1-4	

619   STUART ELLIOTT

Position   Forward

Born   Belfast, 23 July 1978

Clubs   Glentoran; Motherwell; Hull City

Caps   34   Goals   3

Date	Team	Result	G
2 Sep 2000	Malta	1-0	
7 Oct 2000	Denmark	1-1	
11 Oct 2000	Iceland	0-1	
28 Feb 2001	Norway	0-4	
24 Mar 2001	Czech Republic	0-1	
28 Mar 2001	Bulgaria	3-4	
2 Jun 2001	Bulgaria	0-1	
6 Jun 2001	Czech Republic	1-3	
1 Sep 2001	Denmark	1-1	
6 Oct 2001	Malta	1-0	
13 Feb 2002	Poland	1-4	
27 Mar 2002	Liechtenstein	0-0	
17 Apr 2002	Spain	0-5	
12 Feb 2003	Finland	0-1	
29 Mar 2003	Armenia	0-1	
3 Jun 2003	Italy	0-2	
11 Oct 2003	Greece	0-1	
30 May 2004	Barbados	1-1	

Above: Stuart Elliott

2 Jun 2004	St Kitts & Nevis	2-0	
6 Jun 2004	Trinidad & Tobago	3-0	1
18 Aug 2004	Switzerland	0-0	
4 Sep 2004	Poland	0-3	
9 Oct 2004	Azerbaijan	0-0	
13 Oct 2004	Austria	3-3	1
26 Mar 2005	England	0-4	
30 Mar 2005	Poland	0-1	
4 Jun 2005	Germany	1-4	
17 Aug 2005	Malta	1-1	
3 Sep 2005	Azerbaijan	2-0	1
7 Sep 2005	England	1-0	
8 Oct 2005	Wales	2-3	
12 Oct 2005	Austria	0-2	
15 Nov 2005	Portugal	1-1	
1 Mar 2006	Estonia	1-0	

620   GEORGE McCARTNEY

Position   Left-back

Born   Belfast, 29 April 1981

Clubs   Sunderland

Caps   20   Goals   1

Date	Team	Result	G
5 Sep 2001	Iceland	3-0	1
6 Oct 2001	Malta	1-0	
13 Feb 2002	Poland	1-4	
27 Mar 2002	Liechtenstein	0-0	

Date	Team	Result
17 Apr 2002	Spain	0-5
21 Aug 2002	Cyprus	0-0
12 Oct 2002	Spain	0-3
16 Oct 2002	Ukraine	0-0
12 Feb 2003	Finland	0-1
2 Apr 2003	Greece	0-2
3 Jun 2003	Italy	0-2
11 Jun 2003	Spain	0-0
6 Sep 2003	Ukraine	0-0
10 Sep 2003	Armenia	0-1
11 Oct 2003	Greece	0-1
18 Feb 2004	Norway	1-4
8 Sep 2004	Wales	2-2
13 Oct 2004	Austria	3-3
9 Feb 2005	Canada	0-1
4 Jun 2005	Germany	1-4

621   GRANT SAMUEL McCANN

Position   Midfield

Born   Belfast, 14 April 1980

Clubs   West Ham United; Livingston (loan); Notts County (loan); Cheltenham Town (loan); Cheltenham Town

Caps   11

Date	Team	Result	G
6 Oct 2001	Malta	1-0	
13 Feb 2002	Poland	1-4	
27 Mar 2002	Liechtenstein	0-0	
12 Oct 2002	Spain	0-3	
16 Oct 2002	Ukraine	0-0	
29 Mar 2003	Armenia	0-1	
2 Apr 2003	Greece	0-2	
10 Sep 2003	Armenia	0-1	
31 Mar 2004	Estonia	1-0	
15 Nov 2005	Portugal	1-1	
1 Mar 2006	Estonia	1-0	

622   MICHAEL JAMES DUFF

Position   Defender

Born   Belfast, 11 January 1978

Clubs   Cheltenham Town; Burnley

Caps   10

Date	Team	Result	G
13 Feb 2002	Poland	1-4	
21 Aug 2002	Cyprus	0-0	
31 Mar 2004	Estonia	1-0	
18 Aug 2004	Switzerland	0-0	
7 Sep 2005	England	1-0	
8 Oct 2005	Wales	2-3	
12 Oct 2005	Austria	0-2	
1 Mar 2006	Estonia	1-0	
21 May 2006	Uruguay	0-1	
26 May 2006	Romania	0-2	

623   WARREN JAMES FEENEY (junior)

Position   Forward

Born   Belfast, 17 January 1981

Clubs   St Andrew's BC; Leeds United; Bournemouth; Stockport County; Luton Town

Caps   11   Goals   2

Date	Team	Result	G
27 Mar 2002	Liechtenstein	0-0	
17 Apr 2002	Spain	0-5	
21 Aug 2002	Cyprus	0-0	
30 Mar 2005	Poland	0-1	
4 Jun 2005	Germany	1-4	
17 Aug 2005	Malta	1-1	
3 Sep 2005	Azerbaijan	2-0	1
7 Sep 2005	England	1-0	
12 Oct 2005	Austria	0-2	
15 Nov 2005	Portugal	1-1	1
1 Mar 2006	Estonia	1-0	

DID YOU KNOW?
When Warren Feeney junior was capped away to Liechtenstein in March 2002, he became the third generation of his family to play for Northern Ireland. He followed in the footsteps of his grandfather James (capped twice in 1950) and his father Warren senior (once in 1976).

624   SHAUN PAUL HOLMES

Position   Defender

Born   Derry, 27 December 1980

Clubs   Manchester City; Wrexham; Glentoran

Caps   1

Date	Team	Result	G
27 Mar 2002	Liechtenstein	0-0	

625   PATRICK JAMES (Paddy) McCOURT

Position   Winger

Born   Londonderry, 16 December 1983

Clubs   Rochdale

Caps   1

Date	Team	Result	G
17 Apr 2005	Spain	0-5	

626   LEE RICHARD McEVILLY

Position   Forward

Born	Liverpool, 15 April 1982

Clubs	Burscough Town; Rochdale; Accrington Stanley; Wrexham

Caps	1

Date	Team	Result	G
17 Apr 2002	Spain	0-5	

627 STEPHEN CRAIGAN

Position	Defender

Born	Newtonards, 29 October 1976

Clubs	Motherwell; Partick Thistle; Motherwell

Caps	21

Date	Team	Result	G
12 Feb 2003	Finland	0-1	
29 Mar 2003	Armenia	0-1	
2 Apr 2003	Greece	0-2	
31 Mar 2004	Estonia	1-0	
28 Apr 2004	Serbia	1-1	
30 May 2004	Barbados	1-1	
2 Jun 2004	St Kitts & Nevis	2-0	
6 Jun 2004	Trinidad & Tobago	3-0	
18 Aug 2004	Switzerland	0-0	
4 Sep 2004	Poland	0-3	
9 Feb 2005	Canada	0-1	
4 Jun 2005	Germany	1-4	
17 Aug 2005	Malta	1-1	
3 Sep 2005	Azerbaijan	2-0	
7 Sep 2005	England	1-0	
8 Oct 2005	Wales	2-3	
12 Oct 2005	Austria	0-2	
15 Nov 2005	Portugal	1-1	
1 Mar 2006	Estonia	1-0	
21 May 2006	Uruguay	0-1	
26 May 2006	Romania	0-2	

628 CHRISTOPHER PATRICK BAIRD

Position	Right-back

Born	Ballymoney, 25 February 1982

Clubs	Southampton; Walsall (loan); Watford (loan)

Caps	20

Date	Team	Result	G
3 June 2003	Italy	0-2	
11 Jun 2003	Spain	0-0	
6 Sep 2003	Ukraine	0-0	
10 Sep 2003	Armenia	0-1	
11 Oct 2003	Greece	0-1	
18 Feb 2004	Norway	1-4	
31 Mar 2004	Estonia	1-0	
28 Apr 2004	Serbia	1-1	
30 May 2004	Barbados	1-1	

Date	Team	Result	G
2 Jun 2004	St Kitts & Nevis	2-0	
6 Jun 2004	Trinidad & Tobago	3-0	
9 Oct 2004	Azerbaijan	0-0	
9 Feb 2005	Canada	0-1	
26 Mar 2005	England	0-4	
30 Mar 2005	Poland	0-1	
4 Jun 2005	Germany	1-4	
3 Sep 2005	Azerbaijan	2-0	
7 Sep 2005	England	1-0	
12 Oct 2005	Austria	0-2	
1 Mar 2006	Estonia	1-0	

629 THOMAS EDWARD DOHERTY

Position	Midfield

Born	Bristol, 17 March 1979

Clubs	Bristol City

Caps	9

Date	Team	Result	G
3 Jun 2003	Italy	0-2	
11 Jun 2003	Spain	0-0	
6 Sep 2003	Ukraine	0-0	
10 Sep 2003	Armenia	0-1	
28 Apr 2004	Serbia	1-1	
9 Oct 2004	Azerbaijan	0-0	
13 Oct 2004	Austria	3-3	
9 Feb 2005	Canada	0-1	
26 Mar 2005	England	0-4	

630 ANDREW WILLIAM SMITH

Position	Forward

Born	Lisburn, 25 September 1980

Clubs	Ballyclare Comrades; Sheffield United; Bury (loan); Preston North End; Stockport County (loan)

Caps	18

Date	Team	Result	G
3 Jun 2003	Italy	0-2	
11 Jun 2003	Spain	0-0	
6 Sep 2003	Ukraine	0-0	
10 Sep 2003	Armenia	0-1	
11 Oct 2003	Greece	0-1	
18 Feb 2004	Norway	1-4	
31 Mar 2004	Estonia	1-0	
28 Apr 2004	Serbia	1-1	
30 May 2004	Barbados	1-1	
2 Jun 2004	St Kitts & Nevis	2-0	
6 Jun 2004	Trinidad & Tobago	3-0	
18 Aug 2004	Switzerland	0-0	
4 Sep 2004	Poland	0-3	
8 Sep 2004	Wales	2-2	
9 Oct 2004	Azerbaijan	0-0	
9 Feb 2005	Canada	0-1	
30 Mar 2005	Poland	0-1	
4 Jun 2005	Germany	1-4	

631 GARY HAMILTON

Position   Forward

Born   Belfast

Clubs   Portadown; Glentoran

Caps   5

Date	Team	Result	G
3 Jun 2005	Italy	0-2	
28 Apr 2004	Serbia	1-1	
30 May 2004	Barbados	1-1	
2 Jun 2004	St Kitts & Nevis	2-0	
18 Aug 2004	Switzerland	0-0	

632 STEPHEN GRAHAM JONES

Position   Forward

Born   Londonderry, 25 October 1976

Clubs   Chadderton; Blackpool; Bury; Sligo
           Rovers; Bray Wanderers; Chorley; Leigh
           RMI; Crewe Alexandra; Rochdale (loan)

Caps   24

Date	Team	Result	G
3 Jun 2003	Italy	0-2	
11 Jun 2003	Spain	0-0	
6 Sep 2003	Ukraine	0-0	
10 Sep 2003	Armenia	0-1	
11 Oct 2003	Greece	0-1	
18 Feb 2004	Norway	1-4	
31 Mar 2004	Estonia	1-0	
28 Apr 2004	Serbia	1-1	
30 May 2004	Barbados	1-1	
2 Jun 2004	St Kitts & Nevis	2-0	
6 Jun 2004	Trinidad & Tobago	3-0	
4 Sep 2004	Poland	0-3	
13 Oct 2004	Austria	3-3	
9 Feb 2005	Canada	0-1	
26 Mar 2005	England	0-4	
4 Jun 2005	Germany	1-4	
17 Aug 2005	Malta	1-1	
3 Sep 2005	Azerbaijan	2-0	
8 Oct 2005	Wales	2-3	
12 Oct 2005	Austria	0-2	
15 Nov 2005	Portugal	1-1	
1 Mar 2006	Estonia	1-0	
21 May 2006	Uruguay	0-1	
26 May 2006	Romania	0-2	

633 CIARAN TONER

Position   Midfield

Born   Craigavon, 30 June 1981

Clubs   Tottenham Hotspur; Peterborough
           United; Bristol Rovers; Leyton Orient;
           Lincoln City; Cambridge United (loan)

Caps   2

Date	Team	Result	G
3 Jun 2003	Italy	0-2	
11 Jun 2003	Spain	0-0	

634 ANTHONY CHARLES (Tony) CAPALDI

Position   Midfield/Left-back

Born   Porsgrunn, Norway, 12 August 1981

Clubs   Birmingham City; Plymouth Argyle

Caps   18

Date	Team	Result	G
31 Mar 2004	Estonia	1-0	
28 Apr 2004	Serbia	1-1	
30 May 2004	Barbados	1-1	
2 Jun 2004	St Kitts & Nevis	2-0	
6 Jun 2004	Trinidad & Tobago	3-0	
18 Aug 2004	Switzerland	0-0	
4 Sep 2004	Poland	0-3	
8 Sep 2004	Wales	2-2	
9 Feb 2005	Canada	0-1	
26 Mar 2005	England	0-4	
30 Mar 2005	Poland	0-1	
3 Sep 2005	Azerbaijan	2-0	
7 Sep 2005	England	1-0	
8 Oct 2005	Wales	2-3	
15 Nov 2005	Portugal	1-1	
1 Mar 2006	Estonia	1-0	
21 May 2006	Uruguay	0-1	
26 May 2006	Romania	0-2	

635 ALLAN JOHN MANNUS

Position   Goalkeeper

Born   Belfast, 19 May 1982

Clubs   Linfield

Caps   1

Date	Team	Result	G
6 Jun 2004	Trinidad & Tobago	3-0	

636 CHRISTOPHER BRUNT

Position   Midfield

Born   Belfast, 14 December 1984

Clubs   Middlesbrough; Sheffield Wednesday

Caps   7

Date	Team	Result	G
18 Aug 2004	Switzerland	0-0	
4 Jun 2005	Germany	1-4	
17 Aug 2005	Malta	1-1	

Date	Team	Result	G
8 Oct 2005	Wales	2-3	
12 Oct 2005	Austria	0-2	
15 Nov 2005	Portugal	1-1	
1 Mar 2006	Estonia	1-0	

637   MARK GRAHAM CLYDE

Position   Defender

Born   Limavady, 27 December 1982

Clubs   Wolverhampton Wanderers;
Kidderminster Harriers (loan)

Caps   3

Date	Team	Result	G
8 Sep 2004	Wales	2-2	
9 Oct 2004	Azerbaijan	0-0	
4 Jun 2005	Germany	1-4	

638   STEVEN DAVIS

Position   Midfield

Born   Ballymena, 1 January 1985

Clubs   Aston Villa

Caps   13   Goals   1

Date	Team	Result	G
9 Feb 2005	Canada	0-1	
26 Mar 2005	England	0-4	
30 Mar 2005	Poland	0-1	
4 Jun 2005	Germany	1-4	
17 Aug 2005	Malta	1-1	
3 Sep 2005	Azerbaijan	2-0	
7 Sep 2005	England	1-0	
8 Oct 2005	Wales	2-3	1
12 Oct 2005	Austria	0-2	
15 Nov 2005	Portugal	1-1	
1 Mar 2006	Estonia	1-0	
21 May 2006	Uruguay	0-1	
26 May 2006	Romania	0-2	

639   MICHAEL GERARD INGHAM

Position   Goalkeeper

Born   Preston, 7 September 1980

Clubs   Cliftonville; Sunderland; Carlisle United
(loan); Stockport County (loan); Darlington
(loan); York City (loan); Wrexham (loan);
Doncaster Rovers (loan)

Caps   2

Date	Team	Result	G
4 Jun 2005	Germany	1-4	
21 May 2006	Uruguay	0-1	

640   GARETH McAULEY

Position   Defender/Forward

Born   Larne, 5 December 1979

Clubs   Linfield; Crusaders; Coleraine; Lincoln
City

Caps   5

Date	Team	Result	G
4 Jun 2005	Germany	1-4	
15 Nov 2005	Portugal	1-1	
1 Mar 2006	Estonia	1-0	
21 May 2006	Uruguay	0-1	
26 May 2006	Romania	0-2	

641   IVAN SPROULE

Position   Forward

Born   Castlederg, 18 February 1983

Clubs   Hibernian

Caps   5   Goals   1

Date	Team	Result	G
7 Sep 2005	England	1-0	
15 Nov 2005	Portugal	1-1	
1 Mar 2006	Estonia	1-0	1
21 May 2006	Uruguay	0-1	
26 May 2006	Romania	0-2	

642   DEAN SHIELS

Position   Forward

Born   Magherafelt, 1 February 1985

Clubs   Arsenal; Hibernian

Caps   3

Date	Team	Result	G
15 Nov 2005	Portugal	1-1	
21 May 2006	Uruguay	0-1	
26 May 2006	Romania	0-2	

643   PETER THOMPSON

Position   Forward

Born   Belfast, 2 May 1984

Clubs   Linfield

Caps   4

Date	Team	Result	G
15 Nov 2005	Portugal	1-1	
1 Mar 2006	Estonia	1-0	

Date	Team	Result	G
21 May 2006	Uruguay	0-1	
26 May 2006	Romania	0-2	

Position   Forward

Born   Enniskillen, 16 September 1987

Clubs   Burnley; Darlington (loan)

Caps   2

Date	Team	Result	G
21 May 2006	Uruguay	0-1	
26 May 2006	Romania	0-2	

644   BRIAN McLEAN

Position   Defender

Born   Rutherglen, 28 February 1985

Clubs   Glasgow Rangers; Motherwell

Caps   1

Date	Team	Result	G
1 Mar 2006	Estonia	1-0	

649   ALAN BLAYNEY

Position   Goalkeeper

Born   Belfast, 9 October 1981

Clubs   Southampton; Stockport County (loan); Bournemouth (loan); Rushden & Diamonds (loan); Brighton & Hove Albion (loan)

Caps   1

Date	Team	Result	G
26 May 2006	Romania	0-2	

645   SAMUEL GARY CLINGAN

Position   Midfield

Born   Belfast, 13 January 1984

Clubs   Wolverhampton Wanderers; Chesterfield (loan)

Caps   2

Date	Team	Result	G
21 May 2006	Uruguay	0-1	
26 May 2006	Romania	0-2	

650   MARK ANTHONY HUGHES

Position   Midfield

Born   Dungannon, 16 September 1983

Clubs   Tottenham Hotspur; Northampton Town (loan); Oldham Athletic

Caps   1

Date	Team	Result	G
26 May 2006	Romania	0-2	

646   JEFFREY HUGHES

Position   Defender

Born   Larne, 29 May 1985

Clubs   Larne; Ballymena United; Larne; Lincoln City

Caps   2

Date	Team	Result	G
21 May 2006	Uruguay	0-1	
26 May 2006	Romania	0-2	

647   SEAN WEBB

Position   Defender

Born   4 January 1983

Clubs   St Johnstone; Ross County

Caps   2

Date	Team	Result	G
21 May 2006	Uruguay	0-1	
26 May 2006	Romania	0-2	

CHAPTER THREE
NORTHERN IRELAND MANAGERS

PETER DOHERTY

October 1951 – February 1962

There were people who used to say that the flame-haired Doherty who danced his way through English football with Blackpool and Manchester City in the 1930s was a discontented footballer. Doherty was not pompous or petulant, sulky or ill-mannered. Indeed, it would be impossible to meet a more gentle and courteous man. Doherty's discontent was with the system – he was a football trade unionist ahead of his time.

The former Coleraine junior bus conductor who became an Irish national hero won a League Championship medal with Manchester City in 1936-37, and during the war years scored all of Ireland's four goals against the Combined Services. In 1945 he went one better as he helped Derby County win the Midland Cup, scoring five times when the Rams beat Aston Villa in the second leg of the final at the Baseball ground. After a spell with Huddersfield Town, he helped Doncaster Rovers to the Third Division (North) title in 1949-50.

Northern Ireland had never employed a team manager when Doherty took them over in October 1951. They had certainly never even begun to generate the atmosphere of comradeship and dedication he achieved. He was obviously fortunate to have two admirable lieutenants in Spurs' Danny Blanchflower and Jimmy McIlroy of Burnley. Both were rational, gifted and intelligent footballers, just as he had been. The three of them planned the tactics and cut their coat according to their cloth. The first high point was reached in November 1957 when Northern Ireland at long last won in England – and at Wembley.

The following year even this was surpassed when, after drawing 2-2 with Italy at Belfast in a match that was friendly only in name (the Hungarian referee of what was meant to be a World Cup match had been fogbound), the Northern Ireland side proceeded to beat them 2-1 and qualify for the World Cup Finals in Sweden.

There too, they excelled themselves, beating Czechoslovakia and holding West Germany to a draw and in the end beating the Czechs in a play-off to reach the quarter-finals, where their tired and depleted team lost to a rampant France. But even the inspiration and the tactical wisdom of Doherty could not make up for ill-fortune, including the loss of the previous February of the team's gifted centre-half Jackie Blanchflower, shaken by the experience of Manchester United's tragic air crash at Munich.

Doherty returned to England to go on to managing Bristol City. He did so efficiently enough but his chief flair and brilliance were to be seen as an international team manager, fulfilling all the special demands of that task. Above all, he could create the climate of psychological well-being in which matches can be won. He later held scouting posts at a number of clubs and after retiring he lived in Fleetwood, largely shunning publicity until his death in April 1990.

Northern Ireland's Record under Peter Doherty

P	W	D	L	F	A	Success Rate
49	8	14	27	66	112	30.6%

BERTIE PEACOCK

November 1962 – September 1967

Bertie Peacock was a footballer who not only scaled the heights for both club and country, but was also a wonderful ambassador for the game. After beginning his career with Coleraine, he soon joined Glentoran, prior to signing for Celtic in the summer of 1949. He played for the Parkhead club for more than a decade, where his performances earned him 31 international caps for Northern Ireland.

Celtic's team of the 1950s contained such greats as fellow Irish international Charlie Tully and the irrepressible Bobby Evans. Though the Bhoys largely underachieved during that era, Peacock did help them win the domestic double of League and Cup in 1953-54, some three seasons after a victory in the Scottish Cup Final. In 1957 he was a member of the Celtic side that won the League Cup, beating rivals Rangers 7-1 in the final.

Peacock wrote his name into the annals of Northern Ireland football history with his performances in the 1958 World Cup Finals in Sweden, and was dubbed 'The Little Ant' because of his great industry in the Irish midfield. He was also a member of the Great Britain side which met the Rest of Europe in the Irish FA's 75th anniversary match.

After turning down offers to manage both Morton and Blackpool, he returned to Northern Ireland to become player-manager of his first club, Coleraine. He managed Coleraine for 12 years, in the last of which he guided the Showgrounds' club to their only Gibson Cup League triumph. He had led them to success in the Irish Cup in 1965 and 1972 and into Europe but after that League success, he decided to step down, though he remained at the club as a director.

Peacock succeeded Peter Doherty as national team manager in November 1962 and famously gave George Best his international debut against Wales in April 1964. Six months later his Irish side lost 4-3 to England in a seven-goal thriller. Sadly, Peacock had to relinquish his post as national team manager due to business commitments in 1967, and was replaced by former winger Billy Bingham.

Northern Ireland's Record under Bertie Peacock

P	W	D	L	F	A	Success Rate
25	10	4	11	42	45	48.0%

Above: Billy Bingham

BILLY BINGHAM

October 1967 – August 1971 &
February 1980 – November 1993

The father figure of football in Northern Ireland, Billy Bingham holds the record for the longest-serving British international manager, having been in charge of Northern Ireland for a total of 15 years, including one spell of 13 years (1980-1993).

Sunderland paid a large fee for Bingham after an outstanding display for the Irish League against the Football League in 1950. He went on to make 42 consecutive appearances for Northern Ireland in the 1950s. A likeable man with a good sense of humour, Bingham was a superb dribbler and crosser of the ball. His playing days ended after a broken leg in 1965 but before then he had played his part in helping Northern Ireland reach the quarter-finals of the 1958 World Cup Finals in Sweden.

Bingham's first managerial post was at lowly Southport in December 1965. They had a good run to the fifth round of the FA Cup that season and Bingham embarked on a youth campaign, which paid off when the club won promotion to Division Three in 1966-67 as runners-up. Indeed, there was great sadness at Haig Avenue when Bingham moved to take over the reins at Plymouth Argyle. He was not very successful at Home Park, however, and when he was unable to get the club out of the Third Division, the fans began to show their discontent and Bingham was sacked. After spells with Linfield and the Greek national side, he returned to England as manager of one of his former clubs, Everton in 1973. The team was badly in need of reconstruction and with neighbours Liverpool doing so well, it was always going to be a struggle. He brought in some useful players but when honours did not come, he was sacked in January 1977.

A master tactician, Billy Bingham became Northern Ireland's most successful national team manager, taking the country to two World Cup Finals in 1982 and 1986. In 1982 Bingham, who was a member of Doherty's 1958 side that reached the quarter-finals, not only emulated the exploits of that squad but some might say, surpassed it! Appointed manager for a second time in 1980, the Irish began their quest for a place in Spain with a fairly uninspiring goalless draw against Israel but the rest of the qualifying campaign saw victories at Windsor Park against Portugal and Sweden and draws, home and away against the Scots. However, following defeats in Sweden and Portugal, Northern Ireland's hopes of qualification slipped – until Israel surprisingly defeated the Portuguese 4-1.

This left Bingham's side needing a point: in an emotionally charged night at Windsor Park, a Gerry Armstrong goal gave them both points.

In the finals themselves, draws against Honduras and Yugoslavia left them needing either a high-scoring draw or a win against hosts Spain in Valencia. Everyone knows that Gerry Armstrong's goal allowed them to qualify for the second round of the competition. Unfortunately, Northern Ireland went out of the competition at the next stage after a 2-2 draw with Austria and a 4-1 defeat to a very talented French side.

In 1986 Northern Ireland under Bingham continued to be a force to be reckoned with. If they gained a point against England in their final qualifying game, they would win a place in the World Cup Finals in Mexico. A fighting backs-to-the-wall display and a magnificent display of goalkeeping by Pat Jennings saw them play out a goalless draw and qualify for the finals. After a draw against Algeria, Northern Ireland were defeated 2-1 by Spain and needed a point from their final group game against Brazil to progress. However, as expected the Brazilians ran out winners 3-0 and Ireland's World Cup adventure was over. Though Bingham remained manager for a further seven years, this was the end of a golden age, the last occasion when the likes of Pat Jennings, Jimmy Nicholl, Billy Hamilton and Gerry Armstrong would play for their country.

Northern Ireland's Record under Billy Bingham

P	W	D	L	F	A	Success Rate
118	41	33	44	116	129	48.7%

TERRY NEILL

August 1971 – March 1975

Terry Neill's long association with Arsenal began in 1959 when he joined them as a 17-year-old after being spotted playing for Bangor. He made his debut the following season as a wing-half but was later switched to centre-half

by manager Billy Wright. He made 241 League appearances for the Gunners before losing his place to Frank McLintock, who also succeeded him as captain. This intelligent, witty man was a strong, uncompromising player who could be physical or skilful as the situation demanded, making up for his lack of pace with sound positional sense.

He was good enough to make his Northern Ireland debut at 18 against Italy and kept his place for the next 12 years, winning 59 caps and doubling as player-manager and captain in his later years in the side. The most memorable moment of his career came in his 50th international for Northern Ireland when he scored the winning goal against England at Wembley in a rare Irish victory. During his time in charge of the national team, Neill managed with distinction and great professionalism.

He left Highbury to become player-manager at Hull City and at 29 was the youngest boss in the Football League. His management career was eventually to lead him to Tottenham Hotspur in 1974 and then back to Highbury two years later to succeed Bertie Mee. His masterstroke was to bring back coach Don Howe from Leeds United and their partnership guided Arsenal to their three successive FA Cup Finals from 1978-80, plus their near miss in the Cup Winners' Cup in 1980 when they lost to Valencia on penalties. But even this favourite son of Highbury could not escape the usual fate of managers when things begin to go wrong, and after seven years in charge he was sacked at the end of 1983. It was his first real setback in a 25-year career in football. He left football after this to work for a number of charitable organisations before running Terry Neill's Sports Bar in Holborn, London.

Northern Ireland's Record under Terry Neill

P	W	D	L	F	A	Success Rate
20	6	6	8	16	18	45.0%

DAVE CLEMENTS

March 1975 – May 1976

Dave Clements was a man of stature – the epitome of professionalism, principle and integrity. Having played his early football as a winger in his native Northern Ireland for Portadown, he joined Wolverhampton Wanderers. Unable to break into the Molineux club's League side, he moved on to Coventry City.

He soon broke into the Sky Blues' side and just two months after making his League debut for the Highfield Road club, he was making his full international debut for Northern Ireland against Wales. Though he didn't have the best of debuts as the Welsh triumphed 5-0 at Windsor Park, Clements went on to win 48 caps for his country.

At Highfield Road, Clements was converted into a left-back and it was from this position that he netted his first goal at international level in the 1-0 defeat of Scotland in October 1967. On leaving Coventry, Clements signed for Derek Dooley's Sheffield Wednesday where he demonstrated his ability as a cultured passer of the ball who seemed to play the game unhurriedly, in his own time – a sure sign of class. Blessed with a muscular physique, he was adept at retaining possession by shielding the ball and it was rare that an opponent hustled him out of his rather measured stride.

His next club was Everton but like so many of the players at Goodison Park in this era, he suffered from frequent team changes. Whilst on Merseyside, he proved a positive influence on the club's youngsters, and in March 1975 he surprised few when he took the reins of the Northern Ireland side while still a First Division regular.

Not only had Clements succeeded Terry Neill as manager, he also replaced him as captain. In January 1976 he jumped at the opportunity of a transfer from Everton to New York Cosmos – Pele et al – but in doing so, he gave up the chance of a long-term career in international

management. The authorities decided his managerial contract could not be renewed because 'a manager located in the United States was not in the best interests of the Irish FA'.

Northern Ireland's Record under Dave Clements

P	W	D	L	F	A	Success Rate
11	3	2	6	7	15	36.3%

DANNY BLANCHFLOWER

June 1976 – November 1979

Not very quick nor a good tackler, Danny Blanchflower excelled as a reader of the game, a beautiful passer and a player with a rare ability to change tactics in the process of a match. Blanchflower was a thinker, not just a footballer. He was a master tactician with an ability to spot weaknesses in the opposition and exploit them or to plug any deficiencies in his own side.

Although it was Aston Villa who took him into the First Division, after he had played for both Glentoran and Barnsley, club honours did not come his way until he joined Spurs in December 1954 for a fee of £30,000. Under manager Bill Nicholson, Blanchflower became an inspirational figure both on and off the pitch, leading the White Hart Lane club to their greatest-ever achievement – the 1961 League and FA Cup double – and to FA Cup success in 1962 and then on to European Cup Winners' Cup glory the following year. Blanchflower was also Footballer of the Year on two occasions. For Northern Ireland he was the driving force behind one of his country's finest hours, captaining them to the quarter-finals of the World Cup in Sweden in 1958, only to be beaten 4-0 by France.

After a successful spell as a journalist, he was appointed manager of Northern Ireland, succeeding Dave Clements. He was not the most of natural of managers, though he remained in charge for three-and-a-half years. One of Blanchflower's last matches in charge saw Northern Ireland beaten 5-1 by England. Following his departure, he was replaced by

Above: Danny Blanchflower

Billy Bingham, embarking on a second stint in charge of the national side.

Two months later in December 1978, Blanchflower took charge, albeit reluctantly of Chelsea. After just nine months at the helm, he resigned. He felt so alienated by present-day values and what he saw as the absence of loyalty and integrity in the game. Also of course, he had been out of contact with day-to-day football for 15 years and his appointment had looked doomed to failure from the start. One senior player confided: 'He's fascinating to listen to, but we're never quite sure what he's trying to say.'

Northern Ireland's Record under Danny Blanchflower

P	W	D	L	F	A	Success Rate
24	6	5	13	19	38	35.4%

Above: Bryan Hamilton

BRYAN HAMILTON

February 1994 – January 1998

Bryan Hamilton was a terrier-like midfielder who began his career at Linfield and as a £5 part-timer, won his first Northern Ireland cap in 1968. After impressing during the 1971 Home International Championships, Ipswich Town signed him for £26,000 later that year. He moved to Everton in November 1975 for £40,000 but was not a regular at Goodison Park. In October 1980 he was transferred to Tranmere Rovers as their player-manager.

Hamilton made his final appearance in November 1983 but remained in charge at Prenton Park until February 1985 when he was sacked. He had steered the club through a number of crises before his departure. On being appointed manager of Wigan Athletic, he led the club to success in the 1985 Freight Rover Trophy Final at Wembley and the following season to fourth place in the Third Division. He then left Springfield Park to take over the reins at Leicester City. However, he couldn't prevent

their relegation to Division Two and the Foxes were struggling the following season when he was sacked. Hamilton returned to Wigan but had a rather ambiguous role upon his return to the Lancashire club. The club struggled with very low crowds and little success on the pitch, but the genial Irishman managed to keep the side in the Third Division for four seasons, which was a miracle in itself!

Hamilton lost his job in March 1993 but was later a surprise choice to succeed Billy Bingham as Northern Ireland manager – the first full-time occupant. He got off to a flying start as his side pulled off a surprise 2-0 win over Romania. His first major challenge was to lead Northern Ireland to qualification for Euro '96. He failed but his team put up a respectable performance and only just lost out to their neighbours in the Republic of Ireland for a play-off place. The highlights of the campaign included a memorable double over Austria, including a 5-3 home win and a draw with group winners Portugal in Lisbon. Sadly, the next World Cup campaign was a let-down, with the side's worst moment coming in the neutral city of Zürich when Northern Ireland crashed 1-0 to Albania! That defeat and a few other disappointments, along with news that the Northern Ireland boss had lost the respect of his players, saw his contract with the national side terminated.

Northern Ireland's Record under Bryan Hamilton

P	W	D	L	F	A	Success Rate
31	8	8	15	34	41	38.7%

LAWRIE McMENEMY

February 1998 – October 1999

Lawrie McMenemy rocketed to fame as the manager of Southampton. He turned the south coast club into a force to be reckoned with, and his strong personality and ability to communicate with players and fans made him admired by many. McMenemy was a strong disciplinarian, a legacy of his days in the Guards. Behind a warm veneer there was a man ready to make the most difficult of decisions.

As a player, he failed to make the grade at Newcastle United and joined his local club Gateshead, but in 1961 an injury ended his career and he became trainer/coach at the club. In 1964 he was appointed manager of Bishop Auckland and transformed them into Northern Premier League champions. After two years as coach at Sheffield Wednesday, he was appointed manager of Doncaster Rovers and in his first season at Belle Vue took them to the Fourth Division Championship. However, when the Yorkshire club were relegated in 1971, he was sacked. A week later he was appointed manager of Grimsby Town and again at the end of his first season in charge, they too won the Fourth Division title.

In the summer of 1973 he accepted an offer to become Ted Bates' assistant at Southampton but six months later he was appointed the club's full-time manager. At the end of that season, the Saints were relegated and McMenemy came in for a lot of criticism when they did not bounce straight back, but he did take the club to a shock FA Cup victory over Manchester United in 1976.

McMenemy signed a number of experienced professionals and in 1977-78 the Saints won promotion to the First Division and a year later reached the League Cup Final. In 1983-84 Southampton enjoyed their best season in the top flight when they finished runners-up. In June 1985 McMenemy moved to Sunderland but had a tough time at Roker Park, and in April 1987 he was sacked.

After three years out of the game, he returned as assistant-manager to England boss Graham Taylor. His next appointment as Northern Ireland team boss and successor to Bryan Hamilton stunned everyone. Along with coaches Pat Jennings and Joe Jordan, the three were labelled 'The Dream Team' but in truth, his time in charge of the national side was nothing short of a disaster. He started well enough with a couple of victories in friendlies but in competitive games, Northern Ireland continued to fail and in October 1999 McMenemy rejected a new contract.

Northern Ireland's Record under Lawrie McMenemy

P	W	D	L	F	A	Success Rate
14	4	3	7	9	25	39.3%

SAMMY McILROY

January 2000 – October 2003

Sammy McIlroy joined Manchester United in 1969 and two years later made his debut for the Red Devils in the local derby at Maine Road. Yet despite a 63,000 crowd, McIlroy showed considerable maturity and even scored. He made a few more appearances over the next couple of seasons but did not really establish himself until the 1973-74 season as United plunged into the Second Division. He then went on to make over 400 appearances for the club, scoring 68 goals.

McIlroy was a midfielder of energy and attacking purpose whose inspiration was important as United clinched the Second Division championship. He played in the 1976 FA Cup Final and won a winners' medal the following year. In February 1982 he signed for

Above: Sammy McIlroy

Stoke City but after a disappointing time at the Victoria Ground, he returned north to join United's rivals, Manchester City.

On quitting playing McIlroy, who won 88 caps for Northern Ireland, went into management with non-League Macclesfield Town. He had great success with the Silkmen, winning two Conference Championships and triumphing against rivals Northwich Victoria in the 1996 FA Trophy Final. McIlroy helped Macclesfield win promotion to the Football League. In their first season in the League, Macclesfield won promotion to Division Two but in January 2000, McIlroy left the Moss Rose club to manage Northern Ireland. Though spirits in the Northern Ireland camp improved, results in the competitive games didn't!

McIlroy did unearth David Healy and in his first game in charge, Healy scored twice in a 3-0 defeat of Luxembourg. McIlroy's tenure as boss of the national side saw him hampered by problems both on and off the field of play. Players retired and there seemed a never-ending stream of players withdrawing from squads for one reason or another. The former United man was also most unfortunate to be in charge when a number of major controversies caused front page headlines in the newspapers.

In February 2001 came the booing and jeering of Neil Lennon from a small section of home fans in Northern Ireland's 4-0 home defeat at the hands of Norway. Then a few months later came the 'Prague Five' headline in the Czech Republic. Rounding it all off was the death threat made to Lennon prior to him captaining the side against Cyprus at Windsor Park. Sadly, he pulled out of the game and later announced his retirement from international football. After this, both wins and goals proved elusive for the Northern Ireland boss. Following defeats in the home and away games against Armenia, McIlroy left to become manager of Stockport County.

The popular McIlroy is now manager of Nationwide Conference side Morecambe.

Northern Ireland's Record under Sammy McIlroy

P	W	D	L	F	A	Success Rate
29	5	7	17	19	40	29.3%

LAWRIE SANCHEZ

January 2004 –

The son of John Sanchez who played for Arsenal and Watford between 1957 and 1961, he started his career as an associated schoolboy with Reading before leaving to play for Thatcham Town. He later returned to Elm Park and spent seven seasons with Reading, winning a Fourth Division Championship medal in 1978-79. The club were relegated in 1982-93 but he was instrumental in helping the Royals win promotion back to the Third Division at the first time of asking. He had scored 29 goals in 298 games for Reading when Dave Bassett signed him for Wimbledon in December 1984.

Sanchez was an ever-present for the Dons in 1985-86 and helped Bassett achieve his objective of First Division football, when the club finished third in Division two behind

Above: Lawrie Sanchez

Norwich City and Charlton Athletic. Sanchez's outstanding performances for the Dons led to him winning the first of three full caps for Northern Ireland – his mother was from Belfast – in the European Championship qualifier against Turkey.

The highlight of his career came in the 1988 FA Cup Final against Liverpool when he headed home Dennis Wise's free-kick for the only goal of the game. In the seasons that followed, Sanchez struggled with injuries and a loss of form but recovered to win back his place in the side. An excellent club man, he scored 35 goals in 284 games for the Dons before leaving Wimbledon in March 1993 to see out his career with a brief stint at Swindon Town.

He cut his teeth in management with Sligo Rovers in the League of Ireland, taking them to the last four of the FAI Cup before returning to Wimbledon as the Dons' assistant-manager. In February 1999 he was appointed manager of Wycombe Wanderers, helping them stave off relegation which at one time had seemed inevitable. Sanchez stayed at Adams Park until September 2003 when following ten games without a win, he parted company with the club.

Though Jimmy Nicholl had seemed the likely replacement for Sammy McIlroy as Northern Ireland manager, Sanchez shocked everybody by taking the job. On his appointment, Sanchez promised three things – to score a goal, to move up the rankings and to win a game!

In his first game in charge in February 2004, David Healy broke the goalscoring drought of some 1,298 minutes but the Irish were beaten 4-1 by Norway. A month later came Northern Ireland's first victory in three years, when they beat Estonia 1-0 with Healy again the man on target. Following a successful Caribbean tour came Sanchez's first taste of competitive football, but Poland won 3-0 at Windsor Park. There followed entertaining draws against Wales and Austria but in 2005 the team suffered defeats to Canada, England, Poland and Germany as well as playing out a disappointing draw against Malta. After a 2-0 defeat of Azerbaijan, Northern Ireland – thanks to Lawrie Sanchez's tactics and

David Healy's strike – beat the much-fancied England 1-0. Not surprisingly, Sanchez has secured a place in the long and proud football history of Northern Ireland.

Northern Ireland fans have now started to believe that the country can qualify for the finals of Euro 2008 and who knows, with Lawrie Sanchez at the helm, anything is possible!

Northern Ireland's Record under Lawrie Sanchez

P	W	D	L	F	A	Success Rate
23	6	7	10	22	33	41.3%

Above: A Northern Ireland programme from 1958

A Patch from Northern Ireland's World Cup Campaign, 1982

CHAPTER FOUR
THE MATCHES

In addition to listing the date, opposition, team line-up and scorers for every Ireland match since 1882, this section also contains match reports on twenty featured games.

1. 18 February 1882 v ENGLAND at Belfast

J Hamilton	Knock
J McAlery	Cliftonville
D Rattray	Avoniel
DC Martin	Cliftonville
J Hastings	Knock
J Buckle	Cliftonville
WBR McWha	Knock
JR Davison	Cliftonville
J Sinclair	Knock
AH Dill	Knock
D McCaw	Malone
Result	**0-13**

DID YOU KNOW?
On 18 February 1882, England beat Ireland 13-0, the highest score in a Home International.

2. 25 February 1882 v WALES at Wrexham

J Hamilton	Knock
W Crone	Distillery
J McAlery	Cliftonville
DC Martin	Cliftonville
J Hastings	Knock
JR Davison	Cliftonville
WBR McWha	Knock
J Condy	Distillery
J Sinclair	Knock
AH Dill	Knock
RS Johnston	Distillery
Result	**1-7**

RS Johnston

3. 24 February 1883 v ENGLAND at Anfield

J Rankine	Alexander
J Watson	Ulster
D Rattray	Avoniel
TB Molyneux	Ligoniel
DC Martin	Cliftonville

WJ Morrow — Moyola Park
RMC Potts — Cliftonville
WBR McWha — Cliftonville
JR Davison — Cliftonville
J Reid — Ulster
EA Spiller — Cliftonville

Result **0-7**

4. 17 March 1883 v WALES at Belfast

J Rankine	Alexander
J Watson	Ulster
D Rattray	Avoniel
TB Molyneux	Ligoniel
J Hastings	Ulster
WJ Morrow	Moyola Park
RMC Potts	Cliftonville
WBR McWha	Cliftonville
JR Davison	Cliftonville
EA Spiller	Cliftonville
AH Dill	Down Athletic
Result	**1-1**

WJ Morrow

5. 26 January 1884 v SCOTLAND at Belfast

RJ Hunter	Cliftonville
M Wilson	Distillery
W Crone	Distillery
J Hastings	Ulster
TB Molyneux	Cliftonville
AH Dill	Cliftonville
EA Spiller	Cliftonville
JT Gibb	Wellington Park
WJ Morrow	Moyola Park
JR Davison	Cliftonville
AD Gaussen	Moyola Park
Result	**0-5**

6. 9 February 1884 v WALES at Belfast

RJ Hunter	Cliftonville
M Wilson	Distillery
W Crone	Distillery
TB Molyneux	Cliftonville
H Lockhart	Russell School
R Redmond	Cliftonville
JR Davison	Cliftonville
JT Gibb	Wellington Park

J Reid	Ulster
EA Spiller	Cliftonville
AH Dill	Cliftonville

| Result | 0-6 |

7. 23 February 1884 v ENGLAND at Belfast

RJ Hunter	Cliftonville
M Wilson	Distillery
W Crone	Distillery
J Hastings	Ulster
TB Molyneux	Cliftonville
AH Dill	Cliftonville
EA Spiller	Cliftonville
WBR McWha	Cliftonville
RS Johnston	Distillery
JR Davison	Cliftonville
AD Gaussen	Moyola Park

| Result | 1-8 |

WBR McWha

8. 28 February 1885 v ENGLAND at Manchester

AW Henderson	Ulster
G Hewison	Moyola Park
FD Moorehead	Dublin University
TB Molyneux	Cliftonville
WJ Houston	Moyola Park
WLE Eames	Dublin University
WBR McWha	Cliftonville
JR Davison	Cliftonville
JT Gibb	Wellington Park
G Magee	Wellington Park
AH Dill	Cliftonville

| Result | 0-4 |

9. 14 March 1885 v SCOTLAND at Glasgow

AW Henderson	Ulster
G Hewison	Moyola Park
W Johnson	Oldpark
R Muir	Oldpark
WJ Houston	Moyola Park
WLE Eames	Dublin University
T McLean	Limavady
J Sherrard	Limavady
JT Gibb	Wellington Park
G Magee	Wellington Park
AH Dill	Cliftonville

| Result | 2-8 |

JT Gibb (2)

10. 11 April 1885 v WALES at Belfast

AW Henderson	Ulster
W Johnston	Oldpark
WLE Eames	Dublin University

TB Molyneux	Cliftonville
R Muir	Oldpark
WBR McWha	Cliftonville
WJ Hamilton	Dublin Association
WD Hamilton	Dublin Association
JT Gibb	Cliftonville
G Magee	Wellington Park
AH Dill	Cliftonville

| Result | 2-8 |

TB Molyneux; AH Dill

11. 27 February 1866 v WALES at Wrexham

S Gillespie	Hertford
AO Devine	Limavady
J Watson	Ulster
TB Molyneux	Cliftonville
W Crone	Distillery
A McArthur	Distillery
J McClatchey	Distillery
ER Whitfield	Dublin University
RH Smyth	Dublin University
J Lemon	Glentoran
EO Roper	Dublin University

| Result | 0-5 |

12. 12 March 1886 v ENGLAND at Belfast

S Gillespie	Hertford
J Watson	Ulster
AO Devine	Limavady
TB Molyneux	Cliftonville
W Crone	Distillery
J Hastings	Ulster
W Turner	Cliftonville
J Condy	Distillery
S Johnston	Distillery
J McClatchey	Distillery
JR Williams	Ulster

| Result | 1-6 |

JR Williams

13. 20 March 1886 v SCOTLAND at Belfast

S Gillespie	Hertford
J Watson	Ulster
W Crone	Distillery
TB Molyneux	Cliftonville
JR Williams	Ulster
J Hastings	Ulster
J McClatchey	Distillery
S Johnston	Distillery
JT Gibb	Wellington Park
J Condy	Distillery
W Turner	Cliftonville

| Result | 2-7 |

J Condy; S Johnston

S Gillespie	Hertford
F Browne	Cliftonville
WT Fox	Ulster
A Rosbotham	Cliftonville
W Leslie	Belfast YMCA
W Crone	Distillery
J Allen	Limavady
JT Gibb	Wellington Park
OM Stanfield	Distillery
JM Small	Clarence
NM Brown	Limavady

Result	0-7

S Gillespie	Hertford
WT Fox	Ulster
J Watson	Ulster
RL Moore	Ulster
A Rosbotham	Cliftonville
RA Baxter	Cliftonville
J Reid	Ulster
OM Stanfield	Distillery
F Browne	Cliftonville
J Peden	Linfield
JT Gibb	Wellington Park

Result	1-4

F Browne

DID YOU KNOW?
Ireland had to wait until their 16th international for their first win. In that time, they drew one and lost 14 of their first 15 matches. They scored 11 goals and conceded 96!

S Gillespie	Hertford
F Browne	Cliftonville
J Watson	Ulster
J Sherrard	Limavady
A Rosbotham	Cliftonville
AO Devine	Limavady
RL Moore	Ulster
RA Baxter	Cliftonville
JT Gibb	Wellington Park
OM Stanfield	Distillery
J Peden	Linfield

Result	4-1

OM Stanfield; F Browne; J Peden; J Sherrard

J Clugston	Cliftonville
G Forbes	Limavady
W Crone	Distillery

J Sherrard	Limavady
A Rosbotham	Cliftonville
AO Devine	Limavady
AD Gaussen	Magherafelt
OM Stanfield	Distillery
J Barry	Bohemians
JM Wilton	St Columb's Court
J Peden	Linfield

Result	0-11

R Lawther	Distillery
R Wilson	Cliftonville
F Browne	Cliftonville
J Forsythe	Belfast YMCA
A Rosbotham	Cliftonville
TB Molyneux	Cliftonville
W Dalton	Belfast YMCA
OM Stanfield	Distillery
J Barry	Bohemians
J Lemon	Belfast YMCA
W Turner	Cliftonville

Result	2-10

J Lemon; W Dalton

R Lawther	Distillery
M Silo	Belfast YMCA
F Browne	Cliftonville
J Forsythe	Belfast YMCA
A Rosbotham	Cliftonville
W Crone	Distillery
AD Gaussen	Magherafelt
OM Stanfield	Distillery
J McVicker	Linfield
JM Wilton	St Columb's Court
J Peden	Linfield

Result	1-5

W Crone

J Clugston	Cliftonville
MF Goodbody	Dublin University
J Watson	Ulster
A Crawford	Distillery
A Rosbotham	Cliftonville
S Cooke	Belfast YMCA
AD Gaussen	Magherafelt
OM Stanfield	Distillery
J Barry	Bohemians
JM Wilton	St Columb's Court
J Peden	Linfield

Result	1-6

JM Wilton

J Clugston	Cliftonville
J McVicker	Glentoran
R Crone	Distillery
J Thompson	Belfast Athletic
J Christian	Linfield
W Crone	Distillery
S Torrans	Linfield
OM Stanfield	Distillery
JT Gibb	Cliftonville
JM Wilton	St Columb's Court
J Peden	Linfield

| Result | 0-7 |

J Clugston	Cliftonville
AR Elleman	Cliftonville
J Watson	Ulster
A Crawford	Distillery
LV Bennett	Dublin University
J Reid	Ulster
AD Gaussen	Magherafelt
OM Stanfield	Distillery
JC Percy	Belfast YMCA
J Lemon	Belfast YMCA
W Gillespie	West Down

| Result | 1-3 |

J Lemon

W Galbraith	Distillery
R Crone	Distillery
RK Stewart	St Columb's Court
W Crone	Distillery
J Reynolds	Distillery
J Reid	Ulster
W Dalton	Linfield
G Gaffikin	Linfield
S Johnston	Linfield
S Torrans	Linfield
J Peden	Linfield

| Result | 2-5 |

W Dalton (2)

J Clugston	Cliftonville
RK Stewart	St Columb's Court
R Crone	Distillery
J Williamson	Cliftonville
S Spencer	Distillery
S Cooke	Belfast YMCA
AR Elleman	Cliftonville
OM Stanfield	Distillery
JM Wilton	Cliftonville
R McIlvenny	Distillery
J Reynolds	Distillery

| Result | 1-9 |

J Reynolds

J Clugston	Cliftonville
RK Stewart	St Columb's Court
R Crone	Distillery
J Reid	Ulster
S Spencer	Distillery
S Cooke	Belfast YMCA
W Dalton	Linfield
G Gaffikin	Linfield
OM Stanfield	Distillery
S Torrans	Linfield
J Peden	Linfield

| Result | 1-4 |

J Peden

J Clugston	Cliftonville
MF Goodbody	Dublin University
R Morrison	Linfield
A Crawford	Cliftonville
J Reynolds	Ulster
R Moore	Linfield
W Dalton	Linfield
G Gaffikin	Linfield
OM Stanfield	Distillery
S Torrans	Linfield
J Peden	Linfield

| Result | 7-2 |

W Dalton; G Gaffikin; OM Stanfield (4); S Torrans

J Clugston	Cliftonville
G Forbes	Distillery
R Morrison	Linfield
A Crawford	Cliftonville
J Reynolds	Distillery
R Moore	Linfield
T Whiteside	Distillery
OM Stanfield	Distillery
W McCabe	Ulster
R McIlvenny	Ulster
J Peden	Linfield

| Result | 1-6 |

T Whiteside

J Loyal	Clarence
RW Gordon	Linfield
G Forbes	Distillery
A Crawford	Cliftonville
J Reynolds	Ulster
R Moore	Linfield
W Dalton	Linfield
G Gaffikin	Linfield
OM Stanfield	Distillery
D Brisby	Distillery
S Torrans	Linfield

Result	1-2

| OM Stanfield | |

29. 27 February 1892 v WALES at Bangor

J Clugston	Cliftonville
RW Gordon	Linfield
RK Stewart	Cliftonville
N McKeown	Linfield
S Spencer	Distillery
W Cunningham	Ulster
W Dalton	Linfield
G Gaffikin	Linfield
OM Stanfield	Distillery
S Torrans	Linfield
J Peden	Linfield

Result	1-1

| OM Stanfield | |

30. 5 March 1892 v ENGLAND at Belfast

J Clugston	Cliftonville
RW Gordon	Linfield
RK Stewart	Cliftonville
N McKeown	Linfield
S Spencer	Distillery
W Cunningham	Ulster
W Dalton	Linfield
G Gaffikin	Linfield
OM Stanfield	Distillery
S Torrans	Linfield
J Peden	Linfield

Result	0-2

31. 19 March 1892 v SCOTLAND at Belfast

J Clugston	Cliftonville
RW Gordon	Linfield
RK Stewart	Cliftonville
N McKeown	Linfield
S Spencer	Distillery
W Cunningham	Ulster
W Dalton	Linfield
G Gaffikin	Linfield
J Williamson	Cliftonville

OM Stanfield	Distillery
S Torrans	Linfield

Result	2-3

| J Williamson; G Gaffikin | |

32. 25 February 1893 v ENGLAND at Birmingham

J Clugston	Cliftonville
RW Gordon	Linfield
RK Stewart	Cliftonville
N McKeown	Linfield
S Spencer	Distillery
W Cunningham	Ulster
JM Small	Cliftonville
G Gaffikin	Linfield
OM Stanfield	Distillery
S Torrans	Linfield
J Peden	Linfield

Result	1-6

| G Gaffikin | |

> DID YOU KNOW?
> Linfield supplied seven of the players in the Ireland team against Scotland on 25 March 1893 in Glasgow, but the Scots won 6–1.

33. 25 March 1893 v SCOTLAND at Glasgow

J Clugston	Cliftonville
RW Gordon	Linfield
R Torrans	Linfield
N McKeown	Linfield
S Johnston	Linfield
S Torrans	Linfield
JM Small	Cliftonville
G Gaffikin	Linfield
J Williamson	Cliftonville
JM Wilton	St Columb's Court
J Peden	Linfield

Result	1-6

| G Gaffikin | |

34. 5 April 1893 v WALES at Belfast

J Clugston	Cliftonville
RW Gordon	Linfield
RK Stewart	Cliftonville
A Crawford	Cliftonville
N McKeown	Linfield
S Johnston	Linfield
JM Small	Cliftonville
G Gaffikin	Linfield
OM Stanfield	Distillery
JM Wilton	St Columb's Court
J Peden	Linfield

Result	4-3

J Peden (3); JM Wilton

T Gordon	Linfield
RK Stewart	Cliftonville
S Torrans	Linfield
N McKeown	Linfield
J Burnett	Distillery
RG Milne	Linfield
W Dalton	Linfield
G Gaffikin	Linfield
OM Stanfield	Distillery
WK Gibson	Cliftonville
JH Barron	Cliftonville

Result	1-4

OM Stanfield

T Scott	Cliftonville
RK Stewart	Cliftonville
S Torrans	Linfield
S Johnston	Linfield
J Burnett	Distillery
RG Milne	Linfield
W Dalton	Linfield
G Gaffikin	Linfield
OM Stanfield	Distillery
WK Gibson	Cliftonville
JH Barron	Cliftonville

Result	2-2

OM Stanfield; WK Gibson

T Scott	Cliftonville
RK Stewart	Cliftonville
S Torrans	Linfield
N McKeown	Linfield
J Burnett	Distillery
RG Milne	Linfield
W Dalton	Linfield
G Gaffikin	Linfield
OM Stanfield	Distillery
WK Gibson	Cliftonville
JH Barron	Cliftonville

Result	1-2

OM Stanfield

T Gordon	Linfield
H Gordon	Linfield

S Torrans	Linfield
H McKie	Cliftonville
RG Milne	Linfield
J Burnett	Glentoran
T Morrison	Glentoran
G Gaffikin	Linfield
OM Stanfield	Distillery
WC Sherrard	Cliftonville
T Jordan	Linfield

Result	0-9

T Scott	Cliftonville
J Ponsonby	Distillery
LJ Scott	Dublin University
H McKie	Cliftonville
RG Milne	Linfield
J Burnett	Glentoran
T Morrison	Glentoran
WC Sherrard	Cliftonville
T Jordan	Linfield
G Gaukrodger	Linfield
G Gaffikin	Linfield

Result	2-2

G Gaukrodger; WC Sherrard

T Scott	Cliftonville
J Ponsonby	Distillery
LJ Scott	Dublin University
H McKie	Cliftonville
TE Alexander	Cliftonville
T McClatchey	Distillery
T Morrison	Glentoran
WC Sherrard	Cliftonville
OM Stanfield	Distillery
WK Gibson	Cliftonville
JH Barron	Cliftonville

Result	1-3

WC Sherrard

T Scott	Cliftonville
J Ponsonby	Distillery
S Torrans	Linfield
S McCoy	Distillery
RG Milne	Linfield
J Campbell	Cliftonville
E Turner	Cliftonville
G Baird	Distillery
OM Stanfield	Distillery
J McCashin	Cliftonville
J Peden	Distillery

Result	1-6

E Turner

T Scott	Cliftonville
J Ponsonby	Distillery
S Torrans	Linfield
JC Fitzpatrick	Bohemians
RG Milne	Linfield
H Gordon	Linfield
G Baird	Distillery
J Kelly	Glentoran
OM Stanfield	Distillery
E Turner	Cliftonville
J Peden	Distillery

Result	0-2

43. 28 March 1896 v SCOTLAND at Belfast

T Scott	Cliftonville
J Ponsonby	Distillery
S Torrans	Linfield
H Gordon	Linfield
RG Milne	Linfield
JC Fitzpatrick	Bohemians
G Baird	Distillery
D Morrogh	Bohemians
OM Stanfield	Distillery
JH Barron	Cliftonville
J Peden	Distillery

Result	3-3

JH Barron (2); RG Milne (pen)

44. 20 February 1897 v ENGLAND at Nottingham

T Scott	Cliftonville
J Ponsonby	Distillery
S Torrans	Linfield
John Pyper	Cliftonville
RG Milne	Linfield
G McMaster	Glentoran
J Campbell	Cliftonville
G Hall	Distillery
OM Stanfield	Distillery
J Darling	Linfield
JH Barron	Cliftonville

Result	0-6

45. 6 March 1897 v WALES at Belfast

T Scott	Cliftonville
WK Gibson	Cliftonville
S Torrans	Linfield
John Pyper	Cliftonville
J Ponsonby	Distillery
G McMaster	Glentoran
J Campbell	Cliftonville
OM Stanfield	Distillery

James Pyper	Cliftonville
J Peden	Distillery
JH Barron	Cliftonville

Result	4-3

JH Barron; OM Stanfield; John Pyper; J Peden

46. 27 March 1897 v SCOTLAND at Glasgow

J Thompson	Distillery
J Ponsonby	Distillery
S Torrans	Linfield
John Pyper	Cliftonville
RG Milne	Linfield
G McMaster	Glentoran
J Campbell	Cliftonville
OM Stanfield	Distillery
James Pyper	Cliftonville
J Darling	Linfield
J Peden	Distillery

Result	1-5

James Pyper

47. 19 February 1898 v WALES at Llandudno

T Scott	Cliftonville
WK Gibson	Cliftonville
M Cochrane	Distillery
W Anderson	Linfield
RG Milne	Linfield
J Lytle	Glentoran
J Campbell	Cliftonville
JT Mercer	Distillery
James Pyper	Cliftonville
J McCashin	Cliftonville
J Peden	Distillery

Result	1-0

J Peden

48. 5 March 1898 v ENGLAND at Belfast

T Scott	Cliftonville
WK Gibson	Cliftonville
S Torrans	Linfield
W Anderson	Linfield
RG Milne	Linfield
M Cochrane	Distillery
J Campbell	Cliftonville
JT Mercer	Distillery
James Pyper	Cliftonville
J Peden	Distillery
J McAllen	Linfield

Result	2-3

James Pyper; JT Mercer

T Scott	Cliftonville
WK Gibson	Cliftonville
S Torrans	Linfield
W Anderson	Linfield
RG Milne	Linfield
M Cochrane	Distillery
J Campbell	Cliftonville
JT Mercer	Distillery
James Pyper	Cliftonville
J McCashin	Cliftonville
J Peden	Distillery
Result	0-3

50. 18 February 1899 v ENGLAND at Sunderland

J Lewis	Glentoran
John Pyper	Cliftonville
S Torrans	Linfield
J Ponsonby	Distillery
RG Milne	Linfield
M Cochrane	Distillery
J Campbell	Cliftonville
JT Mercer	Distillery
R Waring	Distillery
J Wattie	Distillery
J McAllen	Linfield
Result	2-13

J Campbell; J McAllen (pen)

DID YOU KNOW?
Northern Ireland had played 50 international matches before including a player from a Football League club in their team. In their 51st game on 4 March 1899 against Wales in Belfast, Archie Goodall (Derby County) Bill Taggart (Walsall) and Tom Morrison (Burnley) played in a 1-0 win.

51. 4 March 1899 v WALES at Belfast

J Lewis	Glentoran
John Pyper	Cliftonville
S Torrans	Linfield
AL Goodall	Derby County
RG Milne	Linfield
J Taggart	Walsall
T Morrison	Burnley
J Meldon	Dublin Freebooters
JD Hanna	Royal Artillery, Portsmouth
J McAllen	Linfield
J Peden	Distillery
Result	1-0

J Meldon

52. 25 March 1899 v SCOTLAND at Glasgow

J Lewis	Distillery

S Swan	Linfield
TA Foreman	Cliftonville
W Anderson	Cliftonville
AL Goodall	Derby County
J McShane	Cliftonville
Dr G Sheenan	Bohemians
J Meldon	Dublin Freebooters
James Pyper	Cliftonville
J McCashin	Cliftonville
J McAllen	Linfield
Result	1-9

AL Goodall

53. 24 February 1900 v WALES at Llandudno

T Scott	Cliftonville
John Pyper	Cliftonville
M Cochrane	Distillery
J McShane	Cliftonville
AL Goodall	Derby County
H Maginnis	Linfield
Dr G Sheenan	Bohemians
T Morrison	Burnley
J Kirwan	Tottenham Hotspur
A Kearns	Distillery
J McAllen	Linfield
Result	0-2

54. 3 March 1900 v SCOTLAND at Belfast

J Lewis	Distillery
John Pyper	Cliftonville
M Cochrane	Distillery
J McShane	Cliftonville
J Barry	Bohemians
H Maginnis	Linfield
J Campbell	Cliftonville
J Darling	Linfield
P McAuley	Belfast Celtic
J McAllen	Linfield
A Kearns	Distillery
Result	0-2

55. 17 March 1900 v ENGLAND at Dublin

MM Reilly	Portsmouth
John Pyper	Cliftonville
M Cochrane	Distillery
J McShane	Cliftonville
AL Goodall	Derby County
H Maginnis	Linfield
Dr G Sheenan	Bohemians
J Campbell	Cliftonville
James Pyper	Cliftonville
J McAllen	Linfield
A Kearns	Distillery
Result	0-2

S Alpine	Cliftonville
WK Gibson	Cliftonville
S Torrans	Linfield
P Farrell	Distillery
J Connor	Glentoran
M Cochrane	Leicester Fosse
JE Scott	Cliftonville
JE Smith	Distillery
J Campbell	Cliftonville
H O'Reilly	Dublin Freebooters
R Clarke	Belfast Celtic
Result	0-11

57. 9 March 1901 v ENGLAND at Southampton

JV Nolan-Whelan	Dublin Freebooters
WK Gibson	Cliftonville
P Boyle	Sheffield United
J Connor	Glentoran
AL Goodall	Derby County
J Burnison	Distillery
T Black	Glentoran
R Rea	Glentoran
J Mansfield	Dublin Freebooters
I Doherty	Belfast Celtic
R Clarke	Belfast Celtic
Result	0-3

58. 23 March 1901 v WALES at Belfast

JV Nolan-Whelan	Dublin Freebooters
WK Gibson	Cliftonville
S Torrans	Linfield
P Farrell	Distillery
RG Milne	Linfield
J Burnison	Distillery
J Campbell	Cliftonville
JE Smith	Distillery
H McKelvey	Glentoran
H O'Reilly	Dublin Freebooters
J McAllen	Linfield
Result	0-1

59. 22 February 1902 v WALES at Cardiff

JV Nolan-Whelan	Dublin Freebooters
WK Gibson	Cliftonville
WR McCracken	Distillery
J Darling	Linfield
RG Milne	Linfield
H Nicholl	Belfast Celtic
JT Mercer	Linfield
J Maxwell	Linfield
A Gara	Preston North End
A Kearns	Distillery
J Kirwan	Tottenham Hotspur
Result	3-0

A Gara (3)

60. 1 March 1902 v SCOTLAND at Belfast

JV Nolan-Whelan	Dublin Freebooters
WK Gibson	Cliftonville
John Pyper	Cliftonville
J Darling	Linfield
AL Goodall	Derby County
RG Milne	Linfield
J Campbell	Cliftonville
T Morrison	Glentoran
A Gara	Preston North End
A Kearns	Distillery
J McAllen	Linfield
Result	1-5

RG Milne

61. 22 March 1902 v ENGLAND at Belfast

MM Reilly	Portsmouth
WR McCracken	Distillery
P Boyle	Sheffield United
J Darling	Linfield
RG Milne	Linfield
H Nicholl	Belfast Celtic
JT Mercer	Linfield
T Morrison	Burnley
A Gara	Preston North End
A Kearns	Distillery
J Kirwan	Tottenham Hotspur
Result	0-1

62. 14 February 1903 v ENGLAND at Wolverhampton

W Scott	Linfield
WR McCracken	Distillery
G McMillan	Distillery
J Darling	Linfield
RG Milne	Linfield
AL Goodall	Derby County
J Campbell	Cliftonville
J Maxwell	Linfield
J Sheridan	Everton
HA de B Sloan	Bohemians
J Kirwan	Tottenham Hotspur
Result	0-4

63. 21 March 1903 v SCOTLAND at Glasgow

W Scott	Linfield
A McCartney	Ulster
P Boyle	Sheffield United
J Darling	Linfield
RG Milne	Linfield
H Maginnis	Linfield
JT Mercer	Distillery
J Sheridan	Everton

MJ Connor	Brentford
T Shanks	Woolwich Arsenal
J Kirwan	Tottenham Hotspur
Result	2-0

MJ Connor; J Kirwan

64. 28 March 1903 v WALES at Belfast

W Scott	Linfield
A McCartney	Ulster
P Boyle	Sheffield United
J Darling	Linfield
AL Goodall	Derby County
H Maginnis	Linfield
JT Mercer	Distillery
J Maxwell	Linfield
MJ Connor	Brentford
J Sheridan	Everton
J Kirwan	Tottenham Hotspur
Result	2-0

AL Goodall; J Sheridan

65. 12 March 1904 v ENGLAND at Belfast

W Scott	Linfield
WR McCracken	Distillery
P Boyle	Sheffield United
RG Milne	Linfield
AL Goodall	Glossop
H Maginnis	Linfield
JT Mercer	Derby County
J Sheridan	Everton
MJ Connor	Fulham
J Kirwan	Tottenham Hotspur
HR Buckle	Sunderland
Result	1-3

J Kirwan

66. 21 March 1904 v WALES at Bangor

W Scott	Linfield
WR McCracken	Distillery
A McCartney	Linfield
E McConnell	Cliftonville
RG Milne	Linfield
H Maginnis	Linfield
JT Mercer	Derby County
T Shanks	Woolwich Arsenal
AL Goodall	Glossop
H Kirkwood	Cliftonville
J Kirwan	Tottenham Hotspur
Result	1-0

WR McCracken (pen)

67. 26 March 1904 v SCOTLAND at Dublin

W Scott	Linfield
WR McCracken	Distillery
A McCartney	Linfield
E McConnell	Cliftonville
RG Milne	Linfield
H Maginnis	Linfield
J Campbell	Cliftonville
J Sheridan	Everton
H O'Reilly	Dublin Freebooters
HA de B Sloan	Bohemians
J Kirwan	Tottenham Hotspur
Result	1-1

J Sheridan

68. 25 February 1905 v ENGLAND at Middlesbrough

W Scott	Linfield
WR McCracken	Newcastle United
A McCartney	Linfield
J Darling	Linfield
J Connor	Belfast Celtic
H Nicholl	Belfast Celtic
HA de B Sloan	Dublin Freebooters
J Sheridan	Stoke
N Murphy	Queen's Park Rangers
T Shanks	Brentford
J Kirwan	Tottenham Hotspur
Result	1-1

Williamson (own goal)

69. 18 March 1905 v SCOTLAND at Glasgow

W Scott	Everton
A McCartney	Everton
WR McCracken	Newcastle United
J Darling	Linfield
J Connor	Belfast Celtic
E McConnell	Glentoran
JT Mercer	Derby County
J Maxwell	Glentoran
N Murphy	Queen's Park Rangers
C O'Hagan	Tottenham Hotspur
J Kirwan	Tottenham Hotspur
Result	0-4

70. 8 April 1905 v WALES at Belfast

R Reynolds	Bohemians
WR McCracken	Newcastle United
G McMillan	Distillery
J Darling	Linfield
J Connor	Belfast Celtic
RS Johnston	Distillery
A Hunter	Distillery
J Maxwell	Glentoran
N Murphy	Queen's Park Rangers

C O'Hagan	Tottenham Hotspur
J Kirwan	Tottenham Hotspur
Result	2-2

N Murphy; C O'Hagan

71. 17 February 1906 v ENGLAND at Belfast

JJ Sherry	Bohemians
J Darling	Linfield
H McIlroy	Cliftonville
J Wright	Cliftonville
RG Milne	Linfield
E McConnell	Sunderland
A Hunter	Distillery
S Mulholland	Belfast Celtic
V Harris	Shelbourne
C O'Hagan	Tottenham Hotspur
J Kirwan	Chelsea
Result	0-5

72. 17 March 1906 v SCOTLAND at Dublin

FW McKee	Cliftonville
G Willis	Linfield
J Darling	Linfield
J Wright	Cliftonville
RG Milne	Linfield
JJ Ledwidge	Shelbourne
A Hunter	Distillery
S Mulholland	Belfast Celtic
TMR Waddell	Cliftonville
C O'Hagan	Tottenham Hotspur
J Kirwan	Chelsea
Result	0-1

73. 2 April 1906 v WALES at Wrexham

FW McKee	Cliftonville
G Willis	Linfield
J Darling	Linfield
J Wright	Cliftonville
RG Milne	Linfield
JJ Ledwidge	Shelbourne
A Hunter	Distillery
J Maxwell	Belfast Celtic
C O'Hagan	Tottenham Hotspur
HA de B Sloan	Bohemians
J Kirwan	Chelsea
Result	4-4

J Maxwell (2); HA de B Sloan (2)

74. 16 February 1907 v ENGLAND at Liverpool

W Scott	Everton
WR McCracken	Newcastle United
A McCartney	Belfast Celtic

J Wright	Cliftonville
J Connor	Belfast Celtic
E McConnell	Sunderland
J Blair	Cliftonville
V Harris	Shelbourne
HA de B Sloan	Bohemians
C O'Hagan	Aberdeen
S Young	Linfield
Result	0-1

75. 23 February 1907 v WALES at Belfast

JJ Sherry	Bohemians
J Seymour	Cliftonville
A McCartney	Belfast Celtic
J Wright	Cliftonville
C Crothers	Distillery
G McClure	Cliftonville
J Blair	Cliftonville
V Harris	Shelbourne
HA de B Sloan	Bohemians
C O'Hagan	Aberdeen
J Kirwan	Chelsea
Result	2-3

C O'Hagan; HA de B Sloan

76. 16 March 1907 v SCOTLAND at Glasgow

W Scott	Everton
G Willis	Linfield
A McCartney	Belfast Celtic
J Wright	Cliftonville
J Connor	Belfast Celtic
G McClure	Cliftonville
J Blair	Cliftonville
J Maxwell	Belfast Celtic
E McGuire	Distillery
C O'Hagan	Aberdeen
S Young	Linfield
Result	0-3

77. 15 February 1908 v ENGLAND at Belfast

W Scott	Everton
AB Craig	Glasgow Rangers
A McCartney	Belfast Celtic
V Harris	Shelbourne
J Connor	Belfast Celtic
G McClure	Cliftonville
J Blair	Cliftonville
DJ Hannon	Bohemians
HVA Mercer	Linfield
S Burnison	Distillery
S Young	Linfield
Result	1-3

DJ Hannon

W Scott	Everton
AB Craig	Glasgow Rangers
A McCartney	Belfast Celtic
V Harris	Shelbourne
J Connor	Belfast Celtic
E McConnell	Sunderland
J Blair	Cliftonville
DJ Hannon	Bohemians
W Andrews	Glentoran
C O'Hagan	Aberdeen
S Young	Linfield

Result	0-5

W Scott	Everton
AB Craig	Glasgow Rangers
A McCartney	Belfast Celtic
J Darling	Linfield
E McConnell	Sunderland
V Harris	Shelbourne
A Hunter	Belfast Celtic
WJ Hamilton	Distillery
HA de B Sloan	Bohemians
C O'Hagan	Aberdeen
HR Buckle	Bristol Rovers

Result	1-0

HA de B Sloan

W Scott	Everton
J Balfe	Shelbourne
A McCartney	Glentoran
V Harris	Everton
J Darling	Linfield
G McClure	Distillery
A Hunter	Belfast Celtic
W Lacey	Everton
W Greer	Queen's Park Rangers
C O'Hagan	Aberdeen
S Young	Airdrieonians

Result	0-4

W Scott	Everton
AB Craig	Glasgow Rangers
A McCartney	Glentoran
V Harris	Everton
E McConnell	Sheffield Wednesday
HA de B Sloan	Bohemians
A Hunter	Belfast Celtic
W Lacey	Everton
W Greer	Queen's Park Rangers
CG Webb	Brighton
J Kirwan	Clyde

Result	0-5

W Scott	Everton
J Seymour	Cliftonville
A McCartney	Belfast Celtic
V Harris	Everton
J Connor	Belfast Celtic
E McConnell	Sheffield Wednesday
A Hunter	Belfast Celtic
W Lacey	Everton
W Greer	Queen's Park Rangers
CG Webb	Brighton
JC Slemin	Bohemians

Result	2-3

W Lacey; A Hunter

W Scott	Everton
S Burnison	Distillery
P McCann	Belfast Celtic
V Harris	Everton
E McConnell	Sheffield Wednesday
J Darling	Linfield
WTJ Renneville	Leyton
W Lacey	Everton
JM Murray	Motherwell
J Murphy	Bradford City
FW Thompson	Cliftonville

Result	1-1

FW Thompson

W Scott	Everton
S Burnison	Distillery
P McCann	Belfast Celtic
V Harris	Everton
E McConnell	Sheffield Wednesday
J Darling	Linfield
WTJ Renneville	Leyton
W Lacey	Everton
JM Murray	Motherwell
J Murphy	Bradford City
FW Thompson	Cliftonville

Result	1-0

FW Thompson

JC O'Hehir	Bohemians
J Balfe	Shelbourne
P McCann	Belfast Celtic
V Harris	Everton

E McConnell	Sheffield Wednesday
J Darling	Linfield
WTJ Renneville	Leyton
W Lacey	Everton
JM Murray	Sheffield Wednesday
J Murphy	Bradford City
FW Thompson	Cliftonville

Result	1-4

J Darling (pen)

86. 28 January 1911 v WALES at Belfast

W Scott	Everton
S Burnison	Bradford City
PJ Thunder	Bohemians
V Harris	Everton
J Connor	Belfast Celtic
H Hampton	Bradford City
WTJ Renneville	Leyton
W Lacey	Everton
W Halligan	Derby County
JL McAuley	Huddersfield Town
FW Thompson	Linfield

Result	1-2

W Halligan

87. 11 February 1911 v ENGLAND at Derby

W Scott	Everton
S Burnison	Bradford City
P McCann	Belfast Celtic
V Harris	Everton
J Connor	Belfast Celtic
H Hampton	Bradford City
W Lacey	Everton
DJ Hannon	Bohemians
J McDonnell	Bohemians
JL McAuley	Huddersfield Town
FW Thompson	Bradford City

Result	1-2

JL McAuley

88. 18 March 1911 v SCOTLAND at Glasgow

W Scott	Everton
S Burnison	Bradford City
P McCann	Glentoran
V Harris	Everton
J Connor	Belfast Celtic
H Hampton	Bradford City
W Lacey	Everton
DJ Hannon	Bohemians
J McDonnell	Bohemians
CG Webb	Brighton
T Walker	Bury

Result	0-2

89. 10 February 1912 v ENGLAND at Dublin

W Scott	Everton
S Burnison	Distillery
P McCann	Glentoran
V Harris	Everton
P O'Connell	Sheffield Wednesday
H Hampton	Bradford City
W Lacey	Everton
M Hamill	Manchester United
W Halligan	Wolverhampton Wanderers
JL McAuley	Huddersfield Town
FW Thompson	Bradford City

Result	1-6

M Hamill

90. 6 March 1912 v SCOTLAND at Belfast

J Hanna	Nottingham Forest
G Willis	Linfield
AB Craig	Morton
J Darling	Linfield
P O'Connell	Sheffield Wednesday
J Moran	Leeds City
J Houston	Linfield
J McKnight	Preston North End
JL McAuley	Huddersfield Town
J Enright	Leeds City
S Young	Airdrieonians

Result	1-4

J McKnight (pen)

91. 13 April 1912 v WALES at Cardiff

J Hanna	Nottingham Forest
AB Craig	Morton
WG McConnell	Bohemians
H Hampton	Bradford City
B Brennan	Bohemians
D Rollo	Linfield
J Houston	Linfield
DJ Hannon	Bohemians
J McDonnell	Bohemians
J McCandless	Bradford Park Avenue
FW Thompson	Bradford City

Result	3-2

J McCandless (2); B Brennan

92. 18 January 1913 v WALES at Belfast

W Scott	Leeds City
S Burnison	Distillery
P McCann	Glentoran
D Rollo	Linfield
L Donnelly	Distillery
H Hampton	Bradford City
J Houston	Linfield

W Lacey	Liverpool
J McDonnell	Bohemians
J McCandless	Bradford Park Avenue
FW Thompson	Bradford City

| Result | 0-1 |

93. 15 February 1913 v ENGLAND at Belfast

W Scott	Leeds City
WG McConnell	Bohemians
P Warren	Shelbourne
H Hampton	Bradford City
V Harris	Everton
W Andrews	Grimsby Town
J Houston	Everton
DJ Hannon	Bohemians
W Gillespie	Sheffield United
JL McAuley	Huddersfield Town
FW Thompson	Bradford City

| Result | 2-1 |

W Gillespie (2)

94. 15 March 1913 v SCOTLAND at Dublin

W Scott	Leeds City
WG McConnell	Bohemians
P Warren	Shelbourne
W Andrews	Grimsby Town
V Harris	Everton
H Hampton	Bradford City
J Houston	Everton
J McKnight	Glentoran
W Gillespie	Sheffield United
JL McAuley	Huddersfield Town
FW Thompson	Bradford City

| Result | 1-2 |

J McKnight

95. 19 January 1914 v WALES at Wrexham

FW McKee	Belfast Celtic
WG McConnell	Bohemians
AB Craig	Morton
V Harris	Everton
P O'Connell	Hull City
D Rollo	Linfield
HC Seymour	Bohemians
S Young	Linfield
W Gillespie	Sheffield United
W Lacey	Liverpool
LJO Bookman	Bradford City

| Result | 2-1 |

S Young; W Gillespie

96. 14 February 1914 v ENGLAND at Middlesbrough

FW McKee	Belfast Celtic
WG McConnell	Bohemians
AB Craig	Morton
H Hampton	Bradford City
P O'Connell	Hull City
M Hamill	Manchester United
D Rollo	Linfield
S Young	Linfield
W Gillespie	Sheffield United
W Lacey	Liverpool
FW Thompson	Clyde

| Result | 3-0 |

W Lacey (2); W Gillespie

97. 14 March 1914 v SCOTLAND at Belfast

FW McKee	Belfast Celtic
WG McConnell	Bohemians
AB Craig	Morton
V Harris	Everton
P O'Connell	Hull City
M Hamill	Manchester United
J Houston	Everton
R Nixon	Linfield
S Young	Linfield
W Lacey	Liverpool
FW Thompson	Clyde

| Result | 1-1 |

S Young

98. 25 October 1919 v ENGLAND at Belfast

W O'Hagan	St Mirren
W McCandless	Linfield
WR McCracken	Newcastle United
W Emerson	Glentoran
M Hamill	Belfast Celtic
W Lacey	Liverpool
J Ferris	Belfast Celtic
A Snape	Airdrieonians
J Gowdy	Glentoran
P Gallagher	Glasgow Celtic
DR Lyner	Glentoran

| Result | 1-1 |

J Ferris

99. 14 February 1919 v WALES at Belfast

W O'Hagan	St Mirren
R Manderson	Glasgow Rangers
D Rollo	Blackburn Rovers
W McCandless	Linfield
M Hamill	Belfast Celtic
W Emerson	Glentoran
DR Lyner	Glentoran

W Lacey	Liverpool
W Gillespie	Sheffield United
J Ferris	Belfast Celtic
J McCandless	Bradford Park Avenue

| Result | 2-2 |

W McCandless; W Emerson

100. 13 March 1919 v SCOTLAND at Glasgow

E Scott	Liverpool
R Manderson	Glasgow Rangers
D Rollo	Northern Ireland
M Hamill	Belfast Celtic
W Lacey	Liverpool
W Emerson	Glentoran
P Robinson	Distillery
P Gallagher	Glasgow Celtic
EA Brookes	Shelbourne
W Gillespie	Sheffield United
J McCandless	Bradford Park Avenue

| Result | 0-3 |

101. 23 October 1920 v ENGLAND at Sunderland

E Scott	Liverpool
D Rollo	Blackburn Rovers
W McCandless	Linfield
R McCracken	Crystal Palace
W Lacey	Liverpool
W Emerson	Glentoran
PJ Kelly	Manchester City
J Ferris	Chelsea
JF Doran	Brighton & Hove Albion
W Gillespie	Sheffield United
J McCandless	Bradford Park Avenue

| Result | 0-2 |

102. 26 February 1921 v SCOTLAND at Belfast

E Scott	Liverpool
J Mulligan	Manchester City
D Rollo	Blackburn Rovers
W Lacey	Liverpool
EE Smith	Cardiff City
MT O'Brien	Queen's Park Rangers
S McGregor	Glentoran
J Ferris	Chelsea
D McKinney	Hull City
M Hamill	Manchester City
LJO Bookman	Luton Town

| Result | 0-2 |

103. 9 April 1921 v WALES at Swansea

E Scott	Liverpool
D Rollo	Blackburn Rovers
W McCandless	Glasgow Rangers

W Lacey	Liverpool
MJ Scraggs	Glentoran
J Harris	Cliftonville
P Robinson	Blackburn Rovers
J Brown	Glenavon
RJ Chambers	Distillery
A Mathieson	Luton Town
LJO Bookman	Luton Town

| Result | 1-2 |

RJ Chambers

104. 22 October 1921 v ENGLAND at Belfast

E Scott	Liverpool
WR McCracken	Newcastle United
D Rollo	Blackburn Rovers
R McCracken	Crystal Palace
MJ Scraggs	Glentoran
W Emerson	Glentoran
W Lacey	Liverpool
W Gillespie	Sheffield United
JF Doran	Brighton & Hove Albion
A Mathieson	Luton Town
LJO Bookman	Luton Town

| Result | 1-1 |

W Gillespie

105. 4 March 1922 v SCOTLAND at Glasgow

F Collins	Glasgow Celtic
WR McCracken	Newcastle United
W McCandless	Glasgow Rangers
R McCracken	Crystal Palace
MT O'Brien	Leicester City
W Emerson	Glentoran
W Lacey	Liverpool
P Gallagher	Glasgow Celtic
RW Irvine	Everton
W Gillespie	Sheffield United
DR Lyner	Glentoran

| Result | 1-2 |

W Gillespie

106. 1 April 1922 v WALES at Belfast

JAC Mehaffey	Queen's Island
WR McCracken	Newcastle United
JJ Curran	Glenavon
R McCracken	Crystal Palace
MT O'Brien	Leicester City
W Emerson	Burnley
DR Lyner	Glentoran
WJ Crooks	Manchester United
JF Doran	Brighton & Hove Albion
W Gillespie	Sheffield United
J Toner	Arsenal

Result	1-1

W Gillespie

107. 21 October 1922 v ENGLAND at West Bromwich

Al Harland	Linfield
D Rollo	Blackburn Rovers
JJ Curran	Pontyprid
W Emerson	Burnley
EE Smith	Cardiff City
FG Morgan	Linfield
DR Lyner	Manchester United
RW Irvine	Everton
P Nelis	Nottingham Forest
W Gillespie	Sheffield United
J Burns	Glenavon

Result	0-2

108. 3 March 1923 v SCOTLAND at Belfast

TG Farquharson	Cardiff City
WR McCracken	Hull City
JJ Curran	Pontypridd
SJ Irving	Dundee
G Moorehead	Linfield
W Emerson	Burnley
H McKenzie	Distillery
P Gallagher	Glasgow Celtic
GH Reid	Cardiff City
W Gillespie	Sheffield United
W Moore	Falkirk

Result	0-1

109. 14 April 1923 v WALES at Wrexham

TG Farquharson	Cardiff City
J Mackie	Arsenal
AL Kennedy	Arsenal
SJ Irving	Dundee
EE Smith	Cardiff City
W Emerson	Burnley
DR Lyner	Kilmarnock
P Gallagher	Glasgow Celtic
RW Irvine	Everton
W Gillespie	Sheffield United
J Toner	Arsenal

Result	3-0

RW Irvine (2); W Gillespie

110. 20 October 1923 v ENGLAND at Belfast

TG Farquharson	Cardiff City
A McCluggage	Bradford Park Avenue
JJ Curran	Glenavon
SJ Irving	Dundee
EE Smith	Cardiff City
W Emerson	Burnley

J Brown	Tranmere Rovers
T Croft	Queen's Island
RW Irvine	Everton
W Gillespie	Sheffield United
J Toner	Arsenal

Result	2-1

W Gillespie; T Croft

111. 1 March 1924 v SCOTLAND at Glasgow

TG Farquharson	Cardiff City
D Rollo	Blackburn Rovers
W McCandless	Glasgow Rangers
SJ Irving	Dundee
MT O'Brien	Leicester City
FG Morgan	Nottingham Forest
D McKinney	Bradford City
P Gallagher	Glasgow Celtic
RW Irvine	Everton
W Gillespie	Sheffield United
J McGrillen	Clyde

Result	0-2

112. 15 March 1924 v WALES at Belfast

TG Farquharson	Cardiff City
D Rollo	Blackburn Rovers
W McCandless	Glasgow Rangers
J Gowdy	Queen's Island
MT O'Brien	Leicester City
SJ Irving	Dundee
J Brown	Tranmere Rovers
P Gallagher	Glasgow Celtic
P McIlvenny	Distillery
W Gillespie	Sheffield United
J Toner	Arsenal

Result	0-1

113. 22 October 1924 v ENGLAND at Liverpool

TG Farquharson	Cardiff City
R Manderson	Glasgow Rangers
AL Kennedy	Arsenal
HA Chatton	Partick Thistle
MT O'Brien	Hull City
SJ Irving	Dundee
W Lacey	New Brighton
P Gallagher	Glasgow Celtic
RW Irvine	Everton
W Gillespie	Sheffield United
J Toner	Arsenal

Result	1-3

W Gillespie

TG Farquharson	Cardiff City
R Manderson	Glasgow Rangers
W McCandless	Glasgow Rangers
HA Chatton	Partick Thistle
MT O'Brien	Hull City
SJ Irving	Dundee
D Martin	Bo'ness
P Gallagher	Glasgow Celtic
E Carroll	Glenavon
W Gillespie	Sheffield United
J Toner	Arsenal
Result	0-3

115. 18 April 1925 v WALES at Wrexham

E Scott	Liverpool
D Rollo	Blackburn Rovers
WH McConnell	Reading
J Garrett	Distillery
MT O'Brien	Hull City
SJ Irving	Dundee
TS Cowan	Queen's Island
P Gallagher	Glasgow Celtic
AS Sloan	London Caledonians
HL Meek	Glentoran
H Wilson	Linfield
Result	0-0

116. 24 October 1925 v ENGLAND at Belfast

E Scott	Liverpool
D Rollo	Blackburn Rovers
WH McConnell	Reading
J Gowdy	Falkirk
HA Chatton	Partick Thistle
T Sloan	Cardiff City
AW Bothwell	Ards
RW Irvine	Everton
HH Davey	Reading
J Hopkins	Brighton & Hove Albion
D McMullan	Liverpool
Result	0-0

117. 13 February 1926 v WALES at Belfast

E Scott	Liverpool
WG Brown	Glenavon
WH McConnell	Reading
SJ Irving	Dundee
MT O'Brien	Hull City
T Sloan	Cardiff City
AW Bothwell	Ards
A Steele	Charlton Athletic
S Curran	Belfast Celtic
W Gillespie	Sheffield United
D McMullan	Liverpool
Result	3-0

W Gillespie; S Curran (2)

E Scott	Liverpool
R Manderson	Glasgow Rangers
T Watson	Cardiff City
SJ Irving	Dundee
J Gowdy	Falkirk
T Sloan	Cardiff City
AW Bothwell	Ards
A Steele	Charlton Athletic
S Curran	Belfast Celtic
W Gillespie	Sheffield United
J Mahood	Belfast Celtic
Result	0-4

119. 20 October 1926 v ENGLAND at Liverpool

E Scott	Liverpool
D Rollo	Blackburn Rovers
WH McConnell	Reading
J Gowdy	Falkirk
FG Morgan	Nottingham Forest
SJ Irving	Dundee
AW Bothwell	Ards
RW Irvine	Everton
HH Davey	Reading
W Gillespie	Sheffield United
J Toner	St Johnstone
Result	3-3

W Gillespie; HH Davey; RW Irvine

FEATURED MATCH NO.1

ENGLAND 3   NORTHERN IRELAND 3

At ANFIELD, LIVERPOOL, 20 OCTOBER 1926.

English football critics openly boasted that this season would see mighty England once again on the pedestal of fame and the game against the Irish at Anfield would provide them with their first victory of the season – a victory which was to lay the foundation of the Home International Championships.

With two splendid, fighting sides battling for victory, there was never a dull moment. For an hour and a half, the spectators saw football as it should be played. They saw goals scored and the only disappointment in terms of the travelling Irish fans was the referee, who was perhaps the only man in the ground who didn't think England's second goal was yards offside!

England did all the early attacking and Elisha Scott playing on his home ground produced the game's first save when he turned Bullock's effort round the post. However, it wasn't too long before the home side opened the scoring. Eight minutes had been played

when George BROWN turned home Ruffell's cross from the left-wing. The Irish drew level through the Sheffield United forward GILLESPIE, after Toner had easily beaten Cresswell before flighting his cross to the far post. Sunderland's Bert McInroy in the England goal appeared jumpy after this goal and never settled down. Indeed, it wasn't long before the visitors had taken the lead through Everton's IRVINE. Ireland completely dominated the first-half and went further ahead towards the interval when Hugh DAVEY who led the line well, headed home Irving's deep cross.

Early in the second-half a fine through ball from Green found SPENCE and though he looked yards offside, the referee waved away Irish claims and allowed the Manchester United winger to go on and shoot past the advancing Scott. England pressed hard for the equaliser and it was only the brilliance of Elisha Scott that prevented them from doing so. Twice in quick succession he denied goalbound shots from Bullock and Walker and even when he was beaten, full-backs Rollo and McConnell made goal-line clearances. However, there was little he could do when BULLOCK forced the ball home from close range following good work by Spence.

A division of the spoils was a fitting termination to one of the best games played between the two countries, though in the dying moments, only a brave save by Scott at the feet of George Brown denied England from scoring a fourth!

120. 26 February 1927 v SCOTLAND at Belfast

E Scott	Liverpool
A McCluggage	Burnley
WH McConnell	Reading
J Gowdy	Falkirk
T Sloan	Cardiff City
D McMullan	Liverpool
J McGrillen	Belfast Celtic
P Gallagher	Falkirk
HH Davey	Reading
SJ Irving	Cardiff City
J Toner	St Johnstone

Result	0-2

121. 9 April 1927 v WALES at Cardiff

E Scott	Liverpool
A McCluggage	Burnley
WH McConnell	Reading
SJ Irving	Cardiff City
T Sloan	Cardiff City
MT O'Brien	Derby County
AW Bothwell	Ards
RW Irvine	Everton
H Johnston	Portadown
W Gillespie	Sheffield United
JH McCaw	Linfield

Result	2-2

H Johnston (2)

122. 22 October 1927 v ENGLAND at Belfast

E Scott	Liverpool
A McCluggage	Burnley
WH McConnell	Reading
SJ Irving	Cardiff City
FG Morgan	Nottingham Forest
T Sloan	Cardiff City
RJ Chambers	Bury
RW Irvine	Everton
HH Davey	Reading
W Gillespie	Sheffield United
J Mahood	Belfast Celtic

Result	2-0

H Jones (own goal); J Mahood

123. 4 February 1928 v WALES at Belfast

E Scott	Liverpool
A McCluggage	Burnley
WH McConnell	Reading
SJ Irving	Cardiff City
FG Morgan	Nottingham Forest
T Sloan	Cardiff City
RJ Chambers	Bury
J Dunne	Sheffield United
HH Davey	Portsmouth
P McConnell	Doncaster Rovers
J Mahood	Belfast Celtic

Result	1-2

RJ Chambers

124. 25 February 1928 v SCOTLAND at Glasgow

E Scott	Liverpool
A McCluggage	Burnley
R Hamilton	Glasgow Rangers
SJ Irving	Cardiff City
G Moorhead	Linfield
FG Morgan	Nottingham Forest
RJ Chambers	Bury
RW Irvine	Everton
S Curran	Belfast Celtic
J Ferris	Belfast Celtic
J Mahood	Belfast Celtic

Result	1-0

RJ Chambers

125. 22 October 1928 v ENGLAND at Liverpool

E Scott	Liverpool
A McCluggage	Burnley
R Hamilton	Glasgow Rangers
SJ Irving	Chelsea

T Sloan	Cardiff City
FG Morgan	Nottingham Forest
RJ Chambers	Bury
RW Irvine	Portsmouth
J Bambrick	Linfield
W Gillespie	Sheffield United
J Mahood	Belfast Celtic
Result	1-2

J Bambrick

126. 2 February 1929 v WALES at Wrexham

E Scott	Liverpool
A McCluggage	Burnley
W McCandless	Glasgow Rangers
J Miller	Middlesbrough
JH Elwood	Bradford Park Avenue
A Steele	Fulham
RJ Chambers	Bury
RWM Rowley	Southampton
J Bambrick	Linfield
L Cumming	Huddersfield Town
J Mahood	Belfast Celtic
Result	2-2

J Mahood; A McCluggage (pen)

127. 23 February 1929 v SCOTLAND at Belfast

E Scott	Liverpool
A McCluggage	Burnley
H Flack	Burnley
J Miller	Middlesbrough
G Moorhead	Linfield
A Steele	Fulham
RJ Chambers	Bury
RWM Rowley	Southampton
J Bambrick	Linfield
L Cumming	Huddersfield Town
J Mahood	Belfast Celtic
Result	3-7

J Bambrick (2); RWM Rowley

128. 19 October 1929 v ENGLAND at Belfast

E Scott	Liverpool
SR Russell	Bradford City
R Hamilton	Glasgow Rangers
J Miller	Middlesbrough
JH Elwood	Bradford Park Avenue
W McCleery	Linfield
HA Duggan	Leeds United
RWM Rowley	Southampton
J Bambrick	Linfield
L Cumming	Oldham Athletic
PJ Kavanagh	Glasgow Celtic
Result	0-3

129. 1 February 1930 v WALES at Belfast

A Gardiner	Cliftonville
A McCluggage	Burnley
RP Fulton	Belfast Celtic
W McCleery	Linfield
J Jones	Linfield
T Sloan	Linfield
RJ Chambers	Bury
RWM Rowley	Southampton
J Bambrick	Linfield
J McCambridge	Ballymena
J Mahood	Belfast Celtic
Result	7-0

J Bambrick (6); A McCluggage (pen)

FEATURED MATCH NO. 2

NORTHERN IRELAND 7   WALES 0

Ireland's greatest ever victory 7-0 over a hapless Welsh side saw Linfield's Joe Bambrick net 6 of his side's goals as the home side tore holes in a poor visitors defence. BAMBRICK opened the scoring in the first few minutes as good work by McCambridge allowed the Ireland centre forward to lose his marker and shoot past Finnegan. Ireland went 2-0 up midway through the first half when a pin-point cross from Chambers who was causing all sorts of problems for the Welsh defence CROSSED for Bambrick to head home. BAMBRICK completed his hat-trick just before half time, finishing off a move that involved Chambers and Rowley before firing high into the roof of the net.

BAMBRICK was again on the score sheet early in the second half as McCambridge beat Keenor and put the ball through for Ireland's number 9 to make it 4-0. The Welsh defence were nowhere to be seen as BAMBRICK who thought he must have been offside went on to take the ball round Finnegan before rolling it into an empty net. Bambrick and McCambridge then combined well before the latter was pulled back by Bennion as he shaped to shoot. The referee had no hesitation in awarding the penalty which McCLUGGAGE tucked away with ease.

With the game heading towards the close BAMBRICK netted his sixth and Ireland's seventh goal following a mis-kick by Russell that inadvertently placed the ball in the Linfield forward's path. The autographed ball was later presented to Joe Bambrick by Fred Keenor, the Welsh captain.

A Gardiner	Cliftonville
J McNinch	Ballymena
RP Fulton	Belfast Celtic
W McCleery	Linfield
J Jones	Linfield
T Sloan	Linfield
H Blair	Portadown
E Falloon	Aberdeen
FC Roberts	Glentoran
J Geary	Glentoran
JH McCaw	Linfield
Result	0-0

133. 22 April 1931 v WALES at Wrexham

W Diffin	Belfast Celtic
A McCluggage	Burnley
RP Fulton	Belfast Celtic
SJ Irving	Chelsea
J Jones	Linfield
W McCleery	Linfield
HA Duggan	Leeds United
RWM Rowley	Tottenham Hotspur
J Dunne	Sheffield United
J McCambridge	Cardiff City
JH McCaw	Linfield
Result	2-3

J Dunne; RWM Rowley

134. 19 September 1931 v SCOTLAND at Glasgow

A Gardiner	Cliftonville
J McNinch	Ballymena
R Hamilton	Glasgow Rangers
W McCleery	Linfield
J Jones	Linfield
WA Gowdy	Hull City
H Blair	Portadown
RWM Rowley	Tottenham Hotspur
J Dunne	Sheffield United
J Geary	Glentoran
RJ Chambers	Nottingham Forest
Result	1-3

J Dunne

130. 22 February 1930 v SCOTLAND at Glasgow

A Gardiner	Cliftonville
SR Russell	Bradford City
R Hamilton	Glasgow Rangers
R McDonald	Glasgow Rangers
J Jones	Linfield
T Sloan	Linfield
RJ Chambers	Bury
RW Irvine	Portsmouth
J Bambrick	Linfield
J McCambridge	Ballymena
JH McCaw	Linfield
Result	1-3

JH McCaw

131. 20 October 1930 v ENGLAND at Sheffield

E Scott	Liverpool
A McCluggage	Burnley
RP Fulton	Belfast Celtic
J Jones	Linfield
W Reid	Heart of Midlothian
W McCleery	Linfield
HA Duggan	Leeds United
RW Irvine	Connah's Quay
J Dunne	Sheffield United
W Gillespie	Sheffield United
JH McCaw	Linfield
Result	1-5

J Dunne

DID YOU KNOW?

Northern Ireland changed from St Patrick's royal blue jersey to the now traditional green on 17 October 1931 against England. There had been complaints that the blue jersey clashed with the dark blue of Scotland.

A Gardiner	Cliftonville
SR Russell	Derry City
RP Fulton	Belfast Celtic
R McDonald	Glasgow Rangers
J Jones	Linfield
W Mitchell	Distillery
RJ Chambers	Nottingham Forest
P McConnell	Southport
J Dunne	Sheffield United
J McCambridge	Cardiff City
J Kelly	Derry City

Result	2-6

J Dunne; J Kelly

136. 5 December 1931 v WALES at Belfast

E Scott	Liverpool
J McNinch	Ballymena
RP Fulton	Belfast Celtic
W McCleery	Linfield
M Pyper	Linfield
W Mitchell	Distillery
RJ Chambers	Nottingham Forest
RW Irvine	Derry City
J Bambrick	Linfield
W Millar	Barrow
J Kelly	Derry City

Result	4-0

J Kelly (2); W Millar; J Bambrick

137. 17 September 1932 v SCOTLAND at Belfast

E Scott	Liverpool
W Cook	Glasgow Celtic
RP Fulton	Belfast Celtic
E Falloon	Aberdeen
J Jones	Linfield
WA Gowdy	Sheffield Wednesday
E Mitchell	Distillery
TJM Priestley	Coleraine
W Millar	Barrow
S English	Glasgow Rangers
J Kelly	Derry City

Result	0-4

138. 17 October 1932 v ENGLAND at Blackpool

E Scott	Liverpool
W Cook	Glasgow Celtic
RP Fulton	Belfast Celtic
W Mitchell	Distillery
J Jones	Linfield
W McCleery	Linfield
HA Duggan	Leeds United
P Moore	Aberdeen
J Dunne	Sheffield United

J Doherty	Cliftonville
J Kelly	Derry City

Result	0-1

139. 7 December 1932 v WALES at Wrexham

E Scott	Liverpool
W Cook	Glasgow Celtic
T Willighan	Burnley
W Mitchell	Distillery
J Jones	Linfield
W McCleery	Linfield
W Houston	Linfield
S English	Glasgow Rangers
J Dunne	Sheffield United
J Doherty	Cliftonville
J Kelly	Derry City

Result	1-4

S English

140. 16 September 1933 v SCOTLAND at Glasgow

E Scott	Liverpool
T Willighan	Burnley
RP Fulton	Belfast Celtic
J McMahon	Bohemians
J Jones	Linfield
W Mitchell	Chelsea
H Blair	Swansea
AE Stevenson	Glasgow Rangers
DK Martin	Belfast Celtic
J Coulter	Belfast Celtic
J Mahood	Ballymena

Result	2-1

DK Martin (2)

141. 14 October 1933 v ENGLAND at Belfast

E Scott	Liverpool
SE Reid	Derby County
RP Fulton	Belfast Celtic
WS McMillen	Manchester United
J Jones	Linfield
S Jones	Distillery
HA Duggan	Leeds United
AE Stevenson	Glasgow Rangers
DK Martin	Belfast Celtic
J Coulter	Belfast Celtic
TJM Priestley	Chelsea

Result	0-3

DID YOU KNOW?
Jack Jones, his brother Sam and their brother-in-law William Mitchell played as Ireland's half-back line in the international against Wales on 4 November 1933.

E Scott	Liverpool
SE Reid	Derby County
RP Fulton	Belfast Celtic
W Mitchell	Chelsea
J Jones	Linfield
S Jones	Blackpool
EJ Mitchell	Glentoran
AE Stevenson	Glasgow Rangers
DK Martin	Belfast Celtic
J Coulter	Belfast Celtic
J Kelly	Derry City
Result	1-1

S Jones

E Scott	Liverpool
J Mackie	Portsmouth
RP Fulton	Belfast Celtic
WS McMillen	Manchester United
J Jones	Linfield
W Mitchell	Chelsea
HA Duggan	Leeds United
WA Gowdy	Linfield
DK Martin	Belfast Celtic
AE Stevenson	Everton
J Coulter	Everton
Result	2-1

DK Martin; J Coulter

FEATURED MATCH NO. 3

NORTHERN IRELAND 2 SCOTLAND 1

AT WINDSOR PARK, BELFAST, 20 OCTOBER 1934

An overhead cable fault at Shaftesbury Square led to a break down in the tram services in Belfast and this meant that several thousands of Irish fans streamed late into Windsor Park.

The early stages of the first-half saw both sides come close to opening the scoring but it was the visitors who took the lead midway through the first-half when Patsy GALLAGHER netted from close range. Elisha Scott in the Ireland goal then saved well from Connor, as the Sunderland forward's header looked like extending Scotland's lead. Ireland too came close with both Martin and Stevenson bringing good saves out of Dawson.

When Ireland came out for the second-half there were gasps of dismay when the home crowd realised they had just 10 men. Goalkeeper Scott had picked up an injury towards the end of the first-half, and he was replaced in goal by Manchester United's Walter McMillen.

The wing-half had a disappointing first-half but he went on to have an outstanding second period, saving everything the Scottish side could throw at him. He saved at the foot of the post from Cook and then tipped Connor's rasping drive round the post. He then smothered Herd's long-range effort before saving from the dangerous Cook.

However, it wasn't all one-way traffic and both Duggan and Stevenson brought fine saves out of Jerry Dawson. Linfield's Joe Gowdy had earned considerable criticism when he was named in the starting line-up for Ireland but there is little doubt that he was Ireland's best player on the day, with an outstanding display of both attacking and defensive football.

Martin missed an easy chance to level the score before Jackie Coulter smashed a shot against the crossbar. There were just five minutes remaining when MARTIN made amends for his earlier miss by shooting home from close range following good work by Duggan. Then with time running out, Joe Gowdy picked up the ball in midfield, beat two Scots and floated the ball across the face of the Scotland goal where COULTER ran in to head into the roof of the net past a startled Jerry Dawson.

The crowd went wild, finding it hard to believe that Ireland's 10 men had come back from being a goal down at half-time to clinch a famous victory. Hats were thrown into the air by the home fans, who did not care if they ever got them back again!

T Breen	Belfast Celtic
W Cook	Everton
RP Fulton	Belfast Celtic
WA Gowdy	Linfield
J Jones	Linfield
W Mitchell	Chelsea
J Brown	Wolverhampton Wanderers
PD Doherty	Blackpool
DK Martin	Wolverhampton Wanderers
AE Stevenson	Everton
J Coulter	Everton
Result	1-2

AE Stevenson

T Breen	Belfast Celtic
J Mackie	Portsmouth
RP Fulton	Belfast Celtic
K McCullough	Belfast Celtic
J Jones	Linfield
WA Gowdy	Linfield
HA Duggan	Leeds United
J Brown	Wolverhampton Wanderers
J Bambrick	Chelsea

PD Doherty	Blackpool
J Coulter	Everton

Result	1-3

J Bambrick

146. 19 October 1935 v ENGLAND at Belfast

E Scott	Belfast Celtic
SE Reid	Derby County
C Allan	Cliftonville
W Mitchell	Chelsea
J Jones	Linfield
RJ Browne	Leeds United
J Brown	Wolverhampton Wanderers
K McCullough	Belfast Celtic
J Bambrick	Chelsea
PD Doherty	Blackpool
J Kelly	Derry City

Result	1-3

J Brown

147. 13 November 1935 v SCOTLAND at Edinburgh

E Scott	Belfast Celtic
W Cook	Everton
RP Fulton	Belfast Celtic
K McCullough	Manchester City
J Jones	Linfield
W Mitchell	Chelsea
HA Duggan	Leeds United
AE Stevenson	Everton
J Bambrick	Chelsea
PD Doherty	Blackpool
J Kelly	Derry City

Result	1-2

J Kelly

148. 11 March 1936 v WALES at Belfast

E Scott	Belfast Celtic
W Cook	Everton
RP Fulton	Belfast Celtic
WA Gowdy	Hibernian
J Jones	Hibernian
RJ Browne	Leeds United
N Kernaghan	Belfast Celtic
TJ Gibb	Cliftonville
DK Martin	Wolverhampton Wanderers
AE Stevenson	Everton
J Kelly	Derry City

Result	3-2

TJ Gibb; AE Stevenson; N Kernaghan

149. 31 October 1936 v SCOTLAND at Belfast

T Breen	Belfast Celtic
W Cook	Everton
RP Fulton	Belfast Celtic
WS McMillen	Manchester United
J Jones	Hibernian
W Mitchell	Chelsea
N Kernaghan	Belfast Celtic
K McCullough	Manchester City
DK Martin	Nottingham Forest
J Coulter	Everton
J Kelly	Derry City

Result	1-3

N Kernaghan

150. 18 November 1936 v ENGLAND at Stoke-on-Trent

T Breen	Belfast Celtic
W Cook	Everton
RP Fulton	Belfast Celtic
K McCullough	Manchester City
J Jones	Hibernian
W Mitchell	Chelsea
J Brown	Coventry City
AE Stevenson	Everton
TL Davis	Oldham Athletic
PD Doherty	Manchester City
J Kelly	Derry City

Result	1-3

TL Davis

151. 17 March 1937 v WALES at Wrexham

T Breen	Manchester United
W Cook	Everton
RP Fulton	Belfast Celtic
TH Brolly	Millwall
J Jones	Hibernian
W Mitchell	Chelsea
J Brown	Coventry City
PD Doherty	Manchester City
SJ Banks	Cliftonville
AE Stevenson	Everton
J Coulter	Everton

Result	1-4

AE Stevenson

152. 23 October 1937 v ENGLAND at Belfast

T Breen	Manchester United
WE Hayes	Huddersfield Town
W Cook	Everton
W Mitchell	Chelsea
J Jones	Hibernian
RJ Browne	Leeds United
N Kernaghan	Belfast Celtic

AE Stevenson	Everton
DK Martin	Nottingham Forest
PD Doherty	Manchester City
O Madden	Norwich City

Result	1-5

AE Stevenson

153. 10 November 1937 v SCOTLAND at Aberdeen

T Breen	Manchester United
WE Hayes	Huddersfield Town
W Cook	Everton
M Doherty	Derry City
WS McMillen	Chesterfield
W Mitchell	Chelsea
J Brown	Coventry City
J McAlinden	Belfast Celtic
DK Martin	Nottingham Forest
PD Doherty	Manchester City
J Coulter	Grimsby Town

Result	1-1

PD Doherty

154. 16 March 1938 v WALES at Belfast

JF Twoomey	Leeds United
W Cook	Everton
RP Fulton	Belfast Celtic
TH Brolly	Millwall
WS McMillen	Chesterfield
RJ Browne	Leeds United
J Brown	Coventry City
P Farrell	Hibernian
J Bambrick	Chelsea
AE Stevenson	Everton
J Coulter	Grimsby Town

Result	1-0

J Bambrick

155. 8 October 1938 v SCOTLAND at Belfast

T Breen	Manchester United
WE Hayes	Huddersfield Town
W Cook	Everton
WS McMillen	Chesterfield
MT O'Mahoney	Bristol Rovers
RJ Browne	Leeds United
J Brown	Birmingham City
J McAlinden	Belfast Celtic
DK Martin	Nottingham Forest
AE Stevenson	Everton
J Coulter	Chelmsford City

Result	0-2

156. 16 November 1938 v ENGLAND at Manchester

JF Twoomey	Leeds United
WE Hayes	Huddersfield Town
W Cook	Everton
TH Brolly	Millwall
WS McMillen	Chesterfield
RJ Browne	Leeds United
D Cochrane	Leeds United
AE Stevenson	Everton
HC Baird	Huddersfield Town
PD Doherty	Manchester City
J Brown	Birmingham City

Result	0-7

157. 15 March 1939 v WALES at Wrexham

T Breen	Manchester United
W Cook	Everton
MP Butler	Blackpool
TH Brolly	Millwall
J Leatham	Belfast Celtic
E Weir	Clyde
D Cochrane	Leeds United
AE Stevenson	Everton
D Milligan	Chesterfield
PD Doherty	Manchester City
J Brown	Birmingham City

Result	1-3

D Milligan

158. 28 September 1946 v ENGLAND at Belfast

A Russell	Linfield
WC Gorman	Brentford
T Aherne	Belfast Celtic
JJ Carey	Manchester United
J Vernon	Belfast Celtic
JP Douglas	Belfast Celtic
D Cochrane	Leeds United
J McAlinden	Portsmouth
EJ McMorran	Belfast Celtic
PD Doherty	Derby County
NH Lockhart	Linfield

Result	2-7

NH Lockhart (2)

159. 27 November 1946 v SCOTLAND at Glasgow

E Hinton	Fulham
WC Gorman	Brentford
JM Feeney	Linfield
CJ Martin	Glentoran
J Vernon	Belfast Celtic
PD Farrell	Everton
D Cochrane	Leeds United
JJ Carey	Manchester United
DJ Walsh	West Bromwich Albion

| AE Stevenson | Everton |
| TJ Eglington | Everton |

| Result | 0-0 |

160. 16 April 1947 v WALES at Belfast

E Hinton	Fulham
WC Gorman	Brentford
JJ Carey	Manchester United
JW Sloan	Arsenal
J Vernon	West Bromwich Albion
PD Farrell	Everton
D Cochrane	Leeds United
AE Stevenson	Everton
DJ Walsh	West Bromwich Albion
PD Doherty	Huddersfield Town
TJ Eglington	Everton

| Result | 2-1 |

AE Stevenson; PD Doherty (pen)

161. 4 October 1947 v SCOTLAND at Belfast

E Hinton	Fulham
CJ Martin	Leeds United
T Aherne	Belfast Celtic
W Walsh	Manchester City
J Vernon	West Bromwich Albion
PD Farrell	Everton
D Cochrane	Leeds United
S Smyth	Wolverhampton Wanderers
DJ Walsh	West Bromwich Albion
AE Stevenson	Everton
TJ Eglington	Everton

| Result | 2-0 |

S Smyth (2)

162. 5 November 1947 v ENGLAND at Liverpool

E Hinton	Fulham
CJ Martin	Leeds United
JJ Carey	Manchester United
W Walsh	Manchester City
J Vernon	West Bromwich Albion
PD Farrell	Everton
D Cochrane	Leeds United
S Smyth	Wolverhampton Wanderers
DJ Walsh	West Bromwich Albion
PD Doherty	Huddersfield Town
TJ Eglington	Everton

| Result | 2-2 |

PD Doherty; DJ Walsh

FEATURED MATCH NO 4

ENGLAND 2 NORTHERN IRELAND 2

AT GOODISON PARK, LIVERPOOL, 5 NOVEMBER 1947

England, victors over Belgium and Wales, faced an Ireland side who in their last game had unexpectedly beaten Scotland 2-0.

A crowd of nearly 55,000 gave the teams a great welcome when they appeared, Ireland resplendent in green jerseys with bold black numbers on a white background and England in their usual white and black outfit.

In the opening minute Wilf Mannion tricked two defenders before finding Matthews on the other wing, but keen Irish tackling relieved the situation. Red-haired Doherty came close to opening the scoring for Ireland but in the main the early exchanges belonged to the home side. Mortensen missed a chance for England by blazing over from 10 yards out and then he and Mannion each failed to cap fine runs by Finney.

Mannion once again could not turn a Finney centre to account, but Hinton in the Irish goal deserved praise for smothering a point-blank shot from Lawton. The home side were relieved when a flying header from Davy Walsh flew inches over Frank Swift's crossbar. Doherty then went close with a long range shot before Matthews' effort from fully 30 yards was inches too high. Just before the interval, Peter Farrell playing on his home ground, shot powerfully from 25 yards but Swift rose to the occasion with a magnificent full length save.

After nine minutes of the second-half, Ireland took the lead when Davy WALSH cleverly diverted a Doherty shot past Swift. Eglington then swept inside Hardwick but Swift stood firm in holding the left-winger's stinging drive.

There were 20 minutes remaining when England were awarded a penalty for a Vernon charge on Matthews. Hinton made a brilliant save from Mannion's spot-kick. In the 80th minute, Mortensen narrowly missed with a flying header but three minutes later, Billy WRIGHT put England level, this despite appeals from Irish defenders who felt the Wolves' player had committed a foul in forcing the ball over the line.

Then on the verge of full-time, Tommy LAWTON gave England the lead but the Irish were not finished and with the referee putting his whistle to his lips to blow for full-time, up popped Peter DOHERTY to earn his side a thoroughly deserved draw.

E Hinton	Fulham
CJ Martin	Leeds United
WC Gorman	Brentford
W Walsh	Manchester City
J Vernon	West Bromwich Albion
PD Farrell	Everton
D Cochrane	Leeds United
S Smyth	Wolverhampton Wanderers
DJ Walsh	West Bromwich Albion
PD Doherty	Huddersfield Town
TJ Eglington	Everton

Result	0-2

W Smyth	Distillery
JJ Carey	Manchester United
CJ Martin	Aston Villa
W Walsh	Manchester City
J Vernon	West Bromwich Albion
PD Farrell	Everton
JF O'Drsicoll	Swansea Town
J McAlinden	Southend United
DJ Walsh	West Bromwich Albion
CP Tully	Glasgow Celtic
TJ Eglington	Everton

Result	2-6

DJ Walsh (2)

W Smyth	Distillery
JJ Carey	Manchester United
TR Keane	Swansea Town
JJ McCabe	Leeds United
J Vernon	West Bromwich Albion
W Walsh	Manchester City
D Cochrane	Leeds United
S Smyth	Wolverhampton Wanderers
DJ Walsh	West Bromwich Albion
PD Doherty	Huddersfield Town
JP O'Driscoll	Swansea Town

Result	2-3

DJ Walsh (2)

C Moore	Glentoran
JJ Carey	Manchester United
T Aherne	Belfast Celtic
JJ McCabe	Leeds United
J Vernon	West Bromwich Albion
PD Farrell	Everton
D Cochrane	Leeds United
S Smyth	Wolverhampton Wanderers
DJ Walsh	West Bromwich Albion

RA Brennan	Luton Town
JF O'Driscoll	Swansea Town

Result	0-2

PM Kelly	Barnsley
GC Bowler	Hull City
A McMichael	Newcastle United
RD Blanchflower	Barnsley
J Vernon	West Bromwich Albion
RO Ferris	Birmingham City
D Cochrane	Leeds United
S Smyth	Wolverhampton Wanderers
RA Brennan	Birmingham City
E Crossan	Blackburn Rovers
J McKenna	Huddersfield Town

Result	2-8

S Smyth (2)

HR Kelly	Fulham
JM Feeney	Swansea Town
A McMichael	Newcastle United
GC Bowler	Hull City
J Vernon	West Bromwich Albion
JJ McCabe	Leeds United
D Cochrane	Leeds United
S Smyth	Wolverhampton Wanderers
RA Brennan	Birmingham City
CP Tully	Glasgow Celtic
J McKenna	Huddersfield Town

Result	2-9

S Smyth; RA Brennan

HR Kelly	Fulham
GC Bowler	Hull City
T Aherne	Luton Town
RD Blanchflower	Barnsley
CJ Martin	Aston Villa
RA Ryan	West Bromwich Albion
J McKenna	Huddersfield Town
S Smyth	Wolverhampton Wanderers
DJ Walsh	West Bromwich Albion
RA Brennan	Birmingham City
NH Lockhart	Coventry City

Result	0-0

HR Kelly	Southampton
C Gallogly	Huddersfield Town
A McMichael	Newcastle United

RD Blanchflower	Barnsley
J Vernon	West Bromwich Albion
WW Cush	Glenavon
JP Campbell	Fulham
E Crossan	Blackburn Rovers
EJ McMorran	Barnsley
RA Brennan	Fulham
J McKenna	Huddersfield Town

Result	1-4

EJ McMorran

171. 1 November 1950 v SCOTLAND at Glasgow

HR Kelly	Southampton
C Gallogly	Huddersfield Town
A McMichael	Newcastle United
RD Blanchflower	Barnsley
J Vernon	West Bromwich Albion
WW Cush	Glenavon
JP Campbell	Fulham
JK McGarry	Cliftonville
EJ McMorran	Barnsley
PD Doherty	Doncaster Rovers
J McKenna	Huddersfield Town

Result	1-6

JK McGarry

172. 7 March 1951 v WALES at Belfast

E Hinton	Millwall
WGL Graham	Doncaster Rovers
WE Cunningham	St Mirren
JJ McCabe	Leeds United
J Vernon	West Bromwich Albion
W Dickson	Chelsea
W Hughes	Bolton Wanderers
EJ McMorran	Barnsley
WJ Simpson	Glasgow Rangers
JK McGarry	Cliftonville
NH Lockhart	Coventry City

Result	1-2

WJ Simpson

DID YOU KNOW?
It was not until 1951 that Northern Ireland played their first international against foreign opposition when they played France in a 2-2 draw in Belfast. Their first away match was against France in Paris in 1952.

173. 12 May 1951 v FRANCE at Belfast

E Hinton	Millwall
WGL Graham	Doncaster Rovers
A McMichael	Newcastle United
RD Blanchflower	Aston Villa
J Vernon	West Bromwich Albion

RO Ferris	Birmingham City
WL Bingham	Sunderland
JK McGarry	Cliftonville
WJ Simpson	Glasgow Rangers
W Dickson	Chelsea
J McKenna	Huddersfield Town

Result	2-2

RO Ferris (pen); WJ Simpson

174. 6 October 1951 v SCOTLAND at Belfast

WMNC Uprichard	Swindon Town
WGL Graham	Doncaster Rovers
A McMichael	Newcastle United
W Dickson	Chelsea
J Vernon	West Bromwich Albion
RO Ferris	Birmingham City
WL Bingham	Sunderland
J McIlroy	Burnley
EJ McMorran	Barnsley
R Peacock	Glasgow Celtic
CP Tully	Glasgow Celtic

Result	0-2

175. 14 November 1951 v ENGLAND at Birmingham

WMNC Uprichard	Swindon Town
WGL Graham	Doncaster Rovers
A McMichael	Newcastle United
W Dickson	Chelsea
J Vernon	West Bromwich Albion
FJ McCourt	Manchester City
WL Bingham	Sunderland
S Smyth	Stoke City
EJ McMorran	Barnsley
J McIlroy	Burnley
J McKenna	Huddersfield Town

Result	0-2

176. 19 March 1952 v WALES at Swansea

WMNC Uprichard	Swindon Town
WGL Graham	Doncaster Rovers
A McMichael	Newcastle United
RD Blanchflower	Aston Villa
W Dickson	Chelsea
FJ McCourt	Manchester City
WL Bingham	Sunderland
SD D'Arcy	Chelsea
EJ McMorran	Barnsley
J McIlroy	Burnley
NH Lockhart	Coventry City

Result	0-3

177. 4 October 1952 v ENGLAND at Belfast

WMNC Uprichard	Swindon Town

WE Cunningham	St Mirren
A McMichael	Newcastle United
RD Blanchflower	Aston Villa
W Dickson	Chelsea
FJ McCourt	Manchester City
WL Bingham	Sunderland
SD D'Arcy	Chelsea
EJ McMorran	Barnsley
J McIlroy	Burnley
CP Tully	Glasgow Celtic
Result	2-2
CP Tully (2)	

178. 5 November 1952 v SCOTLAND at Glasgow

WMNC Uprichard	Swindon Town
WGL Graham	Doncaster Rovers
A McMichael	Newcastle United
RD Blanchflower	Aston Villa
W Dickson	Chelsea
FJ McCourt	Manchester City
WL Bingham	Sunderland
SD D'Arcy	Brentford
EJ McMorran	Barnsley
J McIlroy	Burnley
CP Tully	Glasgow Celtic
Result	1-1
SD D'Arcy	

DID YOU KNOW?
In an international between France and Northern Ireland in Paris in 1952, France played 12 men for a period in the first-half. After Boniface had been injured, a substitute took his place and France saw the half out with 12 men. They won 3-1!

179. 11 November 1952 v FRANCE at Paris

WMNC Uprichard	Portsmouth
WGL Graham	Doncaster Rovers
A McMichael	Newcastle United
RD Blanchflower	Aston Villa
W Dickson	Chelsea
FJ McCourt	Manchester City
WL Bingham	Sunderland
SD D'Arcy	Brentford
EJ McMorran	Barnsley
R Peacock	Glasgow Celtic
CP Tully	Glasgow Celtic
Result	1-3
CP Tully	

FEATURED MATCH NO 5

FRANCE 3 NORTHERN IRELAND 1

AT COLOMBES STADIUM, PARIS, 11 NOVEMBER 1952

This match will be remembered for France's two first-half goals – not because of their brilliance, but for the circumstances surrounding them. The first was scored with 12 French players on the field and the second was made by a player who passed the ball from a position yards offside!

Ireland had the first chance of the game when following a foul on McMorran, McCourt's free-kick passed narrowly outside French keeper Ruminiski's left-hand post. Then the Glasgow Celtic left-wing pairing of Peacock and Tully combined well to set up a chance for McMorran. The Barnsley player gave Jonquet a lot of trouble and came close to getting on the scoresheet on a couple of occasions.

Then the French came into the game and their forwards were shooting at every opportunity. After 26 minutes, Cisowski was injured in a collision with McCourt and was replaced by former French captain Baratte. Then the French trainer instructed the injured Cisowski to take to the field but the substitute Barette did not go off. In fact, it was he who led to the home side's first goal after half-an-hour. He seemed to handle the ball before crossing for UJLAKI to sweep past Uprichard. The entire Irish team clustered round the referee to protest about the goal but in fairness, the referee had not signalled for Cisowski to come on again!

France's second goal came six minutes later. Strappe was so far offside before passing to KOPA, who netted, that the Irish defence just stood still and looked at him.

Ireland pulled a goal back five minutes before the interval. The goal followed a free-kick taken by Blanchflower after a foul on D'Arcy. There was a mix-up in the goalmouth and the ball eventually went to TULLY who gently placed it in the net.

Ireland were fighting like Trojans for the equaliser and Tully narrowly headed over before Danny Blanchflower's shot scraped the bar. France too had their chances but Uprichard saved well from both Kopa and Strappe. McCourt then tried a long range shot which went inches wide. With the minutes ticking away and Ireland hoping for that equaliser, KOPA saw a gap in the Irish defence and raced right down the middle to send a low ground shot past Uprichard and into the net.

WMNC Uprichard	Portsmouth
JJ McCabe	Leeds United
A McMichael	Newcastle United
RD Blanchflower	Aston Villa
W Dickson	Chelsea
FJ McCourt	Manchester City
WL Bingham	Sunderland
J McIlroy	Burnley
EJ McMorran	Doncaster Rovers
SD D'Arcy	Brentford
CP Tully	Glasgow Celtic
Result	2-3

EJ McMorran (2)

W Smyth	Distillery
WE Cunningham	St Mirren
A McMichael	Newcastle United
RD Blanchflower	Aston Villa
JJ McCabe	Leeds United
WW Cush	Glenavon
WL Bingham	Sunderland
J McIlroy	Burnley
WJ Simpson	Glasgow Rangers
CP Tully	Glasgow Celtic
NH Lockhart	Aston Villa
Result	1-3

NH Lockhart (pen)

W Smyth	Distillery
WGL Graham	Doncaster Rovers
A McMichael	Newcastle United
RD Blanchflower	Aston Villa
W Dickson	Arsenal
WW Cush	Glenavon
WL Bingham	Sunderland
J McIlroy	Burnley
WJ Simpson	Glasgow Rangers
EJ McMorran	Doncaster Rovers
NH Lockhart	Aston Villa
Result	1-3

EJ McMorran

H Gregg	Doncaster Rovers
WGL Graham	Doncaster Rovers
A McMichael	Newcastle United
RD Blanchflower	Aston Villa
W Dickson	Arsenal
R Peacock	Glasgow Celtic
WL Bingham	Sunderland

J Blanchflower	Manchester United
WJ McAdams	Manchester City
J McIlroy	Burnley
PJ McParland	Aston Villa
Result	2-1

PJ McParland (2)

WMNC Uprichard	Portsmouth
FJ Montgomery	Coleraine
A McMichael	Newcastle United
RD Blanchflower	Aston Villa
W Dickson	Arsenal
R Peacock	Glasgow Celtic
WL Bingham	Sunderland
J Blanchflower	Manchester United
WJ Simpson	Glasgow Rangers
J McIlroy	Burnley
PJ McParland	Aston Villa
Result	0-2

WMNC Uprichard	Portsmouth
WGL Graham	Doncaster Rovers
WE Cunningham	St Mirren
RD Blanchflower	Aston Villa
WT McCavana	Coleraine
R Peacock	Glasgow Celtic
WL Bingham	Sunderland
J Blanchflower	Manchester United
WJ McAdams	Manchester City
J McIlroy	Burnley
PJ McParland	Aston Villa
Result	2-2

WL Bingham; WJ McAdams

WMNC Uprichard	Portsmouth
WGL Graham	Doncaster Rovers
A McMichael	Newcastle United
RD Blanchflower	Tottenham Hotspur
JW McCleary	Cliftonville
T Casey	Newcastle United
WL Bingham	Sunderland
E Crossan	Blackburn Rovers
J Walker	Doncaster Rovers
J McIlroy	Burnley
PJ McParland	Aston Villa
Result	2-3

E Crossan; J Walker

187. 8 October 1955 v SCOTLAND at Belfast

WMNC Uprichard	Portsmouth
WGL Graham	Doncaster Rovers
WE Cunningham	Leicester City
RD Blanchflower	Tottenham Hotspur
WT McCavana	Coleraine
R Peacock	Glasgow Celtic
WL Bingham	Sunderland
J Blanchflower	Manchester United
F Coyle	Coleraine
J McIlroy	Burnley
PJ McParland	Aston Villa

Result	2-1

J Blanchflower; WL Bingham

188. 2 November 1955 v ENGLAND at Wembley

WMNC Uprichard	Portsmouth
WE Cunningham	Leicester City
WGL Graham	Doncaster Rovers
RD Blanchflower	Tottenham Hotspur
WT McCavana	Coleraine
R Peacock	Glasgow Celtic
WL Bingham	Sunderland
J McIlroy	Burnley
F Coyle	Coleraine
CP Tully	Glasgow Celtic
PJ McParland	Aston Villa

Result	0-3

189. 11 April 1956 v WALES at Cardiff

WMNC Uprichard	Portsmouth
WE Cunningham	Leicester City
A McMichael	Newcastle United
RD Blanchflower	Tottenham Hotspur
J Blanchflower	Manchester United
T Casey	Newcastle United
WL Bingham	Sunderland
J McIlroy	Burnley
J Jones	Glenavon
EJ McMorran	Doncaster Rovers
NH Lockhart	Aston Villa

Result	1-1

J Jones

190. 6 October 1956 v ENGLAND at Belfast

H Gregg	Doncaster Rovers
WE Cunningham	Leicester City
A McMichael	Newcastle United
RD Blanchflower	Tottenham Hotspur
J Blanchflower	Manchester United
T Casey	Newcastle United
WL Bingham	Sunderland
J McIlroy	Burnley
J Jones	Glenavon

WJ McAdams	Manchester City
PJ McParland	Aston Villa

Result	1-1

J McIlroy

191. 7 November 1956 v SCOTLAND at Glasgow

H Gregg	Doncaster Rovers
WE Cunningham	Leicester City
A McMichael	Newcastle United
RD Blanchflower	Tottenham Hotspur
J Blanchflower	Manchester United
T Casey	Newcastle United
WL Bingham	Sunderland
J McIlroy	Burnley
RJ Shields	Southampton
TA Dickson	Linfield
PJ McParland	Aston Villa

Result	0-1

192. 16 January 1957 v PORTUGAL at Lisbon

H Gregg	Doncaster Rovers
WE Cunningham	Leicester City
A McMichael	Newcastle United
RD Blanchflower	Tottenham Hotspur
J Blanchflower	Manchester United
T Casey	Newcastle United
WL Bingham	Sunderland
J McIlroy	Burnley
F Coyle	Coleraine
WW Cush	Glenavon
PJ McParland	Aston Villa

Result	1-1

WL Bingham

193. 10 April 1957 v WALES at Belfast

H Gregg	Doncaster Rovers
WE Cunningham	Leicester City
A McMichael	Newcastle United
RD Blanchflower	Tottenham Hotspur
WW Cush	Glenavon
R Peacock	Glasgow Celtic
WL Bingham	Sunderland
J McIlroy	Burnley
J Jones	Glenavon
T Casey	Newcastle United
PJ McParland	Aston Villa

Result	0-0

194. 25 April 1957 v ITALY at Rome

H Gregg	Doncaster Rovers
WE Cunningham	Leicester City
A McMichael	Newcastle United

RD Blanchflower	Tottenham Hotspur
WW Cush	Glenavon
T Casey	Newcastle United
WL Bingham	Sunderland
WJ Simpson	Glasgow Rangers
EJ McMorran	Doncaster Rovers
J McIlroy	Burnley
R Peacock	Glasgow Celtic

| Result | 0-1 |

195. 1 May 1957 v PORTUGAL at Belfast

H Gregg	Doncaster Rovers
WE Cunningham	Leicester City
A McMichael	Newcastle United
RD Blanchflower	Tottenham Hotspur
WW Cush	Glenavon
T Casey	Newcastle United
WL Bingham	Sunderland
WJ Simpson	Glasgow Rangers
EJ McMorran	Doncaster Rovers
J McIlroy	Burnley
R Peacock	Glasgow Celtic

| Result | 3-0 |

WJ Simpson; J McIlroy (pen); T Casey

FEATURED MATCH NO 6

NORTHERN IRELAND 3 PORTUGAL 0

AT WINDSOR PARK, BELFAST, 1 MAY 1957

Northern Ireland easily beat Portugal in this World Cup qualifier and in doing so, scored the highest number of goals by an Ireland side in home internationals since 1936. But while the attack followed the Peter Doherty doctrine of shooting hard and often, the marksmanship still left much to be desired!

As well as scoring three goals, Ireland had the ball in the net on a further three occasions. Early chances were missed by McMorran and Simpson as the home side piled on the pressure from the kick-off, but Ireland had to wait until the 22nd minute before opening the scoring. Jimmy McIlroy was fouled some 25 yards out from goal and from the resultant free-kick, Peacock touched the ball to CASEY who shot high into the roof of Gomez's net.

McMorran's lumbering style was causing problems for the Portuguese defence and he created chances for both Simpson and Bingham which were wasted. Cush also came close with a rasping drive which Gomez did well to turn round the post.

Ireland extended their lead on the hour mark when from a Cunningham free-kick, SIMPSON headed home after Pires had made a desperate effort to clear his lines.

Perhaps the most dramatic incident of the night occurred after 76 minutes when McMorran careered

in from the left-wing. Out came Gomez to cut off his shot, but as he dived at the centre-forward's feet, he writhed in pain. He attempted to push it to Pedroto, the right-half but McMorran fastened on to it and flighted the ball into the net. Virgilio pulled it down with his hand and a penalty was awarded.

McIlroy shaped up to take the kick, but flicked it to Blanchflower. The referee ordered it to be re-taken, for he judged Blanchflower to have moved into the penalty area before McIlroy touched the ball. McILROY tried a direct shot in his second attempt and he easily beat Gomez, the Portuguese keeper who played brilliantly.

The result left Ireland with an outside chance of a play-off place in their group, if they could beat Italy in Belfast, and provided Portugal could take a point off the Italians in their two fixtures.

196. 5 October 1957 v SCOTLAND at Belfast

WMNC Uprichard	Portsmouth
WE Cunningham	Leicester City
A McMichael	Newcastle United
RD Blanchflower	Tottenham Hotspur
J Blanchflower	Manchester United
R Peacock	Glasgow Celtic
WL Bingham	Sunderland
WJ Simpson	Glasgow Rangers
WJ McAdams	Manchester City
J McIlroy	Burnley
PJ McParland	Aston Villa

| Result | 1-1 |

WL Bingham

DID YOU KNOW?
In 1957, Northern Ireland ended England's 18-match unbeaten run with a 3-2 win at Wembley.

197. 6 November 1957 v ENGLAND at Wembley

H Gregg	Doncaster Rovers
RM Keith	Newcastle United
A McMichael	Newcastle United
RD Blanchflower	Tottenham Hotspur
J Blanchflower	Manchester United
R Peacock	Glasgow Celtic
WL Bingham	Sunderland
S McCrory	Southend United
WJ Simpson	Glasgow Rangers
J McIlroy	Burnley
PJ McParland	Aston Villa

| Results | 3-2 |

J McIlroy (pen); S McCrory; WJ Simpson

FEATURED MATCH NO 7

ENGLAND 2 NORTHERN IRELAND 3

AT WEMBLEY STADIUM, LONDON, 6 NOVEMBER 1957

Northern Ireland became the third country ever to beat England at Wembley, the others being Hungary and of course Scotland. The crowd of 35,000 was the smallest to watch an international match at Wembley but millions more were watching the game on television.

Dick Keith playing in his first international, soon checked A'Court, England's new cap by kicking into touch when a dangerous left-wing move developed. Manchester United's Tommy Taylor missed a golden chance after just eight minutes when with only Gregg to beat he failed to turn in a low square pass from Kevan. England then put in a spell of furious attacks with Edwards blasting wide and Kevan bringing the best out of Gregg. Ronnie Clayton shot narrowly wide with a terrific volley from a pass from his Blackburn team-mate Bryan Douglas.

After 32 minutes, Jimmy McIlroy was brought down from behind by Billy Wright and the referee had no hesitation in awarding Northern Ireland a penalty. McILROY took the penalty and Hopkinson got his fingers to it, but the ball – after touching the post – glanced in over the goal-line to Hopkinson's evident disgust.

Minutes later Peacock, on the goal-line with Gregg some yards away, prevented an almost certain equaliser by chesting down a header from Taylor. In another England raid, Kevan could not get enough power behind a header and Gregg saved easily.

Early in the second-half, Douglas beat two defenders before Gregg dived at his feet and cleared. Gregg distinguished himself again shortly afterwards by saving a pile-driver by Clayton. In the 58th minute, Derek Kevan gave Alan A'COURT the chance to level the scores – the Liverpool winger shooting past Gregg from an acute angle.

Northern Ireland went ahead again after 67 minutes when Duncan Edwards lost the ball to McCRORY, who seized on it and his shot went in off the far post. Six minutes later, the visitors extended their lead when SIMPSON raced in to meet a pin-point cross from Billy Bingham. England defenders claimed the Rangers' forward was offside but the referee had no hesitation in signalling the goal.

Matthews and Finney did their best to inspire England and with just ten minutes remaining, EDWARDS' hard low shot pulled a goal back for England. Though the home side pressed hard in the minutes that remained and the Irish goal led a charmed life, the visitors held on to record a memorable victory, their first win over England for 30 years!

198. 4 December 1957 v ITALY at Belfast

H Gregg	Doncaster Rovers
RM Keith	Newcastle United
A McMichael	Newcastle United
RD Blanchflower	Tottenham Hotspur
J Blanchflower	Manchester United
R Peacock	Glasgow Celtic
WL Bingham	Sunderland
J McIlroy	Burnley
WJ McAdams	Manchester City
WW Cush	Leeds United
PJ McParland	Aston Villa

Result	2-2

WW Cush (2)	

199. 15 January 1958 v ITALY at Belfast

WMNC Uprichard	Portsmouth
WE Cunningham	Leicester City
A McMichael	Newcastle United
RD Blanchflower	Tottenham Hotspur
J Blanchflower	Manchester United
R Peacock	Glasgow Celtic
WL Bingham	Sunderland
WW Cush	Leeds United
WJ Simpson	Glasgow Rangers
J McIlroy	Burnley
PJ McParland	Aston Villa

Result	1-3

PJ McParland	

200. 16 April 1958 v WALES at Cardiff

H Gregg	Manchester United
WE Cunningham	Leicester City
A McMichael	Newcastle United
RD Blanchflower	Tottenham Hotspur
RM Keith	Newcastle United
R Peacock	Glasgow Celtic
WL Bingham	Sunderland
WW Cush	Leeds United
WJ Simpson	Glasgow Rangers
J McIlroy	Burnley
PJ McParland	Aston Villa

Result	1-1

WJ Simpson	

DID YOU KNOW?
Northern Ireland were ordered not to play two of their three group matches in the 1958 World Cup Finals by the Irish FA, because the games were being played on the Sunday – they refused.

H Gregg	Manchester United
RM Keith	Newcastle United
A McMichael	Newcastle United
RD Blanchflower	Tottenham Hotspur
WE Cunningham	Leicester City
R Peacock	Glasgow Celtic
WL Bingham	Sunderland
WW Cush	Leeds United
AD Dougan	Portsmouth
J McIlroy	Burnley
PJ McParland	Aston Villa

Result	1-0

WW Cush

FEATURED MATCH NO 8

NORTHERN IRELAND 1 CZECHOSLOVAKIA 0

AT HALMSTAD, SWEDEN, 8 JUNE 1958

The only British team to win their own group match in the World Cup Finals of 1958 in Sweden, Northern Ireland's success was a triumph of tactics, gained as much off the field as on it. Manager Peter Doherty and skipper Danny Blanchflower evolved moves to exploit the weakness of the Czechs.

The pitch was slippery after a fall of rain and the Irish players especially in the early stages found great difficulty in keeping on their feet. The Czechs tore into the attack and only a goal-line clearance from Cunningham prevented Horvorka from giving the Czechs the lead. Ireland too had their chances with Wilbur Cush chasing a long ball from defence only to be beaten to it by keeper Dolejsi who clutched it at the second attempt.

Ireland fought hard and it came as no surprise when after 21 minutes they took the lead. McParland forced a corner which he took quickly. He played the ball to McIlroy who got into line to lift it across the face of goal to the waiting CUSH who headed into the roof of the net past Dolejsi.

Docherty's tactics again became evident as Ireland refused to sit back. They attacked with even greater tenacity and a minute later McParland almost scored again from an acutely timed Cush free kick. Cush himself had a chance to extend Ireland's lead but he was tackled by Novak as he shaped to shoot. It was all Northern Ireland: Derek Dougan had two magnificent chances to put his side 2-0 up, but on each occasion he was foiled by good saves by Dolejsi.

In the second-half, the Czechs pushed hard for the equaliser and both Dvorak and Borovicka saw their shots well saved by Harry Gregg. As the game wore on, the Czechs had numerous chances to draw level, but at times it was the luck of the Irish which kept them out. In the end though, Danny Blanchflower and his boys were the victors – victors on merit.

H Gregg	Manchester United
RM Keith	Newcastle United
A McMichael	Newcastle United
RD Blanchflower	Tottenham Hotspur
WE Cunningham	Leicester City
R Peacock	Glasgow Celtic
WL Bingham	Sunderland
WW Cush	Leeds United
F Coyle	Nottingham Forest
J McIlroy	Burnley
PJ McParland	Aston Villa

Result	1-3

PJ McParland

H Gregg	Manchester United
RM Keith	Newcastle United
A McMichael	Newcastle United
RD Blanchflower	Tottenham Hotspur
WE Cunningham	Leicester City
R Peacock	Glasgow Celtic
WL Bingham	Sunderland
WW Cush	Leeds United
T Casey	Newcastle United
J McIlroy	Burnley
PJ McParland	Aston Villa

Result	2-2

PJ McParland (2)

FEATURED MATCH NO 9

NORTHERN IRELAND 2 WEST GERMANY 2

AT MALMO, SWEDEN, 15 JUNE 1958

In a game for sheer excitement, top-class football and honest endeavour, Northern Ireland's 2-2 draw with world champions West Germany is unlikely ever to be surpassed. In fact, the game is still talked about today by many Germans who consider it a classic, in the mould of the Eintrackt Frankfurt-Real Madrid European Cup Final some two years later.

Without doubt, Northern Ireland's hero was goalkeeper Harry Gregg who played with a badly swollen ankle which he twisted in the opening minutes. He bordered on the miraculous and proved that he had regained his confidence following the reactions of the Munich air crash.

In the opening minutes, Gregg produced a couple of fine saves, first from Uwe Seeler and then the dangerous winger Rahn. Yet despite the early pressure coming from the Germans, it was Northern Ireland who took the lead after 18 minutes when McPARLAND fired home from close range after good work by Casey.

However, within two minutes, the Germans were level when their No.1 dangerman RAHN fired through a crowd of players and past the unsighted Gregg. The Irish keeper then saved well from Seeler and full-back Jusowiak whose long-range shot swerved viciously in the air. Helmuth Rahn was through on goal in the closing minutes of the first-half but Gregg was alert to the situation and took the ball off the striker's toe.

Northern Ireland regained the lead just before the hour-mark when Aston Villa winger Peter McPARLAND netted his and his side's second goal. The Irish then had to withstand an awful lot of pressure but with Gregg in such outstanding form and the defence refusing to buckle, they held firm until the 67th minute when SEELER drew the Germans level. Both sides had chances to win it in the closing stages but the Germans came closest in the dying moments when Gregg produced the last of a series of magnificent saves.

It was this performance, when he threw himself about his penalty area with vigour and determination, that earned the Manchester United keeper the title of 'Goalkeeper of the Tournament' – there have been few, if any, better displays from an Irish goalkeeper.

The point was enough to take Germany into the quarter-finals but Northern Ireland – who were applauded off the pitch by the Germans – had to face Czechoslovakia in a play-off at Malmo the following Tuesday.

204. 17 June 1958 v CZECHOSLOVAKIA at Malmo	
WMNC Uprichard	Portsmouth
RM Keith	Newcastle United
A McMichael	Newcastle United
RD Blanchflower	Tottenham Hotspur
WE Cunningham	Leicester City
R Peacock	Glasgow Celtic
WL Bingham	Sunderland
WW Cush	Leeds United
J Scott	Grimsby Town
J McIlroy	Burnley
PJ McParland	Aston Villa
Result	2-1
PJ McParland (2)	

FEATURED MATCH NO 10

NORTHERN IRELAND 2 CZECHOSLOVAKIA 1

AT MALMO, SWEDEN, 17 JUNE 1958

Czechoslovakia, surprisingly defeated Argentina 6-1, finished equal on points with Northern Ireland and so this necessitated a play-off at Malmo, the Tuesday after the Irish had drawn with West Germany. Instead of staying there, the Irish party made the 100-mile journey back to Tylosand, a move that in retrospect was not really conducive to the right preparation.

The hero of the German game, Harry Gregg was not fit and indeed had to hobble to the match with the aid of a stick. The game was only eight-minutes-old when his replacement Norman Uprichard, going for a ball, twisted his ankle. Though the players were tired and it was a hard struggle for supremacy after their battle against the Germans 48 hours earlier, Ireland played superbly, with Blanchflower having his best game of the tournament.

However, after 19 minutes, disaster struck when the unmarked ZIKAN headed home a Popluhar free-kick. But the Czechs failed to press home their advantage and Uprichard was rarely troubled. Almost on half-time, Bingham raced down the right-wing before pushing the ball inside for Cush. He had a couple of shots blocked before deciding against a third and instead crossed the ball for McPARLAND to smash home.

Early in the second-half the Irish suffered more injuries, when Uprichard broke a bone in his hand after colliding with the post in attempting to stop a shot from Dvorak. Then Bertie Peacock strained a muscle – but remarkably the Irish made it to extra-time.

At the break for extra-time, Billy Bingham persuaded the weary Irish players to do an exercise programme of calisthenics. The exhausted Czechs couldn't believe their eyes. The tactical bluff worked and in the 99th minute, Danny Blanchflower curled a free-kick beyond the Czech defence for Peter McPARLAND to volley home what proved to be the winner.

The Czechs then fought like Trojans to level the scores but right-half Bubernik, an ice hockey international went up to the referee – a French gendarme – complaining of being pushed in the back. The referee pushed him aside and the Czech promptly spat in his face. Not surprisingly he received his marching orders! Even then they came close to scoring but the only time the ball went in the net was when Peacock 'scored' at the other end, only for the referee to adjudge his effort to be offside.

Northern Ireland had reached the quarter-finals of the World Cup and though they lost 4-0 to France, they went home as heroes.

205. 19 June 1958 v FRANCE at Norrkoping	
H Gregg	Manchester United
RM Keith	Newcastle United
A McMichael	Newcastle United
RD Blanchflower	Tottenham Hotspur
WE Cunningham	Leicester City
WW Cush	Leeds United
WL Bingham	Sunderland
T Casey	Newcastle United
J Scott	Grimsby Town
J McIlroy	Burnley

PJ McParland	Aston Villa
Result	0-4

H Gregg	Manchester United
RM Keith	Newcastle United
WGL Graham	Doncaster Rovers
RD Blanchflower	Tottenham Hotspur
WE Cunningham	Leicester City
R Peacock	Glasgow Celtic
WL Bingham	Luton Town
WW Cush	Leeds United
T Casey	Portsmouth
J McIlroy	Burnley
PJ McParland	Aston Villa
Result	3-3

WW Cush; R Peacock; T Casey

FEATURED MATCH NO 11

NORTHERN IRELAND 3 ENGLAND 3

AT WINDSOR PARK, BELFAST, 4 OCTOBER 1958

Northern Ireland's first match since the epic days of the World Cup in Sweden saw them entertain England at a very wet Windsor Park. The rain-drenched fans saw the teams share six goals in one of the most dramatic and thrill-packed international matches.

The Irish took the lead through CUSH, the hardworking Leeds United player shooting past Colin McDonald from close range but it wasn't long before England drew level through a superb strike from their best player on the day, Bobby CHARLTON. The young Manchester United forward had already come close to scoring but on each occasion was foiled by the heroics of his club team-mate Harry Gregg.

Northern Ireland went ahead for a second time when Bertie PEACOCK, who suffered an Achilles tendon injury, fired home through a crowded penalty area. Ireland could have extended their lead as McIlroy and McParland combined well on the left to create a goalscoring opportunity for Bingham. His shot was parried by McDonald and the clearance completed by Don Howe. The game was fast flowing and there were chances at both ends before Tom FINNEY levelled the scores. In doing so, the Preston North End forward beat the record of goals for England held by Bolton's Nat Lofthouse.

Tommy CASEY, whose tenacity and bustling tactics were a feature of the game put the home side into the lead for the third time in a most entertaining game. Even then, the visitors were not finished and Finney, who was coming towards the end of a most illustrious career created a chance for the irrepressible CHARLTON to smash the ball past Gregg and make the score 3-3.

England's defence had been out of sorts all afternoon and if any side was going to clinch this thriller, it had to be Northern Ireland. Both McParland and Bingham created havoc down the flanks with Banks and Howe at a loss as how to stop them. Unfortunately, the ball didn't break kindly for the home forwards and the game finished all-square.

Such was the high standard of play that the result was relegated to an irrelevancy though if Northern Ireland had had Bobby Charlton in their ranks, the outcome would have been decided well before half-time!

WMNC Uprichard	Portsmouth
RM Keith	Newcastle United
A McMichael	Newcastle United
RD Blanchflower	Tottenham Hotspur
JT Forde	Ards
T Casey	Portsmouth
WL Bingham	Luton Town
WW Cush	Leeds United
PJ McParland	Aston Villa
J McIlroy	Burnley
CP Tully	Glasgow Celtic
Result	2-6

WW Cush; J McIlroy

WMNC Uprichard	Portsmouth
RM Keith	Newcastle United
A McMichael	Newcastle United
RD Blanchflower	Tottenham Hotspur
WE Cunningham	Leicester City
R Peacock	Glasgow Celtic
WL Bingham	Luton Town
WW Cush	Leeds United
WJ Simpson	Glasgow Rangers
J McIlroy	Burnley
PJ McParland	Aston Villa
Result	2-2

Caldow (own goal); J McIlroy

H Gregg	Manchester United
RM Keith	Newcastle United
A McMichael	Newcastle United
RD Blanchflower	Tottenham Hotspur
WE Cunningham	Leicester City
R Peacock	Glasgow Celtic
WL Bingham	Luton Town
J McIlroy	Burnley
WW Cush	Leeds United
MJ Hill	Norwich City

PJ McParland	Aston Villa

Result	4-1

PJ McParland (2); R Peacock; J McIlroy

H Gregg	Manchester United
RM Keith	Newcastle United
A McMichael	Newcastle United
RD Blanchflower	Tottenham Hotspur
WE Cunningham	Leicester City
R Peacock	Glasgow Celtic
WL Bingham	Luton Town
WW Cush	Leeds United
AD Dougan	Blackburn Rovers
J McIlroy	Burnley
PJ McParland	Aston Villa

Result	0-4

211. 18 November 1959 v ENGLAND at Wembley

H Gregg	Manchester United
RM Keith	Newcastle United
A McMichael	Newcastle United
RD Blanchflower	Tottenham Hotspur
WE Cunningham	Leicester City
R Peacock	Glasgow Celtic
WL Bingham	Luton Town
JA Crossan	Sparta Rotterdam
WW Cush	Leeds United
J McIlroy	Burnley
PJ McParland	Aston Villa

Result	1-2

WL Bingham

212. 6 April 1960 v WALES at Wrexham

H Gregg	Manchester United
AR Elder	Burnley
A McMichael	Newcastle United
RD Blanchflower	Tottenham Hotspur
WE Cunningham	Leicester City
WW Cush	Leeds United
WL Bingham	Luton Town
J McIlroy	Burnley
WI Lawther	Sunderland
MJ Hill	Norwich City
PJ McParland	Aston Villa

Result	2-3

WL Bingham; RD Blanchflower (pen)

DID YOU KNOW?
The biggest ever attendance for an international match at Windsor Park was 60,000 for the visit of England on 8 October 1960, a match England won 5-2.

213. 8 October 1960 v ENGLAND at Belfast

H Gregg	Manchester United
RM Keith	Newcastle United
AR Elder	Burnley
RD Blanchflower	Tottenham Hotspur
JT Forde	Ards
R Peacock	Glasgow Celtic
WL Bingham	Everton
J McIlroy	Burnley
WJ McAdams	Bolton Wanderers
AD Dougan	Blackburn Rovers
PJ McParland	Aston Villa

Result	2-5

WJ McAdams (2)

214. 26 October 1960 v WEST GERMANY at Belfast

JT McClelland	Arsenal
RM Keith	Newcastle United
AR Elder	Burnley
RD Blanchflower	Tottenham Hotspur
JT Forde	Ards
R Peacock	Glasgow Celtic
WL Bingham	Everton
J McIlroy	Burnley
WJ McAdams	Bolton Wanderers
MJ Hill	Norwich City
PJ McParland	Aston Villa

Result	3-4

WJ McAdams (3)

215. 9 November 1960 v SCOTLAND at Glasgow

H Gregg	Manchester United
RM Keith	Newcastle United
AR Elder	Burnley
RD Blanchflower	Tottenham Hotspur
JT Forde	Ards
R Peacock	Glasgow Celtic
WL Bingham	Everton
W Bruce	Glentoran
WJ McAdams	Bolton Wanderers
JJ Nicholson	Manchester United
PJ McParland	Aston Villa

Result	2-5

RD Blanchflower (pen); PJ McParland

216. 12 April 1961 v WALES at Belfast

JT McClelland	Arsenal
RM Keith	Newcastle United
AR Elder	Burnley
RD Blanchflower	Tottenham Hotspur
WE Cunningham	Dunfermline Athletic
JJ Nicholson	Manchester United

TC Stewart	Linfield
AD Dougan	Blackburn Rovers
WJ McAdams	Bolton Wanderers
J McIlroy	Burnley
PJ McParland	Aston Villa

Result	1-5

AD Dougan

217. 25 April 1961 v ITALY at Bologna

JT McClelland	Arsenal
RM Keith	Newcastle United
WJ McCullough	Arsenal
M Harvey	Sunderland
WJT Neill	Arsenal
R Peacock	Glasgow Celtic
WL Bingham	Everton
AD Dougan	Blackburn Rovers
WI Lawther	Sunderland
WJ McAdams	Bolton Wanderers
PJ McParland	Aston Villa

Result	2-3

AD Dougan; WJ McAdams

218. 3 May 1961 v GREECE at Athens

JT McClelland	Arsenal
RM Keith	Newcastle United
AR Elder	Burnley
WW Cush	Leeds United
WJT Neill	Arsenal
R Peacock	Glasgow Celtic
WL Bingham	Everton
J McIlroy	Burnley
WJ McAdams	Bolton Wanderers
AD Dougan	Blackburn Rovers
PJ McParland	Aston Villa

Result	1-2

J McIlroy

219. 10 May 1961 v WEST GERMANY at Berlin

JT McClelland	Arsenal
RM Keith	Newcastle United
AR Elder	Burnley
RD Blanchflower	Tottenham Hotspur
WJT Neill	Arsenal
R Peacock	Glasgow Celtic
WL Bingham	Everton
WW Cush	Portadown
WJ McAdams	Bolton Wanderers
J McIlroy	Burnley
PJ McParland	Aston Villa

Result	1-2

J McIlroy

220. 7 October 1961 v SCOTLAND at Belfast

H Gregg	Manchester United
EJ Magill	Arsenal
AR Elder	Burnley
RD Blanchflower	Tottenham Hotspur
WJT Neill	Arsenal
R Peacock	Glasgow Celtic
SJ Wilson	Glenavon
J McIlroy	Burnley
WI Lawther	Blackburn Rovers
MJ Hill	Norwich City
JC McLaughlin	Shrewsbury Town

Result	1-6

JC McLaughlin

221. 17 October 1961 v GREECE at Belfast

H Gregg	Manchester United
EJ Magill	Arsenal
AR Elder	Burnley
RD Blanchflower	Tottenham Hotspur
WJT Neill	Arsenal
JJ Nicholson	Manchester United
WL Bingham	Everton
J McIlroy	Burnley
WJ McAdams	Bolton Wanderers
WW Cush	Portadown
JC McLaughlin	Shrewsbury Town

Result	2-0

JC McLaughlin (2)

222. 22 November 1961 v ENGLAND at Wembley

V Hunter	Coleraine
EJ Magill	Arsenal
AR Elder	Burnley
RD Blanchflower	Tottenham Hotspur
WJT Neill	Arsenal
JJ Nicholson	Manchester United
WL Bingham	Everton
HH Barr	Linfield
WJ McAdams	Bolton Wanderers
J McIlroy	Burnley
JC McLaughlin	Shrewsbury Town

Result	1-1

J McIlroy

223. 11 April 1962 v WALES at Cardiff

WR Briggs	Manchester United
RM Keith	Newcastle United
WE Cunningham	Dunfermline Athletic
RD Blanchflower	Tottenham Hotspur
WJT Neill	Arsenal
JJ Nicholson	Manchester United
WM Humphries	Ards
WC Johnston	Glenavon

J O'Neill	Sunderland
JC McLaughlin	Shrewsbury Town
RM Braithwaite	Linfield

Result	0-4

224. 9 May 1962 v HOLLAND at Rotterdam

RJ Irvine	Linfield
RM Keith	Newcastle United
WE Cunningham	Dunfermline Athletic
M Harvey	Sunderland
RD Blanchflower	Tottenham Hotspur
JJ Nicholson	Manchester United
WM Humphries	Coventry City
WI Lawther	Blackburn Rovers
WJ McAdams	Leeds United
J McIlroy	Burnley
PJ McParland	Wolverhampton Wanderers

Result	0-4

225. 10 October 1962 v POLAND at Katowice

RJ Irvine	Linfield
EJ Magill	Arsenal
AR Elder	Burnley
RD Blanchflower	Tottenham Hotspur
S Hatton	Linfield
JJ Nicholson	Manchester United
WM Humphries	Coventry City
HH Barr	Coventry City
AD Dougan	Aston Villa
J McIlroy	Burnley
WL Bingham	Everton

Result	2-0

AD Dougan; WM Humphries

226. 20 October 1962 v ENGLAND at Belfast

RJ Irvine	Linfield
EJ Magill	Arsenal
AR Elder	Burnley
RD Blanchflower	Tottenham Hotspur
WJT Neill	Arsenal
JJ Nicholson	Manchester United
WM Humphries	Coventry City
HH Barr	Coventry City
ST McMillan	Manchester United
J McIlroy	Burnley
WL Bingham	Everton

Result	1-3

HH Barr

227. 7 November 1962 v SCOTLAND at Glasgow

RJ Irvine	Linfield
EJ Magill	Arsenal

AR Elder	Burnley
RD Blanchflower	Tottenham Hotspur
S Hatton	Linfield
JJ Nicholson	Manchester United
WM Humphries	Coventry City
ST McMillan	Manchester United
AD Dougan	Aston Villa
J McIlroy	Burnley
WL Bingham	Everton

Result	1-5

WL Bingham

228. 28 November 1962 v POLAND at Belfast

RJ Irvine	Linfield
EJ Magill	Arsenal
AR Elder	Burnley
RD Blanchflower	Tottenham Hotspur
WJT Neill	Arsenal
JJ Nicholson	Manchester United
WL Bingham	Everton
JA Crossan	Sunderland
AD Dougan	Aston Villa
J McIlroy	Burnley
RM Braithwaite	Linfield

Result	2-0

JA Crossan; WL Bingham

229. 3 April 1963 v WALES at Belfast

RJ Irvine	Linfield
EJ Magill	Arsenal
AR Elder	Burnley
M Harvey	Sunderland
AC Campbell	Crusaders
WJT Neill	Arsenal
WM Humphries	Coventry City
JA Crossan	Sunderland
WJ Irvine	Burnley
J McIlroy	Stoke City
JC McLaughlin	Shrewsbury Town

Result	1-4

M Harvey

230. 30 May 1963 v SPAIN at Bilbao

RJ Irvine	Linfield
EJ Magill	Arsenal
AR Elder	Burnley
M Harvey	Sunderland
WJT Neill	Arsenal
WJ McCullough	Arsenal
WL Bingham	Everton
WM Humphries	Coventry City
WJ Irvine	Burnley
JA Crossan	Sunderland
RM Braithwaite	Linfield

Result   1-1

WJ Irvine

H Gregg	Manchester United
EJ Magill	Arsenal
J Parke	Linfield
M Harvey	Sunderland
WJT Neill	Arsenal
WJ McCullough	Arsenal
WL Bingham	Port Vale
WM Humphries	Coventry City
SJ Wilson	Glenavon
JA Crossan	Sunderland
MJ Hill	Everton

Result   2-1

WL Bingham; SJ Wilson

V Hunter	Coleraine
EJ Magill	Arsenal
J Parke	Hibernian
M Harvey	Sunderland
WJT Neill	Arsenal
WJ McCullough	Arsenal
WL Bingham	Port Vale
WM Humphries	Coventry City
SJ Wilson	Falkirk
JA Crossan	Sunderland
MJ Hill	Everton

Result   0-1

H Gregg	Manchester United
EJ Magill	Arsenal
J Parke	Hibernian
M Harvey	Sunderland
WJT Neill	Arsenal
WJ McCullough	Arsenal
WL Bingham	Port Vale
WM Humphries	Coventry City
SJ Wilson	Falkirk
JA Crossan	Sunderland
MJ Hill	Everton

Result   3-8

JA Crossan; SJ Wilson (2)

DID YOU KNOW?
Northern Ireland's 8-3 defeat by England on 20 November 1963, was the first international at Wembley to be played entirely under floodlights.

PA Jennings	Watford
EJ Magill	Arsenal
AR Elder	Burnley
M Harvey	Sunderland
WJT Neill	Arsenal
WJ McCullough	Arsenal
G Best	Manchester United
JA Crossan	Sunderland
SJ Wilson	Falkirk
JC McLaughlin	Swansea Town
RM Braithwaite	Middlesbrough

Result   3-2

JC McLaughlin; SJ Wilson; M Harvey

PA Jennings	Watford
EJ Magill	Arsenal
AR Elder	Burnley
M Harvey	Sunderland
WJT Neill	Arsenal
WJ McCullough	Arsenal
G Best	Manchester United
JA Crossan	Sunderland
SJ Wilson	Falkirk
JC McLaughlin	Swansea Town
RM Braithwaite	Middlesbrough

Result   3-0

JA Crossan (2) (2 pens); SJ Wilson

PA Jennings	Tottenham Hotspur
EJ Magill	Arsenal
AR Elder	Burnley
M Harvey	Sunderland
WJT Neill	Arsenal
WJ McCullough	Arsenal
G Best	Manchester United
JA Crossan	Sunderland
SJ Wilson	Falkirk
JC McLaughlin	Swansea Town
RM Braithwaite	Middlesbrough

Result   3-4

SJ Wilson; JC McLaughlin (2)

PA Jennings	Tottenham Hotspur
EJ Magill	Arsenal
AR Elder	Burnley
M Harvey	Sunderland
WJT Neill	Arsenal
WJ McCullough	Arsenal
G Best	Manchester United

JA Crossan	Sunderland
SJ Wilson	Falkirk
JC McLaughlin	Swansea Town
RM Braithwaite	Middlesbrough

Result	1-0

JA Crossan (pen)

238. 14 November 1964 v SWITZERLAND at Lausanne

PA Jennings	Tottenham Hotspur
EJ Magill	Arsenal
AR Elder	Burnley
M Harvey	Sunderland
AC Campbell	Crusaders
J Parke	Sunderland
G Best	Manchester United
JA Crossan	Sunderland
WJ Irvine	Burnley
JC McLaughlin	Swansea Town
RM Braithwaite	Middlesbrough

Result	1-2

G Best

239. 25 November 1964 v SCOTLAND at Glasgow

PA Jennings	Tottenham Hotspur
EJ Magill	Arsenal
AR Elder	Burnley
M Harvey	Sunderland
WJT Neill	Arsenal
J Parke	Sunderland
G Best	Manchester United
WM Humphries	Coventry City
WJ Irvine	Burnley
JA Crossan	Sunderland
RM Braithwaite	Middlesbrough

Result	2-3

G Best; WJ Irvine

240. 17 March 1965 v HOLLAND at Belfast

W Briggs	Swansea Town
J Parke	Sunderland
AR Elder	Burnley
M Harvey	Sunderland
WJT Neill	Arsenal
JJ Nicholson	Huddersfield Town
WM Humphries	Swansea Town
JA Crossan	Manchester City
WJ Irvine	Burnley
D Clements	Coventry City
G Best	Manchester United

Result	2-1

JA Crossan; WJT Neill

241. 31 March 1965 v WALES at Belfast

RJ Irvine	Stoke City
J Parke	Sunderland
AR Elder	Burnley
M Harvey	Sunderland
WJT Neill	Arsenal
JJ Nicholson	Huddersfield Town
WM Humphries	Swansea Town
JA Crossan	Manchester City
WJ Irvine	Burnley
JC McLaughlin	Swansea Town
D Clements	Coventry City

Result	0-5

242. 7 April 1965 v HOLLAND at Rotterdam

PA Jennings	Tottenham Hotspur
EJ Magill	Arsenal
AR Elder	Burnley
M Harvey	Sunderland
WJT Neill	Arsenal
J Parke	Sunderland
G Best	Manchester United
JA Crossan	Manchester City
WJ Irvine	Burnley
JJ Nicholson	Huddersfield Town
RM Braithwaite	Middlesbrough

Result	0-0

243. 7 May 1965 v ALBANIA at Belfast

PA Jennings	Tottenham Hotspur
EJ Magill	Arsenal
AR Elder	Burnley
M Harvey	Sunderland
WJT Neill	Arsenal
J Parke	Sunderland
WM Humphries	Swansea Town
JA Crossan	Manchester City
WJ Irvine	Burnley
JJ Nicholson	Huddersfield Town
G Best	Manchester United

Result	4-1

JA Crossan (3) (1 pen); WJ Irvine

244. 2 October 1965 v SCOTLAND at Glasgow

PA Jennings	Tottenham Hotspur
EJ Magill	Arsenal
AR Elder	Burnley
M Harvey	Sunderland
WJT Neill	Arsenal
JJ Nicholson	Huddersfield Town
J McIlroy	Stoke City
JA Crossan	Manchester City
WJ Irvine	Burnley
AD Dougan	Leicester City
G Best	Manchester United

Result	3-2

AD Dougan; JA Crossan; WJ Irvine

245. 10 November 1965 v ENGLAND at Wembley

PA Jennings	Tottenham Hotspur
EJ Magill	Arsenal
AR Elder	Burnley
M Harvey	Sunderland
WJT Neill	Arsenal
JJ Nicholson	Huddersfield Town
J McIlroy	Stoke City
JA Crossan	Manchester City
WJ Irvine	Burnley
AD Dougan	Leicester City
G Best	Manchester United

Result	1-2

WJ Irvine

246. 24 November 1965 v ALBANIA at Tirana

PA Jennings	Tottenham Hotspur
EJ Magill	Brighton & Hove Albion
AR Elder	Burnley
M Harvey	Sunderland
WJT Neill	Arsenal
JJ Nicholson	Huddersfield Town
J McIlroy	Stoke City
JA Crossan	Manchester City
WJ Irvine	Burnley
AD Dougan	Leicester City
G Best	Manchester United

Result	1-1

WJ Irvine

247. 30 March 1966 v WALES at Cardiff

PA Jennings	Tottenham Hotspur
EJ Magill	Brighton & Hove Albion
AR Elder	Burnley
M Harvey	Sunderland
WJT Neill	Arsenal
JJ Nicholson	Huddersfield Town
E Welsh	Carlisle United
SJ Wilson	Dundee
WJ Irvine	Burnley
AD Dougan	Leicester City
JC McLaughlin	Swansea Town

Result	4-1

WJ Irvine; SJ Wilson; E Welsh; M Harvey

248. 7 May 1966 v WEST GERMANY at Belfast

PA Jennings	Tottenham Hotspur
EJ Magill	Brighton & Hove Albion

J Parke	Sunderland
M Harvey	Sunderland
RJ Napier	Bolton Wanderers
WJT Neill	Arsenal
E Welsh	Carlisle United
JA Crossan	Manchester City
SJ Wilson	Dundee
AD Dougan	Leicester City
VJ McKinney	Falkirk

Result	0-2

249. 22 June 1966 v MEXICO at Belfast

JT McClelland	Fulham
EJ Magill	Brighton & Hove Albion
AR Elder	Burnley
M Harvey	Sunderland
WJT Neill	Arsenal
JJ Nicholson	Huddersfield Town
E Welsh	Carlisle United
W Ferguson	Linfield
WJ Irvine*	Burnley
AD Dougan	Leicester City
D Clements**	Coventry City

Subs	
*W Johnston	Oldham Athletic
**SJ Todd	Burnley

Result	4-1

W Johnston; AR Elder; JJ Nicholson; W Ferguson

250. 22 October 1966 v ENGLAND at Belfast

PA Jennings*	Tottenham Hotspur
J Parke	Sunderland
AR Elder	Burnley
SJ Todd	Burnley
M Harvey	Sunderland
WJ McCullough	Millwall
W Ferguson	Linfield
JA Crossan	Manchester City
WJ Irvine	Burnley
AD Dougan	Leicester City
G Best	Manchester United

Subs	
* WS McFaul	Linfield

Result	0-2

251. 16 November 1966 v SCOTLAND at Glasgow

PA Jennings	Tottenham Hotspur
J Parke	Sunderland
AR Elder	Burnley
M Harvey	Sunderland
WJT Neill	Arsenal
JJ Nicholson	Huddersfield Town
SJ Wilson	Dundee
JA Crossan	Manchester City

WJ Irvine	Burnley
AD Dougan	Leicester City
D Clements	Coventry City
Result	1-2
JJ Nicholson	

252. 12 April 1967 v WALES at Belfast

R McKenzie	Airdrieonians
DJ Craig	Newcastle United
AR Elder	Burnley
A Stewart	Glentoran
WJT Neill	Arsenal
JJ Nicholson	Huddersfield Town
E Welsh	Carlisle United
D Trainor	Crusaders
AD Dougan	Wolverhampton Wanderers
W Bruce	Glentoran
D Clements	Coventry City
Result	0-0

253. 21 October 1967 v SCOTLAND at Belfast

PA Jennings	Tottenham Hotspur
W McKeag	Glentoran
J Parke	Sunderland
A Stewart	Glentoran
WJT Neill	Arsenal
D Clements	Coventry City
WG Campbell	Dundee
JA Crossan	Manchester City
AD Dougan	Wolverhampton Wanderers
JJ Nicholson	Huddersfield Town
G Best	Manchester United
Result	1-0
D Clements	

254. 22 November 1967 v ENGLAND at Wembley

PA Jennings	Tottenham Hotspur
J Parke	Sunderland
AR Elder	Stoke City
A Stewart	Glentoran
WJT Neill	Arsenal
M Harvey	Sunderland
WG Campbell	Dundee
WJ Irvine	Burnley
SJ Wilson	Dundee
JJ Nicholson	Huddersfield Town
D Clements	Coventry City
Result	0-2

255. 28 February 1968 v WALES at Wrexham

| PA Jennings | Tottenham Hotspur |
| DJ Craig | Newcastle United |

AR Elder	Stoke City
M Harvey	Sunderland
SJ Todd	Burnley
W McKeag	Glentoran
WJ Irvine	Burnley
A Stewart	Derby County
AD Dougan	Wolverhampton Wanderers
JJ Nicholson	Huddersfield Town
JT Harkin	Southport
Result	0-2

256. 10 September 1968 v ISRAEL at Tel Aviv

PA Jennings	Tottenham Hotspur
PJ Rice	Arsenal
M Harvey	Sunderland
A Stewart	Derby County
WJT Neill	Arsenal
TA Jackson	Everton
D Sloan	Oxford United
AS McMordie	Middlesbrough
AD Dougan*	Wolverhampton Wanderers
WJ Irvine	Preston North End
WE Ross	Newcastle United
Subs	
* R Gaston	Oxford United
Result	3-2

AD Dougan; WJ Irvine (2)

257. 23 October 1968 v TURKEY at Belfast

PA Jennings	Tottenham Hotspur
DJ Craig*	Newcastle United
M Harvey	Sunderland
JJ Nicholson	Huddersfield Town
WJT Neill	Arsenal
D Clements	Coventry City
WG Campbell	Dundee
AS McMordie	Middlesbrough
AD Dougan	Wolverhampton Wanderers
WJ Irvine	Preston North End
G Best	Manchester United
Subs	
*A Stewart	Derby County
Result	4-1

G Best; AS McMordie; AD Dougan; WG Campbell

258. 11 December 1968 v TURKEY at Istanbul

PA Jennings	Tottenham Hotspur
DJ Craig	Newcastle United
M Harvey	Sunderland
JJ Nicholson	Huddersfield Town
WJT Neill	Arsenal
A Stewart	Derby County
B Hamilton	Linfield

AS McMordie	Middlesbrough
AD Dougan	Wolverhampton Wanderers
JT Harkin	Southport
D Clements	Coventry City

Result	3-0

JT Harkin (2); JJ Nicholson

259. 3 May 1969 v ENGLAND at Belfast

PA Jennings	Tottenham Hotspur
DJ Craig	Newcastle United
M Harvey*	Sunderland
SJ Todd	Burnley
WJT Neill	Arsenal
JJ Nicholson	Huddersfield Town
AS McMordie	Middlesbrough
TA Jackson	Everton
AD Dougan	Wolverhampton Wanderers
WJ Irvine	Preston North End
G Best	Manchester United

Subs	
* AR Elder	Stoke City

Result	1-3

AS McMordie

260. 6 May 1969 v SCOTLAND at Glasgow

PA Jennings	Tottenham Hotspur
DJ Craig	Newcastle United
AR Elder	Stoke City
SJ Todd	Burnley
WJT Neill	Arsenal
JJ Nicholson	Huddersfield Town
G Best	Manchester United
AS McMordie	Middlesbrough
AD Dougan	Wolverhampton Wanderers
TA Jackson	Everton
D Clements	Coventry City

Result	1-1

AS McMordie

DID YOU KNOW?
Only 7,843 people watched Scotland play Northern Ireland at Hampden Park in 1969 – the smallest-ever crowd in the Home Internationals.

261. 19 May 1969 v WALES at Belfast

PA Jennings	Tottenham Hotspur
DJ Craig	Newcastle United
AR Elder	Stoke City
SJ Todd	Burnley
WJT Neill	Arsenal
JJ Nicholson	Huddersfield Town
G Best	Manchester United

AS McMordie	Middlesbrough
AD Dougan	Wolverhampton Wanderers
TA Jackson	Everton
D Clements*	Coventry City

Subs	
* JT Harkin	Shrewsbury Town

Result	0-0

262. 10 September 1969 v USSR at Belfast

PA Jennings	Tottenham Hotspur
PJ Rice	Arsenal
AR Elder	Stoke City
SJ Todd	Burnley
WJT Neill	Arsenal
JJ Nicholson	Huddersfield Town
WG Campbell	Dundee
AS McMordie	Middlesbrough
AD Dougan	Wolverhampton Wanderers
D Clements*	Coventry City
G Best	Manchester United

Subs	
* TA Jackson	Everton

Result	0-0

263. 22 October 1969 v USSR at Moscow

PA Jennings	Tottenham Hotspur
DJ Craig	Newcastle United
M Harvey	Sunderland
A Hunter	Blackburn Rovers
WJT Neill	Arsenal
JJ Nicholson	Huddersfield Town
D Hegan	West Bromwich Albion
TA Jackson	Everton
AD Dougan	Wolverhampton Wanderers
JT Harkin	Shrewsbury Town
D Clements	Coventry City

Result	0-2

264. 18 April 1970 v SCOTLAND at Belfast

PA Jennings	Tottenham Hotspur
DJ Craig	Newcastle United
D Clements	Coventry City
SJ Todd*	Burnley
WJT Neill	Arsenal
JJ Nicholson	Huddersfield Town
WG Campbell**	Dundee
RJ Lutton	Wolverhampton Wanderers
AD Dougan	Wolverhampton Wanderers
AS McMordie	Middlesbrough
G Best	Manchester United

Subs	
* WJ O'Kane	Nottingham Forest
** D Dickson	Coleraine

Result   0-1

265. 21 April 1970 v ENGLAND at Wembley

PA Jennings	Tottenham Hotspur
DJ Craig	Newcastle United
D Clements	Coventry City
WJ O'Kane	Nottingham Forest
WJT Neill	Arsenal
JJ Nicholson	Huddersfield Town
AS McMordie	Middlesbrough
G Best	Manchester United
AD Dougan	Wolverhampton Wanderers
A O'Doherty*	Coleraine
RJ Lutton**	Wolverhampton Wanderers

Subs
* S Nelson	Arsenal
** J Cowan	Newcastle United

Result   1-3

G Best

266. 25 April 1970 v WALES at Swansea

WS McFaul	Newcastle United
DJ Craig	Newcastle United
S Nelson	Arsenal
WJ O'Kane	Nottingham Forest
WJT Neill	Arsenal
JJ Nicholson	Huddersfield Town
WG Campbell*	Dundee
G Best	Manchester United
D Dickson	Coleraine
AS McMordie	Middlesbrough
D Clements	Coventry City

Subs
* A O'Doherty	Coleraine

Result   0-1

267. 11 November 1970 v SPAIN at Seville

WS McFaul	Newcastle United
DJ Craig	Newcastle United
S Nelson	Arsenal
TA Jackson	Nottingham Forest
WJT Neill	Hull City
WJ O'Kane	Nottingham Forest
D Sloan	Oxford United
G Best	Manchester United
AD Dougan	Wolverhampton Wanderers
JT Harkin	Shrewsbury Town
D Clements	Coventry City

Result   0-3

268. 3 February 1971 v CYPRUS at Nicosia

PA Jennings	Tottenham Hotspur
DJ Craig	Newcastle United
S Nelson	Arsenal
A Hunter	Blackburn Rovers
WJT Neill	Hull City
SJ Todd	Sheffield Wednesday
B Hamilton	Linfield
AS McMordie	Middlesbrough
AD Dougan	Wolverhampton Wanderers
JJ Nicholson	Huddersfield Town
G Best	Manchester United

Result   3-0

JJ Nicholson; AD Dougan; G Best (pen)

269. 21 April 1971 v CYPRUS at Belfast

PA Jennings	Tottenham Hotspur
DJ Craig	Newcastle United
D Clements	Coventry City
M Harvey	Sunderland
A Hunter	Blackburn Rovers
SJ Todd*	Sheffield Wednesday
B Hamilton	Linfield
AS McMordie	Middlesbrough
AD Dougan	Wolverhampton Wanderers
JJ Nicholson	Huddersfield Town
G Best	Manchester United

Subs
* P Watson	Distillery

Result   5-0

AD Dougan; G Best (3); J Nicholson

FEATURED MATCH NO 12

NORTHERN IRELAND 5 CYPRUS 0

AT WINDSOR PARK, BELFAST, 21 APRIL 1971

The supremacy of Northern Ireland in this one-sided European Nations Cup tie was never questioned after a 90-second goal from newly appointed captain Derek DOUGAN – a header from a Sammy Todd cross.

The home side piled on the pressure. Jimmy Nicholson's shot was turned round the post by Herodotous before Bryan Hamilton put a shot just wide of the post. Hamilton then had the ball in the net, only for the 'goal' to be disallowed for offside. Hamilton was in the thick of the action and he put Dougan through but the lanky striker's shot landed on the roof of the net. Dave Clements chipped the keeper but the ball clipped the bar prior to Todd just failing to reach a ball after a McMordie-Hamilton move.

The exasperation finally ended in the 44th minute when BEST picked the ball up just outside the penalty

area. His powerful shot struck the upright before landing in the net as the goalkeeper stood motionless assuming it was going wide!

The second-half was only two minutes old when Best struck again. Newcastle full-back David Craig pushed a long ball up to Dougan on the left; on it went to BEST who cut round the full-back and placed it perfectly in the far corner.

Northern Ireland now had the whip hand and the hunger for more goals. George Best smacked a shot against the crossbar and then he hit another just wide. Ireland's third goal came after 56 minutes and was scored by BEST direct from a left-wing corner. Up went McMordie but he missed it and it curled into the net with Allan Hunter and the Cypriot goalkeeper ending up there too!

The home side continued to push forward and a Derek Dougan header went inches past the post before Hamilton's goalbound shot was deflected for a corner. Dougan and Nicholson then went close before Best again smacked a shot against the upright. Northern Ireland's fifth goal came in the 85th minute, shortly after the visitors had made two substitutions. Jimmy NICHOLSON hit a powerful shot that took a deflection off Koureas and so wrong-foot Herodotous.

Despite the mediocrity of the opposition, there was a feeling of satisfaction that at last Northern Ireland had scored goals! The result put them at the top of their Nations Cup qualifying table.

B Hamilton	Linfield
AS McMordie*	Middlesbrough
AD Dougan	Wolverhampton Wanderers
D Clements	Coventry City
G Best	Manchester United
Subs	
* DJ Craig	Newcastle United
Result	1-0

J Greig (own goal)

272. 22 May 1971 v WALES at Belfast

PA Jennings	Tottenham Hotspur
PJ Rice	Arsenal
S Nelson	Arsenal
WJ O'Kane	Nottingham Forest
A Hunter	Blackburn Rovers
JJ Nicholson*	Huddersfield Town
B Hamilton	Linfield
AS McMordie	Middlesbrough
AD Dougan	Wolverhampton Wanderers
D Clements	Coventry City
G Best	Manchester United
Subs	
* M Harvey	Sunderland
Result	1-0

B Hamilton

273. 22 September 1971 v USSR at Moscow

WS McFaul	Newcastle United
DJ Craig*	Newcastle United
S Nelson	Arsenal
A Hunter	Ipswich Town
WJT Neill	Hull City
D Hegan	Wolverhampton Wanderers
WJ O'Kane	Nottingham Forest
JJ Nicholson	Huddersfield Town
AD Dougan	Wolverhampton Wanderers
D Clements	Sheffield Wednesday
G Best	Manchester United
Subs	
* B Hamilton	Ipswich Town
Result	0-1

270. 15 May 1971 v ENGLAND at Belfast

PA Jennings	Tottenham Hotspur
PJ Rice	Arsenal
S Nelson	Arsenal
WJ O'Kane	Nottingham Forest
A Hunter	Blackburn Rovers
JJ Nicholson	Huddersfield Town
B Hamilton	Linfield
AS McMordie*	Middlesbrough
AD Dougan	Wolverhampton Wanderers
D Clements	Coventry City
G Best	Manchester United
Subs	
* T Cassidy	Newcastle United
Result	0-1

271. 18 May 1971 v SCOTLAND at Glasgow

PA Jennings	Tottenham Hotspur
PJ Rice	Arsenal
S Nelson	Arsenal
WJ O'Kane	Nottingham Forest
A Hunter	Blackburn Rovers
JJ Nicholson	Huddersfield Town

274. 13 October 1971 v USSR at Belfast

PA Jennings	Tottenham Hotspur
PJ Rice	Arsenal
S Nelson	Arsenal
JJ Nicholson	Huddersfield Town
A Hunter	Ipswich Town
WJ O'Kane	Nottingham Forest
AS McMordie	Middlesbrough
B Hamilton*	Ipswich Town
WJT Neill	Hull City

AD Dougan**	Wolverhampton Wanderers
D Clements	Sheffield Wednesday
Subs	
* MHM O'Neill	Distillery
** T Cassidy	Newcastle United
Result	**1-1**

JJ Nicholson

275. 16 February 1972 v SPAIN at Hull

PA Jennings	Tottenham Hotspur
PJ Rice	Arsenal
S Nelson	Arsenal
WJT Neill	Hull City
A Hunter	Ipswich Town
D Clements	Sheffield Wednesday
B Hamilton*	Ipswich Town
AS McMordie	Middlesbrough
S Morgan	Port Vale
SB McIlroy	Manchester United
G Best	Manchester United
Subs	
* MHM O'Neill	Nottingham Forest
Result	**1-1**

S Morgan

276. 20 May 1972 v SCOTLAND at Glasgow

PA Jennings	Tottenham Hotspur
PJ Rice	Arsenal
S Nelson	Arsenal
WJT Neill	Hull City
A Hunter	Ipswich Town
D Clements*	Sheffield Wednesday
D Hegan	Wolverhampton Wanderers
AS McMordie**	Middlesbrough
AD Dougan	Wolverhampton Wanderers
WJ Irvine	Brighton & Hove Albion
TA Jackson	Nottingham Forest
Subs	
* DJ Craig	Newcastle United
** SB McIlroy	Manchester United
Result	**0-2**

277. 23 May 1972 v ENGLAND at Wembley

PA Jennings	Tottenham Hotspur

PJ Rice	Arsenal
S Nelson	Arsenal
WJT Neill	Hull City
A Hunter	Ipswich Town
D Clements	Sheffield Wednesday
D Hegan	Wolverhampton Wanderers
AS McMordie	Middlesbrough
AD Dougan	Wolverhampton Wanderers
WJ Irvine	Brighton & Hove Albion
TA Jackson	Nottingham Forest
Result	**1-0**

WJT Neill

FEATURED MATCH NO 13

ENGLAND 0 NORTHERN IRELAND 1

AT WEMBLEY STADIUM, LONDON, 23 MAY 1972

This victory, only Ireland's sixth in 79 meetings with England, was an occasion to savour and to place alongside the 1957 Danny Blanchflower-led triumph on the same ground.

Some of the Irish side were only half-fit, playing defensively and then hitting a goal before containing Alf Ramsey's England team.

All the early pressure came from the home side with Jennings producing outstanding saves from both Marsh and Macdonald before Tony Currie's cross-cum-shot almost caught the Irish keeper out. England continued to mount attack after attack but the Irish defence in which Allan Hunter was outstanding, held firm. There were half chances for Macdonald and Bell but then after 33 minutes, Northern Ireland scored a fairytale goal.

With the rain falling heavily, Wolves' midfielder Danny Hegan took a corner on the left – a planned set piece. He put a short one to the near post, but with Derek Dougan having wandered to the far post and Willie Irvine having missed the ball, it hit player-manager Terry NEILL on the head. It then bounced between Neill and England keeper Shilton before the central defender pivoted and hit it into the net.

Neill was playing in his 50th international for Northern Ireland, and this was only his second goal in a superb international career.

Jennings brought off some remarkable saves from Macdonald, Bell and Marsh before a one-handed effort from a Mike Summerbee cross which must rank among the greatest-ever saves ever seen at Wembley.

England introduced substitutes Martin Peters and Martin Chivers but though they pressed for most of the second-half they were unable to break down the Irish defence. Jennings continued to deny the England forwards. Although the tension at the finish

was almost unbearable, as time was added on for the referee having had treatment for two cramp-related incidents, Northern Ireland held out to record a remarkable win.

This was no fluke win for Northern Ireland. There were no off-the-line clearances, no lucky breaks – they played it tight, snatched the goal and then decided to hold out come what may!

278. 27 May 1972 v WALES at Wrexham

PA Jennings	Tottenham Hotspur
PJ Rice	Arsenal
S Nelson	Arsenal
WJT Neill	Hull City
A Hunter	Ipswich Town
D Clements	Sheffield Wednesday
D Hegan	Wolverhampton Wanderers
AS McMordie	Middlesbrough
AD Dougan*	Wolverhampton Wanderers
WJ Irvine	Brighton & Hove Albion
TA Jackson	Nottingham Forest

Subs	
* MHM O'Neill	Nottingham Forest

Result	0-0

279. 18 October 1972 v BULGARIA at Sofia

PA Jennings	Tottenham Hotspur
PJ Rice	Arsenal
S Nelson	Arsenal
A Hunter	Ipswich Town
WJT Neill	Hull City
D Clements	Sheffield Wednesday
B Hamilton*	Ipswich Town
D Hegan	Wolverhampton Wanderers
AS McMordie	Middlesbrough
AD Dougan	Wolverhampton Wanderers
G Best	Manchester United

Subs	
* S Morgan	Port Vale

Result	0-3

280. 14 February 1973 v CYPRUS at Nicosia

PA Jennings	Tottenham Hotspur
PJ Rice	Arsenal
DJ Craig	Newcastle United
A Hunter	Ipswich Town
WJT Neill	Hull City
D Clements	Sheffield Wednesday
B Hamilton	Ipswich Town
D Hegan	Wolverhampton Wanderers
D Dickson	Coleraine
AD Dougan	Wolverhampton Wanderers
S Nelson	Arsenal

Result	0-1

281. 28 March 1973 v PORTUGAL at Coventry

PA Jennings	Tottenham Hotspur
WJ O'Kane	Nottingham Forest
S Nelson	Arsenal
WJT Neill	Hull City
A Hunter	Ipswich Town
D Clements	Sheffield Wednesday
B Hamilton	Ipswich Town
RI Coyle	Sheffield Wednesday
S Morgan	Port Vale
D Dickson	Coleraine
MHM O'Neill	Nottingham Forest

Result	1-1

MHM O'Neill

282. 8 May 1973 v CYPRUS at London

WS McFaul	Newcastle United
WJ O'Kane	Nottingham Forest
DJ Craig	Newcastle United
WJT Neill	Hull City
A Hunter*	Ipswich Town
D Clements	Sheffield Wednesday
B Hamilton**	Ipswich Town
TA Jackson	Nottingham Forest
S Morgan	Port Vale
MHM O'Neill	Nottingham Forest
T Anderson	Manchester United

Subs	
* RI Coyle	Sheffield Wednesday
** RJ Lutton	Wolverhampton Wanderers

Result	3-0

S Morgan; T Anderson (2)

283. 12 May 1973 v ENGLAND at Liverpool

PA Jennings	Tottenham Hotspur
PJ Rice	Arsenal
DJ Craig	Newcastle United
WJT Neill	Hull City
A Hunter	Ipswich Town
D Clements	Sheffield Wednesday
B Hamilton	Ipswich Town
TA Jackson	Nottingham Forest
S Morgan	Port Vale
MHM O'Neill	Nottingham Forest
T Anderson	Manchester United

Result	1-2

D Clements (pen)

PA Jennings	Tottenham Hotspur
PJ Rice	Arsenal
DJ Craig	Newcastle United
WJT Neill	Hull City
A Hunter	Ipswich Town
D Clements	Sheffield Wednesday
B Hamilton	Ipswich Town
TA Jackson	Nottingham Forest
S Morgan	Port Vale
MHM O'Neill	Nottingham Forest
T Anderson*	Manchester United

Subs	
* RJ Lutton	West Ham United

Result	2-1

MHM O'Neill; T Anderson

PA Jennings	Tottenham Hotspur
PJ Rice	Arsenal
DJ Craig	Newcastle United
WJT Neill	Hull City
A Hunter	Ipswich Town
D Clements	Sheffield Wednesday
B Hamilton*	Ipswich Town
TA Jackson	Nottingham Forest
S Morgan	Port Vale
MHM O'Neill	Nottingham Forest
T Anderson**	Manchester United

Subs	
* RJ Lutton	West Ham United
** RI Coyle	Sheffield Wednesday
Result	1-0

B Hamilton

WS McFaul	Newcastle United
PJ Rice	Arsenal
DJ Craig	Newcastle United
WJ O'Kane	Nottingham Forest
A Hunter	Ipswich Town
D Clements	Everton
B Hamilton	Ipswich Town
TA Jackson*	Nottingham Forest
S Morgan	Aston Villa
T Anderson	Manchester United
MHM O'Neill**	Nottingham Forest

Subs	
* RI Coyle	Sheffield Wednesday
** T Cassidy	Newcastle United

Result	0-0

PA Jennings	Tottenham Hotspur
PJ Rice	Arsenal
DJ Craig	Newcastle United
TA Jackson*	Nottingham Forest
WJ O'Kane	Nottingham Forest
D Clements	Everton
RJ Lutton	West Ham United
MHM O'Neill	Nottingham Forest
S Morgan	Aston Villa
T Anderson	Manchester United
G Best	Manchester United

Subs	
* RI Coyle	Sheffield Wednesday

Result	1 1

WJ O'Kane

PA Jennings	Tottenham Hotspur
PJ Rice	Arsenal
S Nelson	Arsenal
WJ O'Kane	Nottingham Forest
A Hunter	Ipswich Town
D Clements	Everton
B Hamilton*	Ipswich Town
T Cassidy	Newcastle United
S Morgan	Aston Villa
SB McIlroy	Manchester United
RC McGrath	Tottenham Hotspur

Subs	
* TA Jackson	Nottingham Forest

Result	1-0

T Cassidy

PA Jennings	Tottenham Hotspur
PJ Rice	Arsenal
S Nelson*	Arsenal
WJ O'Kane	Nottingham Forest
A Hunter	Ipswich Town
D Clements	Everton
B Hamilton**	Ipswich Town
T Cassidy	Newcastle United
S Morgan	Aston Villa
SB McIlroy	Manchester United
RC McGrath	Tottenham Hotspur

Subs	
* TA Jackson	Nottingham Forest
** MHM O'Neill	Nottingham Forest

Result	0-1

PA Jennings	Tottenham Hotspur
PJ Rice	Arsenal
HO Dowd	Glenavon
WJ O'Kane	Nottingham Forest
A Hunter	Ipswich Town
D Clements	Everton
B Hamilton*	Ipswich Town
T Cassidy	Newcastle United
SB McIlroy	Manchester United
RC McGrath	Tottenham Hotspur
MHM O'Neill	Nottingham Forest

Subs	
* TA Jackson	Nottingham Forest

Result	0-1

PA Jennings	Tottenham Hotspur
PJ Rice	Arsenal
DJ Craig*	Newcastle United
WJ O'Kane	Nottingham Forest
A Hunter	Ipswich Town
D Clements	Everton
B Hamilton	Ipswich Town
T Cassidy	Newcastle United
SB McIlroy	Manchester United
T Finney	Sunderland
RC McGrath**	Tottenham Hotspur

Subs	
* HO Dowd	Sheffield Wednesday
** TA Jackson	Nottingham Forest

Result	1-2

T Finney

PA Jennings	Tottenham Hotspur
WJ O'Kane	Nottingham Forest
S Nelson*	Arsenal
CJ Nicholl	Aston Villa
A Hunter	Ipswich Town
HO Dowd	Sheffield Wednesday
B Hamilton	Ipswich Town
TA Jackson	Nottingham Forest
S Morgan	Aston Villa
MHM O'Neill	Nottingham Forest
SB McIlroy	Manchester United

Subs	
* RV Blair	Oldham Athletic

Result	2-0

CJ Nicholl; MHM O'Neill

PA Jennings	Tottenham Hotspur
PJ Rice	Arsenal
S Nelson	Arsenal
CJ Nicholl	Aston Villa
A Hunter	Ipswich Town
D Clements	Everton
B Hamilton	Ipswich Town
MHM O'Neill	Nottingham Forest
DW Spence	Bury
SB McIlroy	Manchester United
TA Jackson	Nottingham Forest

Result	1-0

B Hamilton

PA Jennings	Tottenham Hotspur
PJ Rice	Arsenal
WJ O'Kane	Nottingham Forest
CJ Nicholl	Aston Villa
A Hunter	Ipswich Town
D Clements	Everton
B Hamilton*	Ipswich Town
MHM O'Neill	Nottingham Forest
DW Spence	Bury
SB McIlroy	Manchester United
TA Jackson	Nottingham Forest

Subs	
* T Finney	Sunderland

Result	0-0

PA Jennings	Tottenham Hotspur
PJ Rice	Arsenal
WJ O'Kane	Nottingham Forest
CJ Nicholl	Aston Villa
A Hunter*	Ipswich Town
D Clements	Everton
T Finney	Sunderland
MHM O'Neill**	Nottingham Forest
DW Spence	Bury
SB McIlroy	Manchester United
TA Jackson	Nottingham Forest

Subs	
* RV Blair	Oldham Athletic
** T Anderson	Swindon Town

Result	0-3

PA Jennings	Tottenham Hotspur
PW Scott	Everton
PJ Rice	Arsenal
CJ Nicholl	Aston Villa

A Hunter	Ipswich Town
D Clements	Everton
RV Blair	Oldham Athletic
TA Jackson	Nottingham Forest
DW Spence	Bury
SB McIlroy	Manchester United
T Finney	Sunderland

Result	1-0

T Finney

297. 3 September 1975 v SWEDEN at Belfast

PA Jennings	Tottenham Hotspur
PJ Rice	Arsenal
S Nelson	Arsenal
CJ Nicholl	Aston Villa
A Hunter	Ipswich Town
D Clements	Everton
RV Blair	Oldham Athletic
B Hamilton*	Ipswich Town
DW Spence	Bury
SB McIlroy	Manchester United
TA Jackson	Nottingham Forest

Subs	
* S Morgan	Aston Villa

Result	1-2

A Hunter

298. 29 October 1975 v NORWAY at Belfast

PA Jennings	Tottenham Hotspur
PJ Rice	Arsenal
S Nelson	Arsenal
CJ Nicholl	Aston Villa
A Hunter	Ipswich Town
TA Jackson	Manchester United
B Hamilton	Norwich City
SB McIlroy	Manchester United
S Morgan*	Aston Villa
J Jamison	Glentoran
T Finney	Sunderland

Subs	
* GT Cochrane	Coleraine

Result	3-0

S Morgan; SB McIlroy; B Hamilton

299. 19 November 1975 v YUGOSLAVIA at Belgrade

PA Jennings	Tottenham Hotspur
PJ Rice	Arsenal
PW Scott	Everton
CJ Nicholl	Aston Villa
A Hunter	Ipswich Town
D Clements	Everton
B Hamilton	Ipswich Town

SB McIlroy	Manchester United
S Morgan	Aston Villa
TA Jackson*	Manchester United
T Finney	Sunderland

Subs	
* MHM O'Neill	Nottingham Forest

Result	0-1

300. 3 March 1976 v ISRAEL at Tel Aviv

PA Jennings*	Tottenham Hotspur
JM Nicholl	Manchester United
PW Scott	York City
A Hunter	Ipswich Town
PJ Rice	Arsenal
RV Blair	Oldham Athletic
S Nelson	Arsenal
B Hamilton	Everton
T Anderson**	Swindon Town
DW Spence	Bury
W Feeney	Glentoran

Subs	
* JA Platt	Middlesbrough
** RC McGrath	Tottenham Hotspur

Result	1-1

W Feeney

301. 8 May 1976 v SCOTLAND at Glasgow

PA Jennings	Tottenham Hotspur
PW Scott	York City
PJ Rice	Arsenal
CJ Nicholl	Aston Villa
A Hunter	Ipswich Town
PG Sharkey*	Ipswich Town
B Hamilton	Everton
SB McIlroy	Manchester United
S Morgan**	Brighton & Hove Albion
T Cassidy	Newcastle United
T Finney	Sunderland

Subs	
* D McCreery	Manchester United
** DW Spence	Bury

Result	0-3

302. 11 May 1976 v ENGLAND at Wembley

PA Jennings	Tottenham Hotspur
PJ Rice	Arsenal
S Nelson*	Arsenal
CJ Nicholl	Aston Villa
A Hunter	Ipswich Town
D Clements	New York Cosmos
B Hamilton	Everton
SB McIlroy	Manchester United
DW Spence	Bury

D McCreery	Manchester United
T Cassidy	Newcastle United

Subs	
* PW Scott	York City

Result	0-4

303. 14 May 1976 v WALES at Swansea

PA Jennings	Tottenham Hotspur
PW Scott	York City
PJ Rice	Arsenal
CJ Nicholl	Aston Villa
A Hunter	Ipswich Town
D Clements	New York Cosmos
B Hamilton	Everton
SB McIlroy	Manchester United
DW Spence*	Bury
T Cassidy**	Newcastle United
D McCreery	Manchester United

Subs	
* S Morgan	Aston Villa
** JM Nicholl	Manchester United

Result	0-1

304. 13 October 1976 v HOLLAND at Rotterdam

PA Jennings	Tottenham Hotspur
JM Nicholl	Manchester United
PJ Rice	Arsenal
TA Jackson	Manchester United
A Hunter	Ipswich Town
B Hamilton	Everton
G Best	Fulham
SB McIlroy	Manchester United
RC McGrath*	Manchester United
D McCreery	Manchester United
T Anderson	Swindon Town

Subs	
* DW Spence	Blackpool

Result	2-2

RC McGrath; DW Spence

305. 10 November 1976 v BELGIUM at Liege

PA Jennings	Tottenham Hotspur
JM Nicholl	Manchester United
PJ Rice*	Arsenal
TA Jackson	Manchester United
A Hunter	Ipswich Tow
B Hamilton	Everton
G Best	Fulham
SB McIlroy	Manchester United
RC McGrath	Manchester United
D McCreery	Manchester United
T Anderson	Swindon Town

Subs	
* S Nelson	Arsenal

Result	0-2

306. 27 April 1977 v WEST GERMANY at Cologne

PA Jennings	Tottenham Hotspur
PJ Rice	Arsenal
S Nelson	Arsenal
TA Jackson	Manchester United
A Hunter	Ipswich Town
D McCreery*	Manchester United
G Best	Fulham
RC McGrath	Manchester United
GJ Armstrong**	Tottenham Hotspur
B Hamilton	Everton
T Anderson	Swindon Town

Subs	
* T Cassidy	Newcastle United
** DW Spence	Blackpool

Result	0-5

307. 28 May 1977 v ENGLAND at Belfast

PA Jennings	Tottenham Hotspur
JM Nicholl	Manchester United
PJ Rice	Arsenal
TA Jackson	Manchester United
A Hunter	Ipswich Town
B Hamilton	Everton
RC McGrath	Manchester United
SB McIlroy	Manchester United
GJ Armstrong*	Tottenham Hotspur
D McCreery	Manchester United
T Anderson**	Swindon Town

Subs	
* MHM O'Neill	Nottingham Forest
** DW Spence	Blackpool

Result	1-2

RC McGrath

308. 1 June 1977 v SCOTLAND at Glasgow

PA Jennings	Tottenham Hotspur
JM Nicholl	Manchester United
PJ Rice	Arsenal
TA Jackson	Manchester United
A Hunter	Ipswich Town
B Hamilton	Everton
MHM O'Neill	Nottingham Forest
SB McIlroy	Manchester United
RC McGrath	Manchester United
D McCreery	Manchester United
T Anderson*	Swindon Town

Subs	
* DW Spence	Blackpool

Result   0-3

PA Jennings	Tottenham Hotspur
JM Nicholl	Manchester United
S Nelson	Arsenal
CJ Nicholl	Aston Villa
A Hunter	Ipswich Town
B Hamilton	Everton
RC McGrath	Manchester United
SB McIlroy	Manchester United
TA Jackson	Manchester United
D McCreery*	Manchester United
T Anderson**	Swindon Town

Subs
* GJ Armstrong	Tottenham Hotspur
** DW Spence	Blackpool

Result   1-1

S Nelson

PA Jennings	Tottenham Hotspur
PJ Rice	Arsenal
S Nelson	Arsenal
JM Nicholl	Manchester United
A Hunter	Ipswich Town
B Hamilton	Everton
RC McGrath	Manchester United
SB McIlroy	Manchester United
TA Jackson*	Manchester United
D McCreery	Manchester United
T Anderson**	Swindon Town

Subs
* DW Spence	Blackpool
** GJ Armstrong	Tottenham Hotspur

Result   0-1

PA Jennings	Arsenal
PJ Rice	Arsenal
S Nelson	Arsenal
JM Nicholl	Manchester United
A Hunter	Ipswich Town
D McCreery	Manchester United
MHM O'Neill	Nottingham Forest
SB McIlroy	Manchester United
RC McGrath	Manchester United
G Best	Fulham
T Anderson	Swindon Town

Result   2-0

RC McGrath; SB McIlroy

PA Jennings	Arsenal
PJ Rice	Arsenal
S Nelson	Arsenal
JM Nicholl	Manchester United
A Hunter	Ipswich Town
D McCreery	Manchester United
MHM O'Neill	Nottingham Forest
SB McIlroy	Manchester United
RC McGrath	Manchester United
G Best	Fulham
T Anderson	Swindon Town

Result   0-1

PA Jennings	Arsenal
PJ Rice	Arsenal
S Nelson	Arsenal
JM Nicholl	Manchester United
A Hunter*	Ipswich Town
SB McIlroy	Manchester United
RC McGrath	Manchester United
D McCreery	Manchester United
GJ Armstrong	Tottenham Hotspur
DC Stewart	Hull City
T Anderson	Swindon Town

Subs
* CJ Nicholl	Southampton

Result   3-0

GJ Armstrong (2); RC McGrath

JA Platt	Middlesbrough
B Hamilton	Millwall
PW Scott	York City
JM Nicholl	Manchester United
CJ Nicholl	Southampton
SB McIlroy	Manchester United
RC McGrath*	Manchester United
MHM O'Neill	Nottingham Forest
GJ Armstrong	Tottenham Hotspur
D McCreery	Manchester United
T Anderson**	Peterborough United

Subs
* WR Hamilton	Queen's Park Rangers
** GT Cochrane	Burnley

Result   1-1

MHM O'Neill

JA Platt	Middlesbrough
B Hamilton	Millwall

PW Scott	York City
JM Nicholl	Manchester United
CJ Nicholl	Southampton
SB McIlroy	Manchester United
RC McGrath*	Manchester United
MHM O'Neill	Nottingham Forest
GJ Armstrong	Tottenham Hotspur
D McCreery	Manchester United
T Anderson	Peterborough United

Subs	
* GT Cochrane	Burnley

Result	0-1

316. 19 May 1978 v WALES at Wrexham

JA Platt	Middlesbrough
B Hamilton	Millwall
PW Scott	York City
JM Nicholl	Manchester United
CJ Nicholl	Southampton
SB McIlroy	Manchester United
RC McGrath	Manchester United
MHM O'Neill	Nottingham Forest
GJ Armstrong	Tottenham Hotspur
D McCreery	Newcastle United
T Anderson*	Peterborough United

Subs	
* GT Cochrane	Burnley

Result	0-1

317. 20 September 1978 v REPUBLIC OF IRELAND at Dublin

PA Jennings	Arsenal
PJ Rice	Arsenal
S Nelson	Arsenal
CJ Nicholl	Southampton
A Hunter*	Ipswich Town
SB McIlroy	Manchester United
D McCreery	Manchester United
MHM O'Neill	Nottingham Forest
GJ Armstrong	Tottenham Hotspur
JM Nicholl	Manchester United
DW Spence**	Blackpool

Subs	
* B Hamilton	Millwall
** GT Cochrane	Burnley

Result	0-0

318. 25 October 1978 v DENMARK at Belfast

PA Jennings	Arsenal
PJ Rice	Arsenal
S Nelson	Arsenal
JM Nicholl	Manchester United
A Hunter	Ipswich Town
D McCreery	Manchester United

MHM O'Neill	Nottingham Forest
SB McIlroy	Manchester United
GJ Armstrong	Tottenham Hotspur
S Morgan*	Sparta Rotterdam
GT Cochrane	Middlesbrough

Subs	
* DW Spence**	Blackpool
** T Anderson	Peterborough United

Result	2-1

DW Spence; T Anderson

319. 29 November 1978 v BULGARIA at Sofia

PA Jennings	Arsenal
B Hamilton	Swindon Town
S Nelson	Arsenal
JM Nicholl	Manchester United
CJ Nicholl	Southampton
D McCreery	Manchester United
MHM O'Neill	Nottingham Forest
SB McIlroy*	Manchester United
GJ Armstrong	Tottenham Hotspur
WT Caskey	Derby County
GT Cochrane**	Middlesbrough

Subs	
* V Moreland	Derby County
** RC McGrath	Manchester United

Result	2-0

GJ Armstrong; WT Caskey

320. 7 February 1979 v ENGLAND at Wembley

PA Jennings	Arsenal
PJ Rice	Arsenal
S Nelson	Arsenal
JM Nicholl	Manchester United
CJ Nicholl	Southampton
D McCreery	Manchester United
MHM O'Neill	Nottingham Forest
SB McIlroy	Manchester United
GJ Armstrong	Tottenham Hotspur
WT Caskey*	Derby County
GT Cochrane**	Middlesbrough

Subs	
* DW Spence	Blackpool
** RC McGrath	Manchester United

Result	0-4

321. 2 May 1979 v BULGARIA at Belfast

PA Jennings	Arsenal
B Hamilton	Swindon Town
S Nelson	Arsenal
JM Nicholl*	Manchester United
CJ Nicholl	Southampton

D McCreery	Manchester United
MHM O'Neill	Nottingham Forest
SB McIlroy	Manchester United
GJ Armstrong	Tottenham Hotspur
WT Caskey**	Derby County
GT Cochrane	Middlesbrough

Subs	
* V Moreland	Derby County
** DW Spence	Blackpool

| Result | 2-0 |

CJ Nicholl; GJ Armstrong

PA Jennings	Arsenal
PJ Rice	Arsenal
S Nelson	Arsenal
JM Nicholl	Manchester United
CJ Nicholl	Southampton
V Moreland*	Derby County
B Hamilton	Swindon Town
SB McIlroy	Manchester United
GJ Armstrong	Tottenham Hotspur
WT Caskey	Derby County
GT Cochrane**	Middlesbrough

Subs	
* RC McGrath	Manchester United
** DW Spence	Blackpool

| Result | 0-2 |

PA Jennings	Arsenal
PJ Rice	Arsenal
S Nelson	Arsenal
JM Nicholl	Manchester United
A Hunter	Ipswich Town
T Sloan	Manchester United
B Hamilton	Swindon Town
SB McIlroy	Manchester United
GJ Armstrong	Tottenham Hotspur
DW Spence*	Blackpool
V Moreland**	Derby County

Subs	
* WT Caskey	Derby County
** PW Scott	York City

| Result | 0-1 |

PA Jennings	Arsenal
PJ Rice	Arsenal
S Nelson	Arsenal
JM Nicholl	Manchester United
A Hunter	Ipswich Town
CJ Nicholl	Southampton

B Hamilton	Swindon Town
D McCreery*	Manchester United
GJ Armstrong	Tottenham Hotspur
SB McIlroy	Manchester United
DW Spence	Blackpool

Subs	
* T Sloan	Manchester United
Result	1-1

DW Spence

PA Jennings	Arsenal
PJ Rice	Arsenal
S Nelson	Arsenal
JM Nicholl	Manchester United
A Hunter	Ipswich Town
D McCreery	Manchester United
MHM O'Neill*	Nottingham Forest
SB McIlroy**	Manchester United
GJ Armstrong	Tottenham Hotspur
DW Spence	Blackpool
B Hamilton	Swindon Town

Subs	
* T Sloan	Manchester United
** WT Caskey	Derby County

| Result | 0-4 |

PA Jennings	Arsenal
PJ Rice	Arsenal
S Nelson	Arsenal
JM Nicholl	Manchester United
A Hunter*	Ipswich Town
D McCreery	Queen's Park Rangers
SB McIlroy	Manchester United
T Cassidy	Newcastle United
GJ Armstrong	Tottenham Hotspur
T Finney**	Cambridge United
V Moreland	Derby County

Subs	
* P Rafferty	Linfield
** WT Caskey	Derby County

| Result | 1-5 |

V Moreland (pen)

PA Jennings	Arsenal
JM Nicholl	Manchester United
S Nelson	Arsenal
CJ Nicholl	Southampton
A Hunter	Ipswich Town
D McCreery	Queen's Park Rangers

MHM O'Neill*	Nottingham Forest
SB McIlroy	Manchester United
GJ Armstrong	Tottenham Hotspur
DW Spence	Blackpool
V Moreland	Derby County

Subs	
* T Cassidy	Newcastle United
Result	1-0

GJ Armstrong

328. 26 March 1980 v ISRAEL at Tel Aviv

PA Jennings	Arsenal
JM Nicholl	Manchester United
S Nelson	Arsenal
JP O'Neill	Leicester City
CJ Nicholl	Southampton
T Cassidy	Newcastle United
MHM O'Neill	Nottingham Forest
SB McIlroy	Manchester United
GJ Armstrong	Tottenham Hotspur
T Finney*	Cambridge United
GT Cochrane	Middlesbrough

Subs	
* DW Spence	Southend United

Result	0-0

329. 16 May 1980 v SCOTLAND at Belfast

JA Platt	Middlesbrough
JM Nicholl	Manchester United
MM Donaghy	Luton Town
JP O'Neill	Leicester City
CJ Nicholl	Southampton
T Cassidy*	Newcastle United
T Finney	Cambridge United
SB McIlroy	Manchester United
GJ Armstrong	Tottenham Hotspur
WR Hamilton**	Burnley
N Brotherston	Blackburn Rovers

Subs	
* D McCreery	Queen's Park Rangers
** J McClelland	Mansfield Town

Result	1-0

WR Hamilton

330. 20 May 1980 v ENGLAND at Wembley

JA Platt	Middlesbrough
JM Nicholl	Manchester United
MM Donaghy	Luton Town
JP O'Neill	Leicester City
CJ Nicholl	Southampton
T Cassidy*	Newcastle United
T Finney	Cambridge United
SB McIlroy	Manchester United

GJ Armstrong	Tottenham Hotspur
WR Hamilton**	Burnley
N Brotherston	Blackburn Rovers

Subs	
* D McCreery	Queen's Park Rangers
** GT Cochrane	Middlesbrough

Result	1-1

GT Cochrane

331. 23 May 1980 v WALES at Cardiff

JA Platt	Middlesbrough
JM Nicholl	Manchester United
MM Donaghy	Luton Town
JP O'Neill	Leicester City
CJ Nicholl	Southampton
T Cassidy*	Newcastle United
T Finney	Cambridge United
SB McIlroy	Manchester United
GJ Armstrong	Tottenham Hotspur
WR Hamilton**	Burnley
N Brotherston	Blackburn Rovers

Subs	
* D McCreery	Queen's Park Rangers
** GT Cochrane	Middlesbrough

Result	1-0

N Brotherston

332. 11 June 1980 v AUSTRALIA at Sydney

JA Platt	Middlesbrough
JM Nicholl	Manchester United
J McClelland	Mansfield Town
JP O'Neill	Leicester City
CJ Nicholl	Southampton
T Cassidy*	Newcastle United
T Finney**	Cambridge United
MHM O'Neill	Nottingham Forest
GJ Armstrong	Tottenham Hotspur
WR Hamilton***	Burnley
N Brotherston****	Blackburn Rovers

Subs	
* D McCreery	Queen's Park Rangers
** B Hamilton	Swindon Town
*** DW Spence	Southend United
**** GT Cochrane	Middlesbrough

Result	2-1

CJ Nicholl; JP O'Neill

333. 15 June 1980 v AUSTRALIA at Melbourne

JA Platt	Middlesbrough
JM Nicholl	Manchester United
J McClelland	Mansfield Town

JP O'Neill	Leicester City
CJ Nicholl	Southampton
T Cassidy	Newcastle United
D McCreery*	Queen's Park Rangers
MHM O'Neill	Nottingham Forest
GJ Armstrong	Tottenham Hotspur
WR Hamilton	Burnley
N Brotherston	Blackburn Rovers
Subs	
* GT Cochrane	Middlesbrough
Result	1-1

MHM O'Neill

JA Platt	Middlesbrough
JM Nicholl	Manchester United
J McClelland	Mansfield Town
JP O'Neill	Leicester City
CJ Nicholl	Southampton
T Cassidy*	Newcastle United
GT Cochrane	Middlesbrough
MHM O'Neill	Nottingham Forest
GJ Armstrong	Tottenham Hotspur
WR Hamilton**	Burnley
N Brotherston	Blackburn Rovers
Subs	
* B Hamilton	Swindon Town
** C McCurdy	Linfield
Result	2-1

N Brotherston; C McCurdy

JA Platt	Middlesbrough
JM Nicholl	Manchester United
MM Donaghy	Luton Town
J McClelland	Mansfield Town
CJ Nicholl	Southampton
T Cassidy*	Burnley
MHM O'Neill	Nottingham Forest
SB McIlroy	Manchester United
GJ Armstrong	Tottenham Hotspur
WR Hamilton**	Burnley
N Brotherston	Blackburn Rovers
Subs	
* D McCreery	Queen's Park Rangers
** GT Cochrane	Middlesbrough
Result	3-0

N Brotherston; SB McIlroy; JM Nicholl

JA Platt	Middlesbrough
JM Nicholl	Manchester United

MM Donaghy	Luton Town
JP O'Neill	Leicester City
CJ Nicholl	Southampton
T Cassidy*	Burnley
MHM O'Neill	Nottingham Forest
SB McIlroy	Manchester United
GJ Armstrong	Watford
WR Hamilton**	Burnley
N Brotherston	Blackburn Rovers
Subs	
* D McCreery	Queen's Park Rangers
** GT Cochrane	Middlesbrough
Result	0-1

PA Jennings	Arsenal
JM Nicholl	Manchester United
S Nelson	Arsenal
JP O'Neill	Leicester City
CJ Nicholl	Southampton
J McClelland	Mansfield Town
D McCreery	Tulsa Roughnecks
SB McIlroy	Manchester United
GJ Armstrong	Watford
WR Hamilton*	Burnley
GT Cochrane	Middlesbrough
Subs	
* DW Spence	Southend United
Result	1-1

WR Hamilton

PA Jennings	Arsenal
JM Nicholl	Manchester United
S Nelson	Arsenal
JP O'Neill	Leicester City
CJ Nicholl	Southampton
D McCreery	Tulsa Roughnecks
MHM O'Neill	Norwich City
SB McIlroy	Manchester United
GJ Armstrong	Watford
WR Hamilton	Burnley
GT Cochrane	Middlesbrough
Result	1-0

GJ Armstrong

PA Jennings	Arsenal
JM Nicholl	Manchester United
S Nelson*	Arsenal
JP O'Neill	Leicester City
CJ Nicholl	Southampton
J McClelland	Glasgow Rangers

MHM O'Neill	Norwich City
SB McIlroy	Manchester United
GJ Armstrong	Watford
WR Hamilton	Burnley
GT Cochrane	Middlesbrough
Subs	
* MM Donaghy	Luton Town
Result	0-2

340. 3 June 1981 v SWEDEN at Stockholm

PA Jennings	Arsenal
JM Nicholl*	Manchester United
S Nelson	Arsenal
JP O'Neill	Leicester City
CJ Nicholl	Southampton
D McCreery	Tulsa Roughnecks
MHM O'Neill	Norwich City
SB McIlroy	Manchester United
GJ Armstrong	Watford
WR Hamilton**	Burnley
GT Cochrane	Middlesbrough
Subs	
* J McClelland	Glasgow Rangers
** DW Spence	Southend United
Result	0-1

341. 14 October 1981 v SCOTLAND at Belfast

PA Jennings	Arsenal
JM Nicholl	Manchester United
MM Donaghy	Luton Town
JP O'Neill	Leicester City
CJ Nicholl	Southampton
MHM O'Neill	Manchester City
GJ Armstrong	Watford
D McCreery	Tulsa Roughnecks
WR Hamilton	Burnley
SB McIlroy	Manchester United
N Brotherston	Blackburn Rovers
Result	0-0

342. 18 November 1981 v ISRAEL at Belfast

PA Jennings	Arsenal
JM Nicholl	Manchester United
MM Donaghy	Luton Town
JP O'Neill	Leicester City
CJ Nicholl	Southampton
D McCreery	Tulsa Roughnecks
SB McIlroy	Manchester United
T Cassidy	Burnley
GJ Armstrong	Watford
WR Hamilton	Burnley
N Brotherston	Blackburn Rovers
Result	1-0

GJ Armstrong	

343. 23 February 1982 v ENGLAND at Wembley

PA Jennings	Arsenal
JM Nicholl	Manchester United
S Nelson	Brighton & Hove Albion
MM Donaghy	Luton Town
CJ Nicholl	Southampton
JP O'Neill	Leicester City
N Brotherston*	Blackburn Rovers
MHM O'Neill**	Norwich City
GJ Armstrong	Watford
SB McIlroy	Stoke City
WR Hamilton	Burnley
Subs	
* GT Cochrane	Middlesbrough
** D McCreery	Tulsa Roughnecks
Result	0-4

344. 24 March 1982 v FRANCE at Paris

JA Platt	Middlesbrough
JM Nicholl	Toronto Blizzard
MM Donaghy	Luton Town
JP O'Neill	Leicester City
CJ Nicholl	Southampton
D McCreery*	Tulsa Roughnecks
MHM O'Neill	Norwich City
SB McIlroy**	Stoke City
GJ Armstrong	Watford
GT Cochrane***	Middlesbrough
N Brotherston	Blackburn Rovers
Subs	
* WT Caskey	Derby County
** DW Spence	Southend United
*** I Stewart	Queen's Park Rangers
Result	0-4

345. 28 April 1982 v SCOTLAND at Belfast

JA Platt	Middlesbrough
MM Donaghy	Luton Town
S Nelson	Brighton & Hove Albion
JP O'Neill	Leicester City
J McClelland	Glasgow Rangers
J Cleary	Glentoran
N Brotherston	Blackburn Rovers
MHM O'Neill	Norwich City
RM Campbell	Bradford City
SB McIlroy	Stoke City
PJ Healy	Coleraine
Result	1-1
SB McIlroy	

PA Jennings*	Arsenal
JM Nicholl	Toronto Blizzard
MM Donaghy	Luton Town
J McClelland	Glasgow Rangers
CJ Nicholl	Southampton
J Cleary**	Glentoran
N Brotherston	Blackburn Rovers
PJ Healy	Coleraine
GJ Armstrong	Watford
SB McIlroy	Stoke City
WR Hamilton	Burnley

Subs	
* JA Platt	Middlesbrough
** RM Campbell	Bradford City

Result	0-3

PA Jennings	Arsenal
JM Nicholl	Toronto Blizzard
MM Donaghy	Luton Town
J McClelland	Glasgow Rangers
CJ Nicholl	Southampton
MHM O'Neill	Norwich City
D McCreery	Tulsa Roughnecks
SB McIlroy	Stoke City
GJ Armstrong	Watford
WR Hamilton	Burnley
N Whiteside	Manchester United

Result	0-0

PA Jennings	Arsenal
JM Nicholl	Toronto Blizzard
MM Donaghy	Luton Town
J McClelland	Glasgow Rangers
CJ Nicholl	Southampton
MHM O'Neill*	Norwich City
D McCreery	Tulsa Roughnecks
SB McIlroy	Stoke City
GJ Armstrong	Watford
WR Hamilton	Burnley
N Whiteside**	Manchester United

Subs	
* PJ Healy	Coleraine
** N Brotherston	Blackburn Rovers

Result	1-1

GJ Armstrong

PA Jennings	Arsenal
JM Nicholl	Toronto Blizzard
MM Donaghy	Luton Town
J McClelland	Glasgow Rangers
CJ Nicholl	Southampton
MHM O'Neill	Norwich City
D McCreery	Tulsa Roughnecks
SB McIlroy*	Stoke City
GJ Armstrong	Watford
WR Hamilton	Burnley
N Whiteside**	Manchester United

Subs	
* T Cassidy	Burnley
** S Nelson	Brighton & Hove Albion

Result	1-0

GJ Armstrong

FEATURED MATCH NO 14

SPAIN 0 NORTHERN IRELAND 1

AT LUIS CASANOVA STADIUM, VALENCIA, 25 JUNE 1982

In defeating Spain 1-0 to qualify for the second phase of the 1982 World Cup, Northern Ireland not only achieved soccer history but produced one of the greatest ever performances by a British team in any World Cup. To do so with just 10 men for the last half-an-hour of a match played in a temperature of 34°C was bordering on the miraculous. As manager Billy Bingham put it, they killed the Spanish bull in its own ring!

After only three minutes, Pat Jennings saved at the feet of Lopez Ufarte, whilst four minutes later, Ufarte forced the Arsenal keeper to make another difficult save. Ireland's first shot of the game came after 27 minutes when 17-year-old Norman Whiteside let fly from outside the box – Arconada saved easily. Just before half-time, referee Ortiz shows Billy Hamilton the yellow card for a foul. Sammy McIlroy protests and is also booked!

A string of hard tackles by the Spaniards went unpunished so Northern Ireland took justice into their own hands shortly after half-time. Armstrong started the move in midfield. Confronted by three defenders he passed the ball wide to Hamilton on his right. Hamilton set off like a greyhound, dogged by Spain's Tendillo all the way down the wing. When he hammered in a low centre, Spanish goalkeeper and captain Arconada could only palm the ball out into the path of Armstrong, who came charging through in support. ARMSTRONG seized the chance to fire home, despite the efforts of the diving Spanish defenders.

In the 53rd minute, Jennings intercepted yet another Lopez Ufarte shot and then two minutes later tipped a rising shot from Quini over the bar. Spain never changed their tactics however – high crosses into the centre where Chris Nicholl promptly headed them away!

On the hour, tragedy struck when Northern Ireland were reduced to 10 men as Mal Donaghy was sent-off for merely pushing away Camacho at the far touchline, with the linesman pointing at the Luton defender as the culprit. The Paraguayan referee – who had never officiated a match in Europe – showed Donaghy the red card!

The Spaniards continued to body check and niggled constantly in the minutes that remained but the Irish who had pulled all their players back into defence, held on. Yet with 11 minutes to go and Spain becoming more desperate, Gordillo broke through the Irish rearguard but shot straight at Jennings. The Irish keeper then brought off a couple of world class saves, the last just two minutes from full-time from Camacho.

Northern Ireland showed top form throughout the game. They displayed great spirit and courage and always looked likely to score on the break. Gerry Armstrong's goal was the 100th scored in the first round's 36 matches – it also proved to be the last!

350. 1 July 1982 v AUSTRIA at Madrid	
JA Platt	Middlesbrough
JM Nicholl	Toronto Blizzard
S Nelson	Brighton & Hove Albion
J McClelland	Glasgow Rangers
CJ Nicholl	Southampton
MHM O'Neill	Norwich City
D McCreery	Tulsa Roughnecks
SB McIlroy	Stoke City
GJ Armstrong	Watford
WR Hamilton	Burnley
N Whiteside*	Manchester United
Subs	
* N Brotherston	Blackburn Rovers
Result	2-2

WR Hamilton (2)

FEATURED MATCH NO 15

AUSTRIA 2 NORTHERN IRELAND 2

AT THE VICENTE CALDERON STADIUM, MADRID, 1 JULY 1982

The national team's stature rose with every game in the 1982 World Cup Finals and perhaps never more so than in this match against Austria, when they came from behind to draw 2-2. It was a game that the Irish could have won, but equally it could so easily have gone the other way.

The Northern Ireland defence in which Jimmy Nicholl was outstanding found itself under early pressure from the Austrians as they went for the game's first goal.

Jim Platt made an outstanding double save, first from Max Hogmayr and then Ernst Baumeister. However, when the Irish broke from defence, there was always danger, especially on the right from Gerry Armstrong's accurate crosses.

It was from this type of build-up that the game's first goal came in the 27th minute. Armstrong accelerated past two Austrian defenders, his sheer strength getting the ball across to the waiting HAMILTON who headed past Koncilia. Just before the interval, Armstrong missed a golden opportunity of extending Ireland's slender lead.

At half-time, Austrian manager George Schmidt made two changes, introducing Reinhold Hintermaier and Kurt Welzl. What a dramatic difference this made as within five minutes of the restart, the Austrians were level. A left-wing corner by Prohaska went straight to Baumeister who hammered it towards goal – Jim Platt had it covered until Bruno PEZZEY just as he was about to be challenged by Chris Nicholl, back-heeled the ball past the Middlesbrough keeper.

In the 67th minute, Austria took the lead after being awarded a free-kick on the edge of the penalty area. Jurtin flicked the ball to HINTERMAIER who scored from 20 yards past a static Platt.

But in the 74th minute came Northern Ireland's equaliser. Armstrong lost the ball in a challenge but it broke for full-back Jimmy Nicholl racing down the right flank. As the keeper came out to meet him, he floated over a perfect cross for HAMILTON to head into the net with an unmarked Martin O'Neill waiting to pounce as well. The Burnley striker who toiled until he almost collapsed had written himself into the record books, by joining Peter McParland as the joint Irish record scorer in a World Cup finals match.

The final minutes were dominated by Northern Ireland who twice came close to snatching the winner. However, they had to be satisfied with a point which put the team in the final second-phase fixture against France – needing a win to reach the semi-final in Seville!

351. 4 July 1982 v FRANCE at Madrid	
PA Jennings	Arsenal
JM Nicholl	Toronto Blizzard
MM Donaghy	Luton Town
J McClelland	Glasgow Rangers
CJ Nicholl	Southampton
MHM O'Neill	Norwich City
D McCreery*	Tulsa Roughnecks
SB McIlroy	Stoke City
GJ Armstrong	Watford
WR Hamilton	Burnley
N Whiteside	Manchester United
Subs	
* JP O'Neill	Leicester City

Result	1-4

GJ Armstrong

JA Platt	Middlesbrough
JM Nicholl	Sunderland
MM Donaghy	Luton Town
J McClelland	Glasgow Rangers
JP O'Neill	Leicester City
MHM O'Neill	Norwich City
D McCreery	Newcastle United
SB McIlroy*	Stoke City
GJ Armstrong	Watford
WR Hamilton	Burnley
I Stewart**	Queen's Park Rangers

Subs	
* N Brotherston	Blackburn Rovers
** PJ Healy	Coleraine

Result	0-2

JA Platt	Middlesbrough
JM Nicholl	Sunderland
MM Donaghy	Luton Town
J McClelland	Glasgow Rangers
JP O'Neill	Leicester City
MHM O'Neill	Norwich City
N Brotherston	Blackburn Rovers
SB McIlroy	Stoke City
WR Hamilton	Burnley
N Whiteside	Manchester United
I Stewart	Queen's Park Rangers

Result	1-0

I Stewart

FEATURED MATCH NO 16

NORTHERN IRELAND 1 WEST GERMANY 0

AT WINDSOR PARK, BELFAST, 17 NOVEMBER 1982

Arguably there has never been a better performance by the national side than when they beat the champions West Germany 1-0 in a European Nations Cup tie.

Right from the start, Northern Ireland went on the offensive, a predetermined plan promised by manager Bingham. Within minutes of the kick-off, the plan almost succeeded as Brotherston flicked on a short corner to Martin O'Neill whose cross found his namesake John O'Neill. His powerful shot cannoned off the upright with an almighty thud!

Then Norman Whiteside, appearing as if he was going

to play the ball out to Stewart on the left-wing, cut inside and unleashed a left-foot drive from fully 35 yards that Schumacher in the German goal could only push out, unable to grasp it cleanly. In the 14th minute, Jimmy Nicholl then hit a long ball across the pitch to Hamilton. The Burnley forward then flicked it on to Ian STEWART on the edge of the box. He went round Manny Kaltz before tucking the ball into the net.

Northern Ireland continued to dominate the first half until the closing stages when Littbarski, an orthodox winger with jinking skills and plenty of pace, beat four Irish players on the left before forcing Platt to tip his shot over the bar. Lothar Mattaus also had his shot beaten away by Platt and the Middlesbrough keeper ended the half by holding on to a powerful header by Hans-Peter Briegel.

During the early stages of the second-half, Littbarski had a 'goal' disallowed (and justifiably so) by the Norwegian referee, for offside. Both sides had chances in front of goal as the minutes ticked away, with Hamilton for Ireland and Schuster for Germany missing the best of those created by their team-mates.

Throughout the majority of the game, there was never any question of Northern Ireland being overrun, although the pressure on them in the final ten minutes as the rain cascaded was intense. When the final whistle eventually went, the fans, drenched to the skin and shivering with cold, remained on the exposed Spion Kop, cheering and waving their flags, having witnessed one of the most glorious chapters in Northern Ireland's football history.

JA Platt	Middlesbrough
JM Nicholl	Sunderland
MM Donaghy	Luton Town
J McClelland	Glasgow Rangers
JP O'Neill	Leicester City
MHM O'Neill	Norwich City
N Brotherston	Blackburn Rovers
SB McIlroy	Stoke City
WR Hamilton	Burnley
N Whiteside	Manchester United
I Stewart	Queen's Park Rangers

Result	0-0

JA Platt	Middlesbrough
JM Nicholl	Sunderland
MM Donaghy	Luton Town
J McClelland	Glasgow Rangers
JP O'Neill	Leicester City
MHM O'Neill	Norwich City
N Brotherston	Blackburn Rovers
SB McIlroy	Stoke City
GJ Armstrong	Watford

N Whiteside	Manchester United
I Stewart	Queen's Park Rangers

Result	2-1

MHM O'Neill; J McClelland

356. 27 April 1983 v ALBANIA at Belfast

PA Jennings	Arsenal
JM Nicholl	Sunderland
MM Donaghy	Luton Town
J McClelland	Glasgow Rangers
JP O'Neill	Leicester City
MHM O'Neill	Norwich City
N Brotherston*	Blackburn Rovers
SB McIlroy	Stoke City
GJ Armstrong	Watford
WR Hamilton	Burnley
I Stewart	Queen's Park Rangers

Subs	
* G Mullan	Glentoran

Result	1-0

I Stewart

357. 24 May 1983 v SCOTLAND at Glasgow

PA Jennings	Arsenal
JM Nicholl	Toronto Blizzard
MM Donaghy	Luton Town
J McClelland	Glasgow Rangers
JP O'Neill*	Leicester City
MHM O'Neill	Norwich City
G Mullan	Glentoran
SB McIlroy	Stoke City
GJ Armstrong	Watford
WR Hamilton**	Burnley
I Stewart	Queen's Park Rangers

Subs	
* CJ Nicholl	Southampton
** N Brotherston	Blackburn Rovers

Result	0-0

358. 28 May 1983 v ENGLAND at Belfast

PA Jennings	Arsenal
JM Nicholl	Toronto Blizzard
MM Donaghy	Luton Town
J McClelland	Glasgow Rangers
CJ Nicholl	Southampton
MHM O'Neill	Norwich City
G Mullan*	Glentoran
SB McIlroy	Stoke City
GJ Armstrong	Watford
WR Hamilton	Burnley
I Stewart	Queen's Park Rangers

Subs	

* N Brotherston	Blackburn Rovers

Result	0-0

359. 31 May 1983 v WALES at Belfast

PA Jennings	Arsenal
JM Nicholl	Toronto Blizzard
MM Donaghy	Luton Town
J McClelland	Glasgow Rangers
CJ Nicholl	Southampton
SB McIlroy	Stoke City
N Brotherston	Blackburn Rovers
GJ Armstrong	Watford
WR Hamilton	Burnley
G Mullan*	Glentoran
I Stewart	Queen's Park Rangers

Subs	
* J Cleary	Glentoran

Result	0-1

360. 21 September 1983 v AUSTRIA at Belfast

PA Jennings	Arsenal
PC Ramsey	Leicester City
MM Donaghy	Luton Town
J McClelland	Glasgow Rangers
CJ Nicholl	Southampton
MHM O'Neill	Notts County
GJ Armstrong	Real Mallorca
SB McIlroy	Stoke City
WR Hamilton	Burnley
N Whiteside	Manchester United
I Stewart	Queen's Park Rangers

Result	3-1

WR Hamilton; N Whiteside; MHM O'Neill

361. 12 October 1983 v TURKEY at Ankara

PA Jennings	Arsenal
JM Nicholl	Toronto Blizzard
MM Donaghy	Luton Town
J McClelland	Glasgow Rangers
CJ Nicholl	Southampton
MHM O'Neill	Notts County
N Brotherston*	Blackburn Rovers
SB McIlroy	Stoke City
WR Hamilton**	Burnley
N Whiteside	Manchester United
I Stewart	Queen's Park Rangers

Subs	
* J Cleary	Glentoran
** D McCreery	Newcastle United

Result	0-1

362. 16 November 1983 v WEST GERMANY at Hamburg	
PA Jennings	Arsenal
JM Nicholl	Glasgow Rangers
MM Donaghy	Luton Town
J McClelland	Glasgow Rangers
GMA McElhinney	Bolton Wanderers
MHM O'Neill	Notts County
GJ Armstrong	Real Mallorca
PC Ramsey	Leicester City
WR Hamilton	Burnley
N Whiteside	Manchester United
I Stewart	Queen's Park Rangers
Result	1-0

N Whiteside

FEATURED MATCH NO 17

WEST GERMANY 0 NORTHERN IRELAND 1

AT VOLKSPARKSTADION, HAMBURG, 16 NOVEMBER 1983

The achievement of defeating one of the world's greatest soccer nations at home in this European Championship qualifier remains as if a dream!

The Germans slumped to the first home defeat by a European country since 1974. They had lost 1-0 in Belfast and now in Hamburg, a city with a greater population than the whole of Northern Ireland.

The Germans had the better of the opening exchanges, with Karl Heinz Rummenigge getting the better of new cap Gerry McElhinney and bringing a fine save out of Pat Jennings. Though McElhinney started shakily, he soon found his feet: a tackle on Meier as he shaped to shoot saved a certain goal.

Northern Ireland hit back midway through the half as Armstrong on the right and Stewart on the left got the better of Briegel and Dremmler respectively. In fact, Stewart repeatedly flashed past the German right-back, creating half-chances for both Hamilton and Whiteside.

As the first-half wore on, Jennings in the Northern Ireland goal produced a couple of world-class saves, first from Meier and then from a fierce drive from Rummenigge that was destined for the top right-hand corner of his net. Just seconds before the interval, McClelland lost Karl Heinz Rummenigge for the only time in the game, but McElhinney's block tackle saved the day.

Then just five minutes into the second-half, Northern Ireland took the lead. It was created by Queen's Park Rangers' winger Ian Stewart, who went down the left-wing, cut in and let fly. Schumacher was unable to hold the powerful shot and pushed the ball out to Ramsey. He passed to WHITESIDE, who pivoted and fired into

the net. The unbelievable had happened. The young Irishman, not one to normally show emotion, raced towards the hordes of Northern Ireland fans before being surrounded by his jubilant team-mates.

The Germans then turned on the heat. Northern Ireland lived dangerously and on occasions luckily! Yet even so, full-back Jimmy Nicholl found time to get forward, beating four German players before shooting inches wide on a mesmerising run from his own half.

Then as the minutes ticked away, the equaliser looked on the cards as German star Lothar Matthaus saw his shot cleared off the line by Nicholl. Yet in a counter-attack, Billy Hamilton should have scored when he tried to take the ball round the keeper instead of shooting.

The Germans had been tactically destroyed by manager Bingham and an Irish team who responded to every command.

363. 13 December 1983 v SCOTLAND at Belfast	
PA Jennings	Arsenal
JM Nicholl	Glasgow Rangers
MM Donaghy	Luton Town
J McClelland	Glasgow Rangers
GMA McElhinney	Bolton Wanderers
PC Ramsey	Leicester City
GT Cochrane*	Gillingham
SB McIlroy	Stoke City
WR Hamilton	Burnley
N Whiteside	Manchester United
I Stewart	Queen's Park Rangers
Subs	
* JP O'Neill	Leicester City
Result	2-0

N Whiteside; SB McIlroy

364. 4 April 1984 v ENGLAND at Wembley	
JA Platt	Middlesbrough
JM Nicholl	Glasgow Rangers
MM Donaghy	Luton Town
J McClelland	Glasgow Rangers
GMA McElhinney	Bolton Wanderers
MHM O'Neill	Notts County
SB McIlroy	Stoke City
GJ Armstrong	Real Mallorca
WR Hamilton	Burnley
N Whiteside	Manchester United
I Stewart	Queen's Park Rangers
Result	0-1

PA Jennings	Arsenal
MM Donaghy	Luton Town
N Worthington	Sheffield Wednesday
J McClelland	Glasgow Rangers
GMA McElhinney	Bolton Wanderers
MHM O'Neill	Notts County
SB McIlroy	Stoke City
GJ Armstrong	Real Mallorca
WR Hamilton	Burnley
N Whiteside	Manchester United
I Stewart	Queen's Park Rangers

Result	1-1

GJ Armstrong

PA Jennings	Arsenal
JM Nicholl	Toronto Blizzard
MM Donaghy	Luton Town
J McClelland	Glasgow Rangers
GMA McElhinney	Bolton Wanderers
MHM O'Neill	Notts County
SB McIlroy*	Stoke City
GJ Armstrong**	Real Mallorca
WR Hamilton	Burnley
N Whiteside	Manchester United
I Stewart	Queen's Park Rangers

Subs	
* N Worthington	Sheffield Wednesday
** GT Cochrane	Gillingham

Result	0-1

PA Jennings	Arsenal
JM Nicholl	Toronto Blizzard
MM Donaghy	Luton Town
J McClelland	Glasgow Rangers
GMA McElhinney	Bolton Wanderers
MHM O'Neill	Notts County
GJ Armstrong	Real Mallorca
D McCreery	Newcastle United
WR Hamilton	Oxford United
N Whiteside	Manchester United
I Stewart	Queen's Park Rangers

Result	3-2

Iorgulescu (own goal); N Whiteside; MHM O'Neill

G Dunlop	Linfield
PC Ramsey	Leicester City
N Worthington	Sheffield Wednesday
J McClelland	Glasgow Rangers
JP O'Neill	Leicester City

J Cleary	Glentoran
S Penney	Brighton & Hove Albion
L Doherty	Linfield
JM Quinn	Blackburn Rovers
N Whiteside*	Manchester United
I Stewart**	Queen's Park Rangers

Subs	
* M McGaughey	Linfield
** N Brotherston	Blackburn Rovers

Result	3-0

N Whiteside; JM Quinn; L Doherty

PA Jennings	Arsenal
JM Nicholl	West Bromwich Albion
MM Donaghy	Luton Town
JP O'Neill	Leicester City
J McClelland	Watford
MHM O'Neill	Notts County
GJ Armstrong	Real Mallorca
SB McIlroy	Stoke City
JM Quinn	Blackburn Rovers
N Whiteside	Manchester United
I Stewart	Queen's Park Rangers

Result	2-1

JP O'Neill; GJ Armstrong (pen)

PA Jennings	Arsenal
JM Nicholl	West Bromwich Albion
MM Donaghy	Luton Town
JP O'Neill	Leicester City
J McClelland	Watford
PC Ramsey	Leicester City
GJ Armstrong	Real Mallorca
SB McIlroy	Stoke City
JM Quinn	Blackburn Rovers
N Whiteside	Manchester United
I Stewart	Queen's Park Rangers

Result	0-1

PA Jennings	Arsenal
JM Nicholl	West Bromwich Albion
MM Donaghy	Luton Town
JP O'Neill	Leicester City
J McClelland	Watford
PC Ramsey	Leicester City
GJ Armstrong*	Real Mallorca
JM Quinn	Blackburn Rovers
WR Hamilton	Oxford United
N Whiteside**	Manchester United
I Stewart	Queen's Park Rangers

Subs	
* N Worthington	Sheffield Wednesday
** D McCreery	Newcastle United

Result	0-0

372. 1 May 1985 v TURKEY at Belfast

PA Jennings	Arsenal
JM Nicholl	West Bromwich Albion
MM Donaghy	Luton Town
JP O'Neill	Leicester City
J McClelland	Watford
PC Ramsey	Leicester City
N Brotherston	Blackburn Rovers
SB McIlroy	Stoke City
JM Quinn	Blackburn Rovers
N Whiteside	Manchester United
I Stewart	Queen's Park Rangers

Result	2-0

N Whiteside (2)

373. 11 September 1985 v TURKEY at Izmir

PA Jennings	Tottenham Hotspur
JM Nicholl	West Bromwich Albion
MM Donaghy	Luton Town
JP O'Neill	Leicester City
J McClelland	Watford
PC Ramsey	Leicester City
S Penney	Brighton & Hove Albion
JM Quinn	Blackburn Rovers
GJ Armstrong	West Bromwich Albion
SB McIlroy*	Manchester City
N Worthington	Sheffield Wednesday

Subs	
* D McCreery	Newcastle United

Result	0-0

374. 18 October 1985 v ROMANIA at Bucharest

PA Jennings	Tottenham Hotspur
JM Nicholl	West Bromwich Albion
MM Donaghy	Luton Town
JP O'Neill	Leicester City
A McDonald	Queen's Park Rangers
D McCreery	Newcastle United
S Penney*	Brighton & Hove Albion
SB McIlroy	Manchester City
JM Quinn	Blackburn Rovers
N Whiteside	Manchester United
I Stewart**	Newcastle United

Subs	
* GJ Armstrong	West Bromwich Albion
** N Worthington	Sheffield Wednesday

Result	1-0

JM Quinn

375. 13 November 1985 v ENGLAND at Wembley

PA Jennings	Tottenham Hotspur
JM Nicholl	West Bromwich Albion
MM Donaghy	Luton Town
JP O'Neill	Leicester City
A McDonald	Queen's Park Rangers
D McCreery	Newcastle United
S Penney*	Brighton & Hove Albion
SB McIlroy	Manchester City
JM Quinn	Blackburn Rovers
N Whiteside	Manchester United
I Stewart**	Newcastle United

Subs	
* GJ Armstrong	West Bromwich Albion
** N Worthington	Sheffield Wednesday

Result	0-0

376. 26 February1986 v FRANCE at Paris

PA Jennings	Tottenham Hotspur
JM Nicholl	West Bromwich Albion
MM Donaghy	Luton Town
JP O'Neill	Leicester City
A McDonald	Queen's Park Rangers
D McCreery*	Newcastle United
S Penney**	Brighton & Hove Albion
SB McIlroy	Manchester City
JM Quinn***	Blackburn Rovers
N Whiteside	Manchester United
CJ Clarke	Bournemouth

Subs	
* J McClelland	Watford
** M Caughey	Linfield
*** GJ Armstrong	West Bromwich Albion

Result	0-0

377. 26 March 1986 v DENMARK at Belfast

PA Jennings	Tottenham Hotspur
MM Donaghy	Luton Town
N Worthington	Sheffield Wednesday
JP O'Neill	Leicester City
A McDonald	Queen's Park Rangers
D McCreery*	Newcastle United
S Penney	Brighton & Hove Albion
SB McIlroy	Manchester City
CJ Clarke**	Bournemouth
N Whiteside	Manchester United
I Stewart***	Newcastle United

Subs	
* GJ Armstrong	Chesterfield
** JM Quinn	Blackburn Rovers
*** M Caughey	Linfield

Result	1-1

A McDonald

PA Jennings*	Everton
PC Ramsey	Leicester City
MM Donaghy	Luton Town
JP O'Neill	Leicester City
A McDonald	Queen's Park Rangers
BA McNally	Shrewsbury Town
S Penney**	Brighton & Hove Albion
SB McIlroy	Manchester City
CJ Clarke	Bournemouth
N Whiteside***	Manchester United
I Stewart****	Newcastle United

Subs	
* JA Platt	Coleraine
** JM Quinn	Blackburn Rovers
*** DA Campbell	Nottingham Forest
**** WR Hamilton	Oxford United

Result	2-1

CJ Clarke; JM Quinn

PA Jennings	Tottenham Hotspur
JM Nicholl	West Bromwich Albion
MM Donaghy	Luton Town
JP O'Neill	Leicester City
A McDonald	Queen's Park Rangers
D McCreery	Newcastle United
S Penney*	Brighton & Hove Albion
SB McIlroy	Manchester City
N Worthington	Sheffield Wednesday
N Whiteside**	Manchester United
WR Hamilton	Oxford United

Subs	
* I Stewart	Newcastle United
** CJ Clarke	Bournemouth

Result	1-1

N Whiteside

PA Jennings	Tottenham Hotspur
JM Nicholl	West Bromwich Albion
MM Donaghy	Luton Town
JP O'Neill	Leicester City
A McDonald	Queen's Park Rangers
D McCreery	Newcastle United
S Penney*	Brighton & Hove Albion
SB McIlroy	Manchester City
N Worthington**	Sheffield Wednesday
N Whiteside	Manchester United
CJ Clarke	Bournemouth

Subs	
* I Stewart	Newcastle United
** WR Hamilton	Oxford United

Result	1-2

CJ Clarke

PA Jennings	Tottenham Hotspur
JM Nicholl	West Bromwich Albion
MM Donaghy	Luton Town
JP O'Neill	Leicester City
A McDonald	Queen's Park Rangers
D McCreery	Newcastle United
DA Campbell*	Nottingham Forest
SB McIlroy	Manchester City
CJ Clarke	Bournemouth
N Whiteside**	Manchester United
I Stewart	Newcastle United

Subs	
* GJ Armstrong	Chesterfield
** WR Hamilton	Oxford United

Result	0-3

PA Hughes	Bury
JG Fleming	Nottingham Forest
N Worthington	Sheffield Wednesday
J McClelland	Watford
A McDonald	Queen's Park Rangers
MM Donaghy	Luton Town
S Penney*	Brighton & Hove Albion
DA Campbell	Nottingham Forest
CJ Clarke	Southampton
N Whiteside**	Manchester United
I Stewart	Newcastle United

Subs	
* JM Quinn	Blackburn Rovers
** SB McIlroy	Manchester City

Result	0-3

PA Hughes	Bury
MM Donaghy	Luton Town
N Worthington	Sheffield Wednesday
J McClelland	Watford
A McDonald	Queen's Park Rangers
DJ Wilson	Brighton & Hove Albion
S Penney	Brighton & Hove Albion
D McCreery	Newcastle United
CJ Clarke	Southampton
JM Quinn*	Blackburn Rovers
DA Campbell**	Nottingham Forest

Subs
| * LP Sanchez | Wimbledon |
| ** BA McNally | Shrewsbury Town |

Result   0-0

PA Hughes	Bury
JG Fleming	Nottingham Forest
MM Donaghy	Luton Town
J McClelland	Watford
A McDonald	Queen's Park Rangers
PC Ramsey	Leicester City
S Penney*	Brighton & Hove Albion
DJ Wilson	Brighton & Hove Albion
KJ Wilson	Ipswich Town
N Whiteside	Manchester United
N Worthington	Sheffield Wednesday

Subs
| * I Stewart | Newcastle United |

Result   1-1

S Penney

G Dunlop	Linfield
JG Fleming	Nottingham Forest
MM Donaghy	Luton Town
J McClelland	Watford
A McDonald	Queen's Park Rangers
PC Ramsey	Leicester City
DA Campbell*	Nottingham Forest
D McCreery	Newcastle United
KJ Wilson	Ipswich Town
N Whiteside	Manchester United
N Worthington	Sheffield Wednesday

Subs
| * DJ Wilson | Brighton & Hove Albion |

Result   0-2

G Dunlop	Linfield
JG Fleming	Nottingham Forest
MM Donaghy	Luton Town
J McClelland	Watford
A McDonald*	Queen's Park Rangers
D McCreery	Newcastle United
DA Campbell**	Nottingham Forest
KJ Wilson	Ipswich Town
CJ Clarke	Southampton
N Whiteside	Manchester United
N Worthington	Sheffield Wednesday

Subs
| * PC Ramsey | Leicester City |
| ** RK McCoy | Coleraine |

Result   1-2

CJ Clarke

AD McKnight	Glasgow Celtic
PC Ramsey	Leicester City
N Worthington	Sheffield Wednesday
MM Donaghy	Luton Town
A McDonald	Queen's Park Rangers
D McCreery	Newcastle United
DA Campbell*	Charlton Athletic
DJ Wilson	Luton Town
CJ Clarke**	Southampton
BA McNally	Shrewsbury Town
KJ Wilson	Chelsea

Subs
| * A Rogan | Glasgow Celtic |
| ** JM Quinn | Swindon Town |

Result   0-3

AD McKnight	Glasgow Celtic
JG Fleming	Nottingham Forest
N Worthington	Sheffield Wednesday
J McClelland	Watford
A McDonald	Queen's Park Rangers
MM Donaghy	Luton Town
DJ Wilson*	Luton Town
JM Quinn	Swindon Town
CJ Clarke	Southampton
N Whiteside	Manchester United
KJ Wilson**	Chelsea

Subs
| * L Doherty | Linfield |
| ** DA Campbell | Charlton Athletic |

Result   1-0

JM Quinn

AD McKnight	Glasgow Celtic
JG Fleming	Nottingham Forest
A Rogan	Glasgow Celtic
J McClelland	Watford
MM Donaghy	Luton Town
BA McNally*	Shrewsbury Town
DJ Wilson	Luton Town
MAM O'Neill**	Newcastle United
CJ Clarke	Southampton
JM Quinn	Swindon Town
N Worthington	Sheffield Wednesday

Subs
| * KJ Wilson | Chelsea |
| ** DA Campbell | Charlton Athletic |

Result	2-3

CJ Clarke (2) (1 pen)

AD McKnight	Glasgow Celtic
JG Fleming	Nottingham Forest
N Worthington	Sheffield Wednesday
MM Donaghy	Luton Town
A McDonald	Queen's Park Rangers
DJ Wilson	Luton Town
S Penney*	Brighton & Hove Albion
JM Quinn**	Swindon Town
CJ Clarke	Southampton
N Whiteside	Manchester United
MAM O'Neill***	Newcastle United

Subs	
* DA Campbell	Charlton Athletic
** KJ Wilson	Chelsea
*** A Rogan	Glasgow Celtic

Result	1-1

DJ Wilson

AD McKnight	Glasgow Celtic
MM Donaghy	Luton Town
N Worthington	Sheffield Wednesday
J McClelland	Watford
A McDonald	Queen's Park Rangers
DJ Wilson	Luton Town
S Penney	Brighton & Hove Albion
MAM O'Neill	Newcastle United
CJ Clarke*	Southampton
N Whiteside**	Manchester United
R Dennison***	Wolverhampton Wanderers

Subs	
* KJ Wilson	Chelsea
** JM Quinn	Swindon Town
*** KT Black	Luton Town

Result	0-0

AD McKnight	Glasgow Celtic
MM Donaghy	Luton Town
N Worthington	Sheffield Wednesday
J McClelland	Watford
A McDonald	Queen's Park Rangers
DJ Wilson	Luton Town
S Penney*	Brighton & Hove Albion
MAM O'Neill	Newcastle United
CJ Clarke	Southampton
JM Quinn	Swindon Town
R Dennison**	Wolverhampton Wanderers

Subs	
* BA McNally	Shrewsbury Town
** KT Black	Luton Town

Result	3-0

JM Quinn; S Penney; CJ Clarke

AD McKnight	West Ham United
MM Donaghy*	Luton Town
N Worthington	Sheffield Wednesday
J McClelland	Watford
A McDonald	Queen's Park Rangers
DJ Wilson	Luton Town
S Penney	Brighton & Hove Albion
JM Quinn	Leicester City
CJ Clarke	Southampton
MAM O'Neill	Newcastle
KT Black	Luton Town

Subs	
* A Rogan	Glasgow Celtic

Result	0-0

AD McKnight	West Ham United
A Rogan	Glasgow Celtic
N Worthington	Sheffield Wednesday
J McClelland	Watford
A McDonald	Queen's Park Rangers
MM Donaghy	Luton Town
R Dennison	Wolverhampton Wanderers
DJ Wilson	Luton Town
CJ Clarke*	Southampton
MAM O'Neill**	Newcastle United
KT Black	Luton Town

Subs	
* JM Quinn	Swindon Town
** KJ Wilson	Chelsea

Result	0-1

AD McKnight	West Ham United
A Rogan	Glasgow Celtic
N Worthington	Sheffield Wednesday
J McClelland	Watford
A McDonald	Queen's Park Rangers
MM Donaghy	Manchester United
S Penney*	Brighton & Hove Albion
D McCreery**	Newcastle United
CJ Clarke	Southampton
KJ Wilson	Chelsea
KT Black	Luton Town

Subs	
* MAM O'Neill	Newcastle United
** JM Quinn	Leicester City
Result	0-4

396. 8 February 1989 v SPAIN at Belfast

AD McKnight	West Ham United
PC Ramsey	Leicester City
A Rogan	Glasgow Celtic
MM Donaghy	Manchester United
J McClelland	Watford
DJ Wilson*	Luton Town
R Dennison**	Wolverhampton Wanderers
LP Sanchez	Wimbledon
JM Quinn	Leicester City
KJ Wilson	Chelsea
KT Black	Luton Town
Subs	
* CJ Clarke	Southampton
** MAM O'Neill	Newcastle United
Result	0-2

397. 26 April 1989 v MALTA at Valetta

TJ Wright	Newcastle United
JG Fleming	Nottingham Forest
N Worthington*	Sheffield Wednesday
MM Donaghy	Manchester United
J McClelland	Watford
DJ Wilson	Luton Town
LP Sanchez**	Wimbledon
D McCreery	Newcastle United
CJ Clarke	Queen's Park Rangers
JM Quinn	Bradford City
KJ Wilson	Chelsea
Subs	
* A Rogan	Glasgow Celtic
** MAM O'Neill	Newcastle United
Result	2-0
CJ Clarke; MAM O'Neill	

DID YOU KNOW?
The smallest crowd to watch a Northern Ireland international match is just 2,500 for the friendly against Chile on 26 May 1989. The game clashed with ITV's live screening of the Liverpool v Arsenal Championship decider.

398. 26 May 1989 v CHILE at Belfast

TJ Wright	Newcastle United
JG Fleming	Nottingham Forest
A Rogan	Glasgow Celtic
MM Donaghy	Manchester United
A McDonald	Queen's Park Rangers
D McCreery*	Newcastle United
DJ Wilson**	Luton Town
MAM O'Neill	Newcastle United
CJ Clarke	Queen's Park Rangers
JM Quinn***	Bradford City
KJ Wilson****	Chelsea
Subs	
* C O'Neill	Motherwell
** R Dennison	Wolverhampton Wanderers
*** L Coyle	Derry City
**** KT Black	Luton Town
Result	0-1

399. 6 September 1989 v HUNGARY at Budapest

TJ Wright	Newcastle United
JG Fleming	Manchester City
N Worthington	Sheffield Wednesday
A Rogan	Glasgow Celtic
A McDonald	Queen's Park Rangers
D McCreery	Heart of Midlothian
DJ Wilson	Luton Town
JM Quinn*	Bradford City
CJ Clarke	Queen's Park Rangers
N Whiteside	Everton
KT Black	Luton Town
Subs	
* MAM O'Neill	Dundee United
Result	1-2
N Whiteside	

400. 11 October 1989 v REPUBLIC OF IRELAND at Dublin

G Dunlop	Linfield
JG Fleming	Manchester City
N Worthington	Sheffield Wednesday
MM Donaghy	Manchester United
A McDonald	Queen's Park Rangers
D McCreery*	Heart of Midlothian
DJ Wilson	Luton Town
MAM O'Neill**	Dundee United
CJ Clarke	Queen's Park Rangers
N Whiteside	Everton
R Dennison	Wolverhampton Wanderers
Subs	
* C O'Neill	Motherwell
** KJ Wilson	Chelsea
Result	0-3

401. 27 March 1990 v NORWAY at Belfast

PV Kee	Oxford United
CF Hill	Sheffield United
MM Donaghy	Manchester United

J McClelland	Leeds United
GP Taggart	Barnsley
D McCreery*	Heart of Midlothian
DJ Wilson	Luton Town
JM Quinn	West Ham United
CJ Clarke**	Queen's Park Rangers
KJ Wilson	Chelsea
KT Black	Luton Town

Subs	
* A Rogan	Glasgow Celtic
** I Dowie	Luton Town

Result	2-3

JM Quinn; KJ Wilson

402. 18 May 1990 v URUGUAY at Belfast

TJ Wright	Newcastle United
CF Hill*	Sheffield United
N Worthington	Sheffield Wednesday
GP Taggart	Barnsley
A McDonald	Queen's Park Rangers
A Rogan**	Glasgow Celtic
R Dennison***	Wolverhampton Wanderers
DJ Wilson	Luton Town
I Dowie	Luton Town
KJ Wilson	Chelsea
KT Black	Luton Town

Subs	
* J Devine	Glentoran
** SJ Morrow	Arsenal
*** D McCreery	Heart of Midlothian

Result	1-0

KJ Wilson

403. 12 September 1990 v YUGOSLAVIA at Belfast

PV Kee	Oxford United
MM Donaghy	Manchester United
N Worthington	Sheffield Wednesday
GP Taggart	Barnsley
A McDonald	Queen's Park Rangers
A Rogan	Glasgow Celtic
R Dennison*	Wolverhampton Wanderers
DJ Wilson	Sheffield Wednesday
I Dowie	Luton Town
KJ Wilson	Chelsea
KT Black	Luton Town

Subs	
* CJ Clarke	Portsmouth

Result	0-2

404. 17 October 1990 v DENMARK at Belfast

PV Kee	Oxford United

MM Donaghy	Manchester United
N Worthington	Sheffield Wednesday
GP Taggart	Barnsley
A McDonald	Queen's Park Rangers
A Rogan	Glasgow Celtic
DJ Wilson	Sheffield Wednesday
C O'Neill*	Motherwell
I Dowie	Luton Town
CJ Clarke	Portsmouth
KT Black	Luton Town

Subs	
* SD McBride	Glenavon

Result	1-1

CJ Clarke

405. 14 November 1990 v AUSTRIA at Vienna

PV Kee	Oxford United
MM Donaghy	Manchester United
N Worthington	Sheffield Wednesday
GP Taggart	Barnsley
A McDonald	Queen's Park Rangers
A Rogan	Glasgow Celtic
R Dennison	Wolverhampton Wanderers
DJ Wilson	Sheffield Wednesday
CJ Clarke*	Portsmouth
KJ Wilson	Chelsea
KT Black**	Luton Town

Subs	
* I Dowie	Luton Town
** SJ Morrow	Arsenal

Result	0-0

406. 5 February 1991 v POLAND at Belfast

PV Kee	Oxford United
CF Hill	Sheffield United
SJ Morrow	Arsenal
GP Taggart	Barnsley
MM Donaghy	Manchester United
J Magilton	Oxford United
R Dennison*	Wolverhampton Wanderers
MAM O'Neill	Dundee United
CJ Clarke	Portsmouth
KJ Wilson	Chelsea
KT Black	Luton Town

Subs	
* SD McBride	Glenavon

Result	3-1

GP Taggart (2); J Magilton (pen)

407. 27 March 1991 v YUGOSLAVIA at Belgrade

PV Kee	Oxford United
JG Fleming	Barnsley

CF Hill	Sheffield United
MM Donaghy	Manchester United
A Rogan	Glasgow Celtic
SJ Morrow	Arsenal
R Dennison*	Wolverhampton Wanderers
J Magilton	Oxford United
KJ Wilson**	Chelsea
I Dowie	West Ham United
KT Black	Luton Town
Subs	
* JM Quinn	West Ham United
** CJ Clarke	Portsmouth
Result	1-4

CF Hill

408. 1 May 1991 v FAROE ISLANDS at Belfast

PV Kee	Oxford United
MM Donaghy	Manchester United
N Worthington	Sheffield Wednesday
GP Taggart	Barnsley
A McDonald	Queen's Park Rangers
J Magilton	Oxford United
DJ Wilson*	Sheffield Wednesday
CJ Clarke	Portsmouth
I Dowie**	West Ham United
KJ Wilson	Chelsea
KT Black	Luton Town
Subs	
* R Dennison	Wolverhampton Wanderers
** PA Williams	West Bromwich Albion
Result	1-1

CJ Clarke

409. 11 September 1991 v FAROE ISLANDS at Landskrona (Sweden)

TJ Wright	Newcastle United
MM Donaghy	Manchester United
SJ Morrow	Arsenal
GP Taggart	Barnsley
A McDonald	Queen's Park Rangers
J Magilton	Oxford United
R Dennison	Wolverhampton Wanderers
KJ Wilson*	Chelsea
I Dowie	West Ham United
CJ Clarke	Portsmouth
KT Black**	Luton Town
Subs	
* MAM O'Neill	Dundee United
** SD McBride	Glenavon
Result	5-0

KJ Wilson; CJ Clark (3) (1 pen); A McDonald

FEATURED MATCH NO 18

FAROE ISLANDS 0 NORTHERN IRELAND 5

AT THE LANDSKRONA STADIUM, SWEDEN, 11 SEPTEMBER 1991

This 5-0 win over the Faroe Islands in a completely one-sided European Championship Group Four qualifying tie, was Northern Ireland's highest-ever away triumph. Portsmouth striker Colin Clarke netted a hat-trick to bring his total to 12 goals in 31 games – equalling the international record held by Joe Bambrick, Billy Gillespie and Gerry Armstrong.

When the two teams met prior to this meeting, they played out a 1-1 draw. This match, watched by just 1,623 spectators was a virtual 'repeat' of that game. There was one significant difference – this time the chances were put away with clinical precision.

Northern Ireland took the lead after just seven minutes when Alan McDonald back-headed Kingsley Black's corner towards the back post. The ball was scrambled off the line but there was Kevin WILSON to stab the ball home.

Five minutes later, Iain Dowie gained possession, and held the ball well on the edge of the area before releasing it to Black. The Nottingham Forest winger sent over a pin-point cross on to the head of Colin CLARKE, who completely unchallenged headed past Faroes keeper Martin Knudsen.

On the quarter-of-an-hour mark, a Robbie Dennison free-kick found Dowie, who headed on for Queen's Park Rangers central defender Alan McDONALD to beat Knudsen with a swivelling volley. It was his second goal for his country and a most brilliantly taken one.

Northern Ireland had many more chances during the remainder of the first-half. The bobble-hatted goalkeeper for the Faroes prevented further goals with a series of saves, the most impressive being when he turned round an Iain Dowie header that was destined for the bottom right-hand corner of his goal.

Three minutes into the second-half and Dowie, always in the action, crossed to the far post where Robbie Dennison knocked it back to CLARKE. Despite a mis-hit, the Portsmouth striker scored his second goal of the game.

After 67 minutes, Dowie again – this time with a long ball – found the head of Gerry Taggart. His header was looping into the net when Morkore used his hands to prevent it crossing the line. The Finnish referee immediately pointed to the spot, ordered off Morkore and up stepped CLARKE to blast the ball past Knudsen and so equal that record.

TJ Wright	Newcastle United
CF Hill	Sheffield United
N Worthington	Sheffield Wednesday
MM Donaghy	Manchester United
GP Taggart	Barnsley
J Magilton	Oxford United
R Dennison	Wolverhampton Wanderers
KJ Wilson	Chelsea
I Dowie	Southampton
CJ Clarke*	Portsmouth
KT Black	Luton Town

Subs	
* DJ Wilson	Sheffield Wednesday

Result	2-1

I Dowie; KT Black

AW Fettis	Hull City
CF Hill	Sheffield United
N Worthington	Sheffield Wednesday
MM Donaghy	Manchester United
GP Taggart	Barnsley
J Magilton	Oxford United
SD McBride	Glenavon
KJ Wilson	Chelsea
CJ Clarke*	Portsmouth
ME Hughes	Manchester City
KT Black**	Nottingham Forest

Subs	
* I Dowie	Southampton
** R Dennison	Wolverhampton Wanderers

Result	1-2

GP Taggart

TJ Wright	Newcastle United
MM Donaghy	Manchester United
N Worthington	Sheffield Wednesday
GP Taggart*	Barnsley
A McDonald	Queen's Park Rangers
J Magilton	Oxford United
KT Black	Nottingham Forest
KJ Wilson**	Chelsea
CJ Clarke***	Portsmouth
DJ Wilson	Sheffield Wednesday
ME Hughes	Manchester City

Subs	
* SJ Morrow	Arsenal
** MAM O'Neill	Dundee United
*** I Dowie	Southampton

Result	0-1

AW Fettis	Hull City
MM Donaghy*	Manchester United
N Worthington	Sheffield Wednesday
GP Taggart	Barnsley
A McDonald	Queen's Park Rangers
J Magilton	Oxford United
KT Black	Nottingham Forest
JM Quinn	Bournemouth
I Dowie**	Southampton
KJ Wilson	Notts County
ME Hughes	Manchester City

Subs	
* JG Fleming	Barnsley
** A Rogan	Sunderland

Result	2-2

KJ Wilson; GP Taggart

TJ Wright	Newcastle United
JG Fleming	Barnsley
N Worthington	Sheffield Wednesday
GP Taggart	Barnsley
A McDonald	Queen's Park Rangers
MM Donaghy	Manchester United
KT Black*	Nottingham Forest
J Magilton	Oxford United
CJ Clarke**	Portsmouth
KJ Wilson	Notts County
ME Hughes	Manchester City

Subs	
* SJ Morrow	Arsenal
** MAM O'Neill	Dundee United

Result	1-1

ME Hughes

TJ Wright	Newcastle United
JG Fleming	Barnsley
N Worthington	Sheffield Wednesday
GP Taggart	Barnsley
A McDonald	Queen's Park Rangers
MM Donaghy	Chelsea
KJ Wilson	Notts County
J Magilton	Oxford United
CJ Clarke*	Portsmouth
I Dowie	Southampton
ME Hughes	Strasbourg

Subs	
* MAM O'Neill	Dundee United

Result	3-0

CJ Clarke; KJ Wilson; J Magilton

TJ Wright	Newcastle United
JG Fleming	Barnsley
N Worthington	Sheffield Wednesday
GP Taggart	Barnsley
A McDonald	Queen's Park Rangers
MM Donaghy	Chelsea
KT Black*	Nottingham Forest
KJ Wilson	Notts County
CJ Clarke	Portsmouth
JM Quinn	Reading
ME Hughes	Strasbourg

Subs	
* SJ Morrow	Arsenal

Result	0-0

AW Fettis	Hull City
JG Fleming	Barnsley
N Worthington	Sheffield Wednesday
GP Taggart	Barnsley
A McDonald	Queen's Park Rangers
MM Donaghy	Chelsea
J Magilton	Oxford United
KJ Wilson*	Notts County
CJ Clarke**	Portsmouth
JM Quinn	Reading
ME Hughes	Strasbourg

Subs	
* KT Black	Nottingham Forest
** P Gray	Luton Town

Result	0-1

TJ Wright	Newcastle United
JG Fleming	Barnsley
SJ Morrow	Arsenal
GP Taggart	Barnsley
A McDonald	Queen's Park Rangers
MM Donaghy	Chelsea
J Magilton	Oxford United
P Gray	Luton Town
I Dowie*	Southampton
MAM O'Neill	Dundee United
KT Black	Nottingham Forest

Subs	
* JM Quinn	Reading

Result	2-1

J Magilton; A McDonald

TJ Wright	Newcastle United
MM Donaghy	Chelsea
N Worthington	Sheffield Wednesday
GP Taggart	Barnsley
A McDonald	Queen's Park Rangers
SJ Morrow	Arsenal
J Magilton*	Oxford United
MAM O'Neill**	Dundee United
I Dowie	Southampton
P Gray	Luton Town
ME Hughes	Strasbourg

Subs	
* JM Quinn	Reading
** KT Black	Nottingham Forest

Result	0-3

TJ Wright	Newcastle United
JG Fleming	Barnsley
N Worthington	Sheffield Wednesday
GP Taggart	Barnsley
A McDonald	Queen's Park Rangers
MM Donaghy	Chelsea
KT Black*	Nottingham Forest
KJ Wilson	Notts County
P Gray	Luton Town
MAM O'Neill**	Dundee United
ME Hughes	Strasbourg

Subs	
* R Dennison	Wolverhampton Wanderers
** I Dowie	Southampton

Result	1-3

KJ Wilson

TJ Wright	Newcastle United
JG Fleming	Barnsley
N Worthington	Sheffield Wednesday
GP Taggart	Barnsley
A McDonald	Queen's Park Rangers
MM Donaghy	Chelsea
J Magilton	Oxford United
MAM O'Neill	Dundee United
I Dowie	Southampton
KJ Wilson	Notts County
ME Hughes	Strasbourg

Result	1-0

I Dowie

TJ Wright	Newcastle United
JG Fleming	Barnsley
N Worthington	Sheffield Wednesday
GP Taggart	Barnsley
A McDonald	Queen's Park Rangers
MM Donaghy	Chelsea
MAM O'Neill*	Dundee United
J Magilton	Oxford United
KJ Wilson	Notts County
I Dowie	Southampton
ME Hughes	Strasbourg
Subs	
* JM Quinn	Reading
Result	2-1

J Magilton; GP Taggart

TJ Wright	Newcastle United
JG Fleming	Barnsley
N Worthington	Sheffield Wednesday
GP Taggart	Barnsley
MM Donaghy	Chelsea
J Magilton*	Oxford United
KJ Wilson	Notts County
JM Quinn	Reading
I Dowie	Southampton
P Gray	Sunderland
ME Hughes	Strasbourg
Subs	
* K Rowland	West Ham United
Result	2-0

JM Quinn; P Gray

TJ Wright	Nottingham Forest
JG Fleming	Barnsley
N Worthington	Sheffield Wednesday
GP Taggart	Barnsley
A McDonald	Queen's Park Rangers
MM Donaghy	Chelsea
KJ Wilson*	Notts County
J Magilton	Oxford United
I Dowie**	Southampton
P Gray	Sunderland
ME Hughes	Strasbourg
Subs	
* KT Black	Nottingham Forest
** JM Quinn	Reading
Result	0-1

TJ Wright	Nottingham Forest
JG Fleming	Barnsley
N Worthington	Sheffield Wednesday
GP Taggart	Barnsley
A McDonald	Queen's Park Rangers
MM Donaghy	Chelsea
J Magilton	Oxford United
KJ Wilson*	Notts County
JM Quinn	Reading
P Gray**	Sunderland
ME Hughes	Strasbourg
Subs	
* KT Black	Nottingham Forest
** I Dowie	Southampton
Result	1-1

JM Quinn

TJ Wright	Nottingham Forest
JG Fleming	Barnsley
SJ Morrow	Arsenal
GP Taggart	Barnsley
MM Donaghy	Chelsea
J Magilton	Southampton
KJ Wilson	Notts County
SM Lomas	Manchester City
JM Quinn*	Reading
P Gray	Sunderland
ME Hughes**	Strasbourg
Subs	
* I Dowie	Southampton
** KT Black	Nottingham Forest
Result	2-0

SJ Morrow; P Gray

TJ Wright	Nottingham Forest
JG Fleming	Barnsley
N Worthington	Sheffield Wednesday
GP Taggart	Barnsley
MM Donaghy	Chelsea
J Magilton	Southampton
KJ Wilson	Notts County
SM Lomas*	Manchester City
JM Quinn	Reading
I Dowie**	Southampton
ME Hughes	Strasbourg
Subs	
* MAM O'Neill	Hibernian
** P Gray	Sunderland
Result	4-1

JM Quinn (2); SM Lomas; I Dowie

TJ Wright	Nottingham Forest
JG Fleming	Barnsley
N Worthington	Sheffield Wednesday
GP Taggart	Barnsley
MM Donaghy	Chelsea
J Magilton*	Southampton
KJ Wilson**	Notts County
SJ Morrow	Arsenal
JM Quinn***	Reading
I Dowie****	Southampton
ME Hughes	Strasbourg

Subs	
* R Dennison	Wolverhampton Wanderers
** SM Lomas	Manchester City
*** G O'Boyle	Dunfermline Athletic
**** DJ Patterson	Crystal Palace

Result	0-2

AW Fettis*	Hull City
JG Fleming**	Barnsley
N Worthington	Sheffield Wednesday
GP Taggart	Barnsley
MM Donaghy	Chelsea
J Magilton***	Southampton
KJ Wilson****	Notts County
SM Lomas	Manchester City
JM Quinn*****	Reading
G O'Boyle	Dunfermline Athletic
ME Hughes	Strasbourg

Subs	
* TJ Wright	Nottingham Forest
** SJ Morrow	Arsenal
*** DJ Patterson	Crystal Palace
**** NF Lennon	Crewe Alexandra
***** I Dowie	Southampton

Result	0-3

AW Fettis	Hull City
JG Fleming	Barnsley
N Worthington	Leeds United
SJ Morrow*	Arsenal
A McDonald	Queen's Park Rangers
SM Lomas	Manchester City
KR Gillespie**	Manchester United
J Magilton	Southampton
JM Quinn	Reading
P Gray	Sunderland
ME Hughes	Strasbourg

Subs	
* GP Taggart	Barnsley
** G O'Boyle	Dunfermline Athletic

Result	1-2

JM Quinn (pen)

PV Kee	Ards
JG Fleming	Barnsley
N Worthington	Leeds United
GP Taggart	Barnsley
A McDonald	Queen's Park Rangers
SM Lomas	Manchester City
KR Gillespie*	Manchester United
J Magilton	Southampton
I Dowie**	Southampton
P Gray	Sunderland
ME Hughes	Strasbourg

Subs	
* MAM O'Neill	Hibernian
** JM Quinn	Reading

Result	2-1

KR Gillespie; P Gray

PV Kee	Ards
JG Fleming	Barnsley
N Worthington	Leeds United
GP Taggart	Barnsley
SJ Morrow	Arsenal
MAM O'Neill*	Hibernian
KR Gillespie**	Manchester United
J Magilton	Southampton
I Dowie	Crystal Palace
P Gray	Sunderland
ME Hughes	Strasbourg

Subs	
* DJ Patterson	Crystal Palace
** KJ Wilson	Walsall

Result	0-4

AW Fettis	Hull City
DJ Patterson	Crystal Palace
N Worthington	Leeds United
GP Taggart	Barnsley
A McDonald	Queen's Park Rangers
SJ Morrow	Arsenal
KR Gillespie	Newcastle United
J Magilton	Southampton
I Dowie	Crystal Palace

CF Hill	Leicester City
ME Hughes	Strasbourg

Result	1-1

I Dowie

434. 26 April 1995 v LATVIA at Riga

AW Fettis	Hull City
DJ Patterson	Crystal Palace
N Worthington	Leeds United
BV Hunter	Wrexham
A McDonald	Queen's Park Rangers
CF Hill	Leicester City
KR Gillespie*	Newcastle United
KJ Wilson	Walsall
I Dowie**	Crystal Palace
K Horlock	Swindon Town
ME Hughes	Strasbourg

Subs	
* G O'Boyle	St Johnstone
** JM Quinn	Reading

Result	1-0

I Dowie (pen)

435. 22 May 1995 v CANADA at Edmonton

AW Fettis	Hull City
DJ Patterson	Crystal Palace
K Rowland	West Ham United
GP Taggart	Barnsley
A McDonald*	Queen's Park Rangers
K Horlock**	Swindon Town
KR Gillespie***	Newcastle United
J Magilton	Southampton
P Gray	Sunderland
I Dowie****	Crystal Palace
ME Hughes	Strasbourg

Subs	
* PCG McGibbon	Manchester United
** N Worthington	Leeds United
*** GJ McMahon	Tottenham Hotspur
**** G O'Boyle	St Johnstone

Result	0-2

436. 25 May 1995 v CHILE at Edmonton

AW Fettis	Hull City
PCG McGibbon*	Manchester United
N Worthington	Leeds United
GP Taggart	Barnsley
A McDonald	Queen's Park Rangers
K Rowland	West Ham United
GJ McMahon**	Tottenham Hotspur
J Magilton***	Southampton
NF Lennon	Crewe Alexandra
I Dowie****	Crystal Palace

ME Hughes	Strasbourg

Subs	
* DJ Patterson	Crystal Palace
** KR Gillespie	Newcastle United
*** G O'Boyle	St Johnstone
**** P Gray	Sunderland

Result	1-2

I Dowie

437. 7 June 1995 v LATVIA at Belfast

AW Fettis	Hull City
PCG McGibbon*	Manchester United
N Worthington	Leeds United
GP Taggart	Barnsley
A McDonald	Queen's Park Rangers
SJ Morrow	Arsenal
GJ McMahon	Tottenham Hotspur
J Magilton	Southampton
I Dowie	Crystal Palace
K Rowland**	West Ham United
ME Hughes	Strasbourg

Subs	
* DJ Patterson	Crystal Palace
** KR Gillespie	Newcastle United

Result	1-2

I Dowie

438. 3 September 1995 v PORTUGAL at Oporto

AW Fettis	Hull City
SJ Morrow	Arsenal
N Worthington	Leeds United
CF Hill	Leicester City
BV Hunter	Wrexham
SM Lomas	Manchester City
KR Gillespie	Newcastle United
J Magilton*	Southampton
I Dowie**	West Ham United
NF Lennon	Crewe Alexandra
ME Hughes	Strasbourg

Subs	
* K Rowland	West Ham United
** P Gray	Sunderland

Result	1-1

ME Hughes

439. 11 October 1995 v LIECHTENSTEIN at Eschen-Mauren

AW Fettis*	Hull City
SM Lomas	Manchester City
N Worthington	Leeds United
CF Hill	Leicester City

BV Hunter	Wrexham
NF Lennon	Crewe Alexandra
GJ McMahon**	Tottenham Hotspur
MAM O'Neill	Hibernian
JM Quinn	Reading
P Gray	Sunderland
ME Hughes***	Strasbourg
Subs	
* TJ Wood	Walsall
** PCG McGibbon	Manchester United
*** K Rowland	West Ham United
Result	4-0

MAM O'Neill; GJ McMahon; JM Quinn; P Gray

440. 15 November 1995 v AUSTRIA at Belfast

AW Fettis	Hull City
SM Lomas	Manchester City
N Worthington	Leeds United
BV Hunter	Wrexham
CF Hill	Leicester City
NF Lennon	Crewe Alexandra
KR Gillespie	Newcastle United
MAM O'Neill	Hibernian
I Dowie*	West Ham United
P Gray**	Sunderland
ME Hughes	Strasbourg
Subs	
* JM Quinn	Reading
** A McDonald	Queen's Park Rangers
Result	5-3

MAM O'Neill (2); I Dowie (pen); BV Hunter; P Gray

FEATURED MATCH NO 19

NORTHERN IRELAND 5 AUSTRIA 3

AT WINDSOR PARK, BELFAST, 15 NOVEMBER 1995

In one of the most entertaining games at Windsor Park for many years, the crowd of 8,400 saw eight goals, with five of them scored by Northern Ireland. The national side hadn't scored five goals in a home game since George Best netted a hat-trick in a 5-0 defeat of Cyprus some 24 years earlier!

Neil Lennon was at the centre of most of Northern Ireland's early moves in the game, setting up chances for both Gray and Dowie. Michael Hughes and Keith Gillespie were giving the Austrian full-backs a torrid time and it seemed that the first goal wouldn't be too far away. However, it took until the 27th minute for the home side to open their account when a cross from Hughes reached Dowie. The West Ham man knocked it into the path of O'NEILL and his unerring left-foot shot found the net.

That goal had been coming for a long time and so it was no surprise when five minutes later, Northern Ireland extended their lead. Iain DOWIE upended in the penalty box, smashed the resultant penalty past Austrian keeper Michael Konsel.

Even with the winds at their backs in the first-half, Austria struggled and went in at half-time 2-0 down. The second-half was only eight-minutes-old when Wrexham defender Barry Hunter marked his home debut by hooking home a Michael Hughes cross.

The Austrians pulled a goal back through SCHOPP before Phil GRAY got the final touch to another Hunter effort. Northern Ireland extended their lead even further when Mike O'NEILL netted his second goal of the evening – a marvellous chip following great work from Hughes who chased after, and then raced away with, Alan Fettis' punched clearance.

Austria's two substitutes STUMPF and WETL reduced the arrears for the visitors but by then it was too little too late. Northern Ireland had saved the best to last, but unfortunately it was too late to salvage anything from the European Championships Group Six except pride, pleasure and promise.

441. 27 March 1996 v NORWAY at Belfast

AW Fettis	Nottingham Forest
SM Lomas	Manchester City
N Worthington*	Leeds United
CF Hill	Leicester City
A McDonald	Queen's Park Rangers
NF Lennon	Leicester City
KR Gillespie	Newcastle United
MAM O'Neill**	Hibernian
I Dowie	West Ham United
J Magilton***	Southampton
ME Hughes	Strasbourg
Subs	
* K Rowland	West Ham United
** GJ McMahon	Tottenham Hotspur
*** DJ Patterson	Luton Town
Result	0-2

442. 24 April 1996 v SWEDEN at Belfast

AJ Davison	Bolton Wanderers
DJ Patterson	Luton Town
N Worthington*	Leeds United
CF Hill	Leicester City
BV Hunter	Wrexham
SJ Morrow	Arsenal
JD McCarthy	Port Vale
SM Lomas	Manchester City
GJ McMahon	Tottenham Hotspur
MAM O'Neill**	Hibernian
K Rowland	West Ham United

Subs	
* SJ Quinn	Blackpool
** G O'Boyle	St Johnstone

Result	1-2

GJ McMahon

443. 29 May 1996 v GERMANY at Belfast

AW Fettis	Nottingham Forest
DJ Griffin	St Johnstone
N Worthington*	Leeds United
CF Hill	Leicester City
BV Hunter	Wrexham
SM Lomas	Manchester City
KR Gillespie**	Newcastle United
J Magilton	Southampton
I Dowie	West Ham United
GJ McMahon	Tottenham Hotspur
ME Hughes	Strasbourg

Subs	
* K Rowland	West Ham United
** G O'Boyle	St Johnstone

Result	1-1

G O'Boyle

444. 31 August 1996 v UKRAINE at Belfast

AW Fettis	Nottingham Forest
DJ Griffin*	St Johnstone
K Rowland**	West Ham United
CF Hill	Leicester City
SJ Morrow	Arsenal
SM Lomas	Manchester City
KR Gillespie	Newcastle United
NF Lennon	Leicester City
I Dowie	West Ham United
P Gray	Nancy
ME Hughes	West Ham United

Subs	
* MAM O'Neill	Hibernian
** J Magilton	Southampton

Result	0-1

445. 5 October 1996 v ARMENIA at Belfast

AW Fettis	Nottingham Forest
IR Nolan	Sheffield Wednesday
K Rowland	West Ham United
CF Hill	Leicester City
BV Hunter	Reading
SM Lomas	Manchester City
KR Gillespie*	Newcastle United
NF Lennon**	Leicester City
I Dowie	West Ham United
P Gray***	Nancy
ME Hughes	West Ham United

Subs	
* MAM O'Neill	Hibernian
** J Magilton	Southampton
*** GJ McMahon	Stoke City

Result	1-1

NF Lennon

446. 9 November 1996 v GERMANY at Nuremberg

TJ Wright	Reading
IR Nolan	Sheffield Wednesday
GP Taggart	Bolton Wanderers
CF Hill	Leicester City
BV Hunter	Reading
K Horlock	Swindon Town
SJ Morrow	Arsenal
SM Lomas	Manchester City
I Dowie*	West Ham United
NF Lennon**	Leicester City
ME Hughes	West Ham United

Subs	
* P Gray	Nancy
** A Rogan	Millwall

Result	1-1

GP Taggart

447. 14 December 1996 v ALBANIA at Belfast

TJ Wright	Reading
IR Nolan	Sheffield Wednesday
GP Taggart	Bolton Wanderers
CF Hill	Leicester City
BV Hunter	Reading
K Horlock	Swindon Town
SJ Morrow*	Arsenal
SM Lomas	Manchester City
I Dowie**	West Ham United
NF Lennon	Leicester City
ME Hughes	West Ham United

Subs	
* GJ McMahon	Stoke City
** SJ Quinn	Blackpool

Result	2-0

I Dowie (2)

448. 22 January 1997 v ITALY at Palermo

TJ Wright	Reading
DJ Griffin	St Johnstone
N Worthington	Stoke City
GP Taggart	Bolton Wanderers
BV Hunter	Reading
SJ Morrow	Arsenal
JD McCarthy*	Port Vale
SM Lomas	Manchester City

SJ Quinn**	Blackpool
K Horlock	Swindon Town
ME Hughes***	West Ham United

Subs	
* R Dennison	Wolverhampton Wanderers
** G O'Boyle	St Johnstone
*** K Rowland	West Ham United

Result 0-2	

449. 11 February 1997 v BELGIUM at Belfast

TJ Wright	Manchester City
GP Taggart	Bolton Wanderers
SJ Morrow	Arsenal
J Magilton	Southampton
BV Hunter*	Reading
SM Lomas	Manchester City
KR Gillespie	Newcastle United
NF Lennon**	Leicester City
SJ Quinn***	Blackpool
GJ McMahon****	Stoke City
K Horlock*****	Manchester City

Subs	
* DJ Griffin	St Johnstone
** N Worthington	Stoke City
*** G O'Boyle	St Johnstone
**** PP Mulryne	Manchester United
***** Jeff Whitely	Manchester City

Result	3-0

SJ Quinn; J Magilton; PP Mulryne

450. 29 March 1997 v PORTUGAL at Belfast

TJ Wright	Manchester City
IR Nolan	Sheffield Wednesday
SJ Morrow	Queen's Park Rangers
CF Hill	Leicester City
GP Taggart	Bolton Wanderers
SM Lomas	West Ham United
KR Gillespie	Newcastle United
NF Lennon	Leicester City
I Dowie	West Ham United
J Magilton	Southampton
SJ Quinn*	Blackpool

Subs	
* GJ McMahon	Stoke City

Result	0-0

451. 2 April 1997 v UKRAINE at Kiev

TJ Wright	Manchester City
IR Nolan	Sheffield Wednesday
SJ Morrow	Queen's Park Rangers
CF Hill	Leicester City
GP Taggart	Bolton Wanderers

SM Lomas	West Ham United
KR Gillespie*	Newcastle United
K Horlock	Manchester City
I Dowie	West Ham United
NF Lennon**	Leicester City
ME Hughes	West Ham United

Subs	
* GJ McMahon	Stoke City
** SJ Quinn	Blackpool

Result	1-2

I Dowie (pen)

452. 30 April 1997 v ARMENIA at Yerevan

AW Fettis	Nottingham Forest
I Jenkins	Chester City
SJ Morrow	Queen's Park Rangers
CF Hill	Leicester City
GP Taggart	Bolton Wanderers
SM Lomas	West Ham United
JD McCarthy*	Port Vale
K Horlock	Manchester City
I Dowie	West Ham United
NF Lennon	Leicester City
SJ Quinn**	Blackpool

Subs	
* PP Mulryne	Manchester United
** GJ McMahon	Stoke City

Result	0-0

453. 21 May 1997 v THAILAND at Bangkok

AJ Davison*	Bradford City
DJ Griffin	St Johnstone
I Jenkins**	Chester City
CF Hill	Leicester City
PCG McGibbon	Manchester United
SM Lomas	West Ham United
JD McCarthy***	Port Vale
K Horlock	Manchester City
I Dowie****	West Ham United
NF Lennon	Leicester City
PP Mulryne*****	Manchester United

Subs	
* RE Carroll	Wigan Athletic
** Jeff Whitely	Manchester City
*** GJ McMahon	Stoke City
**** S Robinson	Bournemouth
***** SJ Quinn	Blackpool

Result	0-0

454. 20 August 1997 v GERMANY at Belfast

AJ Davison	Grimsby Town
IR Nolan	Sheffield Wednesday
SJ Morrow	Queen's Park Rangers

CF Hill	Trellsborgs
GP Taggart	Bolton Wanderers
J Magilton	Southampton
KR Gillespie*	Newcastle United
NF Lennon**	Leicester City
SJ Quinn	Blackpool
K Horlock	Manchester City
ME Hughes	West Ham United

Subs	
* GJ McMahon	Stoke City
** DJ Griffin	St Johnstone

Result	1-3

ME Hughes

455. 10 September 1997 v ALBANIA at Zurich

TJ Wright	Manchester City
DJ Griffin	St Johnstone
K Rowland*	West Ham United
CF Hill	Trellsborgs
PCG McGibbon	Wigan Athletic
SM Lomas	West Ham United
KR Gillespie	Newcastle United
NF Lennon**	Leicester City
I Dowie	West Ham United
SJ Quinn***	Blackpool
K Horlock	Manchester City

Subs	
* PP Mulryne	Manchester United
** DJ Sonner	Ipswich Town
*** GJ McMahon	Stoke City

Result	0-1

456. 11 October 1997 v PORTUGAL at Lisbon

AW Fettis	Blackburn Rovers
IR Nolan	Sheffield Wednesday
SJ Morrow	Queen's Park Rangers
GP Taggart	Bolton Wanderers
CF Hill*	Trellsborgs
SM Lomas	West Ham United
J Magilton	Sheffield Wednesday
NF Lennon**	Leicester City
I Dowie	West Ham United
K Horlock	Manchester City
ME Hughes	Wimbledon

Subs	
* GJ McMahon	Stoke City
** JD McCarthy	Birmingham City

Result	0-1

457. 25 March 1998 v SLOVAKIA at Belfast

AW Fettis	Blackburn Rovers
I Jenkins	Chester City
AW Hughes	Newcastle United

SM Lomas	West Ham United
SJ Morrow	Queen's Park Rangers
CF Hill	Northampton Town
KR Gillespie*	Newcastle United
NF Lennon	Leicester City
SJ Quinn**	West Bromwich Albion
I Dowie	Queen's Park Rangers
ME Hughes	Wimbledon

Subs	
* JD McCarthy	Birmingham City
** G O'Boyle	St Johnstone

Result	1-0

SM Lomas

458. 22 April 1998 v SWITZERLAND at Belfast

AW Fettis	Blackburn Rovers
I Jenkins	Dundee United
AW Hughes	Newcastle United
DJ Patterson	Luton Town
SJ Morrow	Queen's Park Rangers
SM Lomas	West Ham United
KR Gillespie	Newcastle United
NF Lennon	Leicester City
SJ Quinn*	West Bromwich Albion
I Dowie	Queen's Park Rangers
ME Hughes	Wimbledon

Subs	
* G O'Boyle	St Johnstone

Result	1-0

DJ Patterson

459. 3 June 1998 v SPAIN at Santander

AW Fettis	Blackburn Rovers
I Jenkins	Dundee United
GP Taggart	Bolton Wanderers
SJ Morrow	Queen's Park Rangers
DJ Patterson*	Luton Town
JD McCarthy	Birmingham City
J Magilton**	Sheffield Wednesday
NF Lennon***	Leicester City
Jim Whitely	Manchester City
I Dowie	Queen's Park Rangers
ME Hughes	Wimbledon

Subs	
* AW Hughes	Newcastle United
** PP Mulryne	Manchester United
*** Jeff Whitley	Manchester City

Result	1-4

GP Taggart

AW Fettis	Blackburn Rovers
AW Hughes	Newcastle United
K Horlock	Manchester City
PP Mulryne	Manchester United
CF Hill	Northampton Town
SJ Morrow	Queen's Park Rangers
KR Gillespie*	Newcastle United
NF Lennon	Leicester City
I Dowie	Queen's Park Rangers
K Rowland**	Queen's Park Rangers
ME Hughes	Wimbledon

Subs	
* Jim Whitley	Manchester City
** SJ Quinn	West Bromwich Albion

Result	0-3

AW Fettis	Blackburn Rovers
AW Hughes	Newcastle United
K Horlock	Manchester City
PP Mulryne	Manchester United
SJ Morrow	Queen's Park Rangers
DJ Patterson	Dundee United
KR Gillespie*	Newcastle United
NF Lennon	Leicester City
I Dowie**	Queen's Park Rangers
K Rowland***	Queen's Park Rangers
ME Hughes	Wimbledon

Subs	
* JD McCarthy	Birmingham City
** G O'Boyle	St Johnstone
*** SJ Quinn	West Bromwich Albion

Result	1-0

K Rowland

AW Fettis	Blackburn Rovers
DJ Griffin	St Johnstone
PH Kennedy	Watford
SM Lomas	West Ham United
DJ Patterson	Dundee United
SJ Morrow	Queen's Park Rangers
KR Gillespie*	Newcastle United
NF Lennon	Leicester City
I Dowie	Queen's Park Rangers
K Rowland**	Queen's Park Rangers
ME Hughes	Wimbledon

Subs	
* JD McCarthy	Birmingham City
** P Gray	Luton Town

Result	2-2

I Dowie; NF Lennon

MS Taylor	Fulham
DJ Patterson	Dundee United
K Horlock	Manchester City
SM Lomas	West Ham United
MS Williams	Chesterfield
SJ Morrow	Queen's Park Rangers
KR Gillespie*	Blackburn Rovers
NF Lennon**	Leicester City
I Dowie	Queen's Park Rangers
K Rowland***	Queen's Park Rangers
ME Hughes	Wimbledon

Subs	
* JD McCarthy	Birmingham City
** DJ Sonner	Sheffield Wednesday
*** PH Kennedy	Watford

Result	0-3

MS Taylor	Fulham
DJ Patterson*	Dundee United
K Horlock	Manchester City
SM Lomas	West Ham United
MS Williams	Chesterfield
SJ Morrow	Queen's Park Rangers
KR Gillespie	Blackburn Rovers
NF Lennon	Leicester City
I Dowie	Queen's Park Rangers
S Robinson	Bournemouth
ME Hughes	Wimbledon

Subs	
* AW Hughes	Newcastle United

Result	0-0

MS Taylor*	Fulham
AW Hughes	Newcastle United
K Horlock	Manchester City
MS Williams	Chesterfield
BV Hunter	Reading
SM Lomas	West Ham United
JD McCarthy**	Birmingham City
PP Mulryne***	Norwich City
I Dowie****	Queen's Park Rangers
A Coote*****	Norwich City
K Rowland	Queen's Park Rangers

Subs	
* TJ Wright	Manchester City
** R Hamill	Glentoran
*** DJ Sonner	Sheffield Wednesday
**** G Ferguson	Linfield
***** P McVeigh	Tottenham Hotspur

Result	1-1

Parker (own goal)

MS Taylor*	Fulham
DJ Patterson	Dundee United
AW Hughes	Newcastle United
MS Williams	Chesterfield
BV Hunter	Reading
NF Lennon**	Leicester City
JD McCarthy	Birmingham City
S Robinson	Bournemouth
I Dowie***	Queen's Park Rangers
SJ Quinn	West Bromwich Albion
K Rowland****	Queen's Park Rangers
Subs	
* RE Carroll	Wigan Athletic
** DJ Griffin	St Johnstone
*** A Coote	Norwich City
**** DM Johnson	Blackburn Rovers
Result	0-1

MS Taylor*	Fulham
AW Hughes	Newcastle United
K Horlock	Manchester City
SM Lomas	West Ham United
MS Williams	Watford
BV Hunter	Reading
JD McCarthy	Birmingham City
NF Lennon	Leicester City
I Dowie**	Queen's Park Rangers
ME Hughes	Wimbledon
PH Kennedy***	Watford
Subs	
* TJ Wright	Manchester City
** SJ Quinn	West Bromwich Albion
*** KR Gillespie	Blackburn Rovers
Result	0-1

MS Taylor	Fulham
AW Hughes	Newcastle United
K Horlock	Manchester City
SM Lomas	West Ham United
MS Williams	Watford
BV Hunter	Reading
JD McCarthy*	Birmingham City
NF Lennon	Leicester City
I Dowie**	Queen's Park Rangers
ME Hughes	Wimbledon
PH Kennedy	Watford
Subs	
* KR Gillespie	Blackburn Rovers
** SJ Quinn	West Bromwich Albion
Result	0-3

MS Taylor	Fulham
IR Nolan	Sheffield Wednesday
K Horlock	Manchester City
SM Lomas	West Ham United
MS Williams	Watford
SJ Morrow	Queen's Park Rangers
JD McCarthy	Birmingham City
NF Lennon*	Leicester City
I Dowie**	Queen's Park Rangers
ME Hughes	Wimbledon
PH Kennedy	Watford
Subs	
* KR Gillespie	Blackburn Rovers
** SJ Quinn	West Bromwich Albion
Result	0-4

MS Taylor	Fulham
I Jenkins*	Dundee United
IR Nolan	Sheffield Wednesday
NF Lennon	Leicester City
MS Williams	Watford
SJ Morrow	Queen's Park Rangers
JD McCarthy	Birmingham City
Jeff Whitley	Manchester City
SJ Quinn**	West Bromwich Albion
PH Kennedy	Watford
ME Hughes***	Wimbledon
Subs	
* Jim Whitley	Manchester City
** A Coote	Norwich City
*** DM Johnson	Blackburn Rovers
Result	1-4
Jeff Whitley	

RE Carroll*	Wigan Athletic
IR Nolan	Sheffield Wednesday
AW Hughes	Newcastle United
DJ Griffin**	St Johnstone
MS Williams***	Watford
SM Lomas	West Ham United
J Magilton****	Ipswich Town
DM Johnson*****	Blackburn Rovers
SJ Quinn******	West Bromwich Albion
D Healy	Manchester United
KR Gillespie*******	Blackburn Rovers
Subs	
* MS Taylor	Fulham
** PCG McGibbon	Wigan Athletic
*** CJ Murdock	Preston North End
**** DJ Sonner	Sheffield Wednesday
***** ME Hughes	Wimbledon
****** A Coote	Norwich City

******* S Robinson	Bournemouth

Result	3-1

D Healy (2); SJ Quinn

472. 28 March 2000 v MALTA at Valletta

RE Carroll*	Wigan Athletic
IR Nolan	Sheffield Wednesday
DJ Griffin	St Johnstone
SM Lomas	West Ham United
MS Williams	Watford
CJ Murdock**	Preston North End
KR Gillespie***	Blackburn Rovers
NF Lennon	Leicester City
SJ Quinn****	West Bromwich Albion
D Healy	Manchester United
ME Hughes*****	Wimbledon

Subs	
* MS Taylor	Fulham
** DJ Sonner	Sheffield Wednesday
*** DM Johnson	Blackburn Rovers
**** A Coote	Norwich City
***** K Horlock	Manchester City

Result	3-0

ME Hughes; SJ Quinn; D Healy

473. 26 April 2000 v HUNGARY at Belfast

MS Taylor	Fulham
DJ Griffin*	St Johnstone
IR Nolan	Sheffield Wednesday
NF Lennon	Leicester City
AW Hughes	Newcastle United
GP Taggart**	Leicester City
KR Gillespie***	Blackburn Rovers
DJ Sonner	Sheffield Wednesday
AR Kirk****	Heart of Midlothian
D Healy	Manchester United
ME Hughes	Wimbledon

Subs	
* DM Johnson	Blackburn Rovers
** MS Williams	Watford
*** CJ Murdock	Preston North End
**** A Coote	Norwich City

Result	0-1

474. 16 August 2000 v YUGOSLAVIA at Belfast

MS Taylor	Fulham
IR Nolan	Bradford City
AW Hughes	Newcastle United
CJ Murdock*	Preston North End
MS Williams	Watford
K Horlock**	Manchester City
DM Johnson	Blackburn Rovers
PP Mulryne***	Norwich City

D Healy	Manchester United
Jeff Whitley	Manchester City
J Magilton	Ipswich Town

Subs	
* DJ Griffin	Dundee United
** KR Gillespie	Blackburn Rovers
*** SJ Quinn	West Bromwich Albion

Result	1-2

D Healy	

475. 2 September 2000 v MALTA at Belfast

RE Carroll	Wigan Athletic
IR Nolan	Bradford City
AW Hughes	Newcastle United
CJ Murdock	Preston North End
GP Taggart	Leicester City
K Horlock	Manchester City
DM Johnson	Blackburn Rovers
J Magilton	Ipswich Town
D Healy	Manchester United
S Elliott*	Motherwell
SM Lomas	West Ham United

Subs	
* P Gray	Burnley

Result	1-0

P Gray

476. 7 October 2000 v DENMARK at Belfast

RE Carroll	Wigan Athletic
SM Lomas	West Ham United
AW Hughes	Newcastle United
CJ Murdock	Preston North End
GP Taggart	Leicester City
K Horlock	Manchester City
J Magilton	Ipswich Town
Jeff Whitley*	Manchester City
D Healy	Manchester United
S Elliott**	Motherwell
NF Lennon	Leicester City

Subs	
* PP Mulryne	Norwich City
** P Gray	Burnley

Result	1-1

D Healy

477. 11 October 2000 v ICELAND at Reykjavik

RE Carroll	Wigan Athletic
SM Lomas	West Ham United
AW Hughes	Newcastle United
CJ Murdock	Preston North End
GP Taggart*	Leicester City

K Horlock	Manchester City
NF Lennon	Leicester City
DM Johnson	Blackburn Rovers
D Healy	Manchester United
J Magilton	Ipswich Town
S Elliott**	Motherwell

Subs	
* MS Williams	Wimbledon
** P Gray	Burnley

Result	0-1

478. 28 February 2001 v NORWAY at Belfast

MS Taylor	Fulham
JD McCarthy*	Birmingham City
PH Kennedy**	Watford
CJ Murdock	Preston North End
GP Taggart***	Leicester City
AW Hughes	Newcastle United
NF Lennon****	Glasgow Celtic
G Ferguson*****	Linfield
D Healy******	Preston North End
Jeff Whitley*******	Manchester City
J Magilton	Ipswich Town

Subs	
* DM Johnson	Blackburn Rovers
** DJ Griffin	Dundee United
*** MS Williams	Wimbledon
**** S Elliott	Motherwell
***** P Gray	Oxford United
****** AR Kirk	Heart of Midlothian
******* DJ Sonner	Birmingham City

Result	0-4

479. 24 March 2001 v CZECH REPUBLIC at Belfast

RE Carroll	Wigan Athletic
DJ Griffin	Dundee United
AW Hughes	Newcastle United
S Elliott*	Motherwell
MS Williams	Wimbledon
CJ Murdock	Preston North End
KR Gillespie	Blackburn Rovers
NF Lennon	Glasgow Celtic
D Healy**	Preston North End
J Magilton	Ipswich Town
ME Hughes	Wimbledon

Subs	
* P Gray	Oxford United
** G Ferguson	Linfield

Result	0-1

480. 28 March 2001 v BULGARIA at Sofia

RE Carroll	Wigan Athletic
DJ Griffin	Dundee United
IR Nolan*	Bradford City
S Elliott	Motherwell

MS Williams	Wimbledon
CJ Murdock	Preston North End
KR Gillespie**	Blackburn Rovers
NF Lennon***	Glasgow Celtic
D Healy	Preston North End
J Magilton	Ipswich Town
ME Hughes	Wimbledon

Subs	
* JD McCarthy	Birmingham City
** DM Johnson	Blackburn Rovers
*** PH Kennedy	Watford

Result	3-4

MS Williams; D Healy (2)

481. 2 June 2001 v BULGARIA at Belfast

MS Taylor	Fulham
IR Nolan*	Bradford City
DJ Griffin	Dundee United
CJ Murdock	Preston North End
AW Hughes	Newcastle United
NF Lennon**	Glasgow Celtic
KR Gillespie	Blackburn Rovers
DM Johnson	Blackburn Rovers
D Healy	Preston North End
S Elliott***	Motherwell
ME Hughes	Wimbledon

Subs	
* SJ Quinn	West Bromwich Albion
** PP Mulryne	Norwich City
*** G Ferguson	Linfield

Result	0-1

482. 6 June 2001 v CZECH REPUBLIC at Teplice

MS Taylor	Fulham
IR Nolan	Bradford City
AW Hughes	Newcastle United
CJ Murdock	Preston North End
MS Williams	Wimbledon
DJ Griffin	Dundee United
DM Johnson*	Blackburn Rovers
PP Mulryne**	Norwich City
D Healy	Preston North End
S Elliott***	Motherwell
ME Hughes	Wimbledon

Subs	
* G Ferguson	Linfield
** PH Kennedy	Watford
*** SJ Quinn	West Bromwich Albion

Result	1-3

PP Mulryne

MS Taylor	Fulham
DJ Griffin	Dundee United
PH Kennedy	Wigan Athletic
CJ Murdock	Preston North End
AW Hughes	Newcastle United
K Horlock	Manchester City
KR Gillespie	Blackburn Rovers
J Magilton	Ipswich Town
D Healy	Preston North End
PP Mulryne	Norwich City
ME Hughes*	Wimbledon
Subs	
* S Elliott	Motherwell
Result	1-1

PP Mulryne

MS Taylor	Fulham
DJ Griffin	Dundee United
PH Kennedy	Wigan Athletic
K Horlock	Manchester City
AW Hughes	Newcastle United
G McCartney	Sunderland
KR Gillespie*	Blackburn Rovers
J Magilton	Ipswich Town
D Healy	Preston North End
PP Mulryne	Norwich City
ME Hughes	Wimbledon
Subs	
* P McVeigh	Norwich City
Result	3-0

D Healy; ME Hughes; G McCartney

MS Taylor	Fulham
DJ Griffin	Dundee United
PH Kennedy	Wigan Athletic
K Horlock	Manchester City
CJ Murdock	Preston North End
G McCartney	Sunderland
DM Johnson	Blackburn Rovers
J Magilton	Ipswich Town
D Healy*	Preston North End
S Elliott**	Motherwell
ME Hughes	Wimbledon
Subs	
* GS McCann	West Ham United
** SJ Quinn	West Bromwich Albion
Result	1-0

D Healy

MS Taylor	Fulham
DJ Griffin*	Dundee United
PH Kennedy**	Wigan Athletic
PP Mulryne***	Norwich City
AW Hughes	Newcastle United
SM Lomas	West Ham United
KR Gillespie	Blackburn Rovers
J Magilton****	Ipswich Town
DM Johnson*****	Blackburn Rovers
D Healy******	Preston North End
ME Hughes	Wimbledon
Subs	
* G McCartney	Sunderland
** GS McCann	West Ham United
*** NF Lonnon	Glasgow Celtic
**** MJ Duff	Cheltenham Town
***** P McVeigh	Norwich City
****** S Elliott	Motherwell
Result	1-4

SM Lomas

MS Taylor*	Fulham
SM Lomas	West Ham United
GS McCann**	West Ham United
PP Mulryne	Norwich City
MS Williams	Wimbledon
G McCartney	Sunderland
KR Gillespie	Blackburn Rovers
J Magilton	Ipswich Town
DM Johnson	Birmingham City
D Healy***	Preston North End
WJ Feeney****	Bournemouth
Subs	
* RE Carroll	Manchester United
** SP Holmes	Wrexham
*** S Elliott	Motherwell
**** ME Hughes	Wimbledon
Result	0-0

MS Taylor*	Fulham
IR Nolan	Wigan Athletic
G McCartney	Sunderland
K Horlock	Manchester City
AW Hughes	Newcastle United
MS Williams	Wimbledon
KR Gillespie**	Blackburn Rovers
S Elliott	Motherwell
WJ Feeney***	Bournemouth
DM Johnson	Birmingham City
D Healy	Preston North End
Subs	
* RE Carroll	Manchester United

| ** PJ McCourt | Rochdale |
| *** LR McEvilly | Rochdale |

| Result | 0-5 |

489. 21 August 2002 v CYPRUS at Belfast

MS Taylor	Fulham
DJ Griffin*	Dundee United
G McCartney	Sunderland
K Horlock	Manchester City
MS Williams	Wimbledon
CJ Murdock	Preston North End
KR Gillespie**	Blackburn Rovers
DM Johnson	Birmingham City
D Healy	Preston North End
SJ Quinn	Willem II
PH Kennedy	Wigan Athletic

Subs	
* MJ Duff	Cheltenham Town
** WJ Feeney	Bournemouth

| Result | 0-0 |

490. 12 October 2002 v SPAIN at Albacete

MS Taylor	Fulham
AW Hughes	Newcastle United
G McCartney	Sunderland
CJ Murdock	Preston North End
GP Taggart*	Leicester City
SM Lomas	West Ham United
DM Johnson	Birmingham City
PP Mulryne	Norwich City
KR Gillespie	Blackburn Rovers
P McVeigh**	Norwich City
K Horlock***	Manchester City

Subs	
* GS McCann	West Ham United
** D Healy	Preston North End
*** ME Hughes	Wimbledon

| Result | 0-3 |

491. 16 October 2002 v UKRAINE at Belfast

MS Taylor	Fulham
SM Lomas	West Ham United
K Horlock	Manchester City
PP Mulryne*	Norwich City
AW Hughes	Newcastle United
G McCartney	Sunderland
KR Gillespie	Blackburn Rovers
DM Johnson**	Birmingham City
P McVeigh***	Norwich City
D Healy	Preston North End
ME Hughes	Wimbledon

Subs	
* GS McCann	West Ham United
** CJ Murdock	Preston North End

| *** AR Kirk | Heart of Midlothian |

| Result | 0-0 |

492. 12 February 2003 v FINLAND at Belfast

MS Taylor*	Fulham
AW Hughes	Newcastle United
PH Kennedy	Wigan Athletic
MS Williams	Wimbledon
G McCartney**	Sunderland
SM Lomas	West Ham United
KR Gillespie	Blackburn Rovers
DM Johnson	Birmingham City
D Healy	Preston North End
SJ Quinn***	Willem II
P McVeigh****	Norwich City

Subs	
* RE Carroll	Manchester United
** SJ Craigan	Partick Thistle
*** A Kirk	Heart of Midlothian
**** S Elliott	Hull City

| Result | 0-1 |

493. 29 March 2003 v ARMENIA at Erevan

MS Taylor	Fulham
AW Hughes	Newcastle United
GS McCann	West Ham United
SM Lomas	West Ham United
MS Williams	Stoke City
SJ Craigan	Partick Thistle
KR Gillespie	Blackburn Rovers
DM Johnson	Birmingham City
D Healy	Preston North End
SJ Quinn*	Willem II
P McVeigh	Norwich City

| Subs | |
| * S Elliott | Hull City |

| Result | 0-1 |

494. 2 April 2003 v GREECE at Belfast

MS Taylor	Fulham
AW Hughes	Newcastle United
G McCartney	Sunderland
SM Lomas	West Ham United
MS Williams	Stoke City
SJ Craigan	Partick Thistle
KR Gillespie	Blackburn Rovers
DM Johnson	Birmingham City
D Healy*	Preston North End
SJ Quinn	Willem II
GS McCann**	West Ham United

Subs	
* AR Kirk	Heart of Midlothian
** P McVeigh	Norwich City

Result	0-2

** AW Smith	Glentoran
*** SG Jones	Crewe Alexandra

Result	0-0

495. 3 June 2003 v ITALY at Campobasso

MS Taylor*	Fulham
CP Baird	Southampton
PH Kennedy**	Wigan Athletic
DJ Griffin	Dundee United
AW Hughes	Newcastle United
G McCartney	Sunderland
DM Johnson***	Birmingham City
TE Doherty****	Bristol City
D Healy*****	Preston North End
AW Smith	Glentoran
P McVeigh******	Norwich City

Subs	
* RE Carroll	Manchester United
** MS Williams	Stoke City
*** C Toner	Leyton Orient
**** S Elliott	Hull City
***** G Hamilton	Portadown
****** SG Jones	Crewe Alexandra

Result	0-2

498. 10 September 2003 v ARMENIA at Belfast

MS Taylor	Fulham
CP Baird	Southampton
GS McCann	West Ham United
DJ Griffin	Dundee United
AW Hughes	Newcastle United
G McCartney	Sunderland
KR Gillespie*	Leicester City
TE Doherty**	Bristol City
DM Johnson	Birmingham City
D Hoaly***	Preston North End
AW Smith	Glentoran

Subs	
* SG Jones	Crewe Alexandra
** PP Mulryne	Norwich City
*** P McVeigh	Norwich City

Result	0-1

496. 11 June 2003 v SPAIN at Belfast

MS Taylor	Fulham
CP Baird	Southampton
PH Kennedy	Wigan Athletic
DJ Griffin	Dundee United
AW Hughes	Newcastle United
G McCartney	Sunderland
D Healy	Preston North End
DM Johnson	Birmingham City
AW Smith*	Glentoran
SG Jones**	Crewe Alexandra
TE Doherty***	Bristol City

Subs	
* MS Williams	Stoke City
** P McVeigh	Norwich City
*** C Toner	Leyton Orient

Result	0-0

499. 11 October 2003 v GREECE at Athens

MS Taylor	Fulham
CP Baird	Southampton
PH Kennedy	Wigan Athletic
DJ Griffin*	Dundee United
AW Hughes	Newcastle United
G McCartney	Sunderland
KR Gillespie**	Leicester City
Jeff Whitley	Sunderland
D Healy	Preston North End
S Elliott***	Hull City
ME Hughes	Crystal Palace

Subs	
* SG Jones	Crewe Alexandra
** AW Smith	Glentoran
*** CJ Murdock	Hibernian

Result	0-1

497. 6 September 2003 v UKRAINE at Donetsk

MS Taylor	Fulham
CP Baird	Southampton
PH Kennedy	Wigan Athletic
DJ Griffin	Dundee United
AW Hughes	Newcastle United
G McCartney	Sunderland
KR Gillespie	Leicester City
TE Doherty*	Bristol City
DM Johnson	Birmingham City
D Healy**	Preston North End
ME Hughes***	Crystal Palace

Subs	
* PP Mulryne	Norwich City

500. 18 February 2004 v NORWAY at Belfast

MS Taylor	Fulham
CP Baird	Southampton
PH Kennedy*	Wigan Athletic
AW Hughes	Newcastle United
G McCartney	Sunderland
DJ Griffin**	Dundee United
KR Gillespie***	Leicester City
DM Johnson	Birmingham City
D Healy	Preston North End
AW Smith	Glentoran
ME Hughes	Crystal Palace

Subs	
* SG Jones	Crystal Palace

** MS Williams	Wimbledon
*** P McVeigh	Norwich City

Result	1-4

D Healy

501. 31 March 2004 v ESTONIA at Tallinn

MS Taylor	Birmingham City
CP Baird	Southampton
AC Capaldi	Plymouth Argyle
SJ Craigan	Motherwell
MS Williams	Wimbledon
DJ Sonner*	Nottingham Forest
PP Mulryne**	Norwich City
Jeff Whitley	Sunderland
D Healy	Preston North End
AW Smith	Glentoran
SG Jones	Crewe Alexandra

Subs	
* MJ Duff	Cheltenham Town
** GS McCann	West Ham United

Result	1-0

D Healy

502. 28 April 2004 v SERBIA & MONTENEGRO at Belfast

MS Taylor*	Birmingham City
CP Baird	Southampton
AC Capaldi	Plymouth Argyle
SJ Craigan	Motherwell
MS Williams	Wimbledon
TE Doherty**	Bristol City
KR Gillespie***	Leicester City
Jeff Whitley****	Sunderland
D Healy*****	Preston North End
SJ Quinn******	Willem II
PP Mulryne*******	Norwich City

Subs	
* RE Carroll	Manchester United
** ME Hughes	Crystal Palace
*** SG Jones	Crewe Alexandra
**** DJ Sonner	Nottingham Forest
***** G Hamilton	Portadown
****** AW Smith	Glentoran
******* P McVeigh	Norwich City

Result	1-1

SJ Quinn

503. 30 May 2004 v BARBADOS at Waterford

MS Taylor	Birmingham City
CP Baird*	Southampton
AC Capaldi**	Plymouth Argyle
SJ Craigan	Motherwell

MS Williams	Wimbledon
DM Johnson	Birmingham City
KR Gillespie***	Leicester City
DJ Sonner****	Nottingham Forest
D Healy*****	Preston North End
SJ Quinn	Willem II
PP Mulryne******	Norwich City

Subs	
* SG Jones	Crewe Alexandra
** S Elliott	Hull City
*** CJ Murdock	Hibernian
**** P McVeigh	Norwich City
***** G Hamilton	Portadown
****** AW Smith	Glentoran

Result	1-1

D Healy

504. 2 June 2004 v ST KITTS & NEVIS at Basseterre

MS Taylor	Birmingham City
CP Baird	Southampton
AC Capaldi	Plymouth Argyle
SJ Craigan	Motherwell
CJ Murdock	Hibernian
Jeff Whitley*	Sunderland
P McVeigh**	Norwich City
DJ Sonner***	Nottingham Forest
G Hamilton****	Portadown
AW Smith	Glentoran
S Elliott*****	Hull City

Subs	
* DM Johnson	Birmingham City
** PP Mulryne	Norwich City
*** SG Jones	Crewe Alexandra
**** D Healy	Preston North End
***** KR Gillespie	Leicester City

Result	2-0

D Healy; SG Jones

505. 6 June 2004 v TRINIDAD & TOBAGO at Bacolet

MS Taylor*	Birmingham City
CP Baird	Southampton
AC Capaldi	Plymouth Argyle
SJ Craigan**	Motherwell
MS Williams	Wimbledon
Jeff Whitley	Sunderland
DM Johnson***	Birmingham City
PP Mulryne****	Norwich City
D Healy*****	Preston North End
SJ Quinn******	Willem II
S Elliott*******	Hull City

Subs	
* A Mannus	Linfield
** CJ Murdock	Hibernian
*** KR Gillespie	Leicester City

**** DJ Sonner	Nottingham Forest
***** P McVeigh	Norwich City
****** AW Smith	Glentoran
******* SG Jones	Crewe Alexandra

Result	3-0

D Healy (2); S Elliott

506. 18 August 2004 v SWITZERLAND at Zurich

RE Carroll	Manchester United
AW Hughes	Newcastle United
AC Capaldi	Plymouth Argyle
DM Johnson	Birmingham City
MS Williams*	Milton Keynes Dons
SJ Craigan**	Motherwell
KR Gillespie***	Leicester City
DJ Sonner	Peterborough United
D Healy****	Preston North End
AW Smith	Preston North End
S Elliott *****	Hull City

Subs	
* CJ Murdock	Hibernian
** MJ Duff	Burnley
*** P McVeigh	Norwich City
**** G Hamilton	Portadown
***** C Brunt	Sheffield Wednesday

Result	0-0

507. 4 September 2004 v POLAND at Belfast

MS Taylor	Birmingham City
AW Hughes	Newcastle United
AC Capaldi	Plymouth Argyle
Jeff Whitley	Sunderland
MS Williams	Milton Keynes Dons
SJ Craigan	Motherwell
DM Johnson	Birmingham City
ME Hughes*	Crystal Palace
SJ Quinn**	Willem II
D Healy	Preston North End
S Elliott ***	Hull City

Subs	
* SG Jones	Crewe Alexandra
** AW Smith	Preston North End
*** P McVeigh	Norwich City

Result	0-3

508. 8 September 2004 v WALES at Cardiff

MS Taylor	Birmingham City
MG Clyde	Wolverhampton Wanderers
AC Capaldi*	Plymouth Argyle
CJ Murdock	Hibernian
AW Hughes	Newcastle United
MS Williams	Milton Keynes Dons
DM Johnson	Birmingham City
Jeff Whitley	Sunderland
SJ Quinn**	Willem II
D Healy	Preston North End
ME Hughes	Crystal Palace

Subs	
* G McCartney	Sunderland
** AW Smith***	Preston North End
*** P McVeigh	Norwich City

Result	2-2

Jeff Whitley; D Healy

509. 9 October 2004 v AZERBAIJAN at Baku

MS Taylor	Birmingham City
MG Clyde	Wolverhampton Wanderers
AW Hughes	Newcastle United
TE Doherty	Bristol City
MS Williams	Milton Keynes Dons
CJ Murdock	Hibernian
DM Johnson	Birmingham City
Jeff Whitley	Sunderland
SJ Quinn*	Willem II
S Elliott	Hull City
CP Baird**	Southampton

Subs	
* AW Smith	Preston North End
** KR Gillespie	Leicester City

Result	0-0

510. 13 October 2004 v AUSTRIA at Belfast

RE Carroll	Manchester United
G McCartney	Sunderland
AW Hughes	Newcastle United
TE Doherty*	Bristol City
MS Williams	Milton Keynes Dons
CJ Murdock**	Hibernian
KR Gillespie	Leicester City
Jeff Whitley***	Sunderland
SJ Quinn	Willem II
D Healy	Preston North End
DM Johnson	Birmingham City

Subs	
* SG Jones	Crewe Alexandra
** S Elliott	Hull City
*** P McVeigh	Norwich City

Result	3-3

D Healy; CJ Murdock; S Elliott

511. 9 February 2005 v CANADA at Belfast

MS Taylor*	Birmingham City
CP Baird	Southampton
G McCartney	Sunderland
TE Doherty**	Bristol City
AW Hughes	Newcastle United

CJ Murdock***	Crewe Alexandra
KR Gillespie****	Leicester City
Jeff Whitley	Sunderland
D Healy*****	Leeds United
S Davis	Aston Villa
AC Capaldi******	Plymouth Argyle
Subs	
* RE Carroll	Manchester United
** PP Mulryne	Norwich City
*** AR Kirk	Boston United
**** SG Jones	Crewe Alexandra
***** AW Smith	Preston North End
****** SJ Craigan	Motherwell
Result	0-1

512. 26 March 2005 v ENGLAND at Manchester

MS Taylor	Birmingham City
CP Baird	Southampton
AC Capaldi	Plymouth Argyle
TE Doherty*	Bristol City
AW Hughes	Newcastle United
CJ Murdock	Crewe Alexandra
KR Gillespie	Leicester City
DM Johnson	Birmingham City
D Healy**	Leeds United
S Elliott	Hull City
Jeff Whitley***	Sunderland
Subs	
* S Davis	Aston Villa
** AR Kirk	Northampton Town
*** SG Jones	Crewe Alexandra
Result	0-4

513. 30 March 2005 v POLAND at Warsaw

MS Taylor	Birmingham City
CP Baird	Southampton
AC Capaldi	Plymouth Argyle
MS Williams*	Milton Keynes Dons
AW Hughes	Newcastle United
CJ Murdock	Crewe Alexandra
KR Gillespie	Leicester City
S Davis	Aston Villa
SJ Quinn**	Sheffield Wednesday
D Healy***	Leeds United
Jeff Whitley	Sunderland
Subs	
* S Elliott	Hull City
** WJ Feeney	Luton Town
*** AW Smith	Preston North End
Result	0-1

514. 4 June 2005 v GERMANY at Belfast

MS Taylor*	Birmingham City
KR Gillespie**	Leicester City

SJ Craigan***	Motherwell
MG Clyde	Wolverhampton Wanderers
CP Baird	Southampton
G McCartney	Sunderland
DM Johnson	Birmingham City
S Davis	Aston Villa
D Healy****	Leeds United
SG Jones*****	Crewe Alexandra
S Elliott******	Hull City
Subs	
* MG Ingham	Sunderland
** G McAuley	Lincoln City
*** AW Smith	Preston North End
**** C Brunt	Sheffield Wednesday
***** WJ Feeney	Luton Town
****** AR Kirk	Northampton Town
Result	1-4
D Healy	

515. 17 August 2005 v MALTA at Ta'Qali

MS Taylor	Birmingham City
KR Gillespie	Sheffield United
AW Hughes	Aston Villa
S Davis*	Aston Villa
CJ Murdock	Rotherham United
SJ Craigan	Motherwell
DM Johnson	Birmingham City
Jeff Whitley**	Sunderland
SJ Quinn***	Willem II
D Healy	Leeds United
S Elliott****	Hull City
Subs	
* PP Mulryne	Cardiff City
** SG Jones	Crewe Alexandra
*** WJ Feeney	Luton Town
**** C Brunt	Sheffield Wednesday
Result 1-1	
D Healy	

516. 3 September 2005 v AZERBAIJAN at Belfast

MS Taylor	Birmingham City
CP Baird	Southampton
AC Capaldi	Plymouth Argyle
SJ Craigan	Motherwell
AW Hughes	Aston Villa
S Davis	Aston Villa
KR Gillespie	Sheffield United
S Elliott*	Hull City
DM Johnson	Birmingham City
D Healy**	Leeds United
SJ Quinn***	Peterborough United
Subs	
* S Robinson	Luton Town
** SG Jones	Crewe Alexandra

*** WJ Feeney	Luton Town
Result	2-0

S Elliott; WJ Feeney

MS Taylor	Birmingham City
CP Baird	Southampton
AC Capaldi	Plymouth Argyle
SJ Craigan	Motherwell
AW Hughes	Aston Villa
S Davis	Aston Villa
KR Gillespie	Sheffield United
DM Johnson	Birmingham City
S Elliott*	Hull City
D Healy**	Leeds United
SJ Quinn***	Peterborough United

Subs	
* MJ Duff	Burnley
** I Sproule	Hibernian
*** WJ Feeney	Luton Town

Result	1-0

D Healy

FEATURED MATCH NO 20

NORTHERN IRELAND 1 ENGLAND 0

AT WINDSOR PARK, BELFAST, 7 SEPTEMBER 2005

England, with the likes of Wayne Rooney, David Beckham, Steven Gerrard, Frank Lampard and Michael Owen in their side were beaten 1-0 by Northern Ireland. Before this game, it had been 33 years since that last happened – and 78 years since a home win over England had been achieved!

The game was all but eight-seconds-old when the rampaging James Quinn flattened Arsenal's left-back Ashley Cole – this was to become a common theme throughout the evening. In fact, it almost seemed as if different Northern Ireland players took it in turns to tackle and in doing so, rattle England's team of star players.

Midway through the first-half David Beckham's stunning free-kick struck the bar but in open play, the home side coped admirably thanks to the display of central defenders Hughes and Craigan.

After that, chances were few and far between at either end in the first-half but on 43 minutes, wonderkid Wayne Rooney was booked for elbowing Keith Gillespie. The Manchester United striker then unleashed a torrent of abuse at anyone within earshot: even his captain David Beckham, when he tried to calm the young player down came in for the same treatment. Rooney was lucky not to be red-carded

on the stroke of half-time following another reckless challenge, this time on Chris Baird.

England pressed hard at the start of the second-half but Northern Ireland's players never stopped running, tackling and fighting for every loose ball. In fact, the longer this World Cup qualifier went on, the more the Northern Ireland fans believed that the impossible was actually possible and that one goal would do it!

It came in the 74th minute when Aston Villa's Steve Davis controlled a poor clearance from England keeper Paul Robinson and then waited, before delivering a pass into the path of striker David HEALY. He smashed home a tremendous right-foot drive – his 19th goal at international level and without doubt, the most celebrated!

The crowd inside Windsor Park erupted – Northern Ireland fans hugged each other in disbelief. Some twenty minutes later, following four minutes of injury time, the Swiss referee blew the final whistle. This was one of the biggest shocks the game has ever seen.

MS Taylor	Birmingham City
SJ Craigan	Motherwell
AC Capaldi	Plymouth Argyle
MJ Duff	Burnley
CJ Murdock	Rotherham United
S Davis	Aston Villa
KR Gillespie	Sheffield United
DM Johnson	Birmingham City
SJ Quinn	Peterborough United
D Healy	Leeds United
S Elliott*	Hull City

Subs	
* C Brunt	Sheffield Wednesday

Result	2-3

KR Gillespie; S Davis

MS Taylor	Birmingham City
CP Baird	Southampton
SJ Craigan	Motherwell
MJ Duff	Burnley
CJ Murdock	Rotherham United
S Davis	Aston Villa
KR Gillespie	Sheffield United
DM Johnson	Birmingham City
D Healy*	Leeds United
SJ Quinn**	Peterborough United
C Brunt***	Sheffield Wednesday

Subs	
* SG Jones	Crewe Alexandra
** WJ Feeney	Luton Town
*** S Elliott	Hull City

Result	0-2

520. 15 November 2005 v PORTUGAL at Belfast

MS Taylor	Birmingham City
KR Gillespie*	Sheffield United
AC Capaldi	Plymouth Argyle
SJ Craigan	Motherwell
CJ Murdock	Rotherham United
SG Jones**	Crewe Alexandra
S Davis	Aston Villa
C Brunt	Sheffield Wednesday
S Elliott***	Hull City
SJ Quinn⁺****	Peterborough United
WJ Feeney*****	Luton Town

Subs	
* D Shiels	Hibernian
** G McAuley	Lincoln City
*** GS McCann	Cheltenham Town
**** P Thompson	Linfield
***** I Sproule	Hibernian

Result	1-1

WJ Feeney

521. 1 March 2006 v ESTONIA at Belfast

MS Taylor	Birmingham City
G McAuley	Lincoln City
AC Capaldi	Plymouth Argyle
MJ Duff	Burnley
SJ Craigan*	Motherwell
S Davis**	Aston Villa
I Sproule***	Hibernian
CP Baird	Southampton
D Healy****	Leeds United
SJ Quinn*****	Peterborough United
C Brunt******	Sheffield Wednesday

Subs	
* B McLean	Glasgow Rangers
** S Elliott	Hull City
*** SG Jones	Crewe Alexandra
**** WJ Feeney	Luton Town
***** P Thompson	Linfield
****** GS McCann	Cheltenham Town

Result	1-0

I Sproule

522. 21 May 2006 v URUGUAY at East Rutherford (USA)

M Ingham	Sunderland
MJ Duff*	Burnley
AC Capaldi	Plymouth Argyle
CJ Murdock**	Rotherham United
J Hughes***	Lincoln City
SJ Craigan	Motherwell
SG Jones****	Crewe Alexandra

S Davis	Aston Villa
S Clinigan	Wolverhampton Wanderers
SJ Quinn*****	Peterborough United
I Sproule	Hibernian

Subs	
* S Webb	Ross County
** G McAuley	Lincoln City
*** P Thompson	Linfield
**** D Shiels	Hibernian
***** K Lafferty	Burnley

Result	0-1

523. 26 May 2006 v ROMANIA at Chicago

A Blayney	Doncaster Rovers
MJ Duff	Burnley
AC Capaldi*	Plymouth Argyle
SJ Craigan**	Motherwell
G McAuley***	Lincoln City
S Davis	Aston Villa
S Clinigan	Wolverhampton Wanderers
D Shiels****	Hibernian
P Thompson*****	Linfield
I Sproule******	Hibernian
SJ Quinn	Peterborough United

Subs	
* J Hughes	Lincoln City
** S Webb	Ross County
*** CJ Murdock	Rotherham United
**** SG Jones	Crewe Alexandra
***** K Lafferty	Burnley
****** MK Hughes	Oldham Athletic

Result	0-2

Algeria 1   N. Ireland 1

3rd June 1986

A selection of Northern Ireland memorabilia

CHAPTER FIVE
FEATURED PLAYERS

BILL McCRACKEN

Bill McCracken was a colourful character, one of the most famous, yet most controversial personalities the game has seen. He angered fans up and down the country, as his perfection of the offside-trap caused blood to boil wherever he played. He took the taunts – and much physical abuse from spectators – in his stride and always with a smile!

Born in January 1883, he joined the local Belfast Distillery club as a part-timer, being employed as an apprentice in the building trade. On the football field, McCracken was soon among the honours, winning Irish League and full caps when only 19, and twice reached the Irish Cup Final. English and Scottish clubs took notice, and his fast-developing talent held the attention of Everton, both Celtic and Rangers as well as Sunderland and Newcastle United. All the clubs chased the right-back for several months with United eventually securing his signature in May 1904. It was a controversial transfer as the FA immediately announced that an inquiry would take place, to investigate whether McCracken had received illegal payments as part of Newcastle's offer.

McCracken played his part in three League Championship victories during the Edwardian era, and he was also a member of a trio of FA Cup Final teams, picking up a winner's medal in 1910. His organisation at the back proved in many ways the important factor in United's success. Along with another United defender Colin Veitch, McCracken created an offside-trap which caught opposing forwards almost at will.

At Villa Park he was hit on the head by a pipe and had onions thrown his way. At Stamford Bridge his shirt was ripped and he was spat on. At Roker Park he was peppered with oranges, lemons and bananas, while he always collected a

fistful of coins thrown in his direction. Because McCracken was such an expert at the offside game, many spectators lost sight of his brilliance as a defender. His speed of recovery was excellent, and he could use the ball short or long and kick with either foot.

He was born a rebel and had many differences of opinion with referees! Once after being sent-off for questioning a decision, he wrote a four-page letter to the official strongly noting a few points about the game of football. Instead of receiving a seven-day suspension, McCracken was handed a four-week ban! He was also at loggerheads for many years with the Irish FA. A regular for his country since 1902, he would have won a pile of caps but for a personal crusade over payments. He demanded more appearance money, but when it was not forthcoming, he quit the party on the eve of a game with England in the 1907-08 season and was banned until differences were patched up much later in 1919.

McCracken was over 40 when he played in his last international, and was one of the oldest players to represent the Magpies. He went on to score eight goals in 432 games for United and holds record service as a player, on United's books for almost two decades. In February 1923 he was allowed to leave St James Park and become manager of Hull City. He built a useful side, and in 1929-30 took his side within a whisker of reaching Wembley. Hull City reached the semi-finals, knocking out his former club on the way. However, relegation cost McCracken his job and after a brief spell with Gateshead, he took over the reins at Millwall.

After rows with the board and a further relegation he left to join Aldershot, managing the Shots either side of the Second World War. He later became a talent scout – a very respected one – and whilst with Watford, discovered Pat Jennings. He was presented with a special medal by the FA for

his long service to the game in 1978. McCracken died in January 1979, just nine days before his 96th birthday.

BILL LACEY

One of the great characters of Merseyside football, Bill Lacey, an irrepressible little Irish international, could fill any outfield position. Wexford-born Lacey began his career in Dublin with Shelbourne before joining Everton in 1908. Unable to settle at Goodison Park, a deal was struck towards the end of the 1911-12 season that saw Lacey and forward Tom Gracie move to Anfield, with Harry Uren the Liverpool outside-left moving in the opposite direction. Liverpool certainly got the better of the deal, as Lacey went on to make 257 League and FA Cup appearances for the Anfield club over nine seasons in a variety of positions but starring as a winger on either flank.

He immediately went into the Reds' first team, playing in the last 11 games of that season with just one goal to his credit – against Tottenham Hotspur on 16 March 1912. Though he was never renowned as a goalscorer, his tricky wing-play set up numerous chances for his team-mates. After making only 20 League appearances in the Liverpool side in 1912-13, Lacey established himself firmly in the side the following year. Scoring five goals in seven games at inside-forward, he helped Liverpool reach their first major Cup Final – but it was Burnley who took the FA Cup home with them after their 1-0 victory at the old Crystal Palace ground.

Bill Lacey averaged over 30 League games a season for the next five years – effectively a decade because of the First World War – and was an important member of the Liverpool side that won the First Division Championship two years running in 1921-22 and 1922-23, wearing the No.7 jersey both seasons. However, he was only selected nine times during the 1924-25 season, by which time he was approaching his mid-thirties. It was no real surprise when he was allowed to leave Liverpool and move across the Mersey to join the New Brighton club.

Lacey played for Ireland while with both Everton and Liverpool. He made his debut against Wales in 1913, and won 10 and 12 caps respectively, before winning his 23rd and final cap at the age of 36, by which time he was playing for New Brighton. A jovial character with a prominent chin that was a target for cartoonists, he later returned to Ireland to see out his career with his first club Shelbourne.

BILLY GILLESPIE

The son of a policeman, Billy Gillespie spent the early part of his playing career in junior football in Londonderry. It did not take long for the forward's talent to be spotted, and at the age of 17 he signed for Derry Institute. In 1910 he was about to sign for Linfield when Leeds City manager Frank Scott-Walford persuaded him to turn professional and join the West Yorkshire club.

Second Division Leeds City were to be expelled from the Football League just nine years later, because of financial irregularities, but Gillespie spent barely 18 months with them before moving to another Yorkshire outfit. Sheffield United paid £500 for his services and offered him the maximum wage, then £4 a week.

Billy Gillespie's career at Bramall Lane spanned an astonishing 20 years, during which time he scored 137 goals in 492 games for the club. Although he missed out on an FA Cup winner's medal with United in 1915 because of a broken leg, he was instrumental in the Blades lifting the trophy again some ten years later, when they beat Cardiff City 1-0 in the Wembley final.

Whilst with United, he won 25 caps for Ireland, making him to this day, the Blades most capped international. In fact, Gillespie's career at international level got off to a most explosive start, when on his debut he scored twice as Ireland marked their first-ever victory, 2-1 over England. The following year in 1914, Gillespie was a member of the first-ever Irish side to win the British Championship, following victories over England and Wales and a draw against Scotland at Windsor Park.

Gillespie, who was a fierce-looking inside-forward, had quite an incredible record in matches with the old enemy, with seven of his 13 international goals coming against England. His total, which was subsequently equalled by former Portsmouth and Southampton striker Colin Clarke in 1992, was finally beaten after standing for 78 years when David Healy struck his 14th international goal in Northern Ireland's 2004 summer tour of the Caribbean. Gillespie's was an impressive total when you consider that in his era the only international matches that took place were against the other three home nations.

In 1932 he left England and returned to Ireland for a nine-year stint as manager of Derry City. Held in such a high regard by Derry, they changed their strip to red and white stripes in reverence to Gillespie and the Blades. During his tenure as Brandywell boss, he guided the club to two City Cup triumphs, as well as four successive Irish League runners-up spots. He also guided the club to the 1936 Irish Cup Final where they eventually lost 2-1 to Linfield, after the first meeting had ended in a goalless draw in front of a 23,000 strong crowd at Celtic Park.

When he left Derry City as manager in the summer of 1941, he settled in Kent where he lived until dying a month short of his 90th birthday in July 1981.

> **DID YOU KNOW?**
> Ireland's first victory over England saw them make an heroic comeback in the game in Belfast. England led 1-0 when Ireland were reduced to 10-men by an injury to one of their forwards. But two goals from Billy Gillespie lifted them to an historic victory.

PATSY GALLAGHER

The legendary Patsy Gallagher played 464 League and Cup games for Glasgow Celtic. Despite gracing the hallowed turf at Celtic Park in the 1920s, the reverence in which he was held lives on. Patsy Gallagher was born in the old Milford Workhouse in April 1893 and like many of his contemporaries, the family was destined to emigrate to Scotland. His parents went to Glasgow in search of work a few years after Patsy's birth and so began a tale of soccer greatness.

Patsy Gallagher was reputed to live and breathe football, and in 1907 he was playing for a juvenile side called Renfrew St James, one of the most successful sides in the area. He left school at 15 and began to serve his apprenticeship in carpentry at the famous John Brown's Shipyard. Selected to play for the Rest of Scotland against Lanarkshire, his stature and small frame were not seen as being suited to the more physical type of game that was traditional in that era. But Clydebank Juniors were the first to give him a chance and he played for them through the 1910-11 season.

His progress was steadily being brought to the attention of the Celtic manager Willie Maley, but as Gallagher starred for Clydebank, the season at Parkhead was a dismal one by their standards and new talent was urgently needed. The first time he was asked to play for the Bhoys, he was also asked to play for Clyde. Gallagher chose Celtic and so began the legend. He got his name on the scoresheet twice, and then on his next appearance – against an army team – he netted a hat-trick in a 5-0 win. Eventually he broke into the Celtic first team, displacing Paddy Travers. He helped them reach the Scottish Cup Final where they defeated Clyde. Having won a Scottish Cup medal, he nevertheless had to wait until 1914 for a League medal, and as war clouds gathered, he helped Celtic capture the Scottish Cup again.

Following the outbreak of the First World War, he went back to carpentry at John Brown's after being a full-time player for only one season. But the game went on and in 1915, the Parkhead club again won the title, with Gallagher recording a first-team hat-trick for the club in a 6-0 trouncing of Airdrie. He continued doing what he did best, scoring goals and helping his club to another record breaking season in 1916-17, as the Bhoys won another League title.

At the end of the hostilities, Gallagher was still working in the shipyard, as football could not provide sufficient money to keep a family. He went into the pub trade and purchased licensed premises in Clydebank. He continued playing football and in 1921 he had his best season for the club. He scored many memorable goals, including a brilliant individual effort against Hamilton Academicals – Celtic won the title by a narrow margin but it has become a part of the rich legend of the game. By this time, Patsy Gallagher was an international hero, having won the first of his 11 Irish caps and his star was still rising. He won his third Scottish Cup medal in 1923, but his most famous moment came two years later in his last Scottish Cup Final for Celtic.

The Bhoys were a goal down to Dundee and finding it difficult to break down a stubborn defence. Following a free-kick and in the ensuing scramble, Gallagher gathered the ball. Surrounded by defenders, he twisted and turned, weaved and feinted until halted near the goal-line – when he somersaulted over the line and into the net with the ball. A miraculous goal!

In October 1926 he joined Falkirk and remained on their books until his retirement in 1932. His career petered out as he reached 40 years of age and sadly for all his fans, his years at Brockville were not marked with any success. Gallagher was a ferocious competitor, totally committed to winning. However, another aspect to his character was revealed in 1953 after his death. Somebody found a drawer in his Clydebank pub stuffed with IOUs, amounting to hundreds of pounds which he had never bothered to redeem from his customers.

ELISHA SCOTT

Of all the goalkeepers to have pulled on the green jersey of Liverpool, none wore it with more distinction than Elisha Scott. The slim, sharp-faced Irishman – who kept guard between the posts at Anfield for more than 20 years – already followed in a long line of illustrious servants. His immediate predecessor

was Kenny Campbell, the Scottish international who had taken over from the great Sam Hardy, winner of 21 caps for England.

Born in Ulster, Scott initially played for Linfield and Broadway United before moving to Merseyside. He made his Liverpool debut on New Year's Day 1913 in a goalless draw at St James Park, and so impressed Newcastle United that they made an immediate offer for the young Irishman. Scott was keen to accept, arguing that Campbell was so outstanding that he could never hope to replace him at Anfield. The Liverpool manager, Tom Watson, knew better however, and politely refused.

After his debut Scott had to wait until the following season for his second appearance. With Campbell in outstanding form, it was not until the 1914-15 season that he broke into the first team. War then interrupted his career and on the resumption of soccer, it was Campbell who was again the automatic choice. But by now the Scottish keeper was at the end of his Anfield career and decided to move back north. Between 1921 and 1923, he had helped Liverpool to successive League Championships – being ever-present in 1921-22 and conceding only 13 goals at Anfield during the 1922-23 campaign.

The 1920s were also the days of Dixie Dean, and no contest in the Football League was more relished than the clash between Dean and Scott. So fierce was their rivalry that on one occasion, when they were said to have met in the street, Dean nodded in acknowledgement, only to see Scott fling himself to the ground to save some imaginary header. The story is almost certainly apocryphal, but it was typical of the legend that surrounded these two footballing giants.

As the 1933-34 season drew to a close, Scott, who had made 467 appearances for Liverpool, decided to return to Ireland as player-manager of Belfast Celtic. He was capped 27 times while at Anfield and even added a further four caps to his tally after this, making his final international appearance at the grand old age of 42.

Elisha Scott would wear, even in summer, two or three jerseys and a couple of pairs of shorts pulled on over long-johns and knee-pads. This bulky apparel would be donned at least an hour or so before kick-off and he would then spend the remaining hour or so hurling a ball against the dressing-room wall to practise his catching. It was typical of a man who was a perfectionist and who helped turn goalkeeping into a fine art.

JOE BAMBRICK

Describing Joe Bambrick as a 'prolific goalscorer' hardly does justice to a player who is believed to have scored close on 1000 goals during his career. While the majority of Bambrick's goals came during his time with Linfield, the Belfast-born forward will probably be best remembered for netting a double hat-trick for Ireland in a 7-0 drubbing of Wales on 1 February 1930, an Irish record which is unlikely ever to be beaten!

The strongly built and powerful player's first taste of top-class football actually came with Glentoran, for whom he managed to score 44 goals in just 37 games during his one and only season at the Oval. By the start of the 1927-28 season, Bambrick had switched his allegiances to Windsor Park and Glentoran's cross-town rivals Linfield. By the end of his first season, he had found the net an incredible 81 times. However, two years later he was to eclipse even that phenomenal total when he scored an amazing 94 goals – six of which came against the Welsh on that memorable day at Celtic Park.

On the international front, Joe Bambrick had won his first cap against England in 1928, just 12 days short of his 23rd birthday. True to form, he scored an equalising goal at Goodison Park, just half-an-hour into the game. Despite terrorising defences at club level, over the next decade, he was rather surprisingly only chosen for the national side intermittently, eventually finishing with a very impressive tally of 12 goals in just 11 international matches.

In December 1934, Joe Bambrick – who had naturally become a cult figure among Blues supporters – was on his way to England and Chelsea. Although he found the competition across the water a good deal more intense, he still managed a very respectable 37 goals in 66 appearances over three seasons at Stamford Bridge.

A move to Walsall ensued in March 1938 but his stay with the Saddlers was a brief one. It wasn't long before he returned to his beloved Linfield, for whom he eventually coached and scouted following his retirement from the game. Joe Bambrick, who died in October 1983, aged 77, was a true gentleman both on and off the pitch and was without doubt, one of the greatest strikers ever to have graced an Irish side. If he were playing for the modern day Chelsea in the much-hyped Premiership, his value would be incalculable.

> **DID YOU KNOW?**
> On 1 February 1930, Joe Bambrick scored six goals in Northern Ireland's 7-0 victory over Wales, the highest individual tally in a Home International.

PETER DOHERTY

Peter Doherty is regarded by many as the finest footballer ever produced by Ireland. Those who didn't know him regarded him as a discontented footballer, others felt he was a man and a player ahead of his time. He first worked as a bricklayer and bus conductor and started his career with Coleraine prior to a move to Glentoran, who he helped win the Irish FA Cup. In November 1933 he joined Blackpool and soon became conspicuous as a brilliant inside-forward, and in 1935 played against England and Wales.

After two years by the seaside, Doherty joined Manchester City for a club record £10,000 which was only a thousand short of the then British record. The Irishman was a star in the League Championship-winning side of 1936-37, scoring an incredible 30 goals in his 41 League appearances, but there was far more to

Doherty's game than hitting the back of the net. He could tackle like a defender, dribble like a winger and shoot and head as well as any in the game, before and after the Second World War, to which Doherty and many of his generation lost the best years of his career.

From 1939 to 1945 he served in the Royal Air Force as a PT instructor-sergeant. He then joined Derby County for £6,000 and alongside another legend in Raich Carter, he helped the Rams win the 1946 FA Cup Final. He scored one of the goals in the 4-1 win over Charlton Athletic, but not before the ball burst in the last five minutes of normal time with the score at 1-1. Doherty claimed the first goal of extra-time and then laid on number three and number four to take the first post-war FA Cup back to the Baseball Ground.

Unfortunately the strong-willed Irishman fell out with the Derby board after directors refused him permission to take over as a licensee of a hotel near the club's ground, fearing that it would affect his game. Peter Doherty joined Huddersfield Town for £10,000, just seven months after the FA Cup triumph, and with an impressive goal tally of 17 in just 25 matches for County. But he stayed just three seasons at Leeds Road, scoring 36 goals in 87 appearances before leaving to become player-manager of Doncaster Rovers. In his first season at Belle Vue, Doherty scored 26 goals as Rovers won the Third Division, and though he retired as a player in 1949 he remained as manager until January 1958.

It is a travesty that such a distinguished player won just 16 full caps for his country, though he more than compensated for that by steering Northern Ireland to the quarter-finals of the 1958 World Cup as manager. That achievement was a fitting highlight of his 11-year tenure as manager of the national side which ended in 1962.

DANNY BLANCHFLOWER

Danny Blanchflower was not just a wonderfully gifted footballer but also one of the most tactically aware players of his generation. Like many working-class boys of his generation, Danny Blanchflower learned to play football at school and on the streets and waste ground of Belfast. During the early part of the Second World War, he formed his own club, Bloomfield United. He was establishing a reputation for himself and in 1942, shortly before his 16th birthday, he was signed as an amateur by the local professional team Glentoran. He returned from military service fitter and stronger, and soon won a place in Glentoran's first team in the Irish League. In February 1947, Blanchflower played for the Irish League against the Football League, a side containing the likes of Stanley Matthews, Billy Wright, Tom Finney and Tommy Lawton.

He fell out with Glentoran about money, and in 1948-49 their directors agreed that if an English club wanted him, he could have one-third of the transfer fee! Only Second Division Barnsley made an offer and in April 1949 he joined the Oakwell club for a fee of £6,500. Within six months of joining the Yorkshire club, Blanchflower won the first of his 56 caps for Northern Ireland. He played against Scotland at Windsor Park, but it wasn't the happiest of debuts as the Scots won 8-2.

In March 1951 he was transferred to Aston Villa for £15,000 but though he captained the side on many occasions, he became unhappy with the club and the way training was conducted. Blanchflower became one of the first to propose that players should train with a ball, as opposed to merely undertaking physical exercise.

In 1954, Blanchflower was on the verge of signing for Arsenal for a then record fee. At the last moment, the deal fell through and he went to Tottenham Hotspur for £30,000. Arthur Rowe, who had built the stylish Spurs team of the early 1950s, had retired because of illness and his successor Jimmy Anderson was a much more old-fashioned manager. He fell out with Blanchflower and removed him from the captaincy. In October 1958, Bill Nicholson replaced Anderson and though initially he disciplined Blanchflower by dropping him, he later reinstated him as captain. Although very

different in character, they were both keen on new ways of playing, based on what they had seen of the control, passing, movement and possession of the Brazilians and the Hungarians.

Blanchflower had captained Northern Ireland to the quarter-finals of the 1958 World Cup and in the same year was voted Footballer of the Year by the football writers. In his early thirties, he was at the height of his powers and an intelligent creator of time and space on the pitch. In 1959-60 Spurs finished third in the First Division, having finished 18th in 1958-59. The following season, the North London club won the double with a style that made Spurs the second-favourite team of most football enthusiasts. For Blanchflower, it was a personal triumph recognised by a second award as Footballer of the Year. The FA Cup was won again the next year and the European Cup Winners' Cup the year after that, but the glory of 1960-61 could never be recaptured.

Danny Blanchflower was someone who could think and talk about the game as effectively as he played it. He had been writing columns in various papers since his Villa days for the *Birmingham Evening Mail* and then after his move south for the *London Evening News*. By the time of his retirement in 1964, he had ten years' experience and he worked for the *Sunday Express* as a columnist from 1964 to 1988. Blanchflower was a private man and refused to take part in the television programme 'This is your Life' in 1961, but he wanted people to know who he was and became the first professional footballer to appear on Desert Island Discs!

After retiring as a player he withdrew from football for several years, returning briefly as manager of Northern Ireland in 1978 and as manager of Chelsea in 1978-79, whom he failed to save from relegation. He eventually left the job less than a year after his appointment. In the later years of his life, he suffered from Alzheimer's Disease and died at his home in December 1993, aged 67. In 2003, the popular Irishman was inducted into the English Football Hall of Fame in recognition of his talents.

BILLY BINGHAM

Billy Bingham was a small, elusive right-winger who provided fine deliveries from the flank. Among his dribbling skills he would 'pretend' to stumble whilst in control of the ball, a trick which would often throw his opponents off balance.

He started his illustrious playing career with Glentoran and after starring in a representative game for the Irish League in 1951, First Division Sunderland paid £8,000 to take him to Roker Park. Within a couple of years of his arrival in the north-east Bingham, who'd won the first of his 56 caps for Northern Ireland against France in May 1951, was a permanent member of the national side. He had scored 47 goals in 227 games for the Wearsiders when on his return from the 1958 World Cup Finals in Sweden, he joined Luton Town for a fee of £15,000.

For a winger, Billy Bingham was unusually combative in the air – as he showed on numerous occasions – although the majority of his goals came from long distance. In his first season with the Hatters, Bingham scored 14 goals including the winner in the FA Cup semi-final replay against Norwich City at St Andrew's. Though the Kenilworth Road club lost their top flight status the following season, Bingham was the Hatters' top scorer with 16 goals.

In October 1960 Bingham left Luton to join Everton, and though he was by now in his 30th year, he was supremely fit. The winger's penetrating style on the right flank became a key ingredient in the Merseyside club's 1962-63 League Championship-winning side. However, after he had lost his place in the Blues' side to Scottish international Alex Scott, he left Goodison Park to join Port Vale. He hadn't been with the Valiants long when in 1964, a broken leg brought his playing days to an end.

On hanging up his boots, he became manager of Southport and in his first season at Haig Avenue, led the Sandgrounders to promotion for the first time in their history. After spells with Plymouth and Linfield, Bingham took charge of the Greek national side before in the summer of 1973, being appointed manager of Everton.

The club finished seventh in his first season in charge. Having brought in players of the calibre of Martin Dobson and Bob Latchford, it seemed as if the club would win the 1974-75 League title, but after winning just one of their last five games, they finished fourth. After finishing in mid-table the following season, Everton then had a run of eight League games without a win and in January 1977, Bingham was sacked.

Awarded the OBE, Bingham managed the Northern Ireland side in two spells, leading them to the World Cup Finals in 1982 and 1986.

JIMMY McILROY

Though it is perhaps impossible to compare players of the 'modern' era to those who appeared in bygone days, most followers of Burnley would present an overwhelming case that 'Mac', signed from Glentoran for a bargain £8,000 in March 1950, was the finest Clarets' player of all-time. Even in the outstanding Burnley side that was forged in the late 1950s and peaked in the early 1960s as First Division champions, FA Cup finalists and European Cup ambassadors, Jimmy McIlroy was undoubtedly the most skilful individual talent in a team of all the talents. When the great man left Turf Moor in 1963, not only was the team never the same again, somehow the club was never the same either.

Jimmy McIlroy began playing football for the Craigavad Club near Bangor and his performances were soon being monitored by scouts from Glentoran. It wasn't long before he put pen to paper, and he eventually made his first team debut on the final day of the 1948-49 season. The

following campaign saw him become a regular in the Glentoran side, where one of his team-mates was Billy Bingham.

In March 1950, Burnley boss Frank Hill became the latest in a long line of admirers to cross the water to assess the inside-forward's ability. He was treated to a particularly inspiring performance for Glentoran against Distillery and Hill was convinced – contracts were soon exchanged and Glentoran's bank account was boosted by £8,000 as McIlroy moved to Turf Moor.

Early the following season, an unsettled Harry Potts was transferred to Everton, with McIlroy seen as his natural replacement. So in October 1950, four days before his 19th birthday, Jimmy McIlroy made his First Division debut for Burnley, embarking on a truly memorable Football League career.

Within a year, in October 1951, whilst still a teenager, McIlroy won the first of 55 international caps for Northern Ireland against Scotland – his display ensured that he would be virtually a permanent member of his country's line-up as well as that of his club, for the next decade. In August 1955 McIlroy became acknowledged as one of the greatest football talents in these islands, when he was selected for a Great Britain representative side to play the Rest of Europe at Belfast's Windsor Park, to commemorate the 75th anniversary of the formation of the Irish FA.

In Burnley's League Championship-winning season of 1959-60 and the two campaigns that followed, the McIlroy/Adamson partnership was at its magnificent best, the engine room that drove a wonderful team. In 1962 the Clarets came agonisingly close to a League and FA Cup double, but a loss of form by the whole team over the closing weeks deprived the little East Lancashire club of immortality. As it was, McIlroy was just edged into second place in the 'Footballer of the Year' competition by is skipper Jimmy Adamson.

Then in February 1963 the unimaginable happened, as McIlroy was placed on the transfer

list after a series of hush-hush meetings by the club's board of directors. It came as a shock to the genial Irishman, who then joined Stoke City for just £25,000. At the Victoria Ground, he played alongside such greats as Stanley Matthews, Denis Viollet and Jackie Mudie as the Potters went on to win the Second Division Championship at the end of his first season with the club. In 1964 Stoke reached their first-ever major final, but even with McIlroy in the side they were beaten 4-3 on aggregate by Leicester City in a two-legged League Cup Final.

In January 1966 he joined Oldham Athletic, struggling in Division Three as their player-manager, although he had intended to hang up his boots after leaving Stoke. After returning to the Victoria Ground as Stoke's chief coach, he spent just 18 days as team manager of Bolton Wanderers before abruptly leaving Burnden Park.

McIlroy then spent many years as a much respected journalist, primarily as a Sports Reporter but later developing a reputation as a fine features writer. Now retired, Jimmy McIlroy will forever be a sporting hero in his adopted town of Burnley – he was quite simply, the greatest Claret of them all.

PETER McPARLAND

One of Aston Villa's greatest post-war goalscoring wingers, Peter McParland, a hero of the 1958 World Cup, also ranks as his country's greatest outside-left. He first came to the notice of followers of Northern Ireland football when, at the age of 18, he played for Tandragee Rovers against the Irish League champions, Glenavon. He later played for Newry and Dundalk, from where Aston Villa manager George Martin bought him for a fee of just £3,880 in the summer of 1952.

Fast, direct and with a powerful shot in either foot, McParland quickly made his mark with Villa, going on to give them invaluable service for the next decade. His early form led to him winning the first of 34 full caps for Northern Ireland when in March 1954, he scored both his country's goals in a 2-1 defeat of Wales.

McParland was also the scorer of a number of goals for Villa during their run to the FA Cup Final of 1956-57 – one in the third round against Luton, two in the quarter-final against Burnley and another double in the semi-final with West Bromwich Albion. In the final itself, the Irish winger netted both his side's goals in a 2-1 win over Manchester United, a result which denied United the coveted League and Cup double. However, the final is best remembered for McParland's accidental clash with United keeper Ray Wood, who broke his jaw and was taken off to be replaced by Northern Ireland international Jackie Blanchflower in goal.

In 1958, McParland represented Northern Ireland in the World Cup Finals in Sweden, making an immense impact by scoring five goals in the tournament (including doubles against West Germany and in the play-off game against Czechoslovakia). McParland went on to play a major role as the injury-plagued side were beaten 4-0 in the quarter-finals by France.

In 1959-60 he helped Villa win the Second Division Championship and during the course of the campaign, in which he scored 25 League and Cup goals, he represented the Football League against the Italian League. In the two-legged League Cup Final of 1961, he netted the winner against Rotherham United, but the following January, having scored 120 goals in 341 games for Aston Villa – a phenomenal record for an out-and-out winger – he left to play for local rivals Wolverhampton Wanderers.

He never really settled at Molineux and moved to Plymouth Argyle where he ended his League career. Following a spell playing for the Atlanta Chiefs and then non-League Worcester City, he went into management with Glentoran, leading them to an Irish League title. He then spent much of his time afterwards coaching abroad, particularly in Cyprus (where he coached with Ray Wood!), Kuwait and Hong Kong from his base on the south coast.

DEREK DOUGAN

Known wherever he played as simply the 'Doog', Derek Dougan was one of the greatest characters Northern Ireland football has known. He shaved his head, then grew a beard, wore an American Indian headband and fought for players' rights as chairman of the Professional Football Association.

He began his professional career at Fratton Park, Portsmouth in the summer of 1957, having had a brief spell with Distillery, his home-town club. He remained with the south coast club until March 1959 when he was transferred to Blackburn Rovers for £15,000. A year later he had scored the two semi-final goals that defeated Sheffield Wednesday to take Rovers through to the FA Cup final against one of his future clubs, Wolverhampton Wanderers. Unbelievably, he posted a letter to the Lancashire club, seeking a transfer on the morning of their 1960 FA Cup Final, which 10-men Rovers lost 3-0.

Following the departure of Gerry Hitchens to Inter Milan, Aston Villa secured Dougan's services but within two years he was on the move again, this time to Peterborough United. There is little doubt that his spell with Posh in the Third Division helped to restore his sense of perspective, and in the summer of 1966 he took a pay cut to join Leicester City. Leading the Foxes forward line with his unique flair, he lapped up the crowd's adulation, not least on the occasion when he netted a superb hat-trick against his former club, Aston Villa.

The possessor of an excellent football brain, Dougan joined Ronnie Allen's Wolverhampton Wanderers where over the next eight seasons, he became a Molineux Legend, scoring 123 goals in 323 League and Cup games. He helped the Wanderers clinch promotion from Division

Two in 1966-67 and then collected a League Cup winners' medal in 1974. In between times he played his part in Wolves' UEFA Cup run to the final in 1971-72 when he netted a hat-trick against Portuguese side Academica – the only Wolves player to have netted a treble in a major European competition. Four days before that game, Dougan had netted three goals when Wolves beat Nottingham Forest!

While still an active member of the Wolves' side, Dougan became Chairman of the PFA. Capped 43 times by Northern Ireland, he was forever involved with officialdom, being sent-off at least half-a-dozen times in his colourful career.

A stimulating and entertaining TV pundit, he surprised few when he later moved into management, albeit with non-League Kettering Town. In 1982 he returned to Molineux as the club's Chief Executive, a position he held briefly before circumstances made him quit the club. More recently he has been involved in raising money for various charities and has worked on several committees, quite a few relating to the game of football. In the summer of 2006 he appeared on the BBC political debate show 'Question Time', as a representative of UKIP.

GEORGE BEST

George Best was, without doubt, the greatest player to ever pull on the green shirt of Northern Ireland. His death towards the end of November 2005 brought tributes from all over the world, in recognition of his stunning, natural talent.

The son of a shipyard worker, Best was brought up in one of the red-brick streets of Belfast, and his keenness on the game led to him giving up the chance of going to a grammar school, because he wanted to go on playing soccer. Within 48 hours of starting his career with Manchester United, Best, along with another gifted Irishman Eric McMordie, became homesick and returned to Belfast. It was his father who insisted that he return to Old Trafford, and by the age of 17 he was in United's League team.

Above: George Best

22 years of age. That year he also deservedly won the English and European Footballer of the Year awards. He was also United's top scorer with 28 goals, and remained top scorer for the following four seasons. In 1970 he scored six of United's goals as they beat Northampton Town 8-2 at the County ground – the most goals ever scored in a single match by any United player.

His goals, many of which have been captured on television – such as the dazzling runs against Sheffield United and West Ham and the delicate lob against Spurs – have become all-time classics. Nicknamed 'the fifth Beatle', Best was one of the most famous stars in Britain during his time at Old Trafford. He was the first pop-star footballer, a personification of youth culture and the Swinging Sixties. He had the good looks and the style and the girls went mad for him, with Best getting 10,000 fan-mail letters a week! Sadly, it was this pop star image that proved his eventual downfall – for he began to live the lifestyle of a pop star and not a footballer. As he became a casualty of intense media attention, he could not concentrate on the game without being hounded everywhere by paparazzi. He opened a nightclub and a number of boutiques, which were not a success.

Once Sir Matt Busby retired in 1969, it was downhill for the Ulsterman, as United under his successors O'Farrell and Docherty fell into decline. With United being beaten by teams they used to hammer a few years ago, Best took solace in the bottle, with drinking and partying taking over his entire life. He was by now frequently missing training and failing to turn up for games. In 1972 he announced his retirement at only 26, but was persuaded back by Docherty. His comeback was not a success and he played his last game for United against Queen's Park Rangers on New Year's Day 1974. He then played for numerous other clubs, most notably with Fulham. Stockport County and Hibernian followed, then American teams Los Angeles Aztecs, Fort Lauderdale Strikers and San Jose Earthquakes. He finally ended his football career with Bournemouth in 1983 although he went on to play in many charity and friendly matches. In 2000, Best's health hit rock bottom due to liver damage, although in

He made his League debut in a home fixture against West Bromwich Albion and even then, it was plain to see that the young Best had it all: balance, pace, bravery, vision and most of all outstanding dribbling skills. The youngster from the Cregagh Estate had the world at his feet.

He won the first of his 37 international caps for Northern Ireland before he turned 18, in a 3-2 victory over Wales at Swansea. It wasn't long before he was a household name throughout Britain and was the most important member of the great United team which won the League Championship twice in the 1960s. By 1966, 'George Best superstar' had arrived, especially after his magnificent performance in United's 5-1 thrashing of Benfica in Lisbon, where he scored twice.

After five years of playing some breathtaking football, Best secured his place in history in 1968, as United became the first English team to win the European Cup, with the Irishman scoring a superb solo goal in a 4-1 defeat of Benfica. In 1968 Best was at his peak – at only

July 2002 he had a successful liver transplant operation and made a full recovery. Personal problems continued to hound him as he was divorced for a second time and appeared unable to beat the bottle.

In October 2005, Best entered the Cromwell hospital with flu-like symptoms, later diagnosed as a kidney infection. Susceptible to infection because of the medicines needed after his transplant, his condition deteriorated. Though he fought on for far longer than the doctors ever expected, he eventually lost his battle for life. In Belfast, Manchester and around the world, the whole of football mourned at the death of a legend. A week later, the Belfast Boy came home to his native city, where 100,000 people lined the streets and grounds of Stormont for the funeral of Northern Ireland's greatest sporting hero.

Above: Pat Jennings

PAT JENNINGS

Northern Ireland have always had a reputation for producing outstanding goalkeepers but very few would dispute that Pat Jennings is the finest of them all. His career spanned an amazing 22 years, during which time he was not only the best keeper in Britain, but undoubtedly the world.

Having started out by playing Gaelic football for North Down Schools, he turned to football with Newry Town's junior club, Newry United. After just one season with the juniors and a little over six months with Newry Town, Jennings joined Watford for a fee of £6,000. After 48 consecutive appearances for the Hornets, who were then playing in the Third Division of the Football League, Jennings was snapped up by Spurs boss Bill Nicholson, who splashed out the princely sum of £27,000 for him in the summer of 1964.

Prior to arriving at White Hart Lane, Jennings had made his full international debut alongside a 17-year-old George Best against Wales in Swansea in April 1964. This was to be the start of an international career that yielded 119 caps over a 22 year period.

During 13 years with Spurs, 'Big Pat' won numerous trophies including an FA Cup winners' medal in 1967, a UEFA Cup winners' medal in 1972 and two League Cup winners' medals in 1971 and 1973. In August 1967, Jennings performed that coveted and extremely rare feat for a keeper when he scored a goal with a long downfield punt in the 2-2 draw against Manchester United at Old Trafford in the FA Charity Shield.

Jennings was named the Football Writers' Association Player of the Year in 1972-73, as well as the PFA Player of the Year in 1976. He went on to set a record number of appearances for the club, a figure only bettered by Steve Perryman. The popular Irishman was awarded the MBE for his services to the game in the 1976 Queen's Birthday Honours List. His achievements were also honoured by the North London club with a testimonial game against Arsenal. Although he was rarely injured, when he was in 1976-77, Spurs were relegated!

At the end of that season, the Spurs boss Keith Burkinshaw came to the conclusion that at 32,

Jennings' best days were behind him and allowed him to join rivals Arsenal for a paltry fee of just £45,000. He soon came to regret that decision as Jennings proved he was far from over the hill, making nearly 400 appearances for the Gunners and playing in three successive FA Cup Finals, picking up a European Cup Winners' Cup runners-up medal and making a further 42 international appearances for his country.

Jennings' proudest moment came in the 1982 World Cup Finals in Spain, when Northern Ireland defeated the host nation 1-0. Jennings single handedly kept the Spaniards at bay with an outstanding display of goalkeeping. His performance at Wembley against England in 1985 is another that will live long in the memory, as he produced a number of reflex saves to earn his side a goalless draw – and the point they required to make it through to the 1986 World Cup Finals in Mexico.

The tournament was to be Pat Jennings' swansong. Although it was fitting that his 119th and final match would be against the wonderfully talented Brazilians on his 41st birthday, Billy Bingham's side went down 3-0. Though the conclusion of the World Cup saw Jennings officially retire, he later captained the Rest of the World XI against the Americas in a FIFA/UNICEF charity match. He briefly returned to the Northern Ireland fold as goalkeeping coach when Lawrie McMenemy took over the running of the national side in 1998. Nowadays he still resides in London where he occasionally works as a Match Day Host for his beloved Tottenham Hotspur.

Above: Bryan Hamilton

BRYAN HAMILTON

Having played his early football for Distillery and Linfield, where he won the first of his 50 caps for Northern Ireland in a 3-0 defeat of Turkey, Bryan Hamilton moved across the water to play for Ipswich Town in the summer of 1971. It was during his time with the Suffolk club that Hamilton enjoyed his best moments as a player, revelling under manager Bobby Robson in a very talented Ipswich side. After appearing in only a handful of games in 1971-72, Hamilton was an ever-present and joint-top scorer the following season with 11 goals. In 1973-74 he was Town's leading scorer, with 16 goals in 41 games as the Tractor Boys finished fourth in the First Division. Hamilton's only hat-trick for the Portman Road club came in March 1975 as Newcastle United were beaten 5-4. Hamilton had taken his tally of goals to 56 in 199 games when he left Ipswich to join Everton for a fee of £40,000.

Though the Belfast-born midfielder wasn't a prolific scorer at international level, he did have the happy knack of scoring vital goals for his country – three of his four goals for Northern Ireland came in 1-0 wins over Wales (twice) and Yugoslavia.

Hamilton appeared for the Merseyside outfit in the 1977 League Cup Final, although he will always be remembered by the Goodison faithful for scoring the 'goal that never was'. The FA Cup semi-final tie against rivals Liverpool stood at 2-2 when with just seconds remaining, Hamilton's thigh deflected a Duncan McKenzie flick into the Liverpool net. Everyone inside the Maine Road ground thought that the Irish international had put the Blues into the 1977 FA Cup Final. However, it was to become an infamous slice of Goodison folklore when referee Clive Thomas disallowed the effort for alleged handball. The score remained at 2-2 and Liverpool won the replay.

Though his goalscoring tally fell away on Merseyside, he more than compensated by precise passing and mature reading of the game, as well as demonstrating formidable eagerness and phenomenal lung power. Midway through the 1976-77 season, Hamilton lost his place in the Everton side and he joined Millwall for £25,000 in the close season. Hamilton later played for Swindon Town before joining Tranmere Rovers as player-manager. He saw several crises through at Prenton Park, before leaving the Wirral-based club to take over the manager's role at Wigan Athletic.

A Freight Rover Trophy win in May 1985 was the highlight of his time with the Latics, and in June 1986 he was appointed manager of Leicester City. Despite a promising start, the Foxes were relegated in 1986-87, and as he was unable to halt the slide which threatened to lead to Third Division football, he lost his job in December 1987. After returning to Springfield Park as Wigan's Chief Executive, Hamilton later re-assumed control of team matters. After leaving Wigan a second time, Hamilton became a surprise choice to succeed Billy Bingham as manager of Northern Ireland. On parting company with the national side, Hamilton has twice been called in to add his experience to the Ipswich backroom staff and had a spell in charge of rivals Norwich City.

Above: Sammy McIlroy

SAMMY McILROY

As with a number of Belfast schoolboys, the only team Sammy McIlroy set his eyes upon was Manchester United and at 15 years of age, he crossed the Irish Sea to join the Old Trafford club and follow in the footsteps of George Best. McIlroy signed for the Red Devils in September 1969, with the notable distinction of being the last Busby babe. He turned professional two years later, and became one of that rare breed to make their Football League debut in a Manchester derby. He was withdrawn from a reserve game by the club's new manager Frank O'Farrell to wear the No. 10 shirt, and responded in magnificent style to score the first goal in a pulsating 3-3 draw. Sadly, the fairytale soon turned sour when the Irish midfielder was injured in a motorcycle accident, and remained out of action for more than half of the 1972-73 season.

After regaining full fitness, McIlroy gained a regular place in the United side under manager Tommy Docherty, a team that was destined for relegation to Division Two. Like his team-

mates, he learned from the experience and once restored to the top flight, added double-figure goalscoring to his playmaking skills.

McIlroy had won the first of his 88 international caps for Northern Ireland before his accident, and soon became as important a part of the national side as he was to Manchester United. Awarded the MBE as Northern Ireland went on to World Cup glory in Spain in 1982 and Mexico four years later, McIlroy ended his international career with a substitute appearance against England in 1987.

The Irishman was a midfielder full of energy and attacking purpose as the Red Devils clinched the Second Division Championship. After appearing in the 1976 FA Cup Final, McIlroy gained a winners' medal the following season as Liverpool were beaten 2-1. Two years later he made a third appearance only to finish up a loser again.

Despite being a permanent member of the Northern Ireland side, winning 52 caps whilst a Red, United boss Ron Atkinson didn't see him as part of Manchester United's future plans. During the early part of 1982, McIlroy left Old Trafford to join Stoke City, this after scoring 69 goals in 408 League and Cup games. After a fairly discouraging time spent in the Potteries, McIlroy returned to Manchester, this time joining City. He played just a dozen games in blue, including the 3-0 reverse of September 1985, his only derby fixture on the 'other side'.

McIlroy then tried his luck in Sweden with Örgryte before returning to the north-west with Bury. After spending the 1986-87 season with the Shakers, he followed it with another spell abroad in Austria with VFB Mödling before he ended his first-class career with a brief period at Preston North End.

On hanging up his boots, McIlroy became one of the major managers in non-League football, especially with Macclesfield whom he led to two Conference titles and victory in the 1996 FA Trophy Final at Wembley against Northwich Victoria. After helping the Silkmen win promotion to the Football League, he parted company with the club in 2000 to take

over the reins of the Northern Ireland side. The popular midfielder resigned after the last of the 2004 European Championship qualifiers against Greece, later having a spell as manager of Stockport County.

MARTIN O'NEILL

Midfielder Martin O'Neill had just won an Irish Cup winners' medal with his local club Distillery in a 3-0 defeat of Derry City when in October 1971 he joined Nottingham Forest. After making his Football League debut for the injured Scottish international winger John Robertson in a 4-1 win over West Bromwich Albion at the City Ground, a month after signing for Forest, he then faded from the scene and played most of his football for the club's reserves. Indeed, O'Neill was languishing in the second team and had been placed on the transfer list when Brian Clough was appointed Forest manager. He seemed to transform O'Neill into a tenacious midfielder, and it wasn't too long before the Irishman found himself back in Forest's League side.

Above: Martin O'Neill

Throughout his playing career, Martin O'Neill was an automatic choice for Northern Ireland, winning a total of 64 caps. With Forest, he won a League Championship medal in 1977-78, two League Cup winners' medals in 1977-78 and 1978-79, and a European Cup winners' medal in 1980 as the Reds beat German side Hamburg SV – this after he'd been left out of the Forest side to face Swedish champions Malmö the previous season!

Having scored 62 goals in 371 first team games, including a most spectacular hat-trick in a 6-0 mauling of Chelsea, O'Neill was rather surprisingly allowed to leave the City Ground and sign for Norwich City. At Carrow Road he helped the Canaries avoid relegation from the top flight in 1981-82 before leaving to play for Manchester City. He had been at Maine Road for less than a year when he decided to rejoin Norwich for a second spell, eventually helping them win promotion to the First Division. In 1983 he opted for a return to the city of Nottingham but this time to County, where unfortunately injury brought a premature end to his playing career. Following spells in non-League management with both Grantham Town and Shepshed Charterhouse, O'Neill left the game due to his business commitments. However, in February 1990 he was lured back by Wycombe Wanderers and three years later he led them into the Football League.

After resisting offers to manage at the highest level, O'Neill finally returned to take over the reins at one of his former clubs, Norwich City. After just six months in the Carrow Road hot seat, he left to manage Leicester City. The Foxes lost their first nine matches under O'Neill's leadership, but seven wins in their last ten games saw them win a place in the First Division play-offs. In the play-off final at Wembley, Leicester beat Crystal Palace 2-1 to win a place in the top flight.

Also whilst at Filbert Street, he led Leicester to success in the League Cup but in 2000 Celtic came calling, and O'Neill couldn't resist the chance to manage the Parkhead club. Inspired by his motivational skills, the Bhoys swept the board in his first season with the club, and during his five years at the helm continued to win silverware. In 2003 he led Celtic to the UEFA Cup Final, beating English Premiership clubs Blackburn Rovers and Liverpool along the way. Sadly, O'Neill's side failed at the last hurdle, losing 3-2 to José Mourinho's Porto side. More domestic success followed before in May 2005 he decided to resign his post to look after his wife Geraldine, who had been suffering from ill-health for some time.

Once favourite for the England manager's job vacated by Sven-Göran Eriksson, Martin O'Neill, who was awarded the OBE for his work at Celtic, spent the summer of 2006 as a World Cup TV pundit. After months of speculation linking the genial Irishman with a number of top managerial posts, he has recently replaced David O'Leary as manager of Premiership Aston Villa.

GERRY ARMSTRONG

Gerry Armstrong wrote himself into the Northern Ireland history books by hitting the country's winning goal against host nation Spain in Valencia in the 1982 World Cup Finals. When he crossed the Irish Sea to join Tottenham Hotspur from Bangor in 1975, he was raw, hungry and ready for action. One of the game's most best-loved and genuine characters, it might be said that the big striker had barely altered when he left White Hart Lane for Watford five years later. Of course there had been certain refinements to his method, but essentially Gerry Armstrong would always remain a prodigiously strong, selfless workaholic – a colossus in the air and with heart enough for ten men!

Not that he was he was devoid of technique: his team-mates knew that they could knock the ball towards him and, having fought for it and won it, he could retain possession until reinforcements arrived. With the Argentinian influence of Ardiles and Villa placing extra emphasis on touch play, Armstrong was not in his element in North London, and he didn't help his standing with the fans by battling on uncomplainingly when he was injured, thus unable to do himself full justice.

Above: Gerry Armstrong

As stars were bought, his departure became inevitable and in the summer of 1980 he joined Watford for a fee of £250,000. Even so he found it hard to establish himself at Vicarage Road, and it was therefore somewhat surprising that a place in folklore on the international scene was awaiting him.

Having made his debut for Northern Ireland in April 1977 and won 27 caps as a Spurs player, he was already an established member of the province's team when they travelled to Spain for the finals of the 1982 World Cup. The Irish were rated no-hopers by almost every international expert but by the end of the tournament, they had earned respect throughout the game for their spirit, tenacity and skill. After holding Yugoslavia to a 1-1 draw, Armstrong opened the scoring in the game against Honduras. His team failed to hold on to their lead and again they had to be satisfied with a share of the spoils. This meant that Northern Ireland almost certainly had to beat the host nation Spain to qualify for the next round.

Over 49,000 fans crammed into the Luis Casanova Stadium in Valencia expecting to see a Spanish victory, but an Armstrong strike booked Billy Bingham's boys a place in the second phase of the tournament. Confronted by three Spanish defenders, he passed the ball out wide to Billy Hamilton, who hammered in a low centre. Spanish keeper Arconada could only parry the ball into the path of Armstrong, and the Ulsterman seized his chance to fire home the winner, despite the efforts of the Spanish defenders. Not surprisingly his spirited exploits in Spain earned him the award as British Player of the Tournament.

A year later, he left the Hornets and signed for Real Mallorca, spending two years with the Spanish club. On his return to the UK, he joined West Bromwich Albion before following a brief loan spell with Chesterfield, he signed for Brighton and Hove Albion. Though the Seagulls were relegated in 1986-87, Armstrong remained registered as a player as well becoming the club's Youth Development Officer.

His League career came to a sad end in February 1989 when he left the Goldstone Ground after being convicted of assaulting a fan. He then dabbled in the management game at non-League level, before carving out a fairly high-profile career as a television pundit and renowned expert on the European game. It is this knowledge which prompted Northern Ireland boss Lawrie Sanchez to ask the popular Armstrong to become his assistant, and fulfil a position that the former striker last occupied under Bryan Hamilton.

NORMAN WHITESIDE

Norman Whiteside will always be remembered as 'the youngest at everything'. At 17 he was the youngest player to represent Manchester United since Duncan Edwards; the youngest player to score in an FA Cup Final, and also the youngest player ever to appear in a World Cup Finals tournament when in 1982 he was just 17 years and 41 days old.

Born in North Belfast, Whiteside was spotted by United's legendary Ulster scout Bob Bishop, who

Above: Norman Whiteside

His performances for the national side were equally telling. He scored the goal in Northern Ireland's astonishing defeat of West Germany in Hamburg in 1983, and laid the groundwork for Jimmy Quinn's goal in Bucharest, which gave Northern Ireland qualification for the 1986 World Cup Finals at Romania's expense. When Whiteside went to Mexico, he became the youngest player ever to appear in two World Cup tournaments.

It was around this time that Whiteside adopted a position deeper in midfield both for United and Northern Ireland before he began to lose a bit of form and became increasingly upset by injuries. When Alex Ferguson took over as United boss, he decided that the team needed an overhaul. Whiteside's days at Old Trafford were numbered, and in the summer of 1989, with 67 goals in 272 League and Cup games to his name, he left to join Everton in the hope of putting some sparkle back into his game.

After two years at Goodison Park in which his first team appearances were to be limited due to a recurrence of his knee problems, he was forced to retire at the age of only 27. Not the sort of man for self-pity, he went back to University and qualified as a specialist in sports injuries to the feet. The genial Irishman remains an all-time Manchester United hero to this day. A highly gifted player who captured the hearts and imagination of football fans everywhere, he is fondly remembered and appreciated for what he achieved both at Old Trafford and for Northern Ireland.

was also responsible for bringing George Best and Sammy McIlroy to Old Trafford. He made his debut for the Red Devils in the spring of 1982 against Brighton, before making history in the World Cup with Northern Ireland. It was during those finals in which Norman Whiteside first became famous, as he helped the Irish surprise and delight everyone by reaching the quarter-finals. The following season United won the League Cup, beating Liverpool in the final, when Whiteside scored another 'youngest ever' goal and then later that campaign scored in the FA Cup Final replay 4-0 win against Brighton.

The next few years were the high point of his career both for United and Northern Ireland. Perhaps his most famous moment came in 1985 when United played the then champions Everton in the FA Cup Final. At 0-0 in extra-time, reduced to ten men, United were up against it and an Everton winner seemed likely. Big Norman went on a run down the right wing and curled in a superb bending shot from 20 yards to beat Everton keeper Southall. It won 'goal of the season' and sealed one of the great FA Cup Final wins.

DID YOU KNOW?
When Norman Whiteside scored for Manchester United in the FA Cup Final on 26 May 1983, he was just 18 years and 19 days old, the youngest player to score during an FA Cup Final.

Above: David Healy

impact in United's first team squad.

In December 2000, Healy joined Preston North End for a Deepdale club record fee of £1.5 million. The young Irishman provided an immediate return on the club's investment by scoring after just four minutes of his debut against Sheffield United. Healy went on to score five times in his first seven outings for North End. Possessing an eye for goal, the nippy striker netted his first senior hat-trick in a 6-0 defeat of Stockport County.

However, during the early part of the 2002-03 season, Healy found himself on the bench and unable to displace either Richard Cresswell or Ricardo Fuller. He then had a couple of spells on loan with Norwich City, and during his time at Carrow Road seemed to rediscover some of his confidence. Having almost left Deepdale, he worked hard to win back the home crowd, scoring in four consecutive games and totalling 15 goals in that 2003-04 season.

Healy then made national headlines when he broke Northern Ireland's goalscoring drought against Norway after a remarkable run of 1,298 minutes without a goal! It certainly wasn't for the lack of trying on David Healy's part, because his desire to play for his country has proved an inspiration to all.

After taking his tally of first team goals for North End to 45 in 158 games, Healy turned down a new deal with the Lilywhites and joined Leeds United after a lengthy transfer saga. He opened his scoring account for the Yorkshire club with a double strike in United's 4-2 win at Deepdale!

At international level, he just kept on scoring goals. His shot in the 3-3 draw with Austria in October 2004 was one of the finest ever witnessed inside Windsor Park. That long range volley was a tremendous strike and had the crowd cheering wildly. But that was nothing to the roar that greeted his goal against England on 7 September 2005, a date that has gone down in Northern Ireland football folklore.

The game was goalless when Healy collected a shrewd pass from Steve Davis and ran clear on

DAVID HEALY

In the summer of 2004, the man from Killyleagh scored twice in a 3-0 defeat of Trinidad and Tobago, and in doing so became Northern Ireland's record goalscorer. It wasn't really unexpected because right from the start of his international career, when he bagged a double against Luxembourg, he had been tipped to break the long-standing record. He also netted in his next international as the Irish beat Malta 3-0. After years of desperate searching, Northern Ireland had finally found a natural goalscorer.

David Healy began his career with Manchester United, where he had a penchant for scoring goals. After a disappointing introduction to first team action against Aston Villa in the 1999-2000 League Cup, he went on loan to Port Vale. Despite scoring some important goals for the Valiants he couldn't prevent their relegation to the Second Division. On his return to Old Trafford he signed a four-year contract, and though he continued to impress whenever selected for the national side, he made little

goal, before unleashing a stunning shot which
flew past England keeper Paul Robinson and
into the net. His strike against England will
forever assume the same legendary status in
the hearts of Northern Ireland fans as Gerry
Armstrong's winner against World Cup hosts
Spain in 1982.

A ticket stub from the Northern Ireland Euro 2008 qualifying match against Spain

CHAPTER SIX
STATISTICS

WORLD CUP RESULTS

WORLD CUP 1950

Qualifying Rounds

1 October 1949
Northern Ireland 2 Scotland 8

16 November 1949
England 9 Northern Ireland 2

8 March 1950
Wales 0 Northern Ireland 0

Other results
Wales 1 England 4; Scotland 2 Wales 0; Scotland 0 England 1

British Qualifying Zone (Group 1)

	P	W	D	L	F	A	Pts
England	3	3	0	0	14	3	6
Scotland	3	2	0	1	10	3	4
N IRELAND	3	0	1	2	4	17	1
Wales	3	0	1	2	1	6	1

WORLD CUP 1954

Qualifying Rounds

3 October 1953
Northern Ireland 1 Scotland 3

11 November 1953
England 3 Northern Ireland 1

31 March 1954
Wales 1 Northern Ireland 2

Other results
Wales 1 England 4; Scotland 3 Wales 3; Scotland 2 England 4

British Qualifying Zone (Group 3)

	P	W	D	L	F	A	Pts
England	3	3	0	0	11	4	6
Scotland	3	1	1	1	8	8	3
N IRELAND	3	1	0	2	4	7	2
Wales	3	0	1	2	5	9	1

WORLD CUP 1958

Qualifying Rounds

16 January 1957
Portugal 1 Northern Ireland 1

25 April 1957
Italy 1 Northern Ireland 0

1 May 1957
Northern Ireland 3 Portugal 0

15 January 1958
Northern Ireland 2 Italy 1

Other results
Portugal 3 Italy 0; Italy 3 Portugal 0

Group 8

	P	W	D	L	F	A	Pts
N IRELAND	4	2	1	1	6	3	5
Italy	4	2	0	2	5	5	4
Portugal	4	1	1	2	4	7	3

Northern Ireland qualified for finals

Finals Tournament in Sweden

Group 1
8 June 1958
Northern Ireland 1 Czechoslovakia 0 at Halmstad
Northern Ireland:
Gregg; Keith; McMichael; Blanchflower; Cunningham; Peacock;
Bingham; Cush (1); Dougan; McIlroy; McParland
Czechoslovakia:
Dolejsi; Mraz; Novak; Pluskal; Cadek; Masopust; Hovorka; Dvorak;
Borovicka; Hertl; Krauss

11 June 1958
Argentina 3 Northern Ireland 1 at Halmstad
Argentina:
Carrizo; Dellacha; Vairo; Lombardo; Rossi; Varacka; Corbatta (1 pen);
Avio (1); Menendez (1); Labruna; Boggio
Northern Ireland:
Gregg; Keith; McMichael; Blanchflower; Cunningham; Peacock;
Bingham; Cush; Coyle; McIlroy; McParland (1)

15 June 1958
West Germany 2 Northern Ireland 2 at Malmo
West Germany:
Herkenrath; Stollenwerk; Juskowiak; Eckel; Erhardt; Szymaniak; Rahn
(1); Walter; Seeler (1); Schafer; Klodt
Northern Ireland:
Gregg; Keith; McMichael; Blanchflower; Cunningham; Peacock;
Bingham; Cush; Casey; McIlroy; McParland (2)

Other results
West Germany 3 Argentina 1; West Germany 2 Czechoslovakia 2;
Czechoslovakia 6 Argentina 1

Group 1

	P	W	D	L	F	A	Pts
West Germany	3	1	2	0	7	5	4
N IRELAND	3	1	1	1	4	5	3
Czechoslovakia	3	1	1	1	8	4	3
Argentina	3	1	0	2	5	10	2

Play-off for 2nd Place

17 June 1958
Northern Ireland 2 Czechoslovakia 1 (after extra time) at Malmo

Northern Ireland:
Uprichard; Keith; McMichael; Blanchflower; Cunningham; Peacock;
Bingham; Cush; Scott; McIlroy; McParland (2)
Czechoslovakia:
Dolejsi; Mraz; Novak; Bubernik; Popluhar; Masopust; Dvorak; Molnar;
Farajsl; Borovicka; Zikan (1)

Quarter-Finals

19 June 1958
France 4 Northern Ireland 0 at Norrkoping
France:
Abbes; Kaelbel; Lerond; Penverne; Jonquet; Marcel; Wisnieski (1);
Fontaine (2); Kopa; Plantoni (1); Vincent
Northern Ireland:
Gregg; Keith; McMichael; Blanchflower; Cunningham; Cush;
Bingham; Casey; Scott; McIlroy; McParland

WORLD CUP 1962

Qualifying Rounds

26 October 1960
Northern Ireland 3 West Germany 4

3 May 1961
Greece 2 Northern Ireland 1

10 May 1961
West Germany 2 Northern Ireland 1

17 October 1961
Northern Ireland 2 Greece 0

Other results
Greece 0 West Germany 3; West Germany 2 Greece 1

Group 3

	P	W	D	L	F	A	Pts
West Germany	4	4	0	0	11	5	8
N IRELAND	4	1	0	3	7	8	2
Greece	4	1	0	3	3	8	2

WORLD CUP 1966

Qualifying Rounds

14 October 1964
Northern Ireland 1 Switzerland 0

14 November 1964
Switzerland 2 Northern Ireland 1

17 March 1965
Northern Ireland 2 Holland 1

7 April 1965
Holland 0 Northern Ireland 0

7 May 1965
Northern Ireland 4 Albania 1

24 November 1965
Albania 1 Northern Ireland 1

Other results
Holland 2 Albania 0; Albania 0 Holland 2; Albania 0 Switzerland
2; Switzerland 1 Albania 0; Holland 0 Switzerland 0; Switzerland 2
Holland 1

Group 5

	P	W	D	L	F	A	Pts
Switzerland	6	4	1	1	7	3	9
N IRELAND	6	3	2	1	9	5	8
Holland	6	2	2	2	6	4	6
Albania	6	0	1	5	2	12	1

WORLD CUP 1970

Qualifying Rounds

23 October 1968
Northern Ireland 4 Turkey 1

11 December 1968
Turkey 0 Northern Ireland 3

10 September 1969
Northern Ireland 0 USSR 0

22 October 1969
USSR 2 Northern Ireland 0

Other results
USSR 3 Turkey 0; Turkey 1 USSR 3

Group 4

	P	W	D	L	F	A	Pts
USSR	4	3	1	0	8	1	7
N IRELAND	4	2	1	1	7	3	5
Turkey	4	0	0	4	2	13	0

WORLD CUP 1974

Qualifying Rounds

18 October 1972
Bulgaria 3 Northern Ireland 0

14 February 1973
Cyprus 1 Northern Ireland 0

28 March 1973
Northern Ireland 1 Portugal 1

8 May 1973
Northern Ireland 3 Cyprus 0

26 September 1973
Northern Ireland 0 Bulgaria 0

14 November 1973
Portugal 1 Northern Ireland 1

Other results
Portugal 4 Cyprus 0; Cyprus 0 Portugal 1; Cyprus 0 Bulgaria 4;
Bulgaria 2 Portugal 1; Portugal 2 Bulgaria 2; Bulgaria 2 Cyprus 0

Group 6

	P	W	D	L	F	A	Pts
Bulgaria	6	4	2	0	13	3	10
Portugal	6	2	3	1	10	6	7
N IRELAND	6	1	3	2	5	6	5
Cyprus	6	1	0	5	1	14	2

WORLD CUP 1978

Qualifying Rounds

13 October 1976
Holland 2 Northern Ireland 2

10 November 1976
Belgium 2 Northern Ireland 0

11 June 1977
Iceland 1 Northern Ireland 0

14 September 1977
Northern Ireland 2 Iceland 0

12 October 1977
Northern Ireland 0 Holland 1

16 November 1977
Northern Ireland 3 Belgium 0

Other results
Iceland 0 Belgium 1; Iceland 0 Holland 1; Belgium 0 Holland 2;
Holland 4 Iceland 1; Belgium 4 Iceland 0; Holland 1 Belgium 0

Group 4

	P	W	D	L	F	A	Pts
Holland	6	5	1	0	11	3	11
Belgium	6	3	0	3	7	6	6
N IRELAND	6	2	1	3	7	6	5
Iceland	6	1	0	5	2	12	2

WORLD CUP 1982

Qualifying Rounds

26 March 1980
Israel 0 Northern Ireland 0

15 October 1980
Northern Ireland 3 Sweden 0

19 November 1980
Portugal 1 Northern Ireland 0

25 March 1981
Scotland 1 Northern Ireland 1

29 April 1981
Northern Ireland 1 Portugal 0

3 June 1981
Sweden 1 Northern Ireland 0

14 October 1981
Northern Ireland 0 Scotland 0

18 November 1981
Northern Ireland 1 Israel 0

Other results
Sweden 1 Israel 1; Sweden 0 Scotland 1; Scotland 0 Portugal 0; Israel
0 Sweden 0; Portugal 3 Israel 0; Israel 0 Scotland 1; Scotland 3 Israel
1; Sweden 3 Portugal 0; Scotland 2 Sweden 0; Portugal 1 Sweden 2;
Israel 4 Portugal 1; Portugal 2 Scotland 1

Group 6

	P	W	D	L	F	A	Pts
Scotland	8	4	3	1	9	4	11
N IRELAND	8	3	3	2	6	3	9
Sweden	8	3	2	3	7	8	8
Portugal	8	3	1	4	8	11	7
Israel	8	1	3	4	6	10	5

Northern Ireland qualified for the Finals

Finals Tournament in Spain

Group 5

17 June 1982

Northern Ireland 0 Yugoslavia 0 at Zaragoza
Northern Ireland:
Jennings; Nicholl J; Nicholl C; McClelland; Donaghy; McIlroy;
O'Neill M; McCreery; Armstrong; Hamilton; Whiteside
Yugoslavia:
Pantelic; Gudelj; Zajec; Stojkovic; Petrovic; Sljivo; Zlatko; Vujovic;
Susic; Jovanovic; Hrstic; Surjak

21 June 1982
Honduras 1 Northern Ireland 1 at Zaragoza
Honduras:
Arzu; Gutierrez; Villegas; Cruz JL; Costly; Maradiaga; Gilberto; Zelaya;
Norales (Laing (1)) Betancourt; Figueroa
Northern Ireland:
Jennings; Nicholl J; Nicholl C; McClelland; Donaghy; O,Neill M
(Healy); McCreery; McIlroy; Whiteside (Brotherston); Armstrong (1);
Hamilton

25 June 1982
Northern Ireland 1 Spain 0 at Valencia
Northern Ireland:
Jennings; Nicholl J; Nicholl C; McClelland; Donaghy; O'Neill M;
McCreery; McIlroy (Cassidy); Armstrong (1); Hamilton; Whiteside
(Nelson)
Spain:
Arconada; Camacho; Tendillo; Alesanco; Gordillo; Sanchez; Alonso;
Saura; Juanito; Satrustegui (Quini); Lopez Ufarte (Gallego)

Other results
Spain 1 Honduras 1; Spain 2 Yugoslavia 1; Honduras 0 Yugoslavia 1

Group 5

	P	W	D	L	F	A	Pts
N IRELAND	3	1	2	0	2	1	4
Spain	3	1	1	1	3	3	3
Yugoslavia	3	1	1	1	2	2	3
Honduras	3	0	2	1	2	3	2

Second Round

Group D

1 July 1982
Austria 2 Northern Ireland 2 at Madrid
Austria:
Koncilia; Krauss; Obermayer; Pezzey (1); Schachner; Prohaska; Pichler;
Hagmayr (Welzl); Baumeister; Pregesbauer (Hintermaier (1)); Jurtin
Northern Ireland:
Platt; Nicholl J; Nicholl C; McClelland; Nelson; McCreery; O'Neill
M; McIlroy; Armstrong; Hamilton (2); Whiteside (Brotherston)

4 July 1982
France 4 Northern Ireland 1 at Madrid
France:
Ettori; Amoros; Janvion; Tresor; Bossis; Giresse (2); Genghini; Tigana;
Platini; Soler (Six); Rocheteau (2) (Couriol)
Northern Ireland:
Jennings; Nicholl J; Nicholl C; McClelland; Donaghy; McIlroy;
McCreery (O'Neill J); O'Neill M; Armstrong (1); Hamilton;
Whiteside

Group D

	P	W	D	L	F	A	Pts
France	2	2	0	0	5	1	4
Austria	2	0	1	1	2	3	1
N IRELAND	2	0	1	1	3	6	1

WORLD CUP 1986

Qualifying Rounds

27 May 1984
Finland 1 Northern Ireland 0

12 September 1984

Northern Ireland 3 Romania 2

14 November 1984
Northern Ireland 2 Finland 1

27 February 1985
Northern Ireland 0 England 1

1 May 1985
Northern Ireland 2 Turkey 0

11 September 1985
Turkey 0 Northern Ireland 0

16 October 1985
Romania 0 Northern Ireland 1

13 November 1985
England 0 Northern Ireland 0

Other results
England 5 Finland 0; Turkey 1 Finland 2; Turkey 0 England 8;
Romania 3 Turkey 0; Romania 0 England 0; Finland 1 England 1;
Finland 1 Romania 1; Romania 2 Finland 0; England 1 Romania 1;
Finland 1 Turkey 0; England 5 Turkey 0; Turkey 1 Romania 3

Group 3

	P	W	D	L	F	A	Pts
England	8	4	4	0	21	2	12
N IRELAND	8	4	2	2	8	5	10
Romania	8	3	3	2	12	7	9
Finland	8	3	2	3	7	12	8
Turkey	8	0	1	7	2	24	1

Northern Ireland qualified for the Finals

Finals Tournament in Mexico

Group D

3 June 1986
Algeria 1 Northern Ireland 1 at Guadalajara
Algeria:
Larbi; Medjadi; Mansouri; Kourichi; Guendouz; Kaci Said Assad;
Benmarbrouk; Zidane (1); Maroc (Belloumi); Madjer (Harkouk)
Northern Ireland:
Jennings; Nicholl J; Donaghy; O'Neill; McDonald; Worthington;
Penney (Stewart); McIlroy; McCreery; Hamilton; Whiteside (1)
(Clarke)

7 June 1986
Northern Ireland 1 Spain 2 at Guadalajara
Northern Ireland:
Jennings; Nicholl J; Donaghy; O'Neill; McDonald; Worthington
(Hamilton); Penney (Stewart); McIlroy; McCreery; Clarke (1);
Whiteside
Spain:
Zubizarreta; Tomas; Camacho; Gallego; Giocoechea; Gordillo
(Caldere); Michel; Victor; Butragueno (1); Francisco; Julio Salinas (1)
(Senor)

12 June 1986
Brazil 3 Northern Ireland 0 at Guadalajara
Brazil:
Carlos; Josimar (1); Julio Cesar; Edinho; Branco; Elzo; Alemao; Junior;
Socrates (Zico); Muller (Casagrande); Careca (2)
Northern Ireland:
Jennings; Nicholl J; Donaghy; O'Neill; McDonald; McCreery;
McIlroy; Stewart; Clarke; Whiteside (Hamilton); Campbell
(Armstrong)

Group D

	P	W	D	L	F	A	Pts
Brazil	3	3	0	0	5	0	6
Spain	3	2	0	1	5	2	4
N IRELAND	3	0	1	2	2	6	1
Algeria	3	0	1	2	1	5	1

WORLD CUP 1990

Qualifying Rounds

21 May 1988
Northern Ireland 3 Malta 0

14 September 1988
Northern Ireland 0 Republic of Ireland 0

19 October 1988
Hungary 1 Northern Ireland 0

21 December 1988
Spain 4 Northern Ireland 0

8 February 1989
Northern Ireland 0 Spain 2

26 April 1989
Malta 0 Northern Ireland 2

6 September 1989
Northern Ireland 1 Hungary 2

11 October 1989
Republic of Ireland 3 Northern Ireland 0

Other results
Spain 2 Republic of Ireland 0; Malta 2 Hungary 2; Malta 0 Spain 2;
Hungary 0 Republic of Ireland 0;
Spain 4 Malta 0; Hungary 1 Malta 1; Republic of Ireland 1 Spain 0;
Republic of Ireland 2 Malta 0;
Republic of Ireland 2 Hungary 0; Hungary 2 Spain 2; Spain 4
Hungary 0; Malta 0 Republic of Ireland 2

Group 6

	P	W	D	L	F	A	Pts
Spain	8	6	1	1	20	3	13
Republic of Ireland	8	5	2	1	10	2	12
Hungary	8	2	4	2	8	12	8
N IRELAND	8	2	1	5	6	12	5
Malta	8	0	2	6	3	18	2

WORLD CUP 1994

Qualifying Rounds

28 April 1992
Northern Ireland 2 Lithuania 2

9 September 1992
Northern Ireland 3 Albania 0

14 October 1992
Northern Ireland 0 Spain 0

18 November 1992
Northern Ireland 0 Denmark 1

17 February 1993
Albania 1 Northern Ireland 2

31 March 1993
Republic of Ireland 3 Northern Ireland 0

28 April 1993
Spain 3 Northern Ireland 1

25 May 1993
Lithuania 0 Northern Ireland 1

2 June 1993
Latvia 1 Northern Ireland 2

8 September 1993
Northern Ireland 2 Latvia 0

13 October 1993
Denmark 1 Northern Ireland 0

17 November 1993
Northern Ireland 1 Republic of Ireland 1

Other results
Spain 3 Albania 0; Republic of Ireland 2 Albania 0; Albania 1
Lithuania 0; Latvia 1 Lithuania 2;
Latvia 0 Denmark 0; Republic of Ireland 4 Latvia 0; Lithuania 0
Denmark 0; Latvia 0 Spain 0;
Denmark 0 Republic of Ireland 0; Lithuania 1 Latvia 1; Albania 1
Latvia 1; Spain 0 Republic of Ireland 0;
Spain 5 Latvia 0; Spain 5 Lithuania 0; Denmark 1 Spain 0; Denmark
2 Latvia 0;
Lithuania 3 Albania 1; Republic of Ireland 1 Denmark 1; Latvia 0
Albania 0; Albania 1 Republic of Ireland 2;
Denmark 4 Albania 0; Lithuania 0 Spain 2; Latvia 0 Republic of
Ireland 2; Lithuania 0 Republic of Ireland 1;
Denmark 4 Lithuania 0; Albania 0 Denmark 1; Republic of Ireland 2
Lithuania 0; Albania 1 Spain 5;
Republic of Ireland 1 Spain 3; Spain 1 Denmark 0

Group 3

	P	W	D	L	F	A	Pts
Spain	12	8	3	1	27	4	19
Republic of Ireland	12	7	4	1	19	6	18
Denmark	12	7	4	1	15	2	18
N IRELAND	12	5	3	4	14	13	13
Lithuania	12	2	3	7	8	21	7
Latvia	12	0	5	7	4	21	5
Albania	12	1	2	9	6	26	4

WORLD CUP 1998

Qualifying Rounds

31 August 1996
Northern Ireland 0 Ukraine 1

5 October 1996
Northern Ireland 1 Armenia 1

9 November 1996
Germany 1 Northern Ireland 1

14 December 1996
Northern Ireland 2 Albania 0

29 March 1997
Northern Ireland 0 Portugal 0

2 April 1997
Ukraine 2 Northern Ireland 1

30 April 1997
Armenia 0 Northern Ireland 0

20 August 1997
Northern Ireland 1 Germany 3

10 September 1997
Albania 1 Northern Ireland 0

11 October 1997
Portugal 1 Northern Ireland 0

Other results
Armenia 0 Portugal 0; Ukraine 2 Portugal 1; Albania 0 Portugal 3;
Armenia 1 Germany 5;
Albania 1 Armenia 1; Portugal 1 Ukraine 0; Portugal 0 Germany 0;
Albania 0 Ukraine 1;

Albania 2 Germany 3; Germany 2 Ukraine 0; Ukraine 1 Armenia 1;
Portugal 2 Albania 0;
Ukraine 0 Germany 0; Portugal 3 Armenia 1; Ukraine 1 Albania 0;
Germany 1 Portugal 1;
Armenia 3 Albania 0; Germany 4 Armenia 0; Germany 4 Albania 3;
Armenia 0 Ukraine 2

Group 9

	P	W	D	L	F	A	Pts
Germany	10	6	4	0	23	9	22
Ukraine	10	6	2	2	10	6	20
Portugal	10	5	4	1	12	4	19
Armenia	10	1	5	4	8	17	8
N IRELAND	10	1	4	5	6	10	7
Albania	10	1	1	8	7	20	4

2002 WORLD CUP

Qualifying Rounds

2 September 2000
Northern Ireland 1 Malta 0

7 October 2000
Northern Ireland 1 Denmark 1

11 October 2000
Iceland 1 Northern Ireland 0

24 March 2001
Northern Ireland 0 Czech Republic 1

28 March 2001
Bulgaria 4 Northern Ireland 3

2 June 2001
Northern Ireland 0 Bulgaria 1

6 June 2001
Czech Republic 3 Northern Ireland

1 September 2001
Denmark 1 Northern Ireland 1

5 September 2001
Northern Ireland 3 Iceland 0

6 October 2001
Malta 0 Northern Ireland 1

Other results
Bulgaria 0 Czech Republic 1; Iceland 1 Denmark 2; Bulgaria 3
Malta 0; Czech Republic 4 Iceland 0; Denmark 1 Bulgaria 1; Malta
0 Czech Republic 0; Bulgaria 2 Iceland 1; Malta 0 Denmark 5;
Czech Republic 0 Denmark 0; Malta 1 Iceland 4; Denmark 2 Czech
Republic 1; Iceland 3 Malta 0; Denmark 2 Malta 1; Iceland 1 Bulgaria
1; Iceland 3 Czech Republic 1; Malta 0 Bulgaria 2; Bulgaria 0
Denmark 2; Czech Republic 3 Malta 2; Czech Republic 6 Bulgaria 0;
Denmark 6 Iceland 0

Group 3

	P	W	D	L	F	A	Pts
Denmark	10	6	4	0	22	6	22
Czech Republic	10	6	2	2	20	8	20
Bulgaria	10	5	2	3	14	15	17
Iceland	10	4	1	5	14	20	13
N IRELAND	10	3	2	5	11	12	11
Malta	10	0	1	9	4	24	1

WORLD CUP 2006

Qualifying Rounds

4 September 2004
Northern Ireland 0 Poland 3

8 September 2004
Wales 2 Northern Ireland 2

9 October 2004
Azerbaijan 0 Northern Ireland 0

13 October 2004
Northern Ireland 3 Austria 3

26 March 2005
England 4 Northern Ireland 0

30 March 2005
Poland 1 Northern Ireland 0

3 September 2005
Northern Ireland 2 Azerbaijan 0

7 September 2005
Northern Ireland 1 England 0

8 October 2005
Northern Ireland 2 Wales 3

12 October 2005
Austria 2 Northern Ireland 0

Other results
Austria 2 England 2; Azerbaijan 1 Wales 1; Austria 2 Azerbaijan 0;
Poland 1 England 2; Austria 1 Poland 3; England 2 Wales 0; Azerbaijan
0 England 1; Wales 2 Poland 3; Poland 8 Azerbaijan 0; Wales 0 Austria
2; Austria 1 Wales 0; England 2 Azerbaijan 0; Azerbaijan 0 Poland 3;
Poland 3 Austria 2; Wales 0 England 1; Azerbaijan 0 Austria 0;
Poland 1 Wales 0; England 1 Austria 0; England 2 Poland 1; Wales 2
Azerbaijan 0

Group 6

	P	W	D	L	F	A	Pts
England	10	8	1	1	17	5	25
Poland	10	8	0	2	27	9	24
Austria	10	4	3	3	15	12	15
N IRELAND	10	2	3	5	10	18	9
Wales	10	2	2	6	10	15	8
Azerbaijan	10	0	3	7	1	21	3

EUROPEAN CHAMPIONSHIP RESULTS

EUROPEAN CHAMPIONSHIPS 1964

Qualifying Results

10 October 1962
Poland 0 Northern Ireland 2

28 November 1962
Northern Ireland 2 Poland 0

Second Round

30 May 1963
Spain 1 Northern Ireland 1

30 October 1963
Northern Ireland 0 Spain 1 (Spain won 2-1 on aggregate)

EUROPEAN CHAMPIONSHIPS 1968

Qualifying Results

22 October 1966
Northern Ireland 0 England 2

16 November 1966
Scotland 2 Northern Ireland 1

12 April 1967
Northern Ireland 0 Wales 0

21 October 1967
Northern Ireland 1 Scotland 0

22 November 1967
England 2 Northern Ireland 0

28 February 1968
Wales 2 Northern Ireland 0

Other results
Wales 1 Scotland 1; England 5 Wales 1; England 2 Scotland 3; Wales
0 England 3;
Scotland 3 Wales 2; Scotland 1 England 1

Group 8

	P	W	D	L	F	A	Pts
England	6	4	1	1	15	5	9
Scotland	6	3	2	1	10	8	8
Wales	6	1	2	3	6	12	4
N IRELAND	6	1	1	4	2	8	3

EUROPEAN CHAMPIONSHIPS 1972

Qualifying Results

11 November 1970
Spain 3 Northern Ireland 0

3 February 1971
Cyprus 0 Northern Ireland 3

21 April 1971
Northern Ireland 5 Cyprus 0

22 September 1971
USSR 1 Northern Ireland 0

13 October 1971
Northern Ireland 1 USSR 1

16 February 1972
Northern Ireland 1 Spain 1

Other results
Cyprus 0 Spain 2; USSR 2 Spain 1; USSR 6 Cyprus 1; Spain 0
USSR 0;
Cyprus 1 USSR 3; Spain 7 Cyprus 0

Group 4

	P	W	D	L	F	A	Pts
USSR	6	4	2	0	13	4	10
Spain	6	3	2	1	14	3	8
N IRELAND	6	2	2	2	10	6	6
Cyprus	6	0	0	6	2	26	0

EUROPEAN CHAMPIONSHIPS 1976

Qualifying Results
4 September 1974
Norway 2 Northern Ireland 1

30 October 1974
Sweden 0 Northern Ireland 2

16 April 1975
Northern Ireland 1 Yugoslavia 0

3 September 1975
Northern Ireland 1 Sweden 2

29 October 1975
Northern Ireland 3 Norway 0

19 November 1975
Yugoslavia 1 Northern Ireland 0

Other results
Yugoslavia 3 Norway 1; Sweden 1 Yugoslavia 2; Norway 1 Yugoslavia 3; Sweden 3 Norway 1;
Norway 0 Sweden 2; Yugoslavia 3 Sweden 0

Group 3

	P	W	D	L	F	A	Pts
Yugoslavia	6	5	0	1	12	4	10
N IRELAND	6	3	0	3	8	5	6
Sweden	6	3	0	3	8	9	6
Norway	6	1	0	5	5	15	2

EUROPEAN CHAMPIONSHIPS 1980

Qualifying Results

20 September 1978
Republic of Ireland 0 Northern Ireland 0

25 October 1978
Northern Ireland 2 Denmark 1

29 November 1978
Bulgaria 0 Northern Ireland 2

7 February 1979
England 4 Northern Ireland 0

2 May 1979
Northern Ireland 2 Bulgaria 0

6 June 1979
Denmark 4 Northern Ireland 0

17 October 1979
Northern Ireland 1 England 5

21 November 1979
Northern Ireland 1 Republic of Ireland 0

Other results
Denmark 3 Republic of Ireland 3; Denmark 3 England 4; Denmark 2 Bulgaria 2; Republic of Ireland 1 England 1; Republic of Ireland 2 Denmark 0; Bulgaria 1 Republic of Ireland 0; Bulgaria 0 England 3; England 1 Denmark 0; Republic of Ireland 3 Bulgaria 0; Bulgaria 3 Denmark 0; England 2 Bulgaria 0; England 2 Republic of Ireland 0

Group 1

	P	W	D	L	F	A	Pts
England	8	7	1	0	22	5	15
N IRELAND	8	4	1	3	8	14	9
Republic of Ireland	8	2	3	3	9	8	7
Bulgaria	8	2	1	5	6	14	5
Denmark	8	1	2	5	13	17	4

EUROPEAN CHAMPIONSHIPS 1984

Qualifying Results

13 October 1982
Austria 2 Northern Ireland 0

17 November 1982
Northern Ireland 1 West Germany 0

15 December 1982
Albania 0 Northern Ireland 0

30 March 1983
Northern Ireland 2 Turkey 1

27 April 1983
Northern Ireland 1 Albania 0

21 September 1983
Northern Ireland 3 Austria 1

12 October 1983
Turkey 1 Northern Ireland 0

16 November 1983
West Germany 0 Northern Ireland 1

Other results
Austria 5 Albania 0; Turkey 1 Albania 0; Austria 4 Turkey 0; Albania 1 West Germany 2;
Turkey 0 West Germany 3; Austria 0 West Germany 0; Albania 1 Turkey 1; Albania 1 Austria 2;
West Germany 3 Austria 0; West Germany 5 Turkey 1; Turkey 3 Austria 1; West Germany 2 Albania 1

Group 6

	P	W	D	L	F	A	Pts
West Germany	8	5	1	2	15	5	11
N IRELAND	8	5	1	2	8	5	11
Austria	8	4	1	3	15	10	9
Turkey	8	3	1	4	8	16	7
Albania	8	0	2	6	4	14	2

EUROPEAN CHAMPIONSHIPS 1988

Qualifying Results

15 October 1986
England 3 Northern Ireland 0

12 November 1986
Turkey 0 Northern Ireland 0

1 April 1987
Northern Ireland 0 England 2

29 April 1987
Northern Ireland 1 Yugoslavia 2

14 October 1987
Yugoslavia 3 Northern Ireland 0

11 November 1987
Northern Ireland 1 Turkey 0

Other results
Yugoslavia 4 Turkey 0; England 2 Yugoslavia 0; Turkey 0 England 0;
England 8 Turkey 0; Yugoslavia 1 England 4; Turkey 2 Yugoslavia 3

Group 4

	P	W	D	L	F	A	Pts
England	6	5	1	0	19	1	11
Yugoslavia	6	4	0	2	13	9	8
N IRELAND	6	1	1	4	2	10	3
Turkey	6	0	2	4	2	16	2

EUROPEAN CHAMPIONSHIPS 1992

Qualifying Results

12 September 1990
Northern Ireland 0 Yugoslavia 2

17 October 1990
Northern Ireland 1 Denmark 1

14 November 1990
Austria 0 Northern Ireland 0

27 March 1991
Yugoslavia 4 Northern Ireland 1

1 May 1991
Northern Ireland 1 Faroe Islands 1

11 September 1991
Faroe Islands 0 Northern Ireland 5

16 October 1991
Northern Ireland 2 Austria 1

13 November 1991
Denmark 2 Northern Ireland 1

Other results
Faroe Islands 1 Austria 0; Denmark 4 Faroe Islands 1; Yugoslavia
4 Austria 1; Denmark 0 Yugoslavia 2; Yugoslavia 1 Denmark 2;
Yugoslavia 7 Faroe Islands 0; Austria 3 Faroe Islands 0; Denmark 2
Austria 1; Faroe Islands 0 Denmark 4; Austria 0 Denmark 3; Faroe
Islands 0 Yugoslavia 2; Austria 0 Yugoslavia 2

Group 4

	P	W	D	L	F	A	Pts
Yugoslavia	8	7	0	1	24	4	14
Denmark	8	6	1	1	18	7	13
N IRELAND	8	2	3	3	11	11	7
Austria	8	1	1	6	6	14	3
Faroe Islands	8	1	1	6	3	26	3

EUROPEAN CHAMPIONSHIPS 1996

Qualifying Results

20 April 1994
Northern Ireland 4 Liechtenstein 1

7 September 1994
Northern Ireland 1 Portugal 2

12 October 1994
Austria 1 Northern Ireland 2

16 November 1994
Northern Ireland 0 Republic of Ireland 4

29 March 1995
Republic of Ireland 1 Northern Ireland 1

26 April 1995
Latvia 0 Northern Ireland 1

7 June 1995
Northern Ireland 1 Latvia 2

3 September 1995
Portugal 1 Northern Ireland 1

11 October 1995
Liechtenstein 0 Northern Ireland 4

15 November 1995
Northern Ireland 5 Austria 3

Other results
Liechtenstein 0 Austria 4; Latvia 0 Republic of Ireland 3; Latvia 1
Portugal 3; Republic of Ireland 4 Liechtenstein 0; Portugal 1 Austria 0;
Liechtenstein 0 Latvia 1; Portugal 8 Liechtenstein 0; Austria 5 Latvia 0;
Republic of Ireland 1 Portugal 0; Austria 7 Liechtenstein 0; Portugal
3 Latvia 2; Liechtenstein 0 Republic of Ireland 0; Republic of Ireland
1 Austria 3; Liechtenstein 0 Portugal 7; Latvia 3 Austria 2; Austria 3
Republic of Ireland 1; Latvia 1 Liechtenstein 0; Republic of Ireland 2
Latvia 1; Austria 1 Portugal 1; Portugal 3 Republic of Ireland 0

Group 6

	P	W	D	L	F	A	Pts
Portugal	10	7	2	1	29	7	23
Republic of Ireland	10	5	2	3	17	11	17
N IRELAND	10	5	2	3	20	15	17
Austria	10	5	1	4	29	14	16
Latvia	10	4	0	6	11	20	12
Liechtenstein	10	0	1	9	1	40	1

EUROPEAN CHAMPIONSHIPS 2000

Qualifying Results

5 September 1998
Turkey 3 Northern Ireland 0

10 October 1998
Northern Ireland 1 Finland 0

18 November 1998
Northern Ireland 2 Moldova 2

27 March 1999
Northern Ireland 0 Germany 3

31 March 1999
Moldova 0 Northern Ireland 0

4 September 1999
Northern Ireland 0 Turkey 3

8 September 1999
Germany 4 Northern Ireland 0

9 October 1999
Finland 4 Northern Ireland 1

Other Results
Finland 3 Moldova 2; Turkey 1 Germany 0; Moldova 1 Germany
3; Turkey 1 Finland 3; Turkey 2 Moldova 0; Germany 2 Finland 0;
Germany 6 Moldova 1; Finland 2 Turkey 4; Moldova 0 Finland 0;
Finland 1 Germany 2; Moldova 1 Turkey 1; Germany 0 Turkey 0

Group   2

	P	W	D	L	F	A	Pts
Germany	8	6	1	1	20	4	19
Turkey	8	5	2	1	15	6	17
Finland	8	3	1	4	13	13	10
N IRELAND	8	1	2	5	4	19	5
Moldova	8	0	4	4	7	17	4

EUROPEAN CHAMPIONSHIPS 2004

Qualifying Results

12 October 2002
Spain 3 Northern Ireland 0

16 October 2002
Northern Ireland 0 Ukraine 0

29 March 2003
Armenia 1 Northern Ireland 0

2 April 2003
Northern Ireland 0 Greece 2

11 June 2003
Northern Ireland 0 Spain 0

6 September 2003
Ukraine 0 Northern Ireland 0

10 September 2003
Northern Ireland 0 Armenia 1

11 October 2003
Greece 1 Northern Ireland 0

Other Results
Armenia 2 Ukraine 2; Greece 0 Spain 2; Ukraine 2 Greece 0; Greece 2 Armenia 0; Ukraine 2 Spain 2; Spain 3 Armenia 0; Spain 0 Greece 1; Ukraine 4 Armenia 3; Greece 1 Ukraine 0; Armenia 0 Greece 1; Spain 2 Ukraine 1; Armenia 0 Spain 4

Group 6

	P	W	D	L	F	A	Pts
Greece	8	6	0	2	8	4	18
Spain	8	5	2	1	16	4	17
Ukraine	8	2	4	2	11	10	10
Armenia	8	2	1	5	7	16	7
N IRELAND	8	0	3	5	0	8	3

NORTHERN IRELAND'S RECORD AGAINST THE HOME NATIONS

Northern Ireland v England (including Ireland v England up to 1922)

P	W	D	L	F	A
98	7	16	75	81	323

		Ireland	England
1882	Belfast	0	13
1883	Liverpool	0	7
1884	Belfast	1	8
1885	Manchester	0	4
1886	Belfast	1	6
1887	Sheffield	0	7
1888	Belfast	1	5
1889	Everton	1	6
1890	Belfast	1	9
1891	Wolverhampton	1	6
1892	Belfast	0	2
1893	Birmingham	1	6
1894	Belfast	2	2
1895	Derby	0	9
1896	Belfast	0	2
1897	Nottingham	0	6
1898	Belfast	2	3
1899	Sunderland	2	13
1900	Dublin	0	2
1901	Southampton	0	3
1902	Belfast	0	1
1903	Wolverhampton	0	4
1904	Belfast	1	3
1905	Middlesbrough	1	1
1906	Belfast	0	5
1907	Everton	0	1
1908	Belfast	1	3
1909	Bradford	0	4
1910	Belfast	1	1
1911	Derby	1	2
1912	Dublin	1	6
1913	Belfast	2	1
1914	Middlesbrough	3	0
1919	Belfast	1	1
1920	Sunderland	0	2
1921	Belfast	1	1
1922	West Bromwich	0	2
1923	Belfast	2	1
1924	Everton	1	3
1925	Belfast	0	0
1926	Liverpool	3	3
1927	Belfast	2	0
1928	Everton	1	2
1929	Belfast	0	3
1930	Sheffield	1	5
1931	Belfast	2	6
1932	Blackpool	0	1
1933	Belfast	0	3
1934	Everton	1	2
1935	Belfast	1	3
1936	Stoke	1	3
1937	Belfast	1	5
1938	Manchester	0	7
1946	Belfast	2	7
1947	Everton	2	2
1948	Belfast	2	6
1949	Manchester	2	9
1950	Belfast	1	4
1951	Aston Villa	0	2
1952	Belfast	2	2
1953	Everton	1	3
1954	Belfast	0	2
1955	Wembley	0	3
1956	Belfast	1	1
1957	Wembley	3	2
1958	Belfast	3	3
1959	Wembley	1	2
1960	Belfast	2	5
1961	Wembley	1	1
1962	Belfast	1	3
1963	Wembley	3	8
1964	Belfast	3	4
1965	Wembley	1	2
1966	Belfast	0	2
1967	Wembley	0	2
1969	Belfast	1	3
1970	Wembley	1	3
1971	Belfast	0	1
1972	Wembley	1	0
1973	Everton	1	2
1974	Wembley	0	1

1975	Belfast	0	0
1976	Wembley	0	4
1977	Belfast	1	2
1978	Wembley	0	1
1979	Wembley	0	4
1979	Belfast	0	2
1979	Belfast	1	5
1980	Wembley	1	1
1982	Wembley	0	4
1983	Belfast	0	0
1984	Wembley	0	1
1985	Belfast	0	1
1985	Wembley	0	0
1986	Wembley	0	3
1987	Belfast	0	2
2005	Old Trafford	0	4
2005	Belfast	1	0

DID YOU KNOW?
Ireland's first victory over England saw them make an heroic comeback in the game in Belfast. England led 1-0 when Ireland were reduced to 10-men by an injury to one of their forwards. But two goals from Billy Gillespie lifted them to an historic victory.

Northern Ireland v Scotland

P	W	D	L	F	A
93	15	16	62	81	257

		Ireland	Scotland
1884	Belfast	0	5
1885	Glasgow	2	8
1886	Belfast	2	7
1887	Glasgow	1	4
1888	Belfast	2	10
1889	Glasgow	0	7
1890	Belfast	1	4
1891	Glasgow	1	2
1892	Belfast	2	3
1893	Glasgow	1	6
1894	Belfast	1	2
1895	Glasgow	1	3
1896	Belfast	3	3
1897	Glasgow	1	5
1898	Belfast	0	3
1899	Glasgow	1	9
1900	Belfast	0	3
1901	Glasgow	0	11
1902	Belfast	1	5
1902	Belfast	0	3
1903	Glasgow	2	0
1904	Dublin	1	1
1905	Glasgow	0	4
1906	Dublin	0	1
1907	Glasgow	0	3
1908	Dublin	0	5
1909	Glasgow	0	5
1910	Belfast	1	0
1911	Glasgow	0	2
1912	Belfast	1	4
1913	Dublin	1	2
1914	Belfast	1	1
1920	Glasgow	0	3
1921	Belfast	0	2
1922	Glasgow	1	2
1923	Belfast	0	1
1924	Glasgow	0	2
1925	Belfast	0	3
1926	Glasgow	0	4
1927	Belfast	0	2
1928	Glasgow	1	0
1929	Belfast	3	7
1930	Glasgow	1	3
1931	Belfast	0	0
1931	Glasgow	1	3
1932	Belfast	0	4

1933	Glasgow	2	1
1934	Belfast	2	1
1935	Edinburgh	1	2
1936	Belfast	1	3
1937	Aberdeen	1	1
1938	Belfast	0	2
1946	Glasgow	0	0
1947	Belfast	2	0
1948	Glasgow	2	3
1949	Belfast	2	8
1950	Glasgow	1	6
1951	Belfast	0	3
1952	Glasgow	1	1
1953	Belfast	1	3
1954	Glasgow	2	2
1955	Belfast	2	1
1956	Glasgow	0	1
1957	Belfast	1	1
1958	Glasgow	2	2
1959	Belfast	0	4
1960	Glasgow	2	5
1961	Belfast	1	6
1962	Glasgow	1	5
1963	Belfast	2	1
1964	Glasgow	2	3
1965	Belfast	3	2
1966	Glasgow	1	2
1967	Belfast	1	0
1969	Glasgow	1	1
1970	Belfast	0	1
1971	Glasgow	1	0
1972	Glasgow	0	2
1973	Glasgow	2	1
1974	Glasgow	1	0
1975	Glasgow	0	3
1976	Glasgow	0	3
1977	Glasgow	0	3
1978	Glasgow	1	1
1979	Glasgow	0	1
1980	Belfast	1	0
1981	Glasgow	1	1
1981	Glasgow	0	2
1981	Belfast	0	0
1982	Belfast	1	1
1983	Glasgow	0	0
1983	Belfast	2	0
1992	Glasgow	0	1

DID YOU KNOW?
When Northern Ireland won the Home International Championship with a 1-1 draw against Wales in 1980, it was the first time they had won the competition outright since 1914.

Northern Ireland v Wales

P	W	D	L	F	A
92	27	22	43	131	187

		Ireland	Wales
1882	Wrexham	1	7
1883	Belfast	1	1
1884	Wrexham	0	6
1885	Belfast	2	8
1886	Wrexham	0	5
1887	Belfast	4	1
1888	Wrexham	0	11
1889	Belfast	1	3
1890	Shrewsbury	2	5
1891	Belfast	7	2
1892	Bangor	1	1
1893	Belfast	4	3
1894	Swansea	1	4
1895	Belfast	2	2
1896	Wrexham	1	6

1897	Belfast	4	3
1898	Llandudno	1	0
1899	Belfast	1	0
1900	Llandudno	0	2
1901	Belfast	0	1
1902	Cardiff	3	0
1903	Belfast	2	0
1904	Bangor	1	0
1905	Belfast	2	2
1906	Wrexham	4	4
1907	Belfast	2	3
1908	Aberdare	1	0
1909	Belfast	2	3
1910	Wrexham	1	4
1911	Belfast	1	2
1912	Cardiff	3	2
1913	Belfast	0	1
1914	Wrexham	2	1
1920	Belfast	2	2
1921	Swansea	1	2
1922	Belfast	1	1
1923	Wrexham	3	0
1924	Belfast	0	1
1925	Wrexham	0	0
1926	Belfast	3	0
1927	Cardiff	2	2
1928	Belfast	1	2
1929	Wrexham	2	2
1930	Belfast	7	0
1931	Wrexham	2	3
1931	Belfast	4	0
1932	Wrexham	1	4
1933	Belfast	1	1
1935	Wrexham	1	3
1936	Belfast	3	2
1937	Wrexham	1	4
1938	Belfast	1	0
1939	Wrexham	1	3
1947	Belfast	2	1
1948	Wrexham	0	2
1949	Belfast	0	2
1950	Wrexham	0	0
1951	Belfast	1	2
1952	Swansea	0	3
1953	Belfast	2	3
1954	Wrexham	2	1
1955	Belfast	2	3
1956	Cardiff	1	1
1957	Belfast	0	0
1958	Cardiff	1	1
1959	Belfast	4	1
1960	Wrexham	2	3
1961	Belfast	1	5
1962	Cardiff	0	4
1963	Belfast	1	4
1964	Cardiff	3	2
1965	Belfast	0	5
1966	Cardiff	4	1
1967	Belfast	0	0
1968	Wrexham	0	2
1969	Belfast	0	0
1970	Swansea	0	1
1971	Belfast	1	0
1972	Wrexham	0	0
1973	Everton	1	0
1974	Wrexham	0	1
1975	Belfast	1	0
1976	Swansea	0	1
1977	Belfast	1	1
1978	Wrexham	0	1
1979	Belfast	1	1
1980	Cardiff	1	0
1982	Wrexham	0	3
1983	Belfast	0	1
1984	Swansea	1	1
2004	Cardiff	2	2
2005	Belfast	2	3

NORTHERN IRELAND'S RECORD AGAINST ALL NATIONS

	P	W	D	L	F	A
Albania	8	5	2	1	13	4
Algeria	1	0	1	0	1	1
Argentina	1	0	0	1	1	3
Armenia	4	0	2	2	1	3
Australia	3	2	1	0	5	3
Austria	9	4	3	2	17	15
Azerbaijan	2	1	1	0	2	0
Barbados	1	0	1	0	1	1
Belgium	3	2	0	1	6	2
Brazil	1	0	0	1	0	3
Bulgaria	6	2	1	3	7	8
Canada	3	0	1	2	1	4
Chile	2	0	0	2	1	3
Colombia	1	0	0	1	0	2
Cyprus	5	3	1	1	11	1
Czech Republic	2	0	0	2	1	4
Czechoslovakia	2	2	0	0	3	1
Denmark	9	1	4	4	7	13
England	98	7	16	75	81	323
Estonia	2	2	0	0	2	0
Faroe Islands	2	1	1	0	6	1
Finland	5	2	0	3	4	7
France	8	0	3	5	4	18
Germany	7	0	3	4	5	17
West Germany	7	2	1	4	8	15
Greece	5	1	0	4	5	8
Holland	5	1	2	2	4	8
Honduras	1	0	1	0	1	1
Hungary	3	0	0	3	1	4
Iceland	4	2	0	2	5	2
Israel	6	3	3	0	9	4
Italy	6	1	1	4	6	11
Latvia	4	3	0	1	6	3
Liechtenstein	3	2	1	0	8	1
Lithuania	2	1	1	0	3	2
Luxembourg	1	1	0	0	3	1
Malta	6	5	1	0	11	1
Mexico	2	1	0	1	4	4
Moldova	2	0	2	0	2	2
Morocco	1	1	0	0	2	1
Norway	6	1	0	5	7	15
Poland	7	3	1	3	9	10
Portugal	11	2	6	3	10	9
Republic of Ireland	9	2	4	3	4	12
Romania	4	3	0	1	6	4
Scotland	92	14	16	62	81	257
Serbia & Montenegro	1	0	1	0	1	1
Slovakia	1	1	0	0	1	0
Spain	16	1	5	10	8	35
St Kitts & Nevis	1	1	0	0	2	0
Sweden	5	2	0	3	7	5
Switzerland	4	2	1	1	3	2
Thailand	1	0	1	0	0	0
Trinidad & Tobago	1	1	0	0	3	0
Turkey	10	5	2	3	12	9
Ukraine	4	0	2	2	1	3
Uruguay	3	2	0	1	4	1
USSR	4	0	2	2	1	4
Wales	92	27	22	43	131	187
Yugoslavia	8	1	1	6	4	14

Played	523	
Won	126	
Drawn	118	
Lost	279	
Goals Scored	553	
Goals Conceded	1073	

DID YOU KNOW?
James Quinn scored Northern Ireland's 500th goal in a 3-0 friendly international victory against Belgium in February 1997.

TOP 50 APPEARANCES

As with League football, Pat Jennings takes the top spot. He was 19 when he won his first cap against Wales in April 1994 and played the last of his 119 internationals against Brazil in June 1986 on what was his 41st birthday!

	Player	Career Dates	Total Appearances
1	Pat Jennings	1964-1986	119
2	Mal Donaghy	1980-1994	91
3	Sammy McIlroy	1972-1986	88
4	Jimmy Nicholl	1976-1986	73
5	Michael Hughes	1991-2005	71
6	Keith Gillespie	1994-present	68
7	David McCreery	1976-1990	67
8	Nigel Worthington	1984-1997	66
9	Martin O'Neill	1972-1985	64
10	Gerry Armstrong	1977-1986	63
11=	Iain Dowie	1990-2000	59
	Terry Neill	1961-1973	59
13=	Billy Bingham	1951-1964	56
	Danny Blanchflower	1950-1963	56
15	Jimmy McIlroy	1952-1966	55
16=	Allan Hunter	1970-1980	53
	John McClelland	1980-1990	53
18=	Alan McDonald	1986-1996	52
	Jim Magilton	1991-2002	52
	Maik Taylor	1999-present	52
21=	Sammy Nelson	1970-1982	51
	Chris Nicholl	1975-1984	51
	Gerry Taggart	1990-2003	51
24	Bryan Hamilton	1969-1980	50
25=	David Healy	2000-present	49
	Pat Rice	1969-1980	49
27	Dave Clements	1965-1976	48
28=	Aaron Hughes	1998-present	46
	James Quinn	1996-present	46
	Jimmy Quinn	1985-1996	46
31	Steve Lomas	1994-2003	45
32	Derek Dougan	1958-1973	43
33=	Damien Johnson	1999-present	42
	Kevin Wilson	1987-1995	42
35=	Billy Hamilton	1978-1986	41
	Jimmy Nicholson	1961-1972	41
37=	Alex Elder	1960-1970	40
	Neil Lennon	1994-2002	40
	Alf McMichael	1950-1960	40
40=	Steve Morrow	1990-2000	39
	John O'Neill	1980-1986	39
42=	Colin Clarke	1986-1993	38
	Norman Whiteside	1982-1990	38
44	George Best	1964-1978	37
45	Mark Williams	1999-present	36
46	Tommy Jackson	1969-1977	35
47=	Stuart Elliott	2001-present	34
	Martin Harvey	1961-1971	34
	Peter McParland	1954-1962	34
50	Kevin Horlock	1995-2003	32

DID YOU KNOW?
On 1 February 1930, Joe Bambrick scored six goals in Northern Ireland's 7-0 victory over Wales, the highest individual tally in a Home International.

TOP 50 GOALSCORERS

No one player has yet scored a quarter-century of goals for Northern Ireland but Leeds United striker David Healy is well on his way to achieving this feat.

In terms of strike-rate (dividing goals scored by games played) the leader of the pack is Joe Bambrick who scored 12 goals in 11 games. It should be remembered though, that substitute appearances are included as full games in these totals.

	Player	Career Dates	Total	Games Played	Strike Rate
1	David Healy	2000-present	19	49	0.38
2=	Colin Clarke	1986-1993	13	38	0.34
	Billy Gillespie	1913-1931	13	25	0.52
4=	Gerry Armstrong	1977-1986	12	63	0.19
	Joe Bambrick	1929-1938	12	11	1.09
	Iain Dowie	1990-2000	12	59	0.20
	Jimmy Quinn	1985-1996	12	46	0.26
8	Ollie Stansfield	1887-1897	11	30	0.36
9=	Billy Bingham	1951-1964	10	56	0.17
	Johnny Crossan	1960-1968	10	24	0.41
	Jimmy McIlroy	1952-1966	10	55	0.18
	Peter McParland	1954-1962	10	34	0.29
13=	George Best	1964-1978	9	37	0.24
	Norman Whiteside	1982-1990	9	38	0.23
15=	Derek Dougan	1958-1973	8	43	0.18
	Willie Irvine	1963-1972	8	23	0.34
	Martin O'Neill	1972-1985	8	64	0.12
18=	Billy McAdams	1954-1962	7	15	0.46
	John Peden	1887-1899	7	24	0.29
	Gerry Taggart	1990-2003	7	51	0.13
	Sammy Wilson	1962-1968	7	12	0.58
22=	Phil Gray	1993-2001	6	26	0.23
	Jimmy McLaughlin	1962-1966	6	12	0.50
	Jimmy Nicholson	1961-1972	6	41	0.14
	Kevin Wilson	1987-1995	6	42	0.14
26=	Wilbur Cush	1951-1962	5	26	0.19
	Billy Hamilton	1978-1986	5	41	0.12
	Michael Hughes	1991-2005	5	71	0.07
	Jim Magilton	1991-2002	5	52	0.09
	Sammy McIlroy	1972-1986	5	88	0.05
	Billy Simpson	1951-1959	5	12	0.41
	Sammy Smyth	1948-1952	5	9	0.55
	Alex Stevenson	1934-1948	5	17	0.29
	Davy Walsh	1947-1950	5	9	0.55
35=	Trevor Anderson	1973-1979	4	22	0.18
	William Dalton	1888-1894	4	11	0.36
	Jimmy Dunne	1928-1933	4	7	0.57
	Stuart Elliott	2001-present	4	34	0.11
	James Gaffikin	1890-1895	4	15	0.26
	Bryan Hamilton	1969-1980	4	50	0.08
	John Kelly	1932-1937	4	11	0.36
	Chris McGrath	1974-1979	4	21	0.19
	Eddie McMorran	1947-1957	4	15	0.26
	Mike O'Neill	1988-1997	4	31	0.12
	James Quinn	1996-present	4	46	0.08
	HA de B Sloan	1903-1909	4	8	0.50
47=	JH Barron	1894-1897	3	7	0.42
	Noel Brotherston	1980-1985	3	27	0.11
	James Chambers	1921-1932	3	12	0.25
	Peter Doherty	1935-1961	3	16	0.18
	Andrew Gara	1902	3	3	1.00
	Martin Harvey	1961-1971	3	34	0.08
	Bobby Irvine	1922-1932	3	15	0.20
	Bill Lacey	1909-1925	3	23	0.13
	Norman Lockhart	1947-1956	3	8	0.37
	Steve Lomas	1994-2003	3	45	0.06
	David Martin	1934-1939	3	10	0.30
	Jim McCandless	1912-1921	3	5	0.60
	Alan McDonald	1986-1996	3	52	0.05
	Eric McMordie	1969-1973	3	21	0.14
	Sammy Morgan	1972-1979	3	18	0.16
	Phil Mulryne	1997-present	3	27	0.11
	Derek Spence	1975-1982	3	29	0.10
	Charlie Tully	1949-1959	3	10	0.30

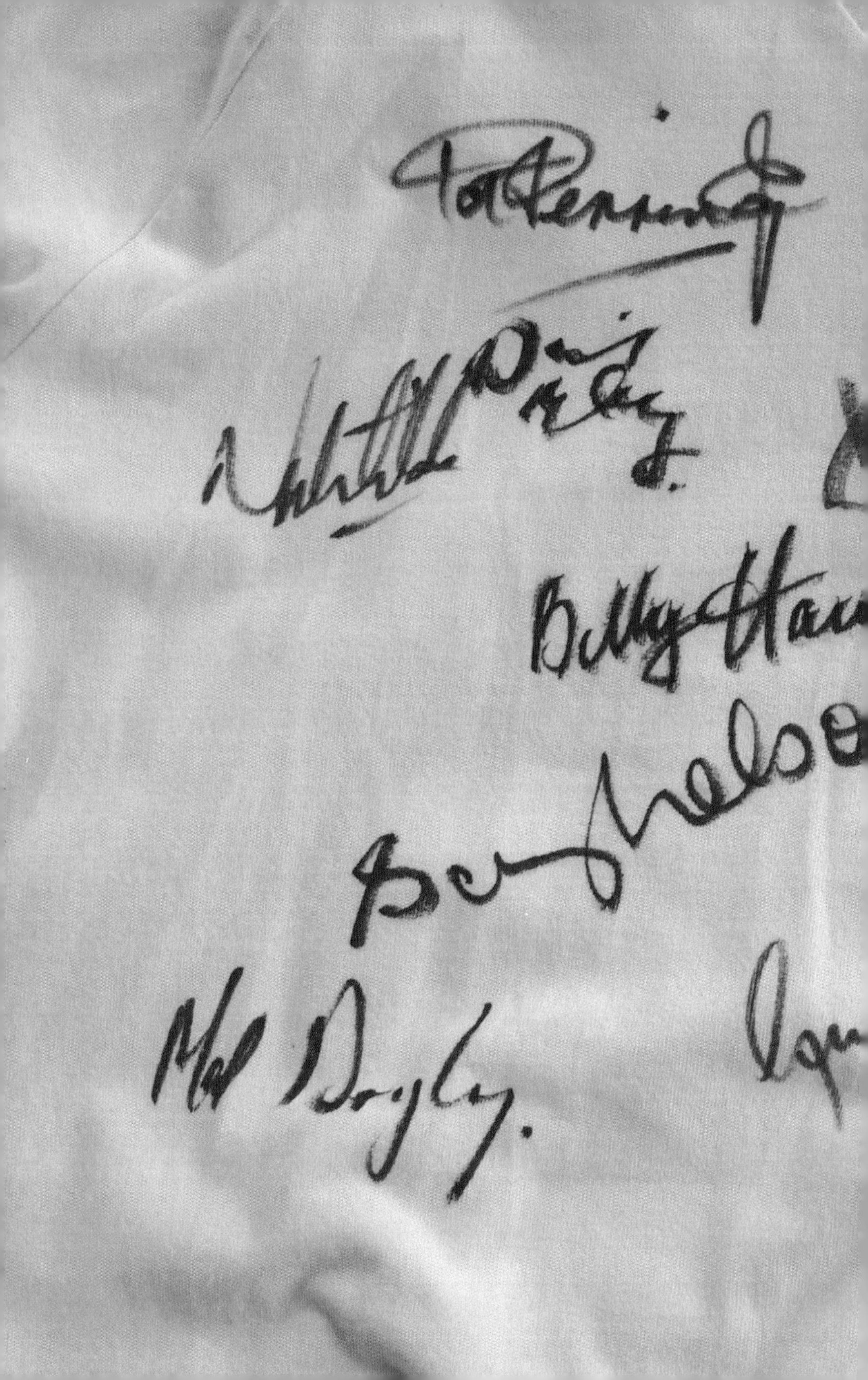